D1130337

E.S.E.A.
TITLE II

Imperialism

A volume
in
THE DOCUMENTARY HISTORY
of
WESTERN CIVILIZATION

Imperialism

Edited by

PHILIP D. CURTIN

WALKER AND COMPANY

New York

JC
359
.C85
1972

Copyright © 1971 by Philip D. Curtin

All rights reserved. No part of this book may
be reproduced or transmitted in any form or by
any means, electronic or mechanical, including
photocopying, recording, or by any information
storage and retrieval system, without permission
in writing from the Publisher.

Published simultaneously in Canada by Fitzhenry &
Whiteside, Limited, Toronto.

Library of Congress Catalog Card Number: 75-142853
ISBN: 0-8027-2046-3
Printed in the United States of America.

Published in the United States of America in 1972
by Walker and Company, a division of Walker
Publishing Company, Inc.

Volumes in this series are published in association
with Harper & Row, Publishers, Inc., from
whom paperback editions are available in Harper
Torchbooks.

CONTENTS

78-156

Introduction:
Imperialism as Intellectual History

"Imperialism" is a word of many meanings—too many to keep it fully useful in historical discussion. To take only examples from European history over the past century and a half, in mid-nine-teenth-century France it meant belief in *l'empire*, the Napoleonic form of government, or even the somewhat mythical recall of glories that had once been, and might again be, French. In this context, its opposite was likely to be republicanism or monarchism. Or, moving across the Channel to England of the 1860's, an imperialist was someone who favored the empire, in this case the British Empire; but the word called up an image of Australia or Canada as valued parts of Greater Britain, whose loyalty to the crown was to be cherished. It still lacked the later connotation of jingo expansionism, though its opposite would already have been Little Englander. It was not until the 1890's that the English sense of the term had clearly shifted from the idea of valuing the empire to that of making it bigger, and even this was soon overtaken by a strong competitor. At least for the European Left, the Leninist view that overseas expansion represented the final or "imperialist" phase of capitalism began to capture the world during the interwar period. After the Second World War, the meaning of the term had so altered that its opposite could be socialist, democratic, or even peace-loving.

This book makes no pretense of following all these meanings, only a narrow aspect of one of them. It is concerned with imperial-ism as the body of European ideas about the conquest and adminis-tration of non-Western countries and peoples—not the acts or the diplomacy of conquest, or the way overseas empires were actually run, only the intellectual history of the movement as it reached its peak in the nineteenth and early twentieth centuries.

The history of ideas is sometimes presented with value judg-ments, the "great ideas" of Western man or the "intellectual heritage" of Western civilization. This book seeks to avoid any such judgment. The selections from imperial theory are chosen because they were typical of their time—of the attitudes, values, and goals of the imperialists. If anything, they are the bad ideas of Western man, his moments of self-righteous arrogance, his justifications for using the power recently presented to him by industrial technology. But neither are the texts that follow chosen as examples for condemnation. Few are admirable for what they say, almost none can be considered a contribution to man's better understanding of his society; but they were part of an empire-building era, which had a great deal to do with the making of the world today. That era is now finished, and the great empires are liquidated. The imperialists are beyond the useful range of moral judgment, but it remains important to understand their place in history; and one key to understanding is to know what they thought they were doing, and why they thought they should do it.

The body of European thought about the world beyond that small peninsula and its nearby islands is vast. Even the segment that might be labeled imperial theory extends beyond the matter of conquering and ruling over non-Western people. Alongside the true empires of alien culture, the Europeans sent out their own people to settle in true colonies, ruled initially from Europe but Western in culture from the beginning. The existence of these true colonies overseas posed problems, which generated their own body of colonial theory. But the European thought about true colonization was quite different from imperialist theory. It had to do with economic development, land and immigration policy, or constitutional relations. These questions are familiar to Americans in the setting of United States history. They occurred with different ramifications to Canadians, Australians, and New Zealanders; to Russian settlers in the Ukraine and much of Siberia north of the present Soviet Central Asia; to the Hispanic-American settlers in central and southern Brazil, Argentina, Uruguay, and Chile. The theory of true colonization, where it concerned the internal relations of an expanding Western society, can nevertheless be left aside from the theory of true empire.

But the settlement colonies shared the concerns of empire in two respects. Some areas of European settlement were already densely inhabited before the settlers arrived. In these, the immigrants could neither absorb the original inhabitants nor easily push them aside. Instead of establishing a completely Western, immigrant society on the model of Canada, the Europeans merely succeeded in establishing a Western community within the alien society. This happened in such places as Algeria, South Africa, Soviet Central Asia, and Rhodesia. By the nineteenth century, the early true empires established by the Spanish in Mexico and Peru had evolved into plural societies of this type, where two cultures existed side by side, often in uneasy or hostile relations. Within the plural societies produced by European settlement, many of the problems of empire and imperial theory came to the fore. In effect, the rule over an alien society was internalized, and "native policy" became a domestic issue.

"Native policy" in another form had a temporary importance where settler societies were expanding behind a moving frontier. Even though the aborigines were relatively few in places like Canada and the United States, and even though many died in contact with European disease, their presence beyond the frontier was at least a transitional military problem until the frontier passed on and the survivors were encapsulated as a cultural minority in the Western mass. Canada and the United States thus had a "native policy" toward Indians and Eskimos. So did Chile toward the Araucanians, or New Zealand toward the Maori. In either case, imperial theory was not confined to the imperial powers of Europe; it was also generated in the offshoot European communities all around the world, especially those that became independent of Europe or partially self-governing—which normally meant not merely governing themselves but governing their non-European neighbors as well.

A comprehensive study of European imperial thought, therefore, would have to be concerned with imperial policies—and the thought lying behind the policies—in as many as fifteen different political units. It would have to take in the intellectual justification of apartheid in South Africa and the Russian efforts to assimilate the Muslim population in Central Asia, as well as the better-known British discussion of policies appropriate to the Indian Empire. The great bulk of imperialist writing was policy-oriented, and policy was made at the national level; European imperial theory is therefore divided into a series of national compartments.

This compartmentalization makes European imperial thought an

unhandy subject for study, and historians have never treated it as a
whole. It *was* a whole, however, because theorists in different
countries were dealing with similar problems and borrowing ideas
and arguments from across the national frontiers. The Russians
debated the role to be assigned to the traditional rulers in Central
Asia, just as the British discussed Indirect Rule for Africa, or the
Dutch beat out a policy in regard to the Javanese regents. In much
the same way, the Juárez government in Mexico developed a body
of theory and enacted a series of laws designed to speed the accul-
turation of the Indians, using many of the ideas and preconceptions
that informed British theory about landholding and social change
in India, or French views of culture change among Algerian
Muslims.

A volume like this one might have been designed to give the
broadest possible view across all the national compartments of
imperial thought. It could have taken account of imperial theory in
Portugal, Holland, and Russia—themes much neglected by English-
speaking historians. It could have looked into special problems
discussed by German imperialists, and the variant readings of
"native policy" on the part of North Americans, Australians,
Brazilians, South Africans, Mexicans, New Zealanders, and
Chileans.

But no such comprehensive view of imperial ideology is attempted here. An editor sometimes has to make hard choices, given
the limitations of a single volume. For this volume, one choice lay
between a broad range of national or geographical examples on one
hand, or a thematic approach on the other. The second of these
alternatives was chosen, with the necessary consequence of concentrating on the imperial theory in France and Great Britain, the two
powers with the largest and most diverse overseas empires. This
limitation makes it possible to illustrate some of the diversity of
imperialist thought, and to show something of the common ground
as well as the national differences between these two powers. But it
is not possible simultaneously to illustrate the whole range of
Western imperial theory.

Even within these limits, imperial thought was not a discrete
body of knowledge. Racism and race theory are obvious and
crucial, yet raciology was also a part of the emerging field of
anthropology. In the same way, administrative theory was part of

an incipient political science, missionology was attached to schools of divinity, and the history of European thought about education overseas belongs with the history of European education in general. Hardly anything in imperial theory belongs under this rubric and nowhere else. It is enmeshed at every point in the web of European intellectual history as a whole, and it sometimes has to be abstracted from the usual categories of Western knowledge in order to see how each contributed to the European belief in empire as it was and should be.

Closely as imperial theory was bound up with the main lines of Western thought, it was also something of a side issue. Its application lay outside of the Western world itself, and Europeans had a chronic tendency to regard the non-West as an exception to the social, historic, or economic patterns they detected in their own society. Non-Europeans were exotic by definition, and they might well behave in curious and unexpected ways. In addition, the social and political goals held out for the empire overseas were rarely identical with those of the metropolis—not, at least, in the eyes of the metropolitan theorist. This exceptionalism in European thought about the non-West was, indeed, an aspect common to almost every subdivision of the imperialist ideology.

The ultimate foundation of that ideology was a conception of the world largely based on self-identification—and identification of "the other people." By the nineteenth century, the European ruling class saw its primary identity as a particular social stratum of a particular European nation-state. Beyond that nation, it recognized its social equals in other Western nations, though they were often thought of as having rather peculiar variants of "civilized standards." Still, they *were* part of the "civilized world," and the perceived gap between any two civilized nations was small indeed compared to the gulf that separated them from the uncivilized who lived beyond the seas or beyond the Urals.

In the past, these others had been identified in various ways, as savages, barbarians, or simply heathen, depending on the form of xenophobia that happened to be fashionable at the moment. Up to the sixteenth century, the division most commonly felt was religious. Christendom was the largest unit claiming the common loyalty of Europeans, and the heathen beyond the pale were seen indistinctly as an amorphous mass whose common characteristic was their heathendom. Europeans knew they had the one true religion, and that knowledge was enough to support their self-identity and feeling of unquestioned superiority.

With the sixteenth century, the nature of the superiority feeling began to change. The maritime revolution meant that European ships could go anywhere in the world. This new capability brought new knowledge of the non-West, and it also marked the beginning of a shift in the balance of world power. Europeans began to discover that other civilizations had played a role in world history. They were still heathen, exotic, and barbarous, but they were skilled and powerful in their own ways. They were, in fact, more powerful than European pride allowed at the time. The Moguls in India and the Turks in the Mediterranean were at least as powerful militarily as any Western state until far into the seventeenth century. Until the nineteenth century, the Chinese and Japanese were able to dictate the times, places, and terms on which Europeans might come as traders or visitors. In tropical Africa, Europeans were no threat to a major African state that was internally strong till after 1800. The only major exception to this changing but relatively equal balance between Western and non-Western force was in the Americas and Oceania. There the indigenous civilizations had been cut off for centuries from the intercommunicating Afro-Eurasian land mass, from its inventions and especially from its diseases. The Americas were therefore the scene of the first true empires controlled from Europe, and Western imperial theory originated in sixteenth-century Spain.

Elsewhere, the Europeans' new knowledge and respect for their barbarous neighbors in Afro-Asia lasted until the second half of the eighteenth century in spite of the gradual shift in the balance of technology and power in their favor. By that time, however, the balance had shifted decisively in most parts of the Old World. Europeans began to exert their authority on land as well as on the sea. Their overseas holdings, previously limited to a series of trading-post enclaves, began to expand into territorial empires, especially in India and Indonesia.

With the industrial revolution of the early nineteenth century, the balance shifted still farther, and much faster. European technological capability reached levels the world had never seen before. In military terms, Western-style armies could now win battles virtually anywhere, and at little cost. In psychological terms,

Europeans could now see and measure their superiority—in factory production, agricultural yields, or the cost of transportation by railway or steamship. Where superiority feelings had once rested on little more than religious arrogance and ordinary xenophobia, they could now be buttressed by demonstrable superiority in power and knowledge. The result for Western thought was a wave of unquestioning cultural arrogance that rose steadily until well into the twentieth century.

Meanwhile, and quite independently, European arrogance was fortified from another direction. Biologists had been at the forefront of the eighteenth-century effort to classify and understand the world around them. The line of investigation from Linnaeus and Buffon through Blumenbach and others reached its culmination with Georges Cuvier in the early nineteenth century. The animal kingdom was neatly labeled and fitted into place, hierarchically organized following the assumptions that a Great Chain of Being reached from God down to his least creature.[1] Man also fell into this system, at the apex of living things, and the races of men were also hierarchically arranged, with European man at the pinnacle, following the dictates of *amour-propre* and the new cultural arrogance.[2] As a result, the groundwork was laid for a new, racially oriented view of human beings and their civilizations. If men were seen to be markedly different from one another in physical racial traits, and if some cultures were seen to be vastly superior to others, it seemed to follow that the racial difference must have been the cause of the cultural superiority.

The full implications of this erroneous confusion of race and culture were not drawn immediately. Revealed religion still held that all men were descended from a common father and mother; those who argued that each race was created separately, that only Europeans had actually descended from Adam and Eve, were still few in the early nineteenth century. But the racism of the biological writers received further support from the new conditions of the overseas world. Europeans were abroad in greater numbers than ever before, with greater power than ever before. The British in

1. See Arthur O. Lovejoy, *The Great Chain of Being: A Study of the History of an Idea* (Cambridge, Mass., 1936); Philip D. Curtin, *The Image of Africa* (Madison, Wis., 1964), pp. 36–48, 227–243.
2. See selection from Cuvier below, pp 4–12.

India, the Dutch in Indonesia, other Europeans in the American tropics dealt with non-Europeans who were manifestly not their equals in the structure of a colonial society. The xenophobia that may be the normal outcome of such confrontations tended to be expressed more and more often in racial terms. The non-Europeans were no longer principally heathen, or even barbarians; they were "niggers." This shift was peculiarly marked in the Americas, where blackness and slave status were synonymous, and where the balance of physical power shifted to the Europeans far earlier than it did in Asia or Africa. Its influence on European thought was especially strong in the eighteenth century by way of the Caribbean sugar colonies, then regarded as the most valuable of all overseas holdings, and in the nineteenth century from North America, the most populous region of overseas settlement.

Full-blown racist theories of history and society began to appear in the first half of the nineteenth century, even before Darwin pushed biological science to a new level of prestige. One of the first was W. F. Edwards' *Caractères physiologiques des races humaines*, which appeared in France in 1829. By 1841, an eminent English scholar, Thomas Arnold, presented a racial theory of world history in his inaugural lecture as Regius Professor of History at Oxford.[3] Before the end of that decade, the imperial implications of the new pseudoscientific racism were drawn out by a British biologist, Robert Knox of Edinburgh.[4]

Darwin actually added little to what Knox had said about the biology of race in more popular language, but he accepted racist premises. Even though he was quite wrong in mistaking acquired immunities for innate racial traits, his growing prestige in the scientific thought of the latter nineteenth century made it easy for others to seize on the evolutionary concept. The social Darwinians shifted from Darwin's theory of a struggle for survival among animal species to a similar hypothesis involving a struggle for survival among varieties within the single species *Homo sapiens*. Most social Darwinians were concerned with racial differences within Europe; but their ideas spilled over into imperial thought as well,

3. Thomas Arnold, *Introductory Lectures on Modern History* (New York, 1842).

4. See selections from Knox's *The Races of Man* (London, 1850) below, pp. 12–22.

and most imperial theory between the 1870's and the 1920's was based on racist assumptions with evolutionary overtones.

Imperial theorists may have agreed in assuming that race was a fundamental determinant of all history and culture, but common assumptions did not lead to identical conclusions. Agreement was actually limited to a number of key beliefs. Simply stated, they were: (a) non-Western culture is far inferior to that of the West; (b) non-Western peoples are racially different from Europeans, and this difference is hereditary; (c) therefore, the cultural inferiority is also hereditary. The range of conclusions seen to follow was enormous. At one extreme was the cold-blooded view that non-Europeans were an inferior stock, doomed by inexorable nature to defeat and extinction in the struggle for survival—this being so, the sooner the better. At the other extreme, some held that racial inferiority was a form of weakness, but "the lower races" deserved the same chivalric protection accorded to women, children, and other weaker forms of life. Between these extremes, the variety of possibilities was enormous and always mixed with other attitudes, outlooks, and prejudices.

One thread running through much imperialist thought was a legalistic concern about rights and duties, those of the ruled and those of the rulers. International law itself responded to the nineteenth-century rise of cultural arrogance. The dominant view of the rights of "savages" before that century had held that all occupied lands were under the sovereignty of their occupiers, no matter how savage. Only vacant land was legally *territorium nullius*, open to seizure by any organized state that discovered and occupied it. There were, however, exceptions. Emer de Vattel, writing in Switzerland in the 1750's, drew a cultural limitation. Sovereignty, in his view, was conditional on the performance of agricultural work. Nomads, hunters, and gatherers held no such right.[5] The nineteenth century drew a tighter line. A substantial minority of international lawyers, represented here by John Westlake writing in the 1890's, held that general cultural inferiority and political disorganization barred certain states (like those in tropical Africa) from membership in the family of nations. He held, for example, that they even lacked the power to sign legal treaties

5. See selection below, pp. 42–45.

transferring their sovereignty to a European power.[6] But discrimination in international law was always explicitly based on culture, not race.[7]

The other side of the coin was the theory that "lower races" deserved special treatment from the organized community of nations.[8] They had certain disabilities, but they also had certain rights, and these were often equated with those of minors in law. The more developed countries were seen in the role of trustee or guardian over the less developed. The most obvious consequence of this line of thought was the mandate system under the League of Nations between the two World Wars, or the Trusteeship Council under the United Nations Charter.[9]

Other offshoots of racial trusteeship are less known, and far more curious in retrospect. One such was the widespread effort to prevent non-Europeans from drinking alcohol. Even though alcohol was sold freely in Europe, it was believed that whites were a strong race capable of drinking wisely, while other races were not. The concept found its way into the legislation of the United States, which at certain periods prohibited the sale of liquor to Indians even when it could be sold freely to Americans of African or European descent. South Africa made a legal distinction for several decades between certain alcoholic beverages that could be sold only to Europeans and others that were available to Africans as well. In tropical Africa, this racial temperance movement reached the level of international agreement. The Brussels Conference of 1890 prohibited the distillation or sale of alcoholic spirits in African colonies, while at the same time allowing a controlled importation of liquor for sale to "non-natives."[10]

This minor effort is only one example of a very pervasive imperial attitude in the late nineteenth century, when the idea of trusteeship was widely used as the moral justification for empire. But trusteeship and racism were not connected in logic—not, at least, explicitly. The roots of trusteeship lie far back in the history

6. See selection below, pp. 45–63.
7. M. F. Lindley, *The Acquisition and Government of Backward Territory in International Law* (London, 1926), pp. 10–23.
8. See selection below, pp.319–37, from J. A. Hobson, *Imperialism: A Study* (London, 1902).
9. See selections below, pp. 64–72.
10. For the text of the Brussels Act, see R. L. Buell, *The Native Problem in Africa*, 2 vols. (New York, 1928), 2:932–934.

of European thought. The most obvious is the chivalric ideal of the Middle Ages, when the knight incurred obligations to help the weak along with his military status. More important still was the Christian tradition, which laid great stress on proselytism from the time of Saint Paul onward. If religious superiority carried an obligation to convert the heathen, cultural superiority might easily carry an obligation to convert the barbarian to civilization. The belief in this obligation, and the effort to carry it out, is sometimes called "conversionism," and conversionism was broadly dominant in Western imperial thought during the first half of the nineteenth century, both in France and in England. In France, the idea of a *mission civilisatrice* was sporadically followed by moves toward the cultural assimilation of its subjects overseas. In England, one of the most famous statements of the conversionist point of view is Macaulay's "Minute" on Indian education, and the belief in a conversionist duty was spelled out by the Parliamentary Committee on Aborigines in 1837.[11]

But conversionism differed from the later belief in trusteeship in crucial ways. It called for missionaries, both cultural and religious, but not necessarily for conquest and control overseas. The obligation to spread Christianity and civilization was a self-imposed obligation on those who thought of themselves as civilized. There was no equivalent duty or limitation on the rights of the uncivilized. They were not so often treated as minors in law, but as adults who would choose civilization and Christianity voluntarily, once it was presented to them. In some variants, a little coercion was called for, and some potential recipients of civilization already lived in European colonies; but the balance of duty lay with the civilizers.[12]

About the middle of the century, the balance began to shift toward the idea of trusteeship, with its emphasis on the minor status of the "natives," its insistence that they come under Western rule with severe limitations on their right of self-direction. This shift owed something to a feeling of disappointment with the first

11. See selections below, pp. 178–91 and 285–91.

12. Perhaps the most important British representative of the conversionist position was Thomas Fowell Buxton, whose ideas for the civilization of Africa are given in most detail in *The Remedy: Being a Sequel to the African Slave Trade* (London, 1840), and for other parts of the empire in the published hearings of the Parliamentary Committee on Aborigines, 1835–37 Parliamentary Papers, 1836, vii (538); and 1837, vii (425). See selection below, pp. 285–91.

results of conversionism. Algerians and Mexicans seemed not to appreciate the French presence in their countries. Former slaves in the French and British West Indies alike seemed to show a lack of gratitude for their emancipation from slavery in 1834 and 1848. Rather than accepting the wages offered on the plantations of their former masters, they followed their own economic advantage and set themselves up as a free peasantry. The Indian mutiny of 1857 was a special shock to complacency in Britain and throughout the British Empire. These disappointments and pseudoscientific racism were mutually reinforcing. The racists said that non-Europeans were born inferior and incapable of accepting civilization. Events overseas seemed to indicate that they were at least unwilling to accept it in the form offered. After the 1860's, the idea of trusteeship was dominant, and it became stronger with each passing decade.

Even then, trusteeship could mean many things to many people. For the sternest imperialists, it came to mean that European rule was a kind of permanent asylum for the "lower races," where enforced labor would pay the costs of colonial benevolence, without hope of ever shaking off the heritage of inferiority. For others, trusteeship kept its humanitarian overtones. J. A. Hobson, better known for his theory of the economic roots of imperialism, argued for a controlled, humanitarian form of trusteeship of this kind, and Lord Olivier defended the rights of the "natives" from his experience as an active ruler in the British Empire.[13]

In these diverse ideas of trusteeship, the crucial variable was the end product—the conditions in which the trust could be terminated. Those who retained conversionist leanings thought of a trust finite in time, to be ended at a future date not far distant, when empire had in fact produced culture change to something approaching the Western model. For them, empire was guardianship over a minor until he reached maturity, not a permanent wardship over the incapacitated. But others held this to be impossible: people of other races could not become truly civilized in the fashion of Europeans. Still others held that full cultural assimilation to the West was not desirable as an immediate goal. Some missionary theorists followed the Reverend Rufus Anderson of the United States in his view that the missionary's proper task was

13. See selections below, pp. 105–31, 319–37.

strictly spiritual—to carry a universal religious message, abstracted
from its context in Western culture. Though this was a minority
position in the nineteenth century, it became important in the mid-
twentieth, just as the imperial era was coming to an end.

The least conversionist of the important advocates of trusteeship
were the British theorists who exalted Indirect Rule through African chiefs and the equivalent French school who took Association
as their watchword, in contrast to Assimilation, which they believed had dominated colonial policy during the nineteenth century. Both the Indirect Rulers and the Associationists began to
formulate their doctrine in the 1890's and to consolidate into a
group of advocates in the decade after 1900. The idea of Association arose in the context of French debates about the aims of
empire, beginning with the National Colonial Congress held in
Paris in 1889–90.[14] The leading figures at that congress were
broadly liberal and republican. They were successful in the passage
of a series of resolutions designed to place colonial affairs more
closely under the direct control of the National Assembly. Some of
them were also conversionist or Assimilationist, and another series
of resolutions were introduced by Senator A. Isaac in that spirit.
The key statement was this:

1. The Section, recognizing that the best mode of colonization
and that closest to the tendencies of the French national character
consists in attracting the native populations increasingly to the
civilization of the mother country, while at the same time respecting the customs of that population that are worthy of respect,
resolves:
That the colonizing effort, in all countries falling under French
authority, be directed toward the propagation among the natives
of the national language, the customs, and the industrious habits
of the motherland.[15]

The resolution was certainly mild enough. It did not call for the
blanket imposition of French culture, or for the political assimilation of the colonies to the French nation, or for the civil and
political equality of the colonized who met the culture test by

14. Congrès colonial national, Paris, 1889–90, *Recueil des délibérations*,
3 vols. (Paris, 1890). See also Hubert Deschamps, *Les méthodes et les
doctrines coloniales de la France (du xvie siècle à nos jours)* (Paris, 1953),
esp. pp. 152–160; and Raymond F. Betts, *Assimilation and Association in
French Colonial Theory, 1890–1914* (New York, 1961).
15. Congrès colonial, *Délibérations*, 3:15.

becoming French. But the key fact for judging the importance of conversionism in French imperial thought was not the moderation of the Isaac resolutions; it was the fact that they were rejected by the congress. Mild as they were, they appeared dangerous to the majority in an era of rapidly increasing racism. The reasoned response came in a series of books and articles by pseudoscientific racists, beginning with Gustave Le Bon's *Les lois psychologiques de l'évolution des peuples* in 1894. Le Bon was a popularizer rather than a scientist of the calibre of Darwin, or even Knox; but his ideas were extremely influential, and their colonial implications were spelled out further by Léopold de Saussure in 1899.[16] Saussure also furthered another tradition among the French racist theorists of empire, that of setting up the theory of Assimilation as a stalking horse in opposition to their own ideas. In fact, French colonial policy as a whole had been no more conversionist than that of Great Britain. Briefly during both the First and the Second Republic, legislation had been passed in France extending the political rights of Frenchmen to a few West Africans and West Indians, but Assimilation was never pursued as a consistent policy, and no well-known colonial theorist argued its merits in a reasoned brief.

The key belief of the Associationists was that culture, like race, is heritable. Culture change is therefore impossible, except within quite narrow limits, and to attempt the impossible is undesirable.[17] The best imperial policy would therefore be one that encouraged "the native" to develop "in his own way." Some elements of this idea were to be found among British racists a half century earlier, like Knox in Scotland, but its principal advocates in Britain were to be the school of Indirect Rule, represented especially by Lord Lugard, Charles Temple, and Sir Hanns Vischer in the prewar decade, with many successors in the 1920's.

The principal difference between the Indirect Rulers and the Associationists was the British emphasis on administrative devices, as opposed to the greater French concern with long-term cultural

16. In *Psychologie de la colonisation française dans ses rapports avec les sociétés indigènes* (Paris, 1899). See selection below, pp.85–92.

17. The most important single theorist of Association was Jules Harmand, who popularized the term in many articles and then presented the whole program in *Domination et colonisation* (Paris, 1910). See selection below, pp. 291–307.

goals. The Indirect Rulers held that Western political institutions, and especially the institutions of local governments, were fundamentally unsuited to the African character—and their principal field of action was tropical Africa. They chose, instead, to preserve traditional institutions intact, only "improving" them gradually and in small stages. In this way, the African authorities would be used as the lower ranks of the imperial administration. In fact, a shortage of European personnel made some such device necessary in the first stages of every European empire, as far back in time as the first Spanish administrations in Mexico and Peru. In this case, necessity was made into a virtue and justified with elaborate theory.

Difference in emphasis, however, should not be allowed to obscure the basic similarity of Indirect Rule and Association. Both were variants of the idea of trusteeship in which conversionism was minimal. Both Indirect Rulers and Associationists were suspicious of religious missions, and both doubted that the values and standards of Western civilization were universally applicable. Both expected a period of imperial tutelage that would extend far into the future. These views were generally dominant in European imperial thought during the last phase of the imperial era, the period between the two World Wars.

I

The "Scientific" Roots: Nineteenth-Century Racism

Not all racists were imperialists, nor were all imperialists racists of the most radical variety; but racism pervaded nineteenth-century European thought about the world overseas. From the 1870's into the 1920's and beyond, virtually every European concerned with imperial theory or imperial administration believed that physical racial appearance was an outward sign of inborn propensities, inclinations, and abilities. The selections that follow are therefore far too few to be truly representative, but they illustrate some of the common tendencies of the period.[1]

One of the roots of racist thought came from the biological sciences, especially from the prestige accorded to biological discovery. Biologists were all too willing to step from their own field of specialization and comment with confidence on human history and society. This tendency was marked in the writings of Georges Cuvier and Charles Darwin, who were genuine scientists of high reputation. It was even more marked among others who stood on the edges of the scientific world, but were anxious to popularize the knowledge of biological advance—men like Gustave Le Bon in France or Robert Knox in England.

Knox was a special case in this respect. His original scientific reputation came from his work in anatomy. In 1828, however, two of the agents who secured corpses for dissection at his school of anatomy turned from grave robbing to murder to fill the demand. Though Knox was not directly implicated, the resulting scandal so tarnished his reputation that he turned from scientific investigation

---

1. For a wider variety of selections, see E. W. Count, *This Is Race* (New York, 1950).

to a new career as lecturer and writer for a more popular audience. He called his new subject "transcendental anatomy," and sought to draw out the fullest possible implications of the new biology. The result was a pre-Darwinian theory of evolution, stressing the competition between human races rather than animal species.

Darwin himself drew something from Knox, though he had comparatively little to say about the possibility of racial competition. He did, however, comment on the apparent fact that different races of men had different chances of survival in the nineteenth century. This differential mortality was the most important biological evidence that race difference was a significant factor in human affairs—and biologists have since found out that it was caused by factors other than race. The nineteenth century nevertheless recognized only that human beings sustained rates of morbidity and mortality from disease that differed in spectacular ways, depending on the time, place, and people involved. Europeans died at much higher rates in the tropics than they did in Europe. American Indians had been decreasing in number since the seventeenth century, and Europeans saw this as a tendency of a "race" to die out on contact with European settlers. Several explanations were tried. High European death rates in the tropics were seen as the result of the "climate," where in fact they were simply the result of unfamiliar diseases among adults who had not acquired a protecting immunity in childhood. In America, the cause of Indian population decline was similar—unfamiliar diseases from the Afro-Eurasian land mass attacking previously isolated populations which lacked the appropriate immunities—and again European explanations fell upon the obvious fact of racial difference and missed the reality of differing disease environments. Some went still further and saw the death of the Indians as the work of a benign God, clearing the way for "civilization" and its superior European bearers.[2]

Both the fact of differential mortality and some explanations had been publicized in Europe in the eighteenth century and even

2. See P. D. Curtin, "Epidemiology and the Slave Trade," *Political Science Quarterly*, 83:190–216 (1968); P. M. Ashburn, *The Ranks of Death. A Medical History of the Conquest of America* (New York, 1947); Woodrow Borah, "América como modelo? El impacto demográfico de la expansión europea sobre el mundo no europeo," *Cuadernos Americanos*, 21:176–185 (1962).

earlier, but humanitarian and scientific interest turned to this subject with renewed concern in the 1830's. A Parliamentary Select Committee met in England in 1835–37 to look into the fate of the aborigines in British colonies. Resulting publicity led to the foundation of the Aborigines Protection Society in Britain, and to the formation of the first professional anthropological societies in both England and France. Major Alexander M. Tulloch of the British Army picked up the problem and conducted an elaborate statistical study of differential mortality among British troops recruited in various parts of the world, a survey which appeared as a series of government publications from 1838 through 1842.[3]

The timing of this new publicity and new evidence in European consciousness was crucial to the development of pseudoscientific racism. Biologists had just completed the classification of animal species and were deeply concerned with the classification of human races. It was only natural to set the new findings in racial terms. Besides, the germ theory of disease was still unknown and would remain unknown for several decades. Virtually nothing was known of immunology, and epidemiology was still in its infancy. Scientists therefore lacked the kind of knowledge necessary to a better understanding. Once started down the road of racial explanations, it was especially hard to backtrack and begin again. Thus, it was far into the twentieth century before it came to be generally recognized that even those immunities to disease that *are* inherited are inherited as a genetic variable independent of race classification. But for biologists of Darwin's generation and those that followed him, race was not merely a matter of appearance. As his discussion of the Tasmanians and Maori showed, it appeared to be a matter of life and death.

These "discoveries" soon moved deeper into European thought. A succession of writers—like Count de Gobineau, Houston Stewart Chamberlain, C. H. Pearson, Madison Grant, and Adolf Hitler —began to emphasize the barely perceptible racial differences within the European community itself. Small wonder, then, that race became such an important factor in the eyes of the imperialists.

3. See P. D. Curtin, *The Image of Africa* (Madison, 1964), esp. pp. 330–331. Tulloch's surveys appeared in the Parliamentary Sessional Papers cited hereafter as PP, 1837–38, xl [C.138]; 1839, xvi [C.166]; 1840, xxx [C.228]; 1842, xxvii [C.358].

1. Georges Cuvier and the Varieties of Mankind

Georges Léopold Chrétien Frédéric Dagobert Cuvier (1769–1832) was a Swiss anatomist considered to be the founder of paleontology. His great work of comparative anatomy appeared in 1817 under the title *Le règne animal, distribué d'après son organisation,* and was published in a fifteen-volume English edition in 1827. The section that follows is from a later English translation as *The Animal Kingdom,* by H. MacMurtrie, published in New York in four volumes in 1831, vol. 1, pp. 44–45 and 48–55. Though his tripartite classification of human races was by no means original, his was an important influence in sustaining that classification, and in perpetuating the term "Caucasian" for peoples with a pinkish-yellow skin color. In retrospect, his treatment of human race is interesting for his narcissistic admiration of his own physical type, combined with a reading of history that was ignorant (even for his period) and culturally arrogant. The passage quoted is all he has to say about human beings, other than a brief anatomical description.

Order I. Bimana.

MAN FORMS but one genus, and that genus the only one of its order. As his history is the more directly interesting to ourselves, and forms the point of comparison to which we refer that of other animals, we will speak of it more in detail.

We will rapidly sketch every thing that is peculiar in each of his organic systems, amidst all that he shares in common with other mammalia; we will examine the advantages he derives from these peculiarities over other species; we will describe the principal varieties of his race and their distinguishing characters, and finally point out the natural order in which his individual and social faculties are developed. . . .

PHYSICAL AND MORAL DEVELOPMENT OF MAN.

The term of gestation in the human species is nine months, and but one child is usually produced at a birth, as in five hundred cases of parturition there is but one of twins; more than the latter is extremely rare. The foetus, a month old, is generally about one inch in height; when two months, it is two inches and a half; when three, five inches; in the fifth month, it is six or seven inches; in the seventh, it is eleven inches; in the eighth, fourteen, and in the ninth, eighteen inches. Those which are born prior to the seventh month usually die. The first or milk teeth begin to appear in a few months, commencing with the incisors. The number increases in two years to twenty, which, about the seventh year, are successively shed to make room for others. Of the twelve posterior molares which are permanent, there are four which make their appearance at four years and a half, and four at nine; the last four are frequently not cut until the twentieth year. The growth of the foetus is proportionably increased as it approaches the time of birth—that of the child, on the contrary, is always less and less. It has more than the fourth of its height when born; it attains the half of it at two years and a half, and the three-fourths at nine or ten years; its growth is completed about the eighteenth year. Man rarely exceeds the height of six feet, and as rarely remains under five. Woman is usually some inches shorter.

Puberty is announced by external symptoms, from the tenth to the twelfth year in girls, and from the twelfth to the sixteenth in boys; it arrives sooner in warm climates, and neither sex, (very rarely at least,) is productive before or after that manifestation.

Scarcely has the body gained the full period of its growth in height, before it begins to increase in bulk; fat accumulates in the cellular tissue, the different vessels become gradually obstructed, the solids become rigid, and, after a life more or less long, more or less agitated, more or less painful, old age arrives with decrepitude, decay, and death. Man rarely lives beyond a hundred years, and most of the species, either from disease, accident, or old age, perish long before that term.

The child needs the assistance of its mother much longer than her milk, from this it obtains an education both moral and physical, and a mutual attachment is created that is fervent and durable. The nearly equal number of the two sexes, the difficulty of supporting more than one wife, when wealth does not supply the want of power, all go to prove that monogamy is the mode of union most natural to our species, and, as wherever this kind of tie exists, the father participates in the education of his offspring, the length of time required for that education allows the birth of others—hence the natural permanence of the conjugal state. From the long period of infantile weakness springs domestic subordination, and the order of society in general, as the young people which compose the new families continue to preserve with their parents those tender relations to which they have so long been accustomed. This disposition to mutual assistance multiplies to an almost unlimited extent those advantages previously derived by insulated man from his intelligence; it has assisted him to tame or repulse other animals, to defend himself from the effects of climate, and thus enabled him to cover the earth with his species.

In other respects, man appears to possess nothing resembling instinct, no regular habit of industry produced by innate ideas; his knowledge is the result of his sensations and of his observation, or of those of his predecessors. Transmitted by speech, increased by meditation, and applied to his necessities and his enjoyments, they have originated all the arts of life. Language and letters, by preserving acquired knowledge, are a source of indefinite perfection to his species. It is thus he has acquired ideas, and made all nature contribute to his wants.

There are very different degrees of development, however, in man.

The first hordes, compelled to live by fishing and hunting, or on wild fruits, and being obliged to devote all their time to search for the means of subsistence, and not being able to multiply greatly, because that would have destroyed the game, advanced but slowly. Their arts were limited to the construction of huts and canoes, to covering themselves with skins and the fabrication of arrows and nets. They observed such stars only as directed them in their journeys, and some few natural objects whose properties were of use to them. They domesticated the Dog, simply because he had a natural inclination for their own kind of life. When they had succeeded in taming the herbivorous animals, they found in the possession of numerous flocks a never failing source of subsistence, and also some leisure, which they employed in extending the sphere of their acquirements. Some industry was then employed in the construction of dwellings and the making of clothes: the idea of property was admitted, and consequently that of barter, as well as wealth and difference of conditions, those fruitful sources of the noblest emulation and the vilest passions: but the necessity of searching for fresh pastures, and of obeying the changes of the seasons, still doomed them to a wandering life, and limited their improvement to a very narrow sphere.

The multiplication of the human species, and its improvement in the arts and sciences, have only been carried to a high degree since the invention of agriculture and the division of the soil into hereditary possessions. By means of agriculture, the manual labour of a portion of society is adequate to the maintenance of the whole, and allows the remainder time for less necessary occupations, at the same time that the hope of acquiring, by industry, a comfortable existence for self and posterity, has given a new spring to emulation. The discovery of a representative of property or a circulating medium, by facilitating exchanges and rendering fortunes more independent and susceptible of being increased, has carried this emulation to its highest degree, but by a necessary consequence it has also equally increased the vices of effeminacy and the furies of ambition.

The natural propensity to reduce every thing to general principles, and to search for the causes of every phenomenon, has produced reflecting men, in every stage of society, who have added new ideas to those already obtained, nearly all of whom, while knowledge was confined to the few, endeavoured to convert their intellectual superiority into the means of domination, by exaggerating their own merit, and disguising the poverty of their knowledge by the propagation of superstitious ideas.

An evil still more irremediable, is the abuse of physical power: now that man only can injure man, he is continually seeking to do so, and is the only animal upon earth that is for ever at war with his own species. Savages fight for a forest, and herdsmen for a pasture, and as often as they can, break in upon the cultivators of the earth to rob them of the fruits of their long and painful labours. Even civilized nations, far from being contented with their blessings, pour out each other's blood for the prerogatives of pride, or the monopoly of trade. Hence, the necessity for governments to direct the national wars, and to repress or reduce to regular forms the quarrels of individuals.

The social condition of man has been restrained, or advanced by circumstances more or less favourable.

The glacial climates of the north of both continents [Asia and Europe], and the impenetrable forests of America are still inhabited by the savage hunter or fisherman. The immense sandy and salt plains of central Asia and Africa are covered with a pastoral people, and innumerable herds. These half civilized hordes assemble at the call of every enthusiastic chief, and rush like a torrent on the cultivated countries that surround them, in which they establish themselves, but to be weakened by luxury, and in their turn to become the prey of others. This is the true cause of that despotism which has always crushed and destroyed the industry of Persia, India, and China.

Mild climates, soils naturally irrigated and rich in vegetables, are the cradles of agriculture and civilization, and when so situated as to be sheltered from the incursions of barbarians, every species of talent is excited; such were (the first in Europe) Italy and Greece, and such is, at present, nearly all that happy portion of the earth.

There are, however, certain intrinsic causes which seem to arrest the progress of particular races, although situated amidst the most favourable circumstances.

VARIETIES OF THE HUMAN SPECIES.

Although the promiscuous intercourse of the human species, which produces individuals capable of propagation, would seem to demonstrate its unity, certain hereditary peculiarities of conformation are observed which constitute what are termed *races*.

Three of them in particular appear very distinct—the *Caucasian* or white, the *Mongolian* or yellow, and the *Ethiopian* or Negro.

The Caucasian, to which we belong, is distinguished by the beauty of the oval formed by his head, varying in complexion and the colour of the hair. To this variety, the most highly civilized nations, and those which have generally held all others in subjection, are indebted for their origin.

The Mongolian is known by his high cheek bones, flat visage, narrow and oblique eyes, straight black hair, scanty beard and olive complexion. Great empires have been established by this race in China and Japan, and their conquests been extended to this side of the Great Desert. In civilization, however, it has always remained stationary.

The Negro race is confined to the south of mount Atlas; it is marked by a black complexion, crisped or woolly hair, compressed cranium, and a flat nose. The projection of the lower parts of the face, and the thick lips, evidently approximate it to the monkey tribe: the hordes of which it consists have always remained in the most complete state of utter barbarism.

The race from which we are descended has been called *Caucasian*, because tradition and the filiation of nations seem to refer its origin to that group of mountains situated between the Caspian and Black seas, whence, as from a centre, it has been extended like the radii of a circle. Various nations in the vicinity of Caucasus, the Georgians and Circassians, are still considered the handsomest on earth. The principal ramifications of this race may be distinguished by the analogies of language. The Armenian or Syrian branch, stretching to the south, produced the Assyrians, the Chaldeans, the hitherto untameable Arabs, who, after Mahomet, were near becoming masters of the world; the Phoenicians, Jews and Abyssinians, which were Arabian colonies; and most probably the Egyptians. It is from this branch, always inclined to mysticism, that have sprung the most widely extended forms of religion—the arts and literature have sometimes flourished among its nations, but always enveloped in a strange disguise and figurative style.

The Indian, German, and Pelasgic branch is much more extended, and was much earlier divided: notwithstanding which, the most numerous affinities may be observed between its four principal languages—the Sanscrit, the present sacred language of the Hindoos, and the parent of the greater number of the dialects of Hindostan; the ancient language of the Pelasgi, common mother of the Greek, Latin, many tongues that are extinct, and of all those of the south of Europe; the Gothic or Teutonic, from which are derived the languages of the north and north-west of Europe, such as the German, Dutch, English, Danish, Swedish, and other dialects; and finally, the Sclavonian, from which spring those of the north-east, the Russian, Polish, Bohemian, &c.

It is by this great and venerable branch of the Caucasian stock, that philosophy, the arts, and the sciences have been carried to the greatest perfection, and remained in the keeping of the nations which compose it for more than three thousand years.

It was preceded in Europe by the Celts, who came from the north, whose tribes, once very numerous, are now confined to its most eastern extremity, and by the Cantabrians, who passed from Africa into Spain, now confounded with the many nations whose posterity have intermingled in that peninsula.

The ancient Persians originate from the same source as the Indians, and their descendants to the present hour bear great marks of resemblance to the people of Europe.

The predatory tribes of the Scythian and Tartar branch, extending at first to the north and north-east, always wandering over the immense plains of those countries, returned only to devastate the happier abodes of their more civilized brethren. The Scythians, who, at so remote a period, made irruptions into upper Asia; the Parthians, who there destroyed the Greek and Roman domination; the Turks, who there subverted that of the Arabs, and subjugated in Europe the unfortunate remnant of the Grecian people, all swarmed from this prolific branch. The Finlanders and Hungarians are tribes of the same division, which have strayed among the Sclavonic and Teutonic nations. Their original country, to the north and north-east of the Caspian sea still contains inhabitants who have the same origin, and speak similar languages, but mingled with other petty nations, variously descended, and of different languages. The Tartars remained unmixed longer than the others in the country included between the mouth of the Danube to beyond the Irtisch, from which they so long menaced Russia, and where they have finally been subjugated by her. The Mongoles, however, have mingled their blood with that of those they conquered, many traces of which may still be found among the inhabitants of lesser Tartary.

It is to the east of this Tartar branch of the Caucasian race that the Mongolian race begins, whence it extends to the eastern ocean. Its branches, the Calmucs, &c. still wandering shepherds, are constantly traversing the desert. Thrice did their ancestors under Attila, Genghis, and Tamerlane, spread far the terror of their name. The Chinese are the earliest and most civilized branch not only of this race, to which they belong, but of all the nations upon earth. A third branch, the Mantchures, recently conquered, and still govern China. The Japanese, Coreans, and nearly all the hordes which extend to the north-east of Siberia, subject to Russia, are also to be considered, in a great measure, as originating from this race; and such also is esteemed the fact, with regard to the original inhabitants of various islands of that Archipelago. With the exception of a few Chinese literati, the different nations of the Mongoles are universally addicted to Buddism, or the religion of Fo.

The origin of this great race appears to have been in the mountains of Atlai, but it is impossible to trace the filiation of its different branches with the same certainty as we have done those of the Caucasian. The history of these wandering nations is as fugitive as their establishments, and that of the Chinese, confined exclusively to their own empire, gives us nothing satisfactory with respect to their neighbours. The affinities of their languages are also too little known to direct us in this labyrinth.

The languages of the north of the Peninsula beyond the Ganges, as well as that of Thibet, are somewhat allied to the Chinese, at least in their monosyllabic structure, and the people who speak them have features somewhat resembling other Mongoles. The south of this Peninsula, however, is inhabited by Malays, whose forms approximate them much nearer to the Indians, whose race and language are extended over all the coasts of the islands of the Indian Archipelago. The innumerable little islands of the southern ocean are also peopled by a handsome race, nearly allied to the Indians, whose language is very similar to the Malay; in the interior of the largest of these islands, particularly in the wilder portions of it, is another race of men with black complexions, crisped hair, and negro faces, called Alfourous. On the coast of New Guinea, and in the neighbouring islands, we find other negroes, nearly similar to those of the eastern coast of Africa, named Papuas; (1) to the latter, are generally referred the people of Van-Diemen's land, and those of New Holland to the Alfourous.

These Malays, and these Papuas are not easily referable to either of the three great races of which we have been speaking, but can the former be clearly distinguished from their neighbours, the Caucasian Hindoos and the Mongolian Chinese? As for us, we confess we cannot discover any sufficient characteristics in them for that purpose. Are the Papuas Negroes, which may formerly have strayed into the Indian ocean? We possess neither figures nor descriptions sufficiently precise to enable us to answer this question.

The northern inhabitants of both continents, the Samoiëdes, the Laplanders, and the Esquimaux spring, according to some, from the Mongolian race, while others assert that they are mere degenerate offsets from the Scythian and Tartar branch of the Caucasian stock.

We have not yet been able to refer the Americans to any of the races of the eastern continent; still, they have no precise nor constant character which can entitle them to be considered as a particular one. Their copper coloured complexion is not sufficient; their generally black hair and scanty beard would induce us to refer them to the Mongoles, if their defined features, projecting nose, large and open eye, did not oppose such a theory, and correspond with the features of the European. Their languages are as numberless as their tribes, and no demonstrative analogy has as yet been obtained, either with each other, or with those of the old world.

2. Robert Knox on the Dark Races of Men

In the nineteenth century, scientific writing for a scientific audience was separated by several stages from popular writing on scientific subjects, and several major scientists wrote for both audiences. Robert Knox (1791–1862) was one of these. After medical school and a period of military service during the Napoleonic Wars, he visited Cape Colony to conduct research on comparative anatomy. Later he founded a school of anatomy in Edinburgh. The supply of corpses for this school involved his name in scandal and led to a period of unpopularity in professional circles, though he was later elected a Fellow of the London Ethnological Society and an honorary curator of its Museum.

In the later 1840's, during his fall from grace, he gave a series of lectures on "transcendental anatomy," which were published in 1850 as *The Races of Man*. The popular platform style is obvious in this selection from his chapter on "The Dark Races of Men." There he assumed that race war will occur—was occurring—and that the whites would win all over the world outside of the tropical zone. There the blacks would win. The idea is clearly derived from the information on differential mortality current at the period, though Knox's error in seeing race where he should have seen disease environment is striking in retrospect. He expected the Xhosa of South Africa to die out, as the American aborigines had done. Instead they increased in number with no apparent ill effects from their contact with the Europeans—not, at least, from European diseases.

Knox's views also illustrate the point that racists were not necessarily imperialists. While he believed that the imperial rule of the "Saxons" was inevitable, he was not an advocate of empire or particular imperial policies; and he had a low opinion of the Colonial Office and the India Office.

The selections are taken from *The Races of Man: A Philosophical Enquiry into the Influence of Race over the Destinies of Nations*, 2nd ed. (London, 1862), pp. 220–230 and 233–244.

Section I.

FROM THE earliest recorded times *might* has always constituted *right*, or been held to do so. By this *right* the Slavonic race crushes down Italy, withering and blasting the grandest section of mankind. By this kind of *right,* that is, *power* or *might,* we seized on North America, dispossessing the native races, to whom America naturally belonged; we drove them back into their primitive forests, slaughtering them piteously; our descendants, the United States men, drove us out by the same *right*—that is, *might.* The same tragedy was repeated in South America; the mingled host of Celtiberian adventurers brought against the feeble Mexican, Peruvian, and Brazilian, the strength and knowledge and arms of European men; the strength of a fair or, at least, of a fairer race. The Popes of Rome sanctified the atrocities; it was the old tragedy again, the fair races of men against the dark races; the strong against the feeble; the united against those who knew not how to place even a sentinel; the progressists against those who stood still—who could not or would not progress. Look all over the globe, it is always the same; the dark races stand still, the fair progress. See how a company of London merchants lord it over a hundred millions of coloured men in Hindostan—I doubt the story of the hundred millions, however; the hot suns of India exalt, I have remarked, the brains of Europeans who sojourn long there; but, be it as they say, the fact is astounding. Whilst I now write, the Celtic race is preparing to seize Northern Africa by the same right as we seized Hindostan—that is, might, physical force—the only real right is physical force; whilst we, not to be behind in the grasp for more acres, annex New Zealand and all its dependencies to the British dominions, to be wrested from us by-and-by by our sons and descendants as the United States were and Canada will be, for no Saxon race can ever hold a colony long. The coolness with which this act of appropriation has been done is, I think, quite unparalleled in the history of aggressions. A slip of parchment signed officially is issued from that den of all abuses, the office of the Colonial Secretary, declaring New Zealand to be a colony of Britain, with all its dependencies, lands, fisheries, mines, inhabitants. The aborigines are to be protected! Now, if the Crown will let them alone, they can protect themselves; but this would not suit the wolf who took care of the sheep. Still, mark the organized hypocrisy of the official opener of the letters of others: the aborigines are not declared Britons; they are merely to be protected!

The Indian empire, as we call it, having turned out so profitable an investment for British capital, although for obvious reasons it never can become a permanent colony of England, suggested to "the Office" the idea of founding a similar empire in the heart of Africa.[1] Everything seemed favourable for the enterprise; Southern Africa had long been ours; the southern extra-tropical part, partly held nominally by the Portuguese—that is, as good as not held at all—a wide desert separating Central Africa from the Morocen, from the Celt (in Alger) and from the present Egyptian ruler; Central Africa, full of wealth, a productive soil, and a feeble, black population! Nothing could be more favourable, and I have not the smallest doubt that the officials at the Colonial-office already contemplated another India in Central Africa; the wealth, the product of the labour of many millions of Africans, in reality slaves, as the natives of Hindostan, but held to be free by a legal fiction, might be poured into the coffers of the office! But, alas for land-seeking colonial secretaries! climate interfered; exterminated the crews of their ships, and scattered the hopes of the patriot lord at the head of the office.

Since the earliest times, then, the dark races have been the slaves of their fairer brethren. Now, how is this? Mr. Gibbon solves the question in his usual dogmatic way; he speaks of the obvious physical inferiority of the Negro; he means, no doubt, the dark races generally, for the remark applies to all. But, notwithstanding the contrary opinion professed by Dr. Tiedemann respecting the great size of some African skulls, which he found in my own museum, sent to me from the western coast of Africa, I feel disposed to think that there must be a physical and, consequently, a psychological inferiority in the dark races generally. This may not depend altogether on deficiency in the size of the brain *en masse*, nor on any partial defects; to which, however, I shall advert presently; but rather, perhaps, to specific characters in the quality of the brain itself. It may, perhaps, be right to consider first the different obvious physical qualities of the dark races, before we enter on the history of their position as regards the mass of mankind, and especially as regards those races which seem destined, if not to destroy

1. The author is referring here to the British Niger expedition of 1841–42, which aimed at establishing a trading post and agricultural settlement at the junction of the Niger and Benue Rivers in what is now Nigeria. In the terminology of the time, this part of Africa was often called Central Africa, though it is now part of the conventional West Africa .

them altogether, at least to limit their position to those regions of the earth where the fair races can neither labour nor live—the equatorial regions and the regions adjoining the tropics, usually termed by romancists and travellers, and not unfairly, the grave of Europeans.

First, as regards mere physical strength, the dark races are generally much inferior to the Saxon and Celt; the bracelets worn by the Kaffirs, when placed on our own arms, prove this. Secondly, in size of brain they seem also considerably inferior to the above races, and no doubt also to the Sarmatian and the Slavonic. Thirdly, the form of the skull differs from ours, and is placed differently on the neck; the texture of the brain is I think generally darker, and the white part more strongly fibrous; but I speak from extremely limited experience. Mr. Tiedemann, I think it is, who says that the convolutions of the upper surface of the two hemispheres of the brain are nearly symmetrical; in our brain the reverse always happens. Lastly, the whole shape of the skeleton differs from ours, and so also I find do the forms of almost every muscle of the body. The upper jaw is uniformly of extraordinary size, and this, together with a peculiarity in the setting on of the face, I find to constitute the most striking differences. I at one time thought that the bones of the nose were peculiar in some races, as in the Bosjeman and Hottentot. In these races, or race, for perhaps they are but one, I fancied that, more frequently at least than in others, the bones of the nose are remarkably narrow, run together to form but one bone, and show even an additional thin germ mesially; perhaps merely the anterior margin of another bone, or an extension of the spine of the frontal. Still the specimens are so few in Europe, that I feel disinclined to attach much importance to this sufficiently singular fact. I think I have seen one of the nasal bones so short and thin as not to reach the frontal.

In the Peruvian skull, at twelve years of age, Von Tchudi thinks he has detected a new germ of bone, an interparietal bone, in fact, peculiar to the native American race; the physical differences in the structure of the Boschjiee women and Hottentots are unmistakeable. Still be it remembered that we have no accurate account of the structural differences of the races of *men* on which we can depend—mere scraps of observations scarcely worthy of notice. The Negro muscles are differently shaped from ours; the curly, corkscrew locks of the Hottentot bear no resemblance to the lank, black hair of the Esquimaux. The Tasmanian and Australian races are said to show many peculiarities in structure.

Let it be remembered, however, that, after all, it is to the exterior we must look for the more remarkable characteristics of animals; it is it alone which nature loves to decorate and to vary: the interior organs of animals, not far removed from each other, vary but little. To this fact I shall advert more particularly in the lecture on transcendental anatomy; the internal structures of animals present details which we read imperfectly, connected as they are, on the one hand, with mechanical arrangements, and on the other with the primitive laws of creation.

There is one thing obvious in the history of the dark races, that they all, more or less, exhibit the outline of the interior more strongly marked than in the fair races generally. Thus the face of the adult Negro or Hottentot resembles, from the want of flesh, a skeleton, over which has been drawn a blackened skin.

But who are the dark races of ancient and modern times? It would not be easy to answer this question. Were the Copts a dark race? Are the Jews a dark race? The Gipsies? The Chinese, &c.? Dark they are to a certain extent; so are all the Mongol tribes—the American Indian and Esquimaux—the inhabitants of nearly all Africa—of the East—of Australia. What a field of extermination lies before the Saxon Celtic and Sarmatian races! The Saxon will not mingle with any dark race, nor will he allow him to hold an acre of land in the country occupied by him; this, at least, is the law of Anglo-Saxon America. The fate, then, of the Mexicans, Peruvians, and Chilians, is in no shape doubtful. Extinction of the race—sure extinction—it is not even denied.

Already, in a few years, we have cleared Van Diemen's Land of every *human* aboriginal; Australia, of course, follows, and New Zealand next; there is no denying the fact, that the Saxon, call him by what name you will, has a perfect horror for his darker brethren. Hence the folly of the war carried on by the philanthropists of Britain against nature: of these persons some are honest, some not. I venture to recommend the honest ones—to try their strength in a practical measure. Let them demand for the natives of Hindostan, of Ceylon, or even of the Cape or New Zealand, the privileges and rights wholly and fairly of Britons; I predict a refusal on the part of the Colonial-office. The office will appoint you as many aborigines protectors as you like—that is, spies; but the extension of equal rights and privileges to all colours is quite another question.

But now, having considered the physical constitution thus briefly of some of these dark races, and shown you that we really know but little of them; that we have not data whereon to base a physical history of mankind; let me now consider the history of a few of them—of those, at least, best known to me. . . .

. . . Our present business is with the primitive race, the aborigines, as they are called, of Southern Africa, called by the Dutch some three hundred years ago Hottentots and Bosjemen,—names unknown in the language of the race, for they call themselves Autniquas, Quoiquoes,[2] &c. Did the Dutch, the Christian Dutch, consider these races to be men and women? I scarcely think so. True, they held as a theory that all men and women came from one pair, like all cows, and pigs, and sheep; but this was a mere theory; in practice they held them to be a something different. The coloured men the Dutch called boys, and the coloured women they called maids; in speaking of the persons composing a Commando, for example, they would say that there were on it thirty *men*, meaning Dutchmen, and fifty boys, meaning black men. *De facto*, then, the Dutch did not hold these races to be the same as their own; the fact is undeniable and incontestable. I care not for theories; the Dutch practically denied the first canon of Scripture in a body, as the United States men do now; there is no denying it. To the strange, perfectly strange, animals around them, every one differing generically and specifically from those of Europe, they gave European names: the beautiful antelope frequenting the bushy ravines of the present colony they called the bosje-bok, or bush-goat, although it be not a goat; they found also the elk or eland, although there are no elks in Africa; the very oxen and miserable sheep of the wretched Hottentot, the Saxon Dutchman adopted, cherished and maintained unaltered, until an irruption from Europe of Englishmen upset them and their soul-destroying self-opiniativeness. But we must not advert at present to these drawbacks on the Saxon character; his onward principle diffused and spread him over the colony; the go-ahead principle was at

2. Modern spelling Khoi-Khoi, now used in preference to the pejorative term "Hottentot."

work; this, of course, led to the seizure of land, the plunder and massacre, wholesale sometimes, of the simple aborigines. Wild principles were let loose on both sides; the gun and bayonet became the law; and whilst I now write, the struggle is recommencing with a dark race (the Caffre), to terminate, of course, in their extinction.[3]

I have said that when the Dutch first landed at the Cape of Good Hope they met with the race called Hottentots—a simple, feeble race of men, living in little groups, almost, indeed, in families, tending their fat-tailed sheep and dreaming away their lives. Of a dirty yellow colour, they slightly resemble the Chinese, but are clearly of a different blood. The face is set on like a baboon's; cranium small but good; jaws very large; feet and hands small; eyes linear in form and of great power; forms generally handsome; hideous when old, and never pretty; lazier than an Irishwoman, which is saying much; and of a blood different and totally distinct from all the rest of the world. The women are not made like other women. Tiedemann says that the two hemispheres of the brain are nearly symmetrical. Though small in stature, they are taller than their cognate race, the Bosjeman; these I take to be nearly allied to the Hottentot, though different in a good many respects. They have the physical qualities of the Hottentot, but exaggerated; they are still shorter in stature. Having no measurements on which I can depend, I offer merely as a conjecture the average height of the male and female Bosjeman,—say four feet six inches for the male, and four feet for the female. Their power of sight is incredible, and this, with all other peculiarities, disappears with a single crossing of the breed.

The extent to which these singular races, if they really be distinct, extend northwards through Central Africa is altogether unknown. Dr. Andrew Smith, so well known for his travels in Southern Africa, informs me, that he saw them within the tropic, and he thinks they extend much higher; moreover, he is of opinion that they form but one race; in Harris's "Ethiopia," mention is

3. The dark race in question is recognized today as being Negro. They are, in fact, the Xhosa people of the eastern Cape and the present Transkei. He is correct in saying that they were racially different from the San and the Khoi-Khoi who lived to the west and northwest. The war in question is probably the frontier war of 1846–48 between the Xhosa and the British in Cape Colony.

made of a race, somewhat resembling the Bosjeman, inhabiting a wild district in Southern Abyssinia, on the equator, deeply hidden amongst woods and mountains. He did not see them, and nothing positive can be gathered from his description.

Diodorus Siculus speaks of the Troglodytes of Northern Africa, who inhabited caves and mountains, a pigmy race and of no courage; whilst the divine Homer places, I think, in Africa, his pigmy men, against whom the cranes waged constant war.

What interesting questions, geographical or ethnological, are here to solve! What a field does Africa still present! Whence came these Bosjemen and Hottentots? They differ as much from their fellow-men as the animals of Southern Africa do from those of South America. They are a dark race; but the sun has not darkened them. Without arts, without religion, and without civilization of any kind, for how many centuries had they occupied their kraals, content to live, and to perish like the beasts of the field, leaving no name behind them that such things were!

Before the go-ahead Dutchmen it was easy to see that this puny, pigmy, miserable race must retire; they did so chiefly, as it seems, towards the northward, towards the Gariepine streams and the Calihari Desert. They could not retire eastward, for this reason, that they there met the Amakosos (whom we call Caffres)—a race I was the first to describe to the scientific world of Europe.

Have we done with the Hottentots and Bosjeman race? I suppose so: they will soon form merely natural curiosities; already there is the skin of one stuffed in England; another in Paris if I mistake not. Their skeleton presents, of course, peculiarities, such as the extreme narrowness of the nasal bones, which run into one in early age not unfrequently, as we find in apes. But it is the exterior which is the most striking; and this, no doubt, is wonderful. No one can believe them to be of the same race with ourselves; yet, unquestionably, they belong to the genus man. They are shrewd, and show powers of mimicry—acquire language readily, but never can be civilized. That I think quite hopeless. The Dutch endeavoured to make soldiers of them; and it is recorded that they alone showed fight at the battle of Blueberg, when all the white men ran away—I state the story as I heard it. We followed and imitated the Dutch in this, as in most things, and got up a Hottentot corps, or rather, perhaps, I ought to say a Cape corps—for John Bull does not like anything he finds useful called by an offensive name. Well, call it Cape corps, or what you will, it is a miserable policy, unworthy the sanction of any statesman.

In a word, they are fast disappearing from the face of the earth; meeting that fate a little earlier from the Dutch which was surely awaiting them on the part of the Caffres. Let us now speak of the Caffre.

When the Hottentot and Bosjeman tribes fled before the warlike Dutch boors, they proceeded almost due north towards the deserts, the Karoos, the Gariepine country, and the Calihari. The reason for this was soon discovered: in their retreat eastward they encountered the Caffre, a warlike, bold, and active race of men, well armed with the assagai, accustomed to war; though somewhat feeble in their arms, yet strongly set upon their limbs, exceedingly daring, and accustomed to act in bodies; dark as Negroes nearly, yet not Negroes; finer made in the limbs, and with more energy; the head, perhaps, a little better than the Negro, or even as good as can be found in any dark race.[4] These Amakosos, or Caffres as we call them, had advanced into the province, now called Albany, when Le Vaillant was in the colony, in 1794 or 1795; they approached or occupied the eastern tract of the country, the seaboard, as it may be called. But they had neither ships nor boats, nor any human arts; properly speaking, they were mere savages, but at that time mild and, to a certain extent, trustworthy; now, by coming into contact with Europeans, they have become treacherous, bloody, and thoroughly savage. Yet they have great and good points about them, which I shall endeavour presently to explain. First let me point out, as I did to Europe, that there is not the slightest foundation for imagining them to be derived in any way from Arabian blood. This is a mere fancy. They are circumcised, eat no fish nor fowl, nor unclean beasts, as they are called; live much on milk, and seem to me capable of being educated and partly civilized. Their extent northward and eastward is unknown, but they join at last the Negroes of the equatorial regions: how far

4. Here and elsewhere, Knox appears to be uncertain as to whether the Xhosa were properly to be classified as Negroes. In this uncertainty, he is echoing a nineteenth-century belief that the Bantu-speaking peoples were racially distinct from the "true Negroes" of West Africa. In fact, the Negroes of Africa represent a variety of racial mixtures, just as the whites of Europe and America do, but the distinction between Bantu-speaking and the rest was based on language and not on any heritable physical features.

they have extended into the interior is not known. Before I speak of the true Negro, let me endeavour to place before you a brief sketch of the race whose contest with the British, but just, as it were, commencing, must end by bestowing on them an unhappy immortality.

The Caffres are closely allied to the Negro race, and probably graduate, as it were, into them; for, as Nature has formed many races of white men whose physical organization and mental disposition differ widely from each other, so also has she formed the swarthy world. It is not necessary, neither perhaps, is it at all correct, to call a Caffre a Negro, or a Negro a Caffre; neither are the Caffres degenerated Bedouins, nor well-fed Hottentots, nor Saxons turned black by the sun, nor Arabs, nor Carthaginians. I would as soon say they were the ten lost tribes. All these theories are on a par, and are worthy of each other, but not worthy of any notice. Their language is soft and melodious, and they seem to have an ear for simple melody. Since I first saw them in 1817 they have acquired firearms and horses; but they want discipline—the firmness of discipline. Individual acts of bravery they have often performed, but combined they can never meet successfully the European. We are now preparing to take possession of their country, and this of course leads to their enslavery and final destruction, for a people without land are most certainly mere bondmen. *Ascripti glebæ*—they would, but they cannot, quit it. The old English yeomen and the modern Dorsetshire labourer, the local tenant of Sutherlandshire and the peasantry of Ireland, are simply bondmen or slaves; there is no avoiding the phrase. The fate of the Caffre race, then, is certain, but centuries may elapse before their final destruction; in the meantime they may retire within the tropic, where in all probability the white man may not be able to follow, as a conqueror at least. There is the retreat for the Caffre—within the tropics, whence he came—to that again must he retire or perish. What travellers and others tell you about tribes of mixed breed, races of mulattoes, has no real existence; I would as soon expect to hear of a generation of mules. When the Negro is crossed with the Hottentot race, the product is a mild-tempered, industrious person; when with the white race, the result is a scoundrel. But, cross as you will, the mulatto cannot hold his ground as a mulatto: back the breed will go to one or other of the pure breeds, white or black. I have already explained all this.

And now for the Negro and Negroland—Central Africa, as yet untrodden and unknown. Look at the Negro, so well known to you, and say, need I describe him? Is he shaped like any white person? Is the anatomy of his frame, of his muscles, or organs like ours? Does he walk like us, think like us, act like us? Not in the least. What an innate hatred the Saxon has for him, and how I have laughed at the mock philanthropy of England! But I have spoken of this already, and it is a painful topic; and yet this despised race drove the warlike French from St. Domingo, and the issue of a struggle with them in Jamaica might be doubtful. But come it will, and then the courage of the Negro will be tried against England. Already they defeated France; but, after all, was it not the climate? for that any body of dark men in this world will ever fight successfully a French army of twenty thousand men I never shall believe. With one thousand white men all the blacks of St. Domingo could be defeated in a single action. This is my opinion of the dark races. . . .

3. Charles Darwin on Racial Extinction

Given his importance for the later theories that placed great weight on a supposed struggle for survival between the various human varieties, Darwin (1809–1882) had remarkably little to say about race— almost nothing in *The Origin of Species*. His principal consideration of race struggle occurs in *The Descent of Man* (1871), which is quoted below from the second edition, reprinted New York, 1922, pp. 185– 196, only the footnotes being omitted. In this selection, he comments on the controversy between monogenesis, the theory that all human races descended from Adam and Eve, and polygenesis, the belief that God created each distinct race separately. Modern anthropology would hold that racial distinctions were created by the isolation of a group of humans, who then interbred over a period of time in such a way as to reinforce the characteristics of the original gene pool. The Darwinian view is not strictly opposed to this one, but Darwin was impressed and puzzled by the population decline among certain groups—in every case, groups that had been isolated for some centuries and then came into contact with people who had long been exposed to a great variety of different diseases from the Afro-Eurasian land mass. He therefore tended to see stronger and weaker peoples, and hence to feed the dogmatic racist views that were present at his time and among his successors.

ONE OTHER question ought not to be passed over without notice, namely, whether, as is sometimes assumed, each sub-species or race of man has sprung from a single pair of progenitors. With our domestic animals a new race can readily be formed by carefully matching the varying offspring from a single pair, or even from a single individual possessing some new character; but most of our races have been formed, not intentionally from a selected pair, but unconsciously by the preservation of many individuals which have varied, however slightly, in some useful or desired manner. If in one country stronger and heavier horses, and in another country lighter and fleeter ones, were habitually preferred, we may feel sure that two distinct sub-breeds would be produced in the course of time, without any one pair having been separated and bred from, in either country. Many races have been thus formed, and their manner of formation is closely analogous to that of natural species. We know, also, that the horses taken to the Falkland Islands have, during successive generations, become smaller and weaker, whilst those which have run wild on the Pampas have acquired larger and coarser heads; and such changes are manifestly due, not to any one pair, but to all the individuals having been subjected to the same conditions, aided, perhaps, by the principle of reversion. The new sub-breeds in such cases are not descended from any single pair, but from many individuals which have varied in different degrees, but in the same general manner; and we may conclude that the races of man have been similarly produced, the modifications being either the direct result of exposure to different conditions, or the indirect result of some form of selection. But to this latter subject we shall presently return.

On the Extinction of the Races of Man.

The partial or complete extinction of many races and sub-races of man is historically known. Humboldt saw in South America a parrot which was the sole living creature that could speak a word of the language of a lost tribe. Ancient monuments and stone implements found in all parts of the world, about which no tradition has been preserved by the present inhabitants, indicate much extinction. Some small and broken tribes, remnants of former races, still survive in isolated and generally mountainous districts. In Europe the ancient races were all, according to Schaaffhausen, "lower

in the scale than the rudest living savages"; they must therefore
have differed, to a certain extent, from any existing race. The remains described by Professor Broca from Les Eyzies, though they
unfortunately appear to have belonged to a single family, indicate a
race with a most singular combination of low or simious, and of
high characteristics. This race is "entirely different from any other,
ancient or modern, that we have heard of." It differed, therefore,
from the quaternary race of the caverns of Belgium.

Man can long resist conditions which appear extremely unfavourable for his existence. He has long lived in the extreme
regions of the North, with no wood for his canoes or implements,
and with only blubber as fuel, and melted snow as drink. In the
southern extremity of America the Fuegians survive without the
protection of clothes, or of any building worthy to be called a
hovel. In South Africa the aborigines wander over arid plains,
where dangerous beasts abound. Man can withstand the deadly
influence of the Terai at the foot of the Himalaya, and the pestilen-
tial shores of tropical Africa.

Extinction follows chiefly from the competition of tribe with
tribe, and race with race. Various checks are always in action,
serving to keep down the numbers of each savage tribe,—such as
periodical famines, nomadic habits and the consequent deaths of
infants, prolonged suckling, wars, accidents, sickness, licentious-
ness, the stealing of women, infanticide, and especially lessened
fertility. If any one of these checks increases in power, even
slightly, the tribe thus affected tends to decrease; and when of two
adjoining tribes one becomes less numerous and less powerful than
the other, the contest is soon settled by war, slaughter, cannibalism,
slavery, and absorption. Even when a weaker tribe is not thus
abruptly swept away, if it once begins to decrease, it generally goes
on decreasing until it becomes extinct.

When civilised nations come into contact with barbarians the
struggle is short, except where a deadly climate gives its aid to the
native race. Of the causes which lead to the victory of civilised
nations, some are plain and simple, others complex and obscure.
We can see that the cultivation of the land will be fatal in many
ways to savages, for they cannot, or will not, change their habits.
New diseases and vices have in some cases proved highly destructive; and it appears that a new disease often causes much death,
until those who are most susceptible to its destructive influence are

gradually weeded out; and so it may be with the evil effects from spirituous liquors, as well as with the unconquerably strong taste for them shewn by so many savages. It further appears, mysterious as is the fact, that the first meeting of distinct and separated people generates disease. Mr. Sproat, who in Vancouver Island closely attended to the subject of extinction, believed that changed habits of life, consequent on the advent of Europeans, induces much ill-health. He lays, also, great stress on the apparently trifling cause that the natives become "bewildered and dull by the new life around them; they lose the motives for exertion, and get no new ones in their place."

The grade of their civilisation seems to be a most important element in the success of competing nations. A few centuries ago Europe feared the inroads of Eastern barbarians; now any such fear would be ridiculous. It is a more curious fact, as Mr. Bagehot has remarked, that savages did not formerly waste away before the classical nations, as they now do before modern civilised nations; had they done so, the old moralists would have mused over the event; but there is no lament in any writer of that period over the perishing barbarians. The most potent of all the causes of extinction, appears in many cases to be lessened fertility and ill-health, especially amongst the children, arising from changed conditions of life, notwithstanding that the new conditions may not be injurious in themselves. I am much indebted to Mr. H. H. Howorth for having called my attention to this subject, and for having given me information respecting it. I have collected the following cases.

When Tasmania was first colonised the natives were roughly estimated by some at 7,000 and by others at 20,000. Their number was soon greatly reduced, chiefly by fighting with the English and with each other. After the famous hunt by all the colonists, when the remaining natives delivered themselves up to the government, they consisted only of 120 individuals, who were in 1832 transported to Flinders Island. This island, situated between Tasmania and Australia, is forty miles long, and from twelve to eighteen miles broad: it seems healthy, and the natives were well treated. Nevertheless, they suffered greatly in health. In 1834 they consisted of forty-seven adult males, forty-eight adult females, and sixteen children, or in all of 111 souls. In 1835 only one hundred were left. As they continued rapidly to decrease, and as they themselves thought that they should not perish so quickly elsewhere, they were removed in 1847 to Oyster Cove in the southern part of Tasmania. They then consisted (Dec. 20th, 1847) of fourteen men, twenty-two women and ten children. But the change of site did no good. Disease and death still pursued them, and in 1864 one man (who died in 1869), and three elderly women alone survived. The infertility of the women is even a more remarkable fact than the liability of all to ill-health and death. At the time when only nine women were left at Oyster Cove, they told Mr. Bonwick, that only two had ever borne children: and these two had together produced only three children!

With respect to the cause of this extraordinary state of things, Dr. Story remarks that death followed the attempts to civilise the natives. "If left to themselves to roam as they were wont and undisturbed, they would have reared more children, and there would have been less mortality." Another careful observer of the natives, Mr. Davis, remarks, "The births have been few and the deaths numerous. This may have been in a great measure owing to their change of living and food; but more so to their banishment from the mainland of Van Diemen's Land, and consequent depression of spirits."

Similar facts have been observed in two widely different parts of Australia. The celebrated explorer, Mr. Gregory, told Mr. Bonwick, that in Queensland "the want of reproduction was being already felt with the blacks, even in the most recently settled parts, and that decay would set in." Of thirteen aborigines from Shark's Bay who visited Murchison River, twelve died of consumption within three months.

The decrease of the Maories of New Zealand has been carefully investigated by Mr. Fenton, in an admirable Report, from which all the following statements, with one exception, are taken. The decrease in number since 1830 is admitted by every one, including the natives themselves, and is still steadily progressing. Although it has hitherto been found impossible to take an actual census of the natives, their numbers were carefully estimated by residents in many districts. The result seems trustworthy, and shows that during the fourteen years, previous to 1858, the decrease was 19.42 per cent. Some of the tribes, thus carefully examined, lived about a hundred miles apart, some on the coast, some inland; and their means of subsistence and habits differed to a certain extent. The total number in 1858 was believed to be 53,700, and in 1872, after a second interval of fourteen years, another census was taken, and the number is given as only 36,359, shewing a decrease of 32.29 per cent! Mr. Fenton, after shewing in detail the insufficiency of the various causes, usually assigned in explanation of this extraordinary decrease, such as new diseases, the profligacy of the women, drunkenness, wars, &c., concludes on weighty grounds that it depends chiefly on the unproductiveness of the women, and on the extraordinary mortality of the young children. In proof of this he shews that in 1844 there was one non-adult for every 2.57 adults; whereas in 1858 there was only one non-adult for every 3.27 adults. The mortality of the adults is also great. He adduces as a further cause of the decrease the inequality of the sexes; for fewer females are born than males. To this latter point, depending perhaps on a widely distinct cause, I shall return in a future chapter. Mr. Fenton contrasts with astonishment the decrease in New Zealand with the increase in Ireland; countries not very dissimilar in climate, and where the inhabitants now follow nearly similar habits. The Maories themselves "attribute their decadence, in some measure, to the introduction of new food and clothing, and the attendant change of habits;" and it will be seen, when we consider the influence of changed conditions on fertility, that they are probably right. The diminution began between the years 1830 and 1840; and Mr. Fenton shews that about 1830, the art of manufacturing putrid corn (maize), by long steeping in water, was discovered and largely practised; and this proves that a change of habits was beginning amongst the natives, even when New Zealand was only thinly inhabited by Europeans. When I visited the Bay of Islands in 1835, the dress and food of the inhabitants had already been much modified: they raised potatoes, maize, and other agricultural produce, and exchanged them for English manufactured goods and tobacco.

It is evident from many statements in the life of Bishop Patteson, that the Melanesians of the New Hebrides and neighbouring archipelagoes, suffered to an extraordinary degree in health, and perished in large numbers, when they were removed to New Zealand, Norfolk Island, and other salubrious places, in order to be educated as missionaries.

The decrease of the native population of the Sandwich Islands [Hawaii] is as notorious as that of New Zealand. It has been roughly estimated by those best capable of judging, that when

Cook discovered the Islands in 1779, the population amounted to about 300,000. According to a loose census in 1823, the numbers then were 142,050. In 1832, and at several subsequent periods, an accurate census was officially taken, but I have been able to obtain only the following returns:

YEAR.	NATIVE POPULATION. —— (Except during 1832 and 1836, when the few foreigners in the islands were included.)	Annual rate of decrease per cent., assuming it to have been uniform between the successive censuses; these censuses being taken at irregular intervals.
1832	130,313	
1836	108,579	4.46
1853	71,019	2.47
1860	67,084	0.81
1866	58,765	2.18
1872	51,531	2.17

We here see that in the interval of forty years, between 1832 and 1872, the population has decreased no less than sixty-eight per cent.! This has been attributed by most writers to the profligacy of the women, to former bloody wars, and to the severe labour imposed on conquered tribes and to newly introduced diseases, which have been on several occasions extremely destructive. No doubt these and other such causes have been highly efficient, and may account for the extraordinary rate of decrease between the years 1832 and 1836; but the most potent of all the causes seems to be lessened fertility. According to Dr. Ruschenberger of the U. S. Navy, who visited these islands between 1835 and 1837, in one district of Hawaii, only twenty-five men out of 1134, and in another district only ten out of 637, had a family with as many as three children. Of eighty married women, only thirty-nine had ever borne children; and "the official report gives an average of half a child to each married couple in the whole island." This is almost exactly the same average as with the Tasmanians at Oyster Cove. Jarves, who published his History in 1843, says that "families who have three children are freed from all taxes; those having more, are rewarded by gifts of land and other encouragements." This unparalleled enactment by the government well shews how infertile the race had become. The Rev. A. Bishop stated in the Hawaiian "Spectator" in 1839, that a large proportion of the children die at early ages, and Bishop Staley informs me that this is still the case, just as in New Zealand. This has been attributed to the neglect of the children by the women, but it is probably in large part due to innate weakness of constitution in the children, in relation to the lessened fertility of their parents. There is, moreover, a further resemblance to the case of New Zealand, in the fact that there is a large excess of male over female births: the census of 1872 gives 31,650 males to 25,247 females of all ages, that is 125.36 males for every 100 females; whereas in all civilised countries the females exceed the males. No doubt the profligacy of the women may in part account for their small fertility; but their changed habits of life is a much more probable cause, and which will at the same time account for the increased mortality, especially of the children. The islands were visited by Cook in 1779, by Vancouver in 1794, and often subsequently by whalers. In 1819 missionaries arrived, and found that idolatry had been already abolished, and other changes effected by the king. After this period there was a rapid change in almost all the habits of life of the natives, and they soon became "the most civilised of the Pacific Islanders." One of my informants, Mr. Coan, who was born on the islands, remarks that the natives have undergone a greater change in their habits of life in the course of fifty years than Englishmen during a thousand years. From information received from Bishop Staley, it does not appear that the poorer classes have ever much changed their diet, although many new kinds of fruit have been introduced, and the sugar-cane is in universal use. Owing, however, to their passion for imitating Europeans, they altered their manner of dressing at an early period, and the use of alcoholic drinks became very general. Although these changes appear inconsiderable, I can well believe, from what is known with respect to animals, that they might suffice to lessen the fertility of the natives.

Lastly, Mr. Macnamara states that the low and degraded inhabitants of the Andaman Islands, on the eastern side of the Gulf of Bengal, are "eminently susceptible to any change of climate: in fact, take them away from their island homes, and they are almost certain to die, and that independently of diet or extraneous influences." He further states that the inhabitants of the Valley of Nepâl, which is extremely hot in summer, and also the various hill

tribes of India, suffer from dysentery and fever when on the plains;
and they die if they attempt to pass the whole year there.

We thus see that many of the wilder races of man are apt to
suffer much in health when subjected to changed conditions or
habits of life, and not exclusively from being transported to a new
climate. Mere alterations in habits, which do not appear injurious in
themselves, seem to have this same effect; and in several cases the
children are particularly liable to suffer. It has often been said, as
Mr. Macnamara remarks, that man can resist with impunity the
greatest diversities of climate and other changes; but this is true
only of the civilised races. Man in his wild condition seems to be in
this respect almost as susceptible as his nearest allies, the anthropoid
apes, which have never yet survived long, when removed from
their native country.

Lessened fertility from changed conditions, as in the case of the
Tasmanians, Maories, Sandwich Islanders, and apparently the Australians, is still more interesting than their liability to ill-health and
death; for even a slight degree of infertility, combined with those
other causes which tend to check the increase of every population,
would sooner or later lead to extinction. The diminution of fertility may be explained in some cases by the profligacy of the
women (as until lately with the Tahitians), but Mr. Fenton has
shewn that this explanation by no means suffices with the New
Zealanders, nor does it with the Tasmanians.

In the paper above quoted, Mr. Macnamara gives reasons for
believing that the inhabitants of districts subject to malaria are apt
to be sterile; but this cannot apply in several of the above cases.
Some writers have suggested that the aborigines of islands have
suffered in fertility and health from long continued inter-breeding;
but in the above cases infertility has coincided too closely with the
arrival of Europeans for us to admit this explanation. Nor have we
at present any reason to believe that man is highly sensitive to the
evil effects of inter-breeding, especially in areas so large as New
Zealand, and the Sandwich archipelago with its diversified stations.
On the contrary, it is known that the present inhabitants of Norfolk Island are nearly all cousins or near relations, as are the Todas
in India, and the inhabitants of some of the Western Islands of
Scotland; and yet they seem not to have suffered in fertility.

A much more probable view is suggested by the analogy of the
lower animals. The reproductive system can be shewn to be

susceptible to an extraordinary degree (though why we know not) to changed conditions of life; and this susceptibility leads both to beneficial and to evil results. A large collection of facts on this subject is given in chap. xviii. of vol. ii. of my "Variation of Animals and Plants under Domestication," I can here give only the briefest abstract; and every one interested in the subject may consult the above work. Very slight changes increase the health, vigour and fertility of most or all organic beings, whilst other changes are known to render a large number of animals sterile. One of the most familiar cases, is that of tamed elephants not breeding in India; though they often breed in Ava, where the females are allowed to roam about the forests to some extent, and are thus placed under more natural conditions. The case of various American monkeys, both sexes of which have been kept for many years together in their own countries, and yet have very rarely or never bred, is a more apposite instance, because of their relationship to man. It is remarkable how slight a change in the conditions often induces sterility in a wild animal when captured; and this is the more strange as all our domesticated animals have become more fertile than they were in a state of nature; and some of them can resist the most unnatural conditions with undiminished fertility. Certain groups of animals are much more liable than others to be affected by captivity; and generally all the species of the same group are affected in the same manner. But sometimes a single species in a group is rendered sterile, whilst the others are not so; on the other hand, a single species may retain its fertility whilst most of the others fail to breed. The males and females of some species when confined, or when allowed to live almost, but not quite free, in their native country, never unite; others thus circumstanced frequently unite but never produce offspring; others again produce some offspring, but fewer than in a state of nature; and as bearing on the above cases of man, it is important to remark that the young are apt to be weak and sickly, or malformed, and to perish at an early age.

Seeing how general is this law of the susceptibility of the reproductive system to changed conditions of life, and that it holds good with our nearest allies, the Quadrumana, can hardly doubt that it applies to man in his primeval state. Hence if savages of any race are induced suddenly to change their habits of life, they become more or less sterile, and their young offspring suffer in health, in the same manner and from the same cause, as do the elephant and hunting-leopard in India, many monkeys in America, and a host of animals of all kinds, on removal from their natural conditions.

We can see why it is that aborigines, who have long inhabited islands, and who must have been long exposed to nearly uniform conditions, should be specially affected by any change in their habits, as seems to be the case. Civilised races can certainly resist changes of all kinds far better than savages; and in this respect they resemble domesticated animals, for though the latter sometimes suffer in health (for instance European dogs in India), yet they are rarely rendered sterile, though a few such instances have been recorded. The immunity of civilised races and domesticated animals is probably due to their having been subjected to a greater extent, and therefore having grown somewhat more accustomed, to diversified or varying conditions, than the majority of wild animals; and to their having formerly immigrated or been carried from country to country, and to different families or sub-races having inter-crossed. It appears that a cross with civilised races at once gives to an aboriginal race an immunity from the evil consequences of changed conditions. Thus the crossed offspring from the Tahitians and English, when settled in Pitcairn Island, increased so rapidly that the Island was soon overstocked; and in June 1856 they were removed to Norfolk Island. They then consisted of 60 married persons and 134 children, making a total of 194. Here they likewise increased so rapidly, that although sixteen of them returned to Pitcairn Island in 1859, they numbered in January 1868, 300 souls; the males and females being in exactly equal numbers. What a contrast does this case present with that of the Tasmanians; the Norfolk Islanders *increased* in only twelve and a half years from 194 to 300; whereas the Tasmanians *decreased* during fifteen years from 120 to 46, of which latter number only ten were children.

So again in the interval between the census of 1866 and 1872 the natives of full blood in the Sandwich Islands decreased by 8,081, whilst the half-castes, who are believed to be healthier, increased by 847; but I do not know whether the latter number includes the offspring from the half-castes, or only the half-castes of the first generation.

The cases which I have here given all relate to aborigines, who have been subjected to new conditions as the result of the immigration of civilised men. But sterility and ill-health would probably follow, if savages were compelled by any cause, such as the inroad of a conquering tribe, to desert their homes and to change their habits. It is an interesting circumstance that the chief check to wild animals becoming domesticated, which implies the power of their breeding freely when first captured, and one chief check to wild men, when brought into contact with civilisation, surviving to form a civilised race, is the same, namely, sterility from changed conditions of life.

Finally, although the gradual decrease and ultimate extinction of the races of man is a highly complex problem, depending on many causes which differ in different places and at different times; it is the same problem as that presented by the extinction of one of the higher animals—of the fossil horse, for instance, which disappeared from South America, soon afterwards to be replaced, within the same districts, by countless troups of the Spanish horse. The New Zealander seems conscious of this parallelism, for he compares his future fate with that of the native rat now almost exterminated by the European rat. Though the difficulty is great to our imagination, and really great, if we wish to ascertain the precise causes and the manner of action, it ought not to be so to our reason, as long as we keep steadily in mind that the increase of each species and each race is constantly checked in various ways; so that if any new check, even a slight one, be superadded, the race will surely decrease in number; and decreasing numbers will sooner or later lead to extinction; the end, in most cases, being promptly determined by the inroads of conquering tribes. . . .

4. Benjamin Kidd
and the Control of the Tropics

Benjamin Kidd (1858–1916) was not a natural scientist, but rather a writer who sought to apply the teachings of "science" to men's affairs. Professionally, he was a minor civil servant until 1894, when the enormous success of his book *Social Evolution* allowed him to resign and devote himself to writing. He is best known for his opposition to the concept of class struggle in Marxian socialism, and to the idea of an individual competitive struggle found in *laissez-faire* economics. Against these two kinds of evolutionary conflict, he opposed a belief in a racial struggle for survival based on racial solidarity. By this time, however, racists were no longer much concerned with opposition between Caucasians and others, but with smaller divisions within Europe. For Kidd, this meant opposition of Celts to Anglo-Saxons, or essentially the old imperial rivalry of France and England in new colors.[1]

The passage below is Chapter III from his book *The Control of the Tropics* (London, 1898), where he develops a racist theory of trusteeship based on the kind of "scientific" finding in Knox's work.

III

WE HAVE to recognize at the outset, as a first principle of the situation, the utter futility of any policy based on the conception that it will be possible in the future to hold our hands and stand aloof from the tropics. There can be no choice in this matter. With the filling up of the temperate regions and the continued development of industrialism throughout the civilized world the rivalry and struggle for the trade of the tropics will, beyond doubt, be the permanent underlying fact in the foreign relations of the Western nations in the twentieth century. This anticipation must be based, in the first place, on the fact of the enormous extent to which our civilization already rests on the productions of the tropics, and, in the second place, on the fact that the principle, underlying all trade—that exchange of products between regions and peoples of different capacities tends to be mutually profitable—finds in commerce between ourselves and these regions its most natural expression. So deeply fixed in the minds of most civilized peoples is this instinct of the future importance of the tropics that, as we have seen, a large part of the attention of our time is already occupied with questions and events arising out of the relations between our civilization and these regions. It has driven the British people to reverse, even under the surprising circumstances to which reference has been made, a policy which has been in the ascendant in the English mind for three generations. It is not even to be expected that existing nations will, in the future, continue to acknowledge any rights in the tropics which are not based both on the intention and the ability to develop these regions. It is a remarkable fact, significant as indicating the current drift of opinion on the subject, that in a recent article from the pen of Baron von Lüttwitz, of

1. For Kidd's relationship to other imperial ideas of his period, see B. Semmel, *Imperialism and Social Reform* (London, 1960), pp. 18–24.

which a translation was printed in England in the *Journal* of the Royal United Service Institution, the writer frankly mentions the prevailing conditions in China and the unstable condition in many South American States as offering opportunities for German expansion in these regions. If the English-speaking world is to face the duty which lies before it in the period upon which we have entered, if it is to raise the rivalry for the control of the tropics above the sordid level at which it has hitherto been carried on, it must be able to meet the subsequent verdict of history with a higher sense of responsibility and a clearer faith in the deep importance of the ideas and forces of which it is the representative, than is to be distinguished in its relations to the tropics either in the past or in the present. It would seem that any future policy of our relations to the tropics, to be permanently successful, must be based on the frank recognition of the following facts:—

In the first place, the attempt to acclimatize the white man in the tropics must be recognized to be a blunder of the first magnitude. All experiments based upon the idea are mere idle and empty enterprises foredoomed to failure. Excepting only the deportation of the African races under the institution of slavery, probably no other idea which has held the mind of our civilization during the last 300 years has led to so much physical and moral suffering and degradation, or has strewn the world with the wrecks of so many gigantic enterprises. In the second place, the question of exploiting any tropical region by regarding it primarily as an estate to be worked for gain must be abandoned. The endeavour of the Continental nations of Europe to base the relationship of the occupying Power to such territories and their inhabitants on the principle of profit, surrounding the regions with laws and tariffs operating in the exclusive interest of the Power in possession, must be regarded as merely a return in modified form to the old Plantation system. Such a system is incompatible with the underlying spirit which is governing the development of the English-speaking peoples themselves, and it could, therefore, never have behind it that larger ethical conception which alone could obtain for it any measure of support as a permanent policy among these people. There will probably be no large measure of dissent from either of those propositions in England, where they have already practically passed into the realm of established truths. Yet, if we are able to give assent to them, it would seem that there must come the conviction that we must also go further. If the white man cannot be permanently acclimatized in the tropics, even where for the time being he has become relatively numerous, under the effects of evil conditions of the past, the government of all such regions must, if the ideas and standards which have prevailed in the past be allowed to continue, tend ultimately in one direction. It must tend to become the government of a large native population by a permanently resident European caste cut off from the moral, ethical, political, and physical conditions, which have produced the European. This is the real problem in many States in the tropical parts of central and northern South America. We cannot look for good government under such conditions; we have no right to expect it. In climatic conditions which are a burden to him; in the midst of races in a different and lower stage of development; divorced from the influences which have produced him, from the moral and political environment from which he sprang, the white man does not in the end, in such circumstances, tend so much to raise the level of the races amongst whom he has made his unnatural home, as he tends himself to sink slowly to the level around him.

The next principle, which it seems must be no less clearly recognized, is one which carries us a great stride forward from the past as soon as we begin to perceive the nature of the consequences which follow from its admission. It is that, nevertheless, there never has been, and there never will be, within any time with which we are practically concerned, such a thing as good government, in the European sense, of the tropics by the natives of these regions. The ultimate fact underlying all the relations of the white man to the tropics is one which really goes to the root of the whole question of the evolution which the race itself has undergone. The human race reached its earliest development where the conditions of life were easiest; namely, in the tropics. But throughout the whole period of human history, the development of the race has taken place outwards from the tropics. Slowly but surely we see the seat of empire and authority moving like the advancing tide northwards. The evolution in character which the race has undergone has been northwards from the tropics. The first step to the solution of the problem before us is simply to acquire the principle that in dealing with the *natural* inhabitants of the tropics we are dealing with peoples who represent the same stage in the history of the development of the race that the child does in the history of the development of the individual. The tropics will not, therefore, be developed by the natives themselves. However we may be inclined to hesitate before reaching this view, it is hard to see how assent to it can be withheld in the face of the consistent verdict of history in the past, and the unvarying support given to it by facts in the present. If there is any one inclined to challenge it, let him reflect for a moment on the evidence on the one side and the difficulty that will present itself to him of producing any serious facts on the other side. If we look to the native social systems of the tropical East, to the primitive savagery of Central Africa, to the West Indian Islands in the past in process of being assisted into the position of modern States by Great Britain, to the Black Republic Hayti in the present, or to modern Liberia in the future, the lesson seems everywhere the same; it is that there will be no development of the resources of the tropics under native government.

We come, therefore, to a clearly defined position. If we have to meet the fact that by force of circumstances the tropics *must* be developed, and if the evidence is equally emphatic that such a development can only take place under the influence of the white man, we are confronted with a larger issue than any mere question of commercial policy or of national selfishness. The tropics in such circumstances can only be governed as a trust for civilization, and with a full sense of the responsibility which such a trust involves. The first principle of success in undertaking such a duty seems to the writer to be a clear recognition of the cardinal fact that in the tropics the white man lives and works only as a diver lives and works under water. Alike in a moral, in an ethical, and in a political sense, the atmosphere he breathes must be that of another region, that which produced him, and to which he belongs. Neither physically, morally, nor politically, can he be acclimatized in the tropics. The people among whom he lives and works are often separated from him by thousands of years of development; he cannot, therefore, be allowed to administer government from any local and lower standard he may develop. If he has any right there at all, he is there in the name of civilization; if our civilization has any right there at all, it is because it represents higher ideals of humanity, a higher type of social order. This is the lesson which, slowly and painfully, and with many a temporary reversion to older ideas, the British peoples have been learning in India for the last fifty years, and which has recently been applied in other cir-

cumstances to the government of Egypt. Under a multitude of
outward aspects, the one principle which separates the new era
from the old in India, a principle the influence of which has come
to extend even to the habits and dress of the governing class, is the
recognition of the fact that the standards according to which India
must be governed have been developed and are nourished elsewhere. The one consistent idea which, through all outward forms,
has in late years been behind the institution of the higher Indian
Civil Service on existing lines is that, even where it is equally open
to natives with Europeans through competitive examination, entrance to it shall be made through an English University. In other
words, it is the best and most distinctive product which England
can give, the higher ideals and standards of her Universities, which
is made to feed the inner life from which the British administration
of India proceeds. It is but the application of the same principle
which we have in the recognition of the fact that no violent hands
must be laid on native insitutions, or native rights, or native systems
of religion, or even on native independence, so far as respect for
existing forms is compatible with the efficient administration of the
government. It is but another form of the recognition of the fact
that we are in the midst of habits and institutions from which our
civilization is separated by a long interval of development, where
progress upwards must be a long, slow process, must proceed on
native lines, and must be the effect of the example and prestige of
higher standards rather than the result of ruder methods. It is on a
like principle that the development of the tropical region occupied
must be held to be the fulfilment of a trust undertaken in the name
of civilization, a duty which allows the occupying country to surround her own position therein with no laws or tariffs operating in
her own interests, and which allows her to retain to herself no
exclusive advantage in the markets which she has assisted in creating. In the case of regions whose inhabitants have made little
progress towards the development of any social organization of
their own, the government for the time being must be prepared for
duties and responsibilities of a different kind to those undertaken
amongst ourselves; for not even under the protection of a civilized
government can it be expected that in such cases the natives will
develop the resources they have in charge under the principles of
our Western individualism. But in this, as in all other matters, the
one underlying principle of success in any future relationship to

the tropics is to keep those who administer the government which represents our civilization in direct and intimate contact with the standards of that civilization at its best; and to keep the acts of the government itself within the closest range of that influence, often irksome, sometimes even misleading, but always absolutely vital,— the continual scrutiny of the public mind at home.

No deeper, no more enduring responsibility, has ever been laid upon the peoples of the whole English-speaking world, than that which presents itself in the situation with which they are confronted, at the end of the nineteenth century, in this matter of our future relations to the tropics. To the writer there seems to be no room here for small-minded comparison between the different merits of civilized races and peoples. The subject goes far deeper than this. There are in reality only two policies before the world. On the one side there is that pursued by the Continental Powers of Western Europe. Reduced to its simplest terms it represents the conception of the relationship to be adopted to territories beyond [the] sea which prevailed throughout Europe more than a hundred years ago and before the secession of the United States. On the other side there is the policy, slowly and painfully learnt after a century of larger experience—the policy which the standards of the English-speaking peoples now represent and of which the logical outcome is the holding of the tropics as a trust for civilization. Every square mile of tropical territory which has been occupied within the last few decades under the first policy rather than under the second has been in part lost to us as a trust to civilization, it has passed definitely backward into the shadow of another century. What it is necessary to remember is that it is idle and useless to trust to any declaration of intentions, however honestly meant, on the acquisition of such territory. Policies in such circumstances grow out of the life of a people and are not permanently regulated by existing intentions. The Congo State was declared neutral and free to the trade of all nations in 1885. It is no longer either neutral or free to trade as at the date of the Declaration; Belgium has acquired the right of annexation and France of preëmption. France undertook the administration of Algeria with many understandings which were doubtless honestly meant at the time but which no longer exist. In 1893 she had obtained the consent of the Powers to confine even the carrying trade between herself and Algeria to French vessels, all foreign Powers, including Great Britain, having given up their right to participate in it. In Madagascar, her latest acquisition, the present trend of policy appears to be in the same direction. A policy in such relations is a matter beyond the control even of governments; it is ultimately regulated only by the development of a people, by standards which are the slow growth of time. If the English-speaking peoples do not mean to shirk the grave responsibility which lies upon them in this matter, they must act at once, with clear purpose and with courage. Neither the purpose nor the courage should be wanting to those who possess a conviction of the far-reaching importance in the future of the ideas and principles for which these peoples now stand in the world.

II

Imperialism and the Law of Nations

ONE OF the problems implicit in international law from the sixteenth century onward was that of dealing with cultural and legal differences between nations. Even within the West, legal provisions concerning such matters as territorial waters did, and still do, differ from one country to another. But the West had at least a common tradition of Roman and canon law and centuries of continuous international relations on which to build some measure of consensus. Dealing with non-Western nations was a far different and far more difficult problem. Conflict between Western and Muslim ideas of correct international dealings was basically irreconcilable, though a *modus vivendi* could be worked out at times. Reconciliation of diverse views between Europe and more alien regions like East Asia was still more difficult. In the longer run of history, differences were not reconciled. The Western community of nations simply spread until all had finally come to accept the European legal framework of international relations, now embodied both in the system of international diplomacy and in the United Nations. From one point of view, this world-wide acceptance of Western norms is one of the more useful long-term results of European imperialism.

At any stage before this general acceptance of Western international law, lawyers had the problem of providing for the existence of states outside the Western community. They were rarely or never concerned with merging Western and non-Western legal concepts but with making allowance for other cultures in the relations between the Western states themselves. One of the key questions over time was therefore the licitness of claims to overseas empire, and the legal object was to provide a basis for settling rival claims, not that of mediating between Europeans and non-Europeans. In this sense, European international law began and continued as an essentially ethnocentric body of ideas and procedures. All four of the selections that follow share in this basic ethnocentricity. All four authors, or sets of authors, accept implicitly the basic premise of European international law, that all states are equal before the law, and each of these authors deals with states or peoples who are outside the law because of cultural difference from European standards. Two selections, those of Emer de Vattel and Westlake, are relevant to imperialist thought because they seek to define the cultural standards that make a non-Western territory liable to European acquisition. The final selections, from the Covenant of the League of Nations and the United Nations Charter, are the other side of the coin of trusteeship. They seek to provide special rights, as well as special disabilities, for those who are seen as outside the "civilized" community.

5. Emer de Vattel
on the Occupation of Territory

Emer de Vattel (1714–67) was perhaps the most widely read of all eighteenth-century authorities on international law. He was not a lawyer by training, but a free-ranging *philosophe* of the Enlightenment. Though he was born and educated in what is now Switzerland, he was a subject of Prussia, and served for a time as Privy Councilor to the King of Saxony. In spite of the royal connection, his political views were close to those that were to emerge in the American and French revolutions. This fact may account for his later influence in the United States.

The selection printed below is Chapter XVIII of *The Law of Nations or the Principles of Natural Law Applied to the Conduct and to the Affairs of Nations and of Sovereigns* (Washington, 1916), translated from the original edition of 1758 by Charles E. Fenwick. Reprinted by permission of Carnegie Institution of Washington, D.C. The chapter is entitled "Occupation of Territory by a Nation," and it is chiefly interesting in contrast to the natural-rights philosophy which pervades the work as a whole, since it denies the right of sovereignty to "wandering tribes" of hunters and gatherers. His emphasis on a human obligation to cultivate the earth was already an old idea, and it was to reappear with some of the nineteenth-century imperialists as an obligation to work, founded on natural law and not merely on human necessity.

THUS FAR we have considered a Nation merely in its political character without regard to the country it inhabits. Let us now regard it as settled in a country which thus becomes its own property and the seat of its national life. The earth belongs to all mankind; and being destined by the Creator to be their common dwelling-place and source of subsistence, all men have a natural right to inhabit it and to draw from it what is necessary for their support and suited to their needs. But when the human race became greatly multiplied in numbers the earth was no longer capable of supporting its inhabitants without their cultivating its soil, and this cultivation could not be carried on properly by the wandering tribes having a common ownership of it. Hence it was necessary for these tribes to settle somewhere and appropriate to themselves certain portions of the earth, in order that, without being disturbed in their labor or deprived of its fruits, they might endeavor to render those lands fertile and thus draw their subsistence from them. Such must have been the origin, as it is the justification, of the rights of *property* and *ownership*. Since their introduction, the common right of all men is restricted in the individual to what he lawfully possesses. The territory which a Nation inhabits, whether the Nation moved into it as a body, or whether the families scattered over the territory came together to form a civil society, forms a national settlement, to which the Nation has a private and exclusive right.

This right contains two elements: (1) *Ownership*, by virtue of which that Nation only may make use of the territory for its needs, may dispose of it, and draw whatever benefits it may yield; (2) *sovereignty*, or the right of supreme jurisdiction, by which the Nation regulates and controls at will whatever goes on in the territory.

When a Nation takes possession of a country which belongs to no one, it is considered as acquiring *sovereignty* over it as well as *ownership*; for, being free and independent, it can not intend, when it settles a territory, to leave to others the right to rule it, nor any other right which belongs to sovereignty. The entire space over which a Nation extends its sovereignty forms the sphere of its jurisdiction, and is called its *domain*.

If a number of free families, scattered over an independent country, come together to form a Nation or State, they acquire as a body sovereignty over the entire territory they inhabit; for they were already owners of their individual parts of the territory, and since they desire to form together a civil society and set up a public authority which each must obey, it is clear that they mean to confer upon this public authority the right to rule the whole country.

All men have an equal right to things which have not yet come into the possession of anyone, and these things belong to the person who first takes possession. When, therefore, a Nation finds a country uninhabited and without an owner, it may lawfully take possession of it, and after it has given sufficient signs of its intention in this respect, it may not be deprived of it by another Nation. In this way navigators setting out upon voyages of discovery and bearing with them a commission from their sovereign, when coming across islands or other uninhabited lands, have taken possession of them in the name of their Nation; and this title has usually been respected, provided actual possession has followed shortly after.

But it is questioned whether a Nation can thus appropriate, by the mere act of taking possession, lands which it does not really occupy, and which are more extensive than it can inhabit or cultivate. It is not difficult to decide that such a claim would be absolutely contrary to the natural law, and would conflict with the designs of nature, which destines the earth for the needs of all mankind, and only confers upon individual Nations the right to appropriate territory so far as they can make use of it, and not merely to hold it against others who may wish to profit by it. Hence the Law of Nations will only recognize the *ownership* and *sovereignty* of a Nation over unoccupied lands when the Nation is in actual occupation of them, when it forms a settlement upon them, or makes some actual use of them. In fact, when explorers have discovered uninhabited lands through which the explorers of other Nations had passed, leaving some sign of their having taken possession, they have no more troubled themselves over such empty forms than over the regulations of Popes, who divided a large part of the world between the crowns of Castile and Portugal.

There is another celebrated question which has arisen principally in connection with the discovery of the New World. It is asked whether a Nation may lawfully occupy any part of a vast territory in which are to be found only wandering tribes whose small numbers can not populate the whole country. We have already pointed out, in speaking of the obligation of cultivating the earth, that these tribes can not take to themselves more land than they have need of or can inhabit and cultivate. Their uncertain occupancy of these vast regions can not be held as a real and lawful taking of possession; and when the Nations of Europe, which are too confined at home, come upon lands which the savages have no special need of and are making no present and continuous use of, they may lawfully take possession of them and establish colonies in them. We have already said that the earth belongs to all mankind as a means of sustaining life. But if each Nation had desired from the beginning to appropriate to itself an extent of territory great enough for it to live merely by hunting, fishing, and gathering wild fruits, the earth would not suffice for a tenth part of the people who now inhabit it. Hence we are not departing from the intentions of nature when we restrict the savages within narrower bounds. However, we can not but admire the moderation of the English Puritans who were the first to settle in New England. Although they bore with them a charter from their sovereign, they bought from the savages the lands they wished to occupy. Their praiseworthy example was followed by William Penn and the colony of Quakers that he conducted into Pennsylvania.

When a Nation takes possession of a distant country and establishes a colony there, that territory, though separated from the mother country, forms naturally a part of the State, as much so as its older possessions. Hence, whenever the public laws or treaties make no distinction between them, all regulations affecting the mother country should be extended equally to the colonies.

6. John Westlake
on the Title to Sovereignty

Unlike Vattel, John Westlake (1828–1913) was a professional international lawyer, holding the Whewell professorship at Cambridge from 1888 to 1908. Among international lawyers of his period, he, more than most a defender of imperialism, advocated a hard line against the pretensions of the "uncivilized." In the era of dominant racism, however, he applied a cultural and not a racial test; the test itself was ethnocentric in the extreme, since he demanded that a non-Western

state be able to act like a Western state in order to be considered
"civilized" and hence worthy of full sovereignty.

The selections printed here are from Chapter IX of his *Chapters
on the Principles of International Law* (1894), as reprinted in *The
Collected Papers of John Westlake on Public International Law* (Cambridge, 1914), pp. 136–157 and 177–181. Many of the footnotes have
been omitted.

Territorial Sovereignty, Especially with Relation to Uncivilised Regions

THE TITLE TO TERRITORIAL SOVEREIGNTY.

LET US consider the old civilised world, including not only the
international society of European origin but those Asiatic and
other countries which we have noticed as possessing different civilisations from ours. All the states in it hold their territory by the
same kind of title by which their subjects hold their property in
land, that is by a series of human dealings—as cession or conquest
in the one case, conveyance *inter vivos* or will in the other—
deduced from a root assumed as presenting an irreducible situation
of fact. But that situation was itself a local distribution of territory
or property, of the same nature as the one which results for the
present time from the deduction of title. You have got no nearer to
an origin of territorial sovereignty or of property. You may discuss
the origin of either by way of philosophical or prehistorical specu-
lation, but with no relevancy to international or to national law.
You may discuss the motives for maintaining either, with some
relevancy to international or national legislation, but with no other
relevancy to law. Thus, the title to territorial sovereignty in old
countries not being capable of discussion apart from the several
dealings, as cession or conquest, which transfer it, we must turn to
new countries.

When a new country is formed by a civilised state into a colony,
the title to land in it may sometimes be deduced by the proprietors
from a situation of fact which existed before the civilised government was established, and which that government has accepted and
clothed with its sanction. This will be the case where the colony
was formed among natives of some advancement, or where its
formation was preceded by the settlement of pioneers of civilisation. But in general the title to land in a colony is traced from a
grant by the state, and the authority of the state to make the grant

resulted from its territorial sovereignty. Or you may say if you please that, at the moment of acquiring the sovereignty, the state assumed to itself the property in so much of the land as it was not morally compelled to acknowledge as belonging to natives or to the pioneers, and that subsequent grants by the state were carried out of the property so assumed. Either way you carry back the property granted to an origin in sovereignty, but the origin of the latter is still to be considered.

But here again all that can really be considered is the extension of territorial sovereignty over new areas. In other words, the question is what facts are necessary and sufficient in order that an uncivilised region may be internationally recognised as appropriated in sovereignty to a particular state? Whatever the answer may be, the international institutions of the old civilised world cannot have arisen in exactly the same manner, for the appropriation with which we are dealing supposes that territorial sovereignty is already known. The states of the old world may have arisen from the settlement of wandering tribes in regions only occupied, if at all, by tribes on a still lower plane of advancement, and that mode of origin would present great similarity to the extension of an existing state over a new locality. Or the states of the old world may have arisen quite differently. In any case the truth will bear repetition that, whatever light philology or archaeology may throw on the early history of mankind, an impassable barrier separates their researches, in spite of the great interest that must be felt in them, from the subjects with which international law has to do.

The form which has been given to the question, namely *what facts are necessary and sufficient in order that an uncivilised region may be internationally appropriated in sovereignty to a particular state?* implies that it is only the recognition of such sovereignty by the members of the international society which concerns us, that of uncivilised natives international law takes no account. This is true, and it does not mean that all rights are denied to such natives, but that the appreciation of their rights is left to the conscience of the state within whose recognised territorial sovereignty they are comprised, the rules of the international society existing only for the purpose of regulating the mutual conduct of its members. Seen from that point of view the proposition, which at first is startling, becomes almost axiomatic. A strongly organised society may enact

rules for the protection of those who are not its members, as is seen
in the case of a state which legislates for the protection of foreigners, or against cruelty to animals. But this is scarcely possible
for a society so weakly organised as the international one, in which,
for want of a central power, the enforcement of rules must be left
in the main to the mutual action of the members as independent
states. In such a society rules intended for the benefit of outsiders
would either fall into desuetude and oblivion, or be made pretexts
for the more specious promotion of selfish interests. The subject,
however, must be treated at greater length.

THE POSITION OF UNCIVILISED NATIVES WITH REGARD TO INTERNATIONAL LAW.

No theorist on law who is pleased to imagine a state of nature
independent of human institutions can introduce into his picture a
difference between civilised and uncivilised man, because it is just
in the presence or absence of certain institutions, or in their greater
or less perfection, that that difference consists for the lawyer. But
in the early times of international law, when the appropriation of a
newly discovered region was referred to the principles which were
held to govern the so-called natural modes of acquisition, the
occupation by uncivilised tribes of a tract, of which according to
our habits a small part ought to have sufficed for them, was not felt
to interpose a serious obstacle to the right of the first civilised
occupant. The region was scarcely distinguished from a *res nullius*.
When again men like Victoria, Soto and Covarruvias maintained
the cause of the American and African natives against the kings
and peoples of Spain and Portugal, they were not so much im-
pugning the title of their country as trying to influence its conduct,
they were the worthy predecessors of those who now make among
us the honourable claim to be "friends of the aborigines." Then
and now such men occupy a field to which international law may
be said to invite them by keeping itself within its own limits. Even
those who, in accordance with the modern tendency, make rights
instead of law their starting point, can hardly avoid admitting that
the rights which are common to civilised and uncivilised humanity
are not among those which it is the special function of international
right to develop and protect. But when the African conference of
Berlin was laying down the rules for the appropriation of territory

on the coasts of that continent, Mr. Kasson, the plenipotentiary of the United States, expressed himself thus:

"Whilst approving the two paragraphs of this declaration as a first step, well directed though short, it is my duty to add two observations to the protocol.

"(1) Modern international law follows closely a line which leads to the recognition of the right of native tribes to dispose freely of themselves and of their hereditary territory. In conformity with this principle my government would gladly adhere to a more extended rule, to be based on a principle which should aim at the voluntary consent of the natives whose country is taken possession of, in all cases where they had not provoked the aggression. (2) I have no doubt as to the conference being agreed in regard to the signification of the preamble. It only points out the minimum of the conditions which must necessarily be fulfilled in order that the recognition of an occupation may be demanded. It is always possible that an occupation may be rendered effective by acts of violence which are foreign to the principles of justice, as well as to national and even international law. Consequently it should be well understood that it is reserved for the respective signatory powers to determine all the other conditions from the point of view of right as well as of fact which must be fulfilled before an occupation can be recognised as valid."

Herr Busch, German under-secretary of state for foreign affairs, was presiding, and

remarked that the first portion of the declaration of Mr. Kasson touched on delicate questions, upon which the conference hesitated to express an opinion. It would suffice to reproduce in the protocol the views put forward by the plenipotentiary of the United States of America. The second portion of the declaration of Mr. Kasson reverted to the explanations exchanged in the commission, from which it resulted that, in the unanimous opinion of the plenipotentiaries, the declaration drawn up by the conference did not limit the right which the powers possessed of causing the recognition of the occupations which might be notified to them to be preceded by such as examination as they might consider necessary.

No more was said on the subject, and the result is that when an accession of territory on the coast of Africa is notified to the powers they will have the opportunity of objecting. It cannot be doubted that if the aggrandisement was made at the expense of a civilised population without its consent, or was attended with proceedings of great inhumanity to an uncivilised population, this would be a good ground of objection on the part of any power that pleased to take up the cause. But it would be going much further, and to a length to which the conference declined to go, if we were to say that, except in the case of unprovoked aggression justifying conquest, an uncivilised population has rights which make its free consent necessary to the establishment over it of a government possessing international validity. Any such principle, had it been adopted, would have tended to defeat one of the chief objects of the conference, namely to avoid collisions between its members by regulating more clearly their mutual position on the African coast. For on that system a power might have fulfilled the conditions of notification and establishment of authority which the conference laid down as necessary for making a new acquisition, but it would have still been exposed to see the validity of its acquisition disputed by another power, under the sanction of the conference itself, on the ground of some native title which it might be pretended had not been duly ceded to it. Is any territorial cession permitted by the ideas of the tribe? What is the authority—chief, elders, body of fighting men—if there is one, which those ideas point out as empowered to make the cession? With what formalities do they require it to be made, if they allow it to be made at all? These questions are too obscure among uncivilised populations, or, if they are clear to them, too obscure for the whites who are in contact with them, for the latter to find much difficulty in picking a hole, when desired, in a cession alleged to have been made by a tribe. And then there would be the controversies whether the irregular violence to which savages are prone amounted to aggression justifying conquest. All these are questions for which, in the general interest, the civilised powers do well not to give occasion in their mutual arrangements, so long as they are unprovided with the means of deciding them in the particular cases which may arise. Those arrangements are not to be construed as denying, because they do not affirm them, the rights of any who are not stipulating parties to the conventions by which they are made. The moral rights of all outside the international society against the several members of that society remain intact, though they have not and scarcely could have been converted into legal rights. Becoming subjects of the power which possesses the international title to the country in which they live, natives have on their governors more than the common claim of the governed, they have the claim of the ignorant and helpless on the enlightened and strong; and that claim is the more likely to receive justice, the freer is the position of the governors from insecurity and vexation.

GOVERNMENT THE INTERNATIONAL TEST OF CIVILISATION.

Civilisation is a term which has often occurred during the last few pages, and we must try to give ourselves an account of what for the present purpose we mean by it. We have nothing here to do with the mental or moral characters which distinguish the civilised from the uncivilised individual, nor even with the domestic or social habits, taking social in a narrow sense, which a traveller may remark. When people of European race come into contact with American or African tribes, the prime necessity is a government under the protection of which the former may carry on the complex life to which they have been accustomed in their homes, which may prevent that life from being disturbed by contests between different European powers for supremacy on the same soil, and which may protect the natives in the enjoyment of a security and well-being at least not less than they enjoyed before the arrival of the strangers. Can the natives furnish such a government, or can it be looked for from the Europeans alone? In the answer to that question lies, for international law, the difference between civilisation and the want of it. If even the natives could furnish such a government after the manner of the Asiatic empires, that would be sufficient. Those empires are formed of populations leading complex lives of their own, so far differing from that of Europe in important particulars, as in the family relations or in the criminal law and its administration, that it is necessary to allow to Europeans among them a system more or less separate under their consuls; but whatever may be the influence with the foreign powers derive from the force which they are known to possess though they do not habitually exercise it, it is the local force of the empire which on all ordinary occasions maintains order and protects each class of inhabitants in the enjoyment of the legal system allowed it. Wherever a population furnishes such a government as this, the law of our own international society has to take account of it. The states which are members of our international society conclude treaties with it as to the special position to be allowed to their subjects in its territory, as to custom duties and the regulation of trade, as to postal and other administrative arrangements. When at war with it, they observe the laws of war as among themselves,

JC
359
.C85
1972

and expect those laws to be observed by it towards them; and they make peace with it by treaties as among themselves. And, what is more particularly to the purpose of the present chapter, they regard its territory as held by a title of the same kind as that by which their own is held, so that the territorial sovereignty of the government in question is a root from which title may be derived to themselves by conquest or cession, and which excludes all modes of acquiring it, whether by discovery occupation or otherwise, which are or pretend to be original modes going back to the inception of sovereignty. But wherever the native inhabitants can furnish no government capable of fulfilling the purposes fulfilled by the Asiatic empires, which is the case of most of the populations with whom Europeans have come into contact in America and Africa, the first necessity is that a government should be furnished. The inflow of the white race cannot be stopped where there is land to cultivate, ore to be mined, commerce to be developed, sport to enjoy, curiosity to be satisfied. If any fanatical admirer of savage life argued that the whites ought to be kept out, he would only be driven to the same conclusion by another route, for a government on the spot would be necessary to keep them out. Accordingly international law has to treat such natives as uncivilised. It regulates, for the mutual benefit of civilised states, the claims which they make to sovereignty over the region, and leaves the treatment of the natives to the conscience of the state to which the sovereignty is awarded, rather than sanction their interest being made an excuse the more for war between civilised claimants, devastating the region and the cause of suffering to the natives themselves.

TREATIES WITH UNCIVILISED TRIBES.

Let us suppose that the officers or private subjects of a European state, or of one of European origin, advance into a region where they find no native government capable of controlling white men or under which white civilisation can exist, and where also no state has yet acquired the sovereignty under the rules which are internationally recognised between white men. We find that one of their first proceedings is to conclude treaties with such chiefs or other authorities as they can discover: and very properly, for no men are so savage as to be incapable of coming to some understanding with other men, and wherever contact has been established between men, some understanding, however incomplete it may be, is a better basis for their mutual relations than force. But what is the scope which it is reasonably possible to give to treaties in such a case, and what the effect which may be reasonably attributed to them?

We have seen that natives in the rudimentary condition supposed take no rights under international law, but that even the fulfillment of the conditions laid down by Art. 34 of the Final Act of Berlin does not preclude the possibility that objection may be made to an appropriation of territory which one civilised state notifies to another. Hence it follows that no document in which such natives are made to cede the sovereignty over any territory can be exhibited as an international title, although an arrangement with them, giving evidence that they have been treated with humanity and consideration, may be valuable as obviating possible objections to what would otherwise be a good international title to sovereignty. And this is reasonable. A stream cannot rise higher than its source, and the right to establish the full system of civilised government, which in these cases is the essence of sovereignty, cannot be based on the consent of those who at the utmost know but a few of the needs which such a government is intended to meet.

Uncivilised tribes partake in various degrees of those elements out of which the full system of civilised society is built up. Settled agricultural populations know property in land, either as belonging to individuals or to families, or, if as belonging in full measure only to the tribe, at least with such rights of a proprietary nature vested in individuals or in families as are necessary for cultivation. Hunting and nomad tribes may have so slight a connection with any land in particular as to share but little, if at all, the ideas which we connect with property in the soil. Both classes may possess, and a settled population can scarcely fail to possess, the practice of trade, by way of barter if not for money, to such an extent as to be familiar with its regulation by the authority which they recognise. To whatever point natives may have advanced, the principle must hold that a cession by them, made in accordance with their ruling customs, may confer a moral title to such property or power as they understand while they cede it, but that no form of cession by them can confer any title to what they do not understand. Hence, while the sovereignty of a European state over an uncivilised region must find its justification, as it easily will, not in treaties with natives but in the nature of the case and compliance with conditions recognised by the civilised world, it is possible that a right of property may be derived from treaties with natives, and this even before any European sovereignty has begun to exist over the spot. In that case the state which afterwards becomes sovereign will be bound to respect such right and give effect to it by its legislation, morally bound if only its own subjects are concerned, but if the previous right of property existed in a subject of another state, there can be no doubt but that respect to it would constitute an international claim as legally valid as any claim between states can be. On the coasts of Africa it would fall within "the obligation to insure the establishment of authority sufficient to protect existing rights," which is recognised in Art. 35 of the Final Act of Berlin.

The principles which I have here sought to lay down have been expressed by the Portuguese statesman J. B. de Martens Ferrão, in a passage which I am the more glad to quote because in their application, and on some further points, England and Portugal have differed.

> "It is clear," he writes, "that in savage tribes as Lubbock describes them we must recognise all natural rights. Natural rights are born with man; they constitute his personality, which the want of cultivation does not extinguish. But international rights cannot be recognised in those tribes, for want of the capacity for government (*capacité dirigeante*). Being nomads or nearly such, they have no international character. For the same reason they have no constituted sovereignty, that being no doubt a political right derived from civilisation, and therefore having civilisation as its base and the condition of its existence. Modern international law is a result of civilisation. On this ground I do not consider successive cessions of sovereignty, made by native chiefs, half or wholly savage, to the chance comer who gives them the most, without any valid sanction of right, as a reasonable base, sufficient to affect rights founded on the facts just mentioned. And all the less can I so consider them because civil property is not their subject, but is left by the negotiators to the possessor of it if there be one. Such cessions of sovereignty can furnish no juridical argument to oppose to the facts which were recognised as lawful titles by the public law in force at the time in question.*

*L'Afrique: la question soulevée dernièrement entre l'Angleterre et le Portugal considérée ou point de vue du droit international, par J. B. de Martens Ferrão: Lisbonne, 1890, p. 6. The passage is on p. 10 of the pamphlet as issued, without the author's name, from a press at Rome.

These principles again do not differ from those on which the European states dealt with the native inhabitants of the American continent north of Mexico, although their enunciation in that connection has often been less clear than it can now be made, partly because of the old confusion between territorial sovereignty and property, and partly because the natives converned were hunters and only to a limited extent cultivators, not possessing so well developed a notion of property in the soil as is possessed by the settled populations of Africa. With Mexico and Peru we have nothing here to do. Those countries had attained a degree of advancement ranking them rather as states than as uncivilised tribes. The history and methods of the British conquest in the more northern parts of the continent were well described by Chief Justice Marshall, in delivering the opinion of the Supreme Court of the United States in the case of *Johnson v. McIntosh* in the year 1823. He observes that

"The potentates of the old world found no difficulty in convincing themselves that they made ample compensation to the inhabitants of the new, by bestowing on them civilisation and Christianity in exchange for unlimited independence. But as they were all in pursuit of nearly the same object, it was necessary, in order to avoid conflicting settlements and consequent war with each other, to establish a principle which all should acknowledge as the law by which the right of acquisition which they all asserted should be regulated as between themselves. This principle was that discovery gave title to the government by whose subjects or by whose authority it was made against all other European governments, which title might be consummated by possession. The exclusion of all other Europeans necessarily gave to the nation making the discovery the sole right of acquiring the soil from the natives and establishing settlements upon it. It was a right with which no Europeans could interfere. It was a right which all asserted for themselves, and to the assertion of which by others all assented. Those relations which were to exist between the discoverer and the natives were to be regulated by themselves. The rights thus acquired being exclusive, no other power could interpose between them. In the establishment of these relations the rights of the original inhabitants were in no instance entirely disregarded, but were necessarily to a considerable extent impaired. They were admitted to be the rightful occupants of the soil, with a legal as well as just claim to retain possession of it and to use it it according to their own discretion; but their rights to complete sovereignty as independent nations were necessarily diminished, and their power to dispose of the soil at their own will to whomsoever they pleased was denied by the original fundamental principle that discovery gave exclusive title to those who made it."

It will be observed that while the Indians passed under political subjection without its being deemed necessary to ask their consent, the right in the soil which they were held to preserve is described as that of occupants, and occupancy is the term used for it in this and all other judgments of the Supreme Court which deal with the question. That it was not a greater right was not due to any incompatibility between a greater civil right of property and political subjection, but to the fact that the Indian hunters knew no greater right among themselves. Such as it was, they could admit a white individual to it, but could not expand it into full property, even in his favour.

> "Admitting," says Chief Justice Marshall, "their power to change their laws or usages so far as to allow an individual to separate a portion of their lands from the common stock and hold it in severalty, still it is a part of their territory and is held under them by a title dependent on their laws. The grant derives its efficacy from their will, and if they choose to resume it and make a different disposition of the land, the courts of the United States cannot interpose for the protection of the title. The person who purchases lands from the Indians within their territory incorporates himself with them so far as respects the property purchased, holds their title under their protection and subject to their laws."

The Indian occupancy, though in them and their grantees it cannot rise higher, is yet so firmly vested in them that even the United States cannot extinguish it otherwise than by a treaty with them. But when the tribe surrenders it by such a treaty, whatever share they may have carved out of it even for a white is surrendered also, unless the Indians reserve or regrant his rights under the sanction of the commissioners with whom the treaty is negotiated. In the absence of such a reservation or regrant it is presumed that any conveyance which the tribe may appear to have previously made to him, and under which he, even though a citizen of the United States, may afterwards claim, was considered by the Indians as invalid. But grants by the British crown passed the full property, and even when they were made before the Indian right of occupancy had been extinguished by treaty, they passed the property subject to that right.

We have here a clear apprehension of the principle that an uncivilised tribe can grant by treaty such rights as it understands and exercises, but nothing more. On the practical aspect of the case as affecting the Indians within the territory of the United States it may be remarked that, although they are precluded from converting their right of occupancy into one of property by their own power, whatever aptitude they may show for imitating the civilisation which is closing in on them, yet tribes which show such an aptitude have been admitted as citizens, not to mention the facilities given for individual Indians to be naturalised as citizens in proper cases. It may also be remarked that the Act of Congress of 3rd March 1871, which transfers the relations with the Indians from the treaty-making to the legislative power of the United States, is by no means inconsistent with a practical observance of the principle that their right of occupancy cannot be extinguished without their free consent. But it would be beside our purpose to enquire into the conduct of Indian affairs either by the United States or by the British government, or even whether the original assumption that the redskins were only hunters, incapable of a larger right than one of occupation, was justified in the case of all the tribes.

In Africa, notwithstanding the caution with which Mr. Kasson's ideas were received at the conference of Berlin, an importance has sometimes been attached to treaties with uncivilised tribes, and a development has sometimes been given to them, which are more calculated to excite laughter than argument. A turn so different from that which things have taken in America is due to several causes. First, the uncivilised populations of Africa are mostly settled agriculturists or cattle-breeders, in a stage of advancement higher than that of the redskins, though still short of that which would relieve the white races, on their arrival among them, from the duty of furnishing a government. Secondly, the climate being less suitable for European settlement, the populations in question long continued to be less known, and hence it was possible, as in the the case of Monomotapa, to exploit their names by vaunting as empires, comparable to those of Asia, what were certainly nothing more than transient agglomerations effected by savage Napoleons. Thirdly, the adventurers—I use the term in no derogatory sense— who in recent times have led the way to the partition of Africa, have had a sufficient tincture of the forms and language of international law to hope for an advantage over European competitors through what have really been travesties of them. Lastly, it may be trusted that some part has been played by a real desire to respect the just, though not well understood, claims of the natives. I am not aware of any national bias in expressing these opinions. During the recent discussions between England and Portugal, if the latter built unsoundly on cessions by the "emperor" of Monomotapa in 1607 and 1629, the former built with as little reason on a treaty by which Lobengula, in 1888, accepted British protection for a region over which he and his father and his people had never been anything but cruel raiders. If the antiquity of the Portuguese treaties exposed them to the answer that, whatever they had been in the beginning, they had lapsed into desuetude at least for the larger part of the territory alleged to be comprised in them, it was all the more difficult to treat the British one seriously, just because the facts relating to what it comprised were so modern and transparent. Leaving instances which have contributed to international dissension rather than to enlightenment, the present section may be brought to a close by two instructive examples of what a treaty with an uncivilised chief should and should not be.

A treaty which exemplifies what one with natives ought not to be is that which Mr. Colquhoun, as "representative of the British South Africa Company," concluded on 14th September 1890 with Umtasa or Mutassa, dignified as "king or chief of Manika." In the "kingdom" of this savage, for so he may be described without disrespect to the much more advanced though still uncivilised natives found elsewhere in Africa, who was such a drunkard as to be subject to *delirium tremens*, adventurers had been prospecting for gold under a Portuguese title; and Mr. Colquhoun, on 21st September, thus described his behaviour in the circumstances. "With regard to the result of the mining, Umtasa says he has till now been 'sitting watching'; while the Portuguese have ignored Umtasa, the latter on his part has ignored the presence of the white men in his country." And during the events of this and the following months, which saw the English and the Portuguese forces alternately at his kraal, fearing only for his skin, he pursued the policy of granting every demand of those who were present, and excusing himself, or even denying what he had done, to those who were absent. Such a pattern adept in all the branches of civilised administration was made to grant to the company:

"The sole absolute and entire perpetual right and power to do the following acts over the whole or any portion of the territory of the said [his] nation or any future extension thereof, including all subject and dependent territories.

(*a*)   To search, prospect, exploit, dig for and keep all metals and minerals.

(*b*)   To construct, improve, equip, work, manage and control public works and conveniences of all kinds, including railways and tramways, docks, harbours, roads, bridges, piers, wharves, canals, reservoirs, waterworks, embankments, viaducts, irrigations, reclamation, improvement, sewage, drainage, sanitary water, gas electric or any other mode of light, telephonic and telegraphic power supply, and all other works and conveniences of general or public utility.

(*c*)   To carry on the business of miners, quarry owners, metallurgists, mechanical engineers, ironfounders, builders and contractors, shipowners, shipbuilders, brickmakers, warehousemen, merchants, importers, exporters; and to buy, sell and deal in goods or property of all kinds.

(*d*)   To carry on the business of banking in all branches.

(*e*)   To buy, sell, refine, manipulate, mint and deal in bullion, specie, coin and precious metals.

(*f*)   To manufacture and import arms and ammunition of all kinds.

(*g*)   To do all such things as are incidental or conducive to the exercise, attainment or protection of all or any of the rights, powers and concessions hereby granted."

And the company agreed:

"That it will, under the King's supervision and authority, aid and assist in the establishment and propagation of the Christian religion and the education and civilisation of the native subjects of the King, by the establishment, maintenance and endowment of such churches, schools and trading stations as may be from time to time mutually agreed upon by the King and the Resident hereinbefore mentioned, and by the extension and equipment of telegraphs and of regular services of postal and transport communications."

It would be superfluous to quote the political stipulations which the treaty also contained. Taken alone they might not have been beyond Umtasa's understanding, but when they were mixed with a farrago which must have been mere jargon to him, the whole must be dismissed as something which could not have received his intelligent consent.

It is pleasant to be able to quote an example to be followed from a British source also. On 26th September 1889 the following treaty was signed with Mr. Buchanan, "Her Majesty's acting Consul for Nyassa," by the chiefs of a nation which for intelligence and character ranks very high among those which must still be called uncivilised.

"We the undersigned Mokololo chiefs (sons of the late Chiputula) do, in the presence of headmen and people assembled at this place, hereby promise:
1. That there shall be peace between the subjects of the queen of England and our subjects.
2. That British subjects shall have free access to all parts of our territory (country), and shall have the right to build houses and possess property according to the laws in force in this country; that they shall have full liberty to carry on such trade or manufacture as may be approved by Her Majesty; and should any difference arise between the aforesaid British subjects and us the said Makololo chiefs, as to the duties or customs to be paid to us the said Makololo chiefs or the headmen of the towns in our country by such British subjects, or as to any other matter, that the dispute shall be referred to a duly authorised representative of Her Majesty, whose decision in the matter shall be binding and final.
3. That we the said Makololo chiefs will at no time whatever cede any of our territory to any other power, or enter into any agreement treaty or arrangement with any foreign government except through and with the consent of the government of Her Majesty the queen of England, &c."

Here we observe that there is nothing beyond the comprehension of the Makololo chiefs; that there is no cession of territorial sovereignty by them, or any pretence of founding on their consent the right which the queen may one day come to exercise of founding a regular government in their country in the character of territorial sovereign, such right being tacitly left to be developed in the progress of events, and in accordance with the rules of international law as between Her Majesty and other European powers; that in the mean time the Makololo are recognised as a nation under their chiefs, capable of entering as such into relations with the queen's government in matters within their comprehension, and acknowledging the final supremacy of the queen's government in such matters, the same government having immediate authority over the white settlers in matters belonging specially to civilisation, as trade and manufacture; that property in land is recognised as among the matters within the comprehension of the chiefs and people, so that white settlers may acquire title to it under native law; and that the exclusion of other powers is stipulated, so far as such exclusion may depend on the Makololo. Every foundation is therefore laid, to the extent admitted by the nature of the case, for the future development of territorial sovereignty in the civilised and international sense, and for the permanence under it of such rights as the Makololo already possessed. To use an expression employed in the United States Supreme Court for the position of the Red Indians, the Makololo are admitted as a "domestic dependent nation," but, as became their condition, with rights beyond that of mere occupancy allowed in the territory of the United States to the tribes of hunters. . . .

Alleged International Title by Civilising Influence Exerted Beyond the Limits of Occupation.

During the recent dissensions between England and Portugal with regard to their mutual limits in Africa, a claim was put forward on behalf of the latter which must be stated in the words of Mr. Martens Ferrão.

"Portugal has possessed for centuries in Western and Eastern Africa vast colonies governed by Portuguese authorities, in which she exercises *dominium* and *imperium:*

She possesses states in *vassalage* according to the system established in Africa by all colonising nations:

She has also countries with which she has established *rudimentary relations*, founded on the right of first discovery, never abandoned and preserved in this manner. With all these tribes Portugal has always maintained relations by the *rudimentary commerce* of which these peoples are barely capable.

I consider these three formulas to be fundamental ones for determining the relations of colonial right in the mysterious dark continent. These typical forms have even been enlarged by England.

The last is recognised by public law, and will long continue to be so, in the great and uncertain enterprise of calling to civilisation tribes which at present are still either in the lowest state of decadence of the species or in the most rudimentary infancy.

That form, as just and well founded as the others, and not demanding less sacrifice, has been recognised as legitimate, and will always be so as long as true civilisation shall not take its place, an event which is still beyond the range of the most penetrating vision."*

The first of the forms thus enumerated needs no remark. It is that of a colony in which a civilised government is in operation under the direct authority of individuals of European race. In the second form the eminent writer appears to contemplate the immediate authority being exercised by the chiefs or other heads of the vassal state, subject to the control of the suzerain state. That is a situation with which we are familiar in the case of a protectorate exercised by a civilised state over another state possessing a civilisation of the same or of a different kind, but it may be doubted whether it is a possible situation where the people dignified with the name of a vassal state is uncivilised. M. Martens Ferrão may have framed his second formula on examples of the former class, such as those of Tunis and Zanzibar; and the traditions of such so-called empires as that of Monomotapa, handed down from the magniloquence of early explorers, may have affected his view of the possibility that natives like those with whom the Portuguese were in contact might be placed in relations similar to those of Tunis or Zanzibar. The third form is that with which we are now concerned, and it contemplates a title to territory having its roots in discovery and kept alive, not by occupation, for in that case it would have been superfluous to mention anything more than the occupation, but by rudimentary relations commercial or other, entertained with tribes whom it is desired gradually to civilise at the cost of some sacrifice to the state maintaining the relations.

There is grave objection to basing an international title on any efforts for the civilisation of native races, because the value and efficacy of such efforts are sure to be differently appreciated by the power which builds on them and by the power against which the title built on them is invoked. The use of an international title is to decide controversies, and to have that effect it ought to be based on facts to which, if I may use the expression, a yard measure can be applied. If the civilising agency of the state to which the discovery belongs is founded on a real occupation of the country accompanied by the establishment of authority in it, the yard measure is

---

* Pamphlet quoted above at p. 9 of the copies with the imprint of Rome. The italics are those of Mr. Martens Ferrão.

found in such occupation. When this is not the case, the civilising agency can mean little, if anything, more than either the work of religious missionaries or the indirect effect of commerce carried on by the natives with the discoverers and their successors. But commerce finds its recompense in itself, and will not justify the proposition that the third form of colonial expansion contemplated by the Portuguese statesman demands not less sacrifice than the other two, each of which involves the burden of government or of control. The profit which a state derives from trade cannot confer any right to exclude other states from the region in which it is carried on.

If on the other hand the civilising agency takes the form of missionary enterprise—which M. Martens Ferrão does not mention, and cannot be supposed to have intended—it is now generally acknowledged that to erect proselytism into an international title to aggrandisement would be highly injurious to sound religion and to peace and goodwill among men. Alluding to the dispute between Spain and Germany which was adjusted by the mediation of the Pope in 1885, Holtzendorff says: "Even the sending of missionaries to convert the natives, on which the Spanish government founded in the controversy about the Caroline Islands, can no longer be considered as an act of occupation because it was the church that sent them."

It is conceivable that the native population of an unoccupied country may be so permeated by influence proceeding in one way or another from a people of European race that they may have gone far towards adopting its distinctive form of civilisation and religion. There is perhaps no instance in which an uncivilised population has made so great an advance without the training and discipline which results from European government or control, but the supposition may be made. In that case it might be morally wrong for another European nation to step in and check or divert so admirable a development. But the state which lost the prospective benefit of colonial expansion over the natives in question would only have to blame itself for not having asserted in good time, over such promising neighbours, an authority which in the supposed circumstances could scarcely have been other than welcome.

On no ground then does it seem possible to admit that an international title to territory can be acquired through civilising influence exerted beyond the limits of occupation.

7. The Mandate System
of the League of Nations

When the Covenant of the League of Nations appeared at the Versailles Conference of 1919, the provisions regarding the former German colonies were hailed as a victory of liberalism over the greed of certain of the Allies, who wished simply to annex them. They were handed over to the Allied powers, but these powers, in turn, were to act as trustees for the League of Nations. At least the principle of an internationally sanctioned trusteeship was established.

In retrospect, however, the document can be seen to incorporate many of the common imperialist attitudes of the era that had just finished. Except for the former Turkish provinces, nothing was said about political development, ultimate self-government, or any other freedom than "freedom of conscience and religion." Implicitly, at least, the trust was expected to be in force for a very long time, if not permanently. In addition, Article 22 of the Covenant called for abolition of the liquor traffic, a prohibition that was nowhere in force in Europe itself—thus giving further international sanction to the racist theory that alcohol is safe for Europeans but not for others.

The provisions of the League of Nations Covenant having to do with overseas empires were Articles 22 and 23, quoted here in full from Allied and Associated Powers, *Treaty of Peace with Germany* (Washington, 1920).

Article 22.

To THOSE colonies and territories which as a consequence of the late war have ceased to be under the sovereignty of the States which formerly governed them and which are inhabited by peoples not yet able to stand by themselves under the strenuous conditions of the modern world, there should be applied the principle that the well-being and development of such peoples form a sacred trust of civilisation and that securities for the performance of this trust should be embodied in this Covenant.

The best method of giving practical effect to this principle is that the tutelage of such peoples should be entrusted to advanced nations who by reason of their resources, their experience or their geographical position can best undertake this responsibility, and who are willing to accept it, and that this tutelage should be exercised by them as Mandatories on behalf of the League.

The character of the mandate must differ according to the stage of the development of the people, the geographical situation of the territory, its economic conditions and other similar circumstances.

Certain communities formerly belonging to the Turkish Empire have reached a stage of development where their existence as independent nations can be provisionally recognised subject to the rendering of administrative advice and assistance by a Mandatory until such time as they are able to stand alone. The wishes of these communities must be a principal consideration in the selection of the Mandatory.

Other peoples, especially those of Central Africa, are at such a stage that the Mandatory must be responsible for the administration of the territory under conditions which will guarantee freedom of conscience and religion, subject only to the maintenance of public order and morals, the prohibition of abuses such as the slave trade, the arms traffic and the liquor traffic, and the prevention of the establishment of fortifications or military and naval bases and of military training of the natives for other than police purposes and the defence of territory, and will also secure equal opportunities for the trade and commerce of other Members of the League.

There are territories, such as South-West Africa and certain of the South Pacific Islands, which, owing to the sparseness of their population, or their small size, or their remoteness from the centres of civilisation, or their geographical contiguity to the territory of the Mandatory, and other circumstances, can be best administered under the laws of the Mandatory as integral portions of its territory, subject to the safeguards above mentioned in the interests of the indigenous population.

In every case of mandate, the Mandatory shall render to the Council an annual report in reference to the territory committed to its charge.

The degree of authority, control, or administration to be exercised by the Mandatory shall, if not previously agreed upon by the Members of the League, be explicitly defined in each case by the Council.

A permanent Commission shall be constituted to receive and examine the annual reports of the Mandatories and to advise the Council on all matters relating to the observance of the mandates.

Article 23.

Subject to and in accordance with the provisions of international conventions existing or hereafter to be agreed upon, the Members of the League:

(a) will endeavour to secure and maintain fair and humane conditions of labour for men, women, and children, both in their own countries and in all countries to which their commercial and industrial relations extend, and for that purpose will establish and maintain the necessary international organisations;

(b) undertake to secure just treatment of the native inhabitants of territories under their control;

(c) will entrust the League with the general supervision over the execution of agreements with regard to the traffic in women and children, and the traffic in opium and other dangerous drugs;

(d) will entrust the League with the general supervision of the trade in arms and ammunition with the countries in which the control of this traffic is necessary in the common interest;

(e) will make provision to secure and maintain freedom of communications and of transit and equitable treatment for the commerce of all Members of the League. In this connection, the special necessities of the regions devastated during the war of 1914–1918 shall be borne in mind;

(f) will endeavour to take steps in matters of international concern for the prevention and control of disease.

8. Trusteeship Under the United Nations

When the Allies met in San Francisco in the summer of 1945 to draft the United Nations Charter, few people realized that the imperial era was as nearly finished as it actually was. Within fifteen years, almost all of the overseas conquests of the past century and a half were to become independent. The intention of the signers, however, was already quite different from that of 1919. The two most important powers, the United States and the U.S.S.R., either had absorbed the imperial conquests of the past, or, in the case of the United States, had already made the decision to liquidate its overseas empire in the Philippines. Both were still concerned about strategic territories, but neither wanted to preserve or extend its rule over alien peoples. Thus, while the tone of Chapter XI of the Charter, dealing with non-self-governing territories, was a far milder kind of anti-imperialism than was heard in the

General Assembly debates of the 1960's, it was even further from the language of the League Covenant.

The idea of trusteeship was continued—and called by that name. But those holding trust territories were now bound to insure "political, economic, social, and educational advancement" with explicit goals of self-government and free political institutions, and the Trusteeship Council was created to watch over the system. Though not stated explicitly in the language of the Charter itself, it was also understood that the role of trustee was to end at the earliest possible date.

Chapters XI, XII, and XIII are quoted here in their entirety from the Charter of the United Nations, signed June 26, 1945, Department of State Publication 2353, Conference Series 74.

Chapter XI
Declaration Regarding Non-self-governing Territories

ARTICLE 73

Members of the United Nations which have or assume responsibilities for the administration of territories whose peoples have not yet attained a full measure of self-government recognize the principle that the interests of the inhabitants of these territories are paramount, and accept as a sacred trust the obligation to promote to the utmost, within the system of international peace and security established by the present Charter, the well-being of the inhabitants of these territories, and, to this end:

a. to ensure, with due respect for the culture of the peoples concerned, their political, economic, social, and educational advancement, their just treatment, and their protection against abuses;

b. to develop self-government, to take due account of the political aspirations of the peoples, and to assist them in the progressive development of their free political institutions, according to the particular circumstances of each territory and its peoples and their varying stages of advancement;

c. to further international peace and security;

d. to promote constructive measures of development, to encourage research, and to cooperate with one another and, when and where appropriate, with specialized international bodies with a view to the practical achievement of the social, economic, and scientific purposes set forth in this Article; and

e. to transmit regularly to the Secretary-General for information purposes, subject to such limitation as security and constitutional considerations may require, statistical and other information of a technical nature relating to economic, social, and educational conditions in the territories for which they are respectively responsible other than those territories to which Chapters XII and XIII apply.

ARTICLE 74

Members of the United Nations also agree that their policy in respect of the territories to which this Chapter applies, no less than in respect of their metropolitan areas, must be based on the general principle of good-neighborliness, due account being taken of the interests and well-being of the rest of the world, in social, economic, and commercial matters.

Chapter XII
International Trusteeship System

ARTICLE 75

The United Nations shall establish under its authority an international trusteeship system for the administration and supervision of such territories as may be placed thereunder by subsequent individual agreements. These territories are hereinafter referred to as trust territories.

ARTICLE 76

The basic objectives of the trusteeship system, in accordance with the Purposes of the United Nations laid down in Article 1 of the present Charter, shall be:

a. to further international peace and security;

b. to promote the political, economic, social, and educational advancement of the inhabitants of the trust territories, and their progressive development towards self-government or independence as may be appropriate to the particular circumstances of each territory and its peoples and the freely expressed wishes of the peoples concerned, and as may be provided by the terms of each trusteeship agreement;

c. to encourage respect for human rights and for fundamental freedoms for all without distinction as to race, sex, language, or religion, and to encourage recognition of the interdependence of the peoples of the world; and

d. to ensure equal treatment in social, economic, and commercial matters for all Members of the United Nations and their nationals, and also equal treatment for the latter in the administration of justice, without prejudice to the attainment of the foregoing objectives and subject to the provisions of Article 80.

ARTICLE 77

1. The trusteeship system shall apply to such territories in the following categories as may be placed thereunder by means of trusteeship agreements:

a. territories now held under mandate;

b. territories which may be detached from enemy states as a result of the Second World War; and

c. territories voluntarily placed under the system by states responsible for their administration.

2. It will be a matter for subsequent agreement as to which territories in the foregoing categories will be brought under the trusteeship system and upon what terms.

ARTICLE 78

The trusteeship system shall not apply to territories which have become Members of the United Nations, relationship among which shall be based on respect for the principle of sovereign equality.

ARTICLE 79

The terms of trusteeship for each territory to be placed under the trusteeship system, including any alteration or amendment, shall be agreed upon by the states directly concerned, including the mandatory power in the case of territories held under mandate by a Member of the United Nations, and shall be approved as provided for in Articles 83 and 85.

ARTICLE 80

1. Except as may be agreed upon in individual trusteeship agreements, made under Articles 77, 79, and 81, placing each territory under the trusteeship system, and until such agreements have been concluded, nothing in this Chapter shall be construed in or of itself to alter in any manner the rights whatsoever of any states or any peoples or the terms of existing international instruments to which Members of the United Nations may respectively be parties.

2. Paragraph 1 of this Article shall not be interpreted as giving grounds for delay or postponement of the negotiation and conclusion of agreements for placing mandated and other territories under the trusteeship system as provided for in Article 77.

ARTICLE 81

The trusteeship agreement shall in each case include the terms under which the trust territory will be administered and designate the authority which will exercise the administration of the trust territory. Such authority, hereinafter called the administering authority, may be one or more states or the Organization itself.

ARTICLE 82

There may be designated, in any trusteeship agreement, a strategic area or areas which may include part or all of the trust territory to which the agreement applies, without prejudice to any special agreement or agreements made under Article 43.

ARTICLE 83

1. All functions of the United Nations relating to stategic areas, including the approval of the terms of the trusteeship agreements and of their alteration or amendment, shall be exercised by the Security Council.

2. The basic objectives set forth in Article 76 shall be applicable to the people of each strategic area.

3. The Security Council shall, subject to the provisions of the trusteeship agreements and without prejudice to security considerations, avail itself of the assistance of the Trusteeship Council to perform those functions of the United Nations under the trusteeship system relating to political, economic, social, and educational matters in the strategic areas.

ARTICLE 84

It shall be the duty of the administering authority to ensure that the trust territory shall play its part in the maintenance of international peace and security. To this end the administering authority may make use of volunteer forces, facilities, and assistance from the trust territory in carrying out the obligations towards the Security Council undertaken in this regard by the administering authority, as well as for local defense and the maintenance of law and order within the trust territory.

ARTICLE 85

1. The functions of the United Nations with regard to trusteeship agreements for all areas not designated as strategic, including the approval of the terms of the trusteeship agreements and of their alteration or amendment, shall be exercised by the General Assembly.

2. The Trusteeship Council, operating under the authority of the General Assembly, shall assist the General Assembly in carrying out these functions.

Chapter XIII
The Trusteeship Council

COMPOSITION

ARTICLE 86

1. The Trusteeship Council shall consist of the following Members of the United Nations:

    a. those Members administering trust territories;

    b. such of those Members mentioned by name in Article 23 as are not administering trust territories; and

    c. as many other Members elected for three-year terms by the General Assembly as may be necessary to ensure that the total number of members of the Trusteeship Council is equally divided between those Members of the United Nations which administer trust territories and those which do not.

2. Each member of the Trusteeship Council shall designate one specially qualified person to represent it therein.

FUNCTION AND POWERS

ARTICLE 87

The General Assembly and, under its authority, the Trusteeship Council, in carrying out their functions, may:

    a. consider reports submitted by the administering authority;

    b. accept petitions and examine them in consultation with the administering authority;

    c. provide for periodic visits to the respective trust territories at times agreed upon with the administering authority; and

d. take these and other actions in conformity with the terms of the trusteeship agreements.

ARTICLE 88

The Trusteeship Council shall formulate a questionnaire on the political, economic, social, and educational advancement of the inhabitants of each trust territory, and the administering authority for each trust territory within the competence of the General Assembly shall make an annual report to the General Assembly upon the basis of such questionnaire.

VOTING

ARTICLE 89

1. Each member of the Trusteeship Council shall have one vote.
2. Decisions of the Trusteeship Council shall be made by a majority of the members present and voting.

PROCEDURE

ARTICLE 90

1. The Trusteeship Council shall adopt its own rules of procedure, including the method of selecting its President.
2. The Trusteeship Council shall meet as required in accordance with its rules, which shall include provision for the convening of meetings on the request of a majority of its members.

ARTICLE 91

The Trusteeship Council shall, when appropriate, avail itself of the assistance of the Economic and Social Council and of the specialized agencies in regard to matters with which they are respectively concerned.

III

The Application of Pseudoscientific Racism

It was remarked in the general introduction that racism was all-pervasive, but led to no particular set of policy decisions or recommendations. Rather, it was a way of looking at the determinants of human action and human history. As such, it could have a powerful influence, but the direction of that influence might be strongly modified by other attitudes. The selections that follow are four illustrations of the way racist doctrines could be used in the hands of imperialist writers, and three of these four writers were men who actually helped to run empires—not merely those who urged them on from the sidelines.

Racism in this context means the belief that physical race is not simply a matter of physical appearance—that it implies a definite heritage of mental abilities, tendencies, strengths, weaknesses, language, and culture. But the degree and kind of difference postulated could vary greatly, leaving the way open for innumerable interpretations. Carl Peters wrote as a German explorer, telling of his experiences in East Africa in 1888–90. As a founder of the German East African Company, and one of the principal advocates of German imperial expansion, he was anxious to show his expedition, and the German imperial effort, in the best possible light. Yet, even by his own account, he regarded instant death for suspected theft as appropriate treatment for Africans. He apparently expected his readers to hold the same opinion, even though it ran counter to German ideas of justice for Germans at home.

At the other extreme is Lord Olivier, a British colonial governor who was also a socialist. His public writings focused on the defense of Negroes against Europeans in Jamaica, South Africa, and elsewhere in the empire. Yet he too was a racist, even though the selection below is actually a defense against the more pejorative aspects of the doctrine. He took the teachings of "science" as he found them and tried to mitigate the consequences. Had he been more a scholar and less a man of affairs, he might have known that pseudoscientific racism was already under attack in some scientific circles. His acceptance of racism, even in a moderate form, is evidence of its enormous influence on imperial thought in the early decades of this century.

The remaining two selections illustrate this influence in different ways. Léopold de Saussure wrote as a political philosopher, based in Europe, and looking mainly at the ultimate aims of French imperial policy. From this point of view, the "fact" of innate mental differences between races was a bar to the older conversionist view that overseas empires bring about the spread of Western civilization. Charles Temple, on the other hand, wrote from experience at the local level of imperial administration. He too accepted the racist position, but he sought solutions in the way the empire was run, without much concern for philosophical principles or ultimate aims.

9. Carl Peters on His Civilizing Mission

Carl Peters (1856–1918) was a controversial figure in his own time and remained one until the Second World War. The British and French used his many atrocities against Africans as a way of attacking German imperialism in general, while the National Socialist regime in Germany tried to make him into a national hero. He was one of the early advocates of a German empire, founder of the German Colonization Society in 1884, and of an unofficial expedition into East Africa to sign treaties of annexation with African authorities. After Bismarck accepted these treaties as the basis of a German East Africa, he returned in 1888–90 to lead a second expedition inland from the coast to Uganda and then southward into present-day Tanzania and back to Zanzibar. The three selections are from the English translation of the published account of this expedition, New Light on Dark Africa (London, 1890), pp. 192–193, 213–215, and 520–531. The first deals with his ideas on the proper way to conduct an expedition, while the second and third deal respectively with his reactions to the Kikuyu of present-day Kenya and the Gogo of the Tanzanian interior.

I HAD made up my mind to practise patience in this country to the utmost possible extent, to get through peacefully; but practically I could not help seeing how impossible it is to get on with natures like these negroes without recourse to corporal punishment. But for this resource, a man is entirely powerless against such breaches of contract and hindrances of every kind; and for these people themselves it is much better, if they are made clearly to understand that lying, thieving, and cheating are not exactly the things that ought to be in this world, but that human society rests upon a certain reciprocity of responsibility and service. Beyond all question, that is the manner in which the way will be best and most safely prepared for the opening up of Africa. To make oneself the object of insolence of the natives is the very way to confirm the blacks in the lowest qualities of their characters, and especially to degrade our race in their eyes. The practice of undertaking such responsibilities, and then leaving them unfulfilled, under all manner of pretexts, is always founded upon a certain under-estimation of the other party. It is quite a mistaken motto of travellers, that in Africa one must learn patience, and that no one who has not patience should travel there. It certainly is far more consonant with our interests and with civilisation if we take it as our motto, on the other hand, that we will impart some of our characteristics to the natives of Africa, instead of simply truckling to their faults. The great principle that makes itself felt through the universe, even in inorganic nature, is the principle of unlimited justice. But this principle is quite as much disregarded when the black man is allowed to overreach the white man, as in the opposite case. During the whole time of my leading the expedition I was always conscious of acting upon this principle. . . .

In Kikuyu seven days of rejoicing refreshed the expedition, which was greatly exhausted by marches on the Upper Tana. Kikuyu is a land that can feed its people, a region literally flowing with milk and honey. It is a mountainous country, with gently-sloping lines, inclining towards the Kenia on the south, richly watered, and with a fresh and verdant appearance everywhere.

There are two divisions of this country: Kikuyu Mbi on the right side of the Tana (Kikuyu 2), where we now were, and Kikuyu Mnea on the left bank of the river (Kikuyu 1). Thomson has much to say of the untameable cruelty of the inhabitants—exaggerated like all the pictures of the dangers among the inhabitants of this steppe offered by Thomson to the wondering European. Count Teleki and Herr von Höhnel had thoroughly impressed the thievish Wakikuyu with the superiority of European weapons; accordingly, as I have already stated, we were brought face to face with a whimsical mixture of impudent, thievish propensities and sentiments of timid submission. The native chiefs hastened to make their peace with us, which was ratified by the slaughter of a goat or a sheep. The younger inhabitants, however, could not restrain a propensity to thieving, confirmed by transmission through many generations, even after, with the concurrence of the elders, I had ordained that every attempt at robbery should be visited with capital punishment, and a number of them had suffered the penalty for indulging their thievish proclivities. If the flocks were driven through the land, luxuriant with grass, a black arm, its possessor entirely hidden in the bush, would be suddenly thrust forth from one side, and seizing a sheep by the hind leg, would endeavour to vanish with the prize as quickly as it had appeared. Then the Somalis would fire into the bushes, out of which a yell of pain would burst forth, proclaiming that just punishment had overtaken the evildoer.

Thus for seven days did we travel through this beauteous Kikuyu, whose flora already exhibits the forms of the temperate zone. Here we met with a kind of tree that reminded us vividly of our European oaks. Here I saw the fresh green clover of the North German borders, on which donkeys, goats, and sheep browsed with much enjoyment. Clear rivulets gushed onward through all the hollows, with an average temperature of only 14–15° C. (55–58° Fahr.). The nights were already bitterly cold; the thermometer fell by ten o'clock to 8–9° C. (44–47° Fahr.). In the morning the hoarfrost lay spread over the fresh landscape. On December 16th the registering "lowest temperature" thermometer for the first time exhibited the register at the freezing-point.

The ways here generally lead along by the far-extending hills. When we had reached the heights, we every morning enjoyed the view of the grave and majestic lines of the Kenia, which appeared more and more prominently in the north. The Wakikuyu snatched greedily at the coloured and white pieces of stuff which we still had with us, and brought in return into our camp quantities of poultry, milk, and honey, besides abundance of grain of all kinds, so that black and white revelled alike in the treasures of this beautiful land. . . .

. . . Of all the countries through which we travelled Ugogo is the ugliest, and, I may add, the most repulsive; and the disposition of the people is in keeping with the character of the country. The Wagogo are originally of Bantu race, but apparently have a considerable admixture of Massai blood. Like the Massais, they are arrogant and addicted to thieving. They look upon strangers simply as enemies; and as for thousands of years traffic has taken its course through their land, they have established for themselves a predaceous custom of exacting tribute, under which all the trade caravans have to suffer grievously.

In his work "In Darkest Africa," vol. ii., p. 406, Stanley thus complains, in a somewhat sentimental strain:—"There is no country in Africa that has excited greater interest in me than this. It is a ferment of trouble and distraction, and a vermin of petty annoyances beset the traveller from day to day while in it. No natives know so well how to aggrieve and be unpleasant to travellers. One would think there was a school somewhere in Ugogo to teach low cunning and vicious malice to the chiefs, who are masters in foxy-craft. Nineteen years ago I looked upon this land and people with desiring eyes. I saw in it a field worth some effort to reclaim. In six months I felt sure Ugogo could be made lovely and orderly, a blessing to the inhabitants and to strangers, without any very great expense or trouble; it would become a pleasant highway of human intercourse with far-away peoples, productive of wealth to the natives, and comfort to caravans. I learned, on arrival in Ugogo, that I was for ever debarred from the hope. It is to be the destiny of the Germans to carry out this work, and I envy them. It is the worst news of all that I shall never be able to drain this cesspool of iniquitous passion, and extinguish the insolence of Wagogo chiefs, and make the land clean, healthy, and even beautiful of view. While my best wishes will accompany German efforts, my mind is clouded with a doubt that it ever will be that fair land of rest and welcome I had dreamed of making it."

What a pity for Ugogo that Stanley cannot carry out his plans respecting this country! It would indeed be an enormous advantage for the whole of Eastern Africa if the caravans, instead of passing through an entirely dried-up savannah at the back of Usagara, could make their way through a verdant and flourishing garden. Certainly Mr. Stanley had a capital opportunity offered him "to extinguish the insolence of Wagogo chiefs" when he last traversed this country, and it is only to be regretted that he took no advantage of it.

On June 9th we found ourselves in the western part of Makenge's country, and on this day I set up the camp at Mtive, once again in an encampment that had been occupied by Mr. Stokes. When Stanley passed through Makenge's country nine months previously the latter had sent to him with the request that he should pay tribute immediately. Stanley, at the head of one thousand men, and possessing a Maxim gun, could have utilised this excellent occasion "to extinguish the insolence of Wagogo chiefs," for a demand of this kind for tribute, in the face of so strong an expedition commanded by nine white men, may well be called insolence.

Instead of setting to work "to drain this cesspool of iniquitous passion," however, Stanley sent Makenge the accustomed tribute paid by caravans. But with this Makenge was not satisfied. He returned the simple tribute, and now demanded of Stanley that he should give him up his men for feudal labour. He desired Stanley to have a fortified camp built for him.

Here was the second opportunity for Mr. Stanley "to extinguish the insolence of Wagogo chiefs." He was certainly sufficiently angry at this demand of Makenge's, but instead of refusing it, and waiting for the consequences, he considered it the wiser course to give way, and sent Makenge four times the usual tribute, with which the latter was graciously pleased to declare himself satisfied.

This small episode, which took place during Stanley's sojourn in Ugogo, is not related by him, and I only mention it to make the following circumstances more intelligible.

It is as clear as possible that if an expedition of the strength of Stanley's in Ugogo consented to pay tribute, one could scarcely expect either great respect or corresponding humility towards the white race from the people of the land. Accordingly, what happened to us in this country is not in any way to be wondered at.

We were still sitting at breakfast, when some rascally Wagogo began to crowd round our tent, and one of them placed himself rudely in front of the entrance. On my requesting him to be off, he grinned impudently, but remained where he was. Hereupon Herr von Tiedemann, who sat nearest to the door, sprang from his seat, seized the fellow, and flung him on one side. I too jumped up, and called out to Hussein to lay hold of him, and to teach him a lesson with the hippopotamus-hide whip. This was done amidst howls of lamentation, whilst the Wangwana informed us that the offender was the son of the Sultan of the country. Whilst this was going on there arose, to the north of the camp, the war-cry of the Wagogo, which we knew so well. These people had driven away my men from the water because I had paid no tribute, and now came rushing towards the camp. I immediately betook myself to the north side of it, and saw how the Wagogo warriors, armed for the most part each with two lances, came dancing along, challenging us to fight.

As they began to shoot their arrows at us, I fired amongst them, knocking one over, and hitting another in the arm. They now took to headlong flight, and immediately some of the chiefs came to me to open peace negotiations. The debate upon these continued all the afternoon, and in the evening it was at last decided to send messengers to Makenge, to whose capital we were to march on the following day, and to leave the settling of the matter to him.

I stationed twelve sentries to guard the camp during the night, and the following morning set out, with beat of drum, on our march eastward, passing great crowds of the Wagogo as we went. Our way led through an almost dried-up river, into the country of Unjanguira. At eleven o'clock we came to a well-cultivated territory, which strongly reminded me of the country bordering Lake Möris, near Alexandria. I remarked that large bodies of men were running about behind the maize fields, and was further disagreeably impressed by the hyena-like howl of the Wagogo, in which I plainly recognised a war-cry.

When we had pursued our way through the maize fields lying east of the villages, I suddenly became aware of several hundred Wagogo warriors, who were kneeling by the left side of the road, with bows bent and lances ready for battle, and one of the chiefs came running towards us, shouting in impudent tones the demand for tribute ("Mahongo! Mahongo!"). My contempt for these rascals had been increased by the occurrences of the previous day. I handed my gun to my servant, and, taking my long knotted stick in my hand, made straight for the Wagogo, calling out to them:—

"Take yourselves off from here, and mind what you are about!"

They all rose, and moved slowly away. I then marched to an

encampment in the south of Makenge's capital, and immediately sent a message to the Sultan, requesting him to put himself in communication with me, as I desired to know whether he wished for war or peace.

The messengers returned with their commission unexecuted. They had been warned by a caravan of Wanjamwesi, encamped in the vicinity, not to enter Makenge's capital, where, they declared, thousands of warriors were collected to attack us. To be prepared for this emergency, as I was almost without ammunition for my muzzle-loaders, I sent in all haste for the only load of wire I had brought with me on the expedition, had it filed into pieces, and distributed these among my men. We then seated ourselves for breakfast, during which messengers, sent from the Wanjamwesi caravan, appeared to offer us their friendship.

Whilst I was speaking to them messengers suddenly arrived from Makenge.

"Our Sultan sends you word that he wishes for peace with you. He wishes to be the friend of the Germans, and you are to pay no tribute in his country."

"Tell your Sultan," I replied, "if he desires to be the friend of the Germans, and our friend, he must exchange presents with me. Let him send me corn and honey, and I will give him powder and cloth stuffs."

We were still in conversation, when the clatter of guns, proceeding from the west of our camp, again near the water, suddenly resounded. In wild haste my men came rushing to the camp from that direction. Seizing my double-barrelled gun, I stepped forth from my tent, and cried,—

"Where are the Wagogo?"

"There, and there, and there! From every side they come!"

And so it was. From every direction I could see the Wagogo in crowds dancing forward.

This sight so roused my anger that I cried out to my men:

"Dererah, Somal!" ("Fight, Somalis!") "To your guns, sons of the Unjamwesi, sons of Usukuma, and sons of Manyema! Forward! Down with the Wagogo!"

The plan of action was soon settled. A few of the Somalis had to protect the east and north side of the camp. To the west and south, from whence the chief attack proceeded, I hastened forward with about twenty men to oppose the enemy. Herr von Tiedemann was at first at my side, but I ordered him back to the eastern side.

The Wagogo, between two and three thousand strong, according to Von Tiedemann's computation, and many of them armed with muzzle-loaders, began the attack. An unfortunate circumstance for me was that my men could only shoot at short distances with those wretched pieces of wire, which somewhat lessened the superiority of our firearms. My double-barrelled gun, however, and the repeating guns of the Somalis, maintained their usual efficiency. In accordance with my old Massai tactics, I gave orders to fire several volleys, so as to begin by knocking down some of their warriors. With loud cheers we then advanced, but in such a way as to carefully watch the movements of our adversaries, and when they halted we halted too, and fired upon them again.

The sun shone fiercely, but in half an hour the Wagogo had been repulsed from the camp towards the south and west; and now I sent a message to Herr von Tiedemann, requesting him to remain in camp and guard it, as I intended to advance against the villages situated about half a mile to the southward, and there to attack the Wagogo in my turn. I was in the act of carrying out this intention, and was pushing forward against the villages, when I was suddenly met by messengers from Makenge.

"The Sultan wishes for peace with you, and will pay you tribute in ivory and oxen."

I replied, "The Sultan shall have peace. It shall be the eternal peace. I will show the Wagogo what the Germans are."

So I advanced against the first village, where the Wagogo at first tried to defend themselves; but after several of them had been shot down, they rushed in wild flight out at the south gate, and the village was in our hands.

"Plunder the village, set fire to the houses, and smash everything to pieces that will not burn!"

But unfortunately it soon became apparent that the Wagogo villages themselves do not burn easily, being composed of wooden buildings covered with clay, with a circular enclosure around them. I ordered large quantities of wood to be placed in the houses, which were systematically set on fire. The axes that I sent for to the camp did their work also in knocking down the walls, so the first village was soon in ruins. Whilst this work was proceeding I placed three Somalis as a guard on the south side, and frightened away the Wagogo with my shots.

Meanwhile, I sent off a message to the neighbouring Wanjamwesi caravan, with which we had already concluded terms of friendship: "Come and help us. If we capture the herds of the Wagogo you shall have a share of the booty."

This was between two and three in the afternoon. The Wanjamwesi, however, did not probably feel very confident about the matter, for they did not appear upon the scene of the encounter until five o'clock. Now Hussein called out to me: "Master, come! the Wagogo are attacking the camp!"

I answered, "I will show you how to drive the Wagogo away from the camp."

We crept through the maize fields, and suddenly began to fire upon the hordes, who were rushing on from the east in flank and in rear. They fled wildly, scattering in every direction. My contempt for the Wagogo was so great, that during this fight I said repeatedly to my men, "I will prove to you what kind of rascals we have to deal with. Stay, all of you, where you are, and I will alone drive the Wagogo away." I went towards the Wagogo, shouted "Hurrah!" and away they ran by hundreds.

I mention this, not to represent our advance as anything heroic, but only to show what all this African population really is, and how exaggerated are the ideas which exist in Europe concerning their warlike capabilities and the means necessary for their subjugation. The Wagogo are considered one of the tribes most to be dreaded in the whole of the German East African Protectorate, before whom the Wangwana of the coast tremble on entering their country; and yet we were able, with bad ammunition and only twenty men, to send thousands of them scampering.

From three in the afternoon I advanced against the other villages in the south. Everywhere the same spectacle was repeated. After a short resistance the Wagogo fled in all directions; burning brands were thrown into the houses, and the axes did their work in hewing in pieces what could not be burnt. By half-past four, twelve villages were thus burnt down; but I was not in a position to seize the herds that were grazing further south on a mountain slope, for I had, as a rule, only six to ten men immediately around me, and I could not but suppose that the Wagogo would here fight more energetically.

Suddenly, at about five o'clock, I saw large numbers coming hurriedly towards me, from the direction of my camp. At first I took them for Wagogo, and was just on the point of firing at them. But my people cried out to me,—

"The Wanjamwesi are coming!"

I now called out to the Wanjamwesi, "Come on, Wanjamwesi! Forward upon the oxen of the Wagogo! There they are, yonder! Hurrah!"

And off we set, rushing wildly past several villages, towards the herds of oxen. The Wagogo endeavoured rapidly to drive their herds away, but we succeeded in seizing two or three hundred head, knocking over those of the herdsmen who did not flee. My gun had become so hot from frequent firing that I could scarcely hold it. The greater part of the firing on that day fell to my share, as I was almost the only person who possessed a sufficient supply of ammunition. My burning thirst I quenched from time to time with some sour milk we had seized.

The sun was sinking in the west when I at last gave the order to retire. My people were so full of fighting spirit, that I could scarcely prevail upon them to return. They were plundering in the various villages, or scoffing at the Wagogo, who were still either standing or lying about in the background in large numbers.

At half-past five we began our return march. The cattle were driven along with us, and the Wagogo followed at a respectful distance, still firing upon us, until we were close to our camp. But they were unable to regain possession of a single head of their cattle. On the following morning, they reported their loss on that afternoon as "over fifty."

When we approached the camp, Herr von Tiedemann and the men there came out joyfully to meet us.

"Well, Herr von Tiedemann, I think those will last us as far as Mpuapua," I said, pointing to the cattle.

We shook hands and walked towards the camp. My men performed warlike and triumphal dances round the animals. On entering my tent, I again quenched my thirst, this time with cognac and water; I then distributed the remaining powder and bits of wire, and posted sentries round the camp. I experienced a peculiar heaviness in the head, from running so much in the hot sun. As became manifest on that very night, I had contracted an affection of the brain, which made itself felt during the next few days in deafness, as well as in feverish temperature and a general feeling of discomfort.

Before turning back from the villages of the Wagogo, I had shouted to them,—

"You now know Kupanda Sharo and the Germans a little better than you did this morning; but you shall learn to know them in quite another fashion. I shall now remain amongst you in your country, so long as a man of you is alive, so long as one of your villages still stands, and a single animal of your herds is to be seized!"

A great slaughtering of cattle was now going on in the camp, and a joyous spirit pervaded the men seated round the camp-fires, before which reclined also the Wanjamwesi, who had been invited to stay till evening.

At nine o'clock Makenge sent his sons to me. They brought some ivory, representing a net value of about one thousand marks, as a first tribute, and requested to know what were my conditions of peace.

"Tell your Sultan that I want no peace with him. The Wagogo are liars, and must be destroyed from off the face of the earth. But if the Sultan wishes to become the slave of the Germans, then he and his people may live. As a proof of your submission, let him send me to-morrow morning a tribute of oxen, sheep and goats, let him send me milk and honey, and then we will negotiate further."

That night I fell into a heavy sleep, from which I was awakened before sunrise by the lowing of cattle. Mankenge had sent me thirty-eight oxen, as well as a number of sheep. In the course of the day, milk and honey and other articles arrived in addition. I now consented to enter into a treaty with him, by virtue of which he was placed under German authority. I promised to send him the flag, as soon as I should reach Mpuapua.

The great Wanjamwesi caravan, which was encamped in the neighbourhood, sent me a deputation on that day to say, "Be our leader; we will be your people." This caravan numbered over twelve hundred men, and possessed, amongst other advantages, a great many drummers.

Having settled everything by June 11th, we started again on our eastward march on the 12th, the black, white, and red flag waving gaily in the morning breeze, the drums beating lustily, and the Wagogo herds in the van. Not a Wagogo was to be seen in the whole country side. . . .

10. *Léopold de Saussure*
as an Opponent of Assimilation

Léopold de Saussure (1866–1925) was born in Switzerland of a family with a broad range of scientific interests. He, however, took French nationality and served in the French navy from 1882 to 1899, participating in colonial wars in East Asia and on the African coast.

Psychologie de la colonisation française was published in the year of his retirement from the navy and was followed by occasional later writings on colonial questions, though Saussure's principal scholarly interest during the remainder of his life was the history of Chinese astronomy.

The selection quoted here is a curious document in intellectual history, being one of the most rigorous—if not *the* most rigorous—statements of the Assimilationist position found in French colonial theory. Its curiosity lies in the fact that it was made by an opponent of Assimilation, not an advocate. If the language is compared to the milder resolution proposed by Senator Isaac in 1889 (see above, p. xxi), the contrast will be clear—and it must be remembered that the Isaac resolution failed to pass at the Colonial Congress of that year. In fact, Saussure was not attacking an actual school of French policy makers, unanimous in their opinions and overwhelmingly supported by the public; he was attacking the rights-of-man philosophy of the Enlightenment, as expressed through the heritage of the French Revolution as it lived on under the Third Republic. This heritage did not actually lead to an Assimilationist imperial policy, in spite of incipient tendencies in that direction at Saussure's time and later. Saussure was really trying to head off the implications that might be drawn from the Revolutionary heritage, and to do this because the "scientific fact" of racism showed how outmoded that heritage was.

The selection is a translation in its entirety, omitting footnotes, of the final chapter of *Psychologie de la colonisation française dans ses rapports avec les sociétés indigènes* (Paris, 1899), pp. 294–311.

FRENCH COLONIAL policy is oriented toward one defined goal—assimilation. The moderate expression presented at the congress of 1899 may have given a false picture and reassured some people, but that makes it all the more dangerous.

At first view, it may seem that this policy, thus defined, is not essentially different from that of other nations: for, even if all colonial expeditions have not been motivated by the purest humanitarianism, all the powers have been pleased to envelop the violence of conquest in the aura of a civilizing mission. They have all proclaimed the moral duty they have contracted in respect to the natives.

From this, it might be conceived that there is no very strict line of demarcation between two policies—that which affirms the principle of assimilation while declaring that it should be followed prudently, and that which, without affirming any principle at all, seizes the occasion to improve the lot of the natives and bring them progress. There is nevertheless an important distinction, for one is based on a dogma and a faith which inspires a whole people, while the other merely follows from experience.

The policy of assimilation not only proposes to bring progress to the natives; it proposes to make them accept the French language, institutions, political and religious beliefs, customs and turn of mind. In so doing, it affirms that that which is suited to the French is equally suited to all races, to Negroes, Annamites, Kanakas, and Arabs. It denies psychological evolution, or at the very least has a very curious idea of it: it denies the intimate relationship linking the moral elements of a civilization with the race that has created it.

It lays down, as the basis for French colonial policy, principles drawn from the philosophy of the eighteenth century whose error is already recognized. While other nations muster all the experience and observation available in order to solve, in conformity to natural facts, the complex, diverse, and obscure problems of managing natives, we impose a preconceived plan on ourselves, which will serve as inspiration for the most important acts, organic decrees, or the conduct of the minister, as much as that of the lowliest official. We have decided in advance on the evolution of all native races, and that evolution will everywhere be uniform: they will pass down the pathway that France has followed. If one considers the variety of temperaments among our native races, he can foresee that this vain effort at uniformization represents useless exertion, heedless expense, and irritating worries.

It claims to be moderate because it recognizes the necessity of being gradual and not trying to transform the natives at the wave of a wand. But that necessity arises from the nature of things: it is self-evident. It is not a question, then, of moderation in the nature of the program, only in the rapidity with which it is put into effect. In carrying out their moderation, the assimilators do not deny making native societies enter into a structure identical to that of

French society; they simply admit (and it would be impossible to do otherwise) that this unification must take place little by little. Taken in isolation, the assimilating measures will be no less in conformity to their principles; they will merely be more spaced out over time.

Furthermore, if the discontent of the natives imposes a certain moderation on the assimilators, one must not forget that they have all public opinion on their side and that they are thus forced to keep this moderation to a strict minimum. We have seen that our most eminent men share the illusions of the crowd on this point; they can conceive of no other solution to the complex problems of ruling over the natives than complete fusion and assimilation.

There is in that unanimity, in that dogmatic candor at the end of the nineteenth century, a principle of general application which shows how the evolution of a dogma can be "compartmentalized," so to speak. It is incontestable that, as a consequence of being applied in the national setting and coming into conflict with reality, the dogmas of the past century have altered in meaning, have lost the virginity and absoluteness of their early days. One no longer encounters, even among the Radicals, the faith of a Condorcet or a Robespierre. A compromise has been established in domestic policy between the ideal and reality. But the minute a new opportunity presents itself to begin the same cycle of experiments in another domain, the old faith returns in all its purity, among the élite as with the masses. It met defeat in the compartment of domestic policy, but it reappeared intact in that of colonial policy.

The doctrine of assimilation, which all factions support, is purely and simply that of the *philosophes* of the reign of Louis XV. A century and a half of geographical discoveries, scientific conquests, and social experiments has not even grazed the confidence it inspired in our ancestors. We ask *them* for solutions to our colonial problems. In regard to colonization, we are still living with "Natural Philosophy."

The point of departure for this philosophy is the definition of man as a complete and unique entity, in possession *ab ovo* of all his attributes of intelligence and sensibility. It is itself derived from another definition (which the *philosophes* accept implicitly without recognizing that they have inherited it from earlier religious systems)—a definition of humanity declared to be of a single origin, presented as a single family, as the posterity of only one father and one mother, as the ruler and master of nature, and as independent of animal kind. The outstanding consequence of this definition, and one whose development is found throughout this philosophy, follows in logic: since an organic moral unity exists in human nature, it follows that moral differences (of which the existence is undeniable) are not organic. They are only superficialities. They are not divergences made cumulative by heredity. They are only the gaudy trappings hiding a common and inalienable core, trappings which one can put on or take off at will.

The philosophers of the last century limited their deductions to the reformation of the social contract; they limited themselves to building, on a basis that seemed to them unassailable, a structure of mutual relations between all members of mankind, whatever their race. They remained silent on everything outside the domain of institutions, the daughters of Reason. They constructed no absolute ideal for other fields of mental development, language, the arts, and so on. Religion, for them, gave way before their deductions, and they did not see the analogy that exists between these divers products of the human mind, any more than they saw the analogy between their development and that of the anatomical structures that distinguish the various races of men.

When this philosophical system took concrete form with the Revolution, France became in a certain sense the elect of the new revelation. She appeared to have an "imminent destiny" and a "providential mission" to fulfill—the conversion of all peoples to the egalitarian religion of mankind. It followed that the transforming virtue which the *philosophes* attributed to the institutions of pure Reason was extended to the language of the new evangel, to the French language and to every manifestation of French civilization.

That extension is so logical, following so closely from the first definition, that, in our times, the apostleship of civilization is conceived in a manner identical to that in which missionaries conceive of their apostleship of the unique and revealed religion. Departing from the same fundamental dogma, Natural Philosophy ended with the same conclusions as the ancient theology, of which it believed itself to be the antithesis. Only it extended the dogmatism that had hitherto remained confined to religious truth to institutions and then to other branches of human thought. It has had no greater success than its initial one of channeling to its own benefit the profoundly religious sentiments of the French, who were then alienated from the Church on account of its solidarity with feudal abuses.

This commonality of origin throws light on the illusions of the assimilative school and on the transforming power it attributes to its program of action. It seeks to impose language and institutions in absolutely the same way missionaries seek to impose religious faith; that is to say, without opportunistic motives and with the conviction that this "conversion" will suppress that sole cause of the inferiority of the native races, that it will regenerate and re-establish the equality they possess in a latent state as members of "mankind."

One group says, "It is by religious belief that we will transform the natives to our own image." For others, "The conversion of Moslems is an unattainable goal; we will assimilate them through our institutions." For still others, "Institutional assimilation is not enough; it is by giving the natives our customs, or 'French spirit,' that we will draw them to us." Depending on the deceptions they use, or the verification they have been able to make, they have differing opinions; but they are all in agreement on the dogma: they assume that there must necessarily be a way of bridging the gap that exists between the different races.

Is that to say that nothing can be done to improve native societies; that it is useless for them to learn our language; that there is nothing in our thought or manners they can adopt? That is to say, that the *status quo* must everywhere be maintained? Certainly not. It is, on the contrary, because so much is to be done that it is important to see things as they are and to decide them in their natural order.

All native societies are capable of progress, but they are not capable of the same progress and none of them is capable of progress identical to that of France, for two societies of different race cannot follow the same path of development. It is even impossible to foresee exactly for a given race the direction its development will take. But conquerors dominated by the idea of proselytization do not understand that impossibility: they want to impose that direction; they devote every effort to it and neglect everything else. The Arabs burned the library at Alexandria to prevent its having an influence different from that of the Koran. The Spanish burned the temples of Mexico, and we burn the native law codes, for the same reason.

Conquerors who have not felt this need to level all and to impose a single direction on every race have done more fruitful work. Rather than defy natural law, they have let it teach them and support them in their plans.

To administer, it has been rightly said, is to foresee. To foresee is to have an intuition (or a reasoned understanding) of natural law. When we drop an object in space, we expect it to fall. When we see the clouds gather, we expect it to rain.

To administer a hundred races while denying the meaning of race, in the name of dogma, is to be condemned to pile up one error upon the next.

The conquerors who have sensed the meaning of race have known how to act: they began by establishing lines of communication (and they had this initial work done by the natives themselves). They then went on to assure security, justice, and individual guarantees, without in any way threatening the manners, beliefs, or institutions of the natives. These diverse measures had the effect of creating ease of transportation and mutual confidence. These are the two conditions necessary for commercial and industrial transactions. These transactions give birth to new ideas and new wants. These ideas and these wants will differ strikingly from those of the conqueror, especially if he is represented in the colony only by a tiny minority. The usage of the conqueror's language will probably be one of these wants. To the extent that it is felt, schools will develop. The desire to be protected by the conqueror's jurisdiction will be another desire, and the native legal code will be modified accordingly. In short, economic development will take place quite naturally and will be followed closely by corollary moral development.

Run through the body of our colonial decrees, our colonial bibliography, and the reports of our congresses, and you will see that we are following an inverse plan of action. We are persuaded that economic development must follow moral development, the transformation of the native on the model of the French people; and our overage dogmas give the illusion that this transformation is easily realizable.

These dogmas explain our colonial policy; they have not been able to fetter our work completely, because economic development has opened up in spite of them. Tonkin, for example, progresses in spite of all our mistakes, thanks to the Chinese businessmen. But the future of our colonization is tied to a certain degree to the development of these dogmas. It is therefore important to know the origins of the present situation.

These dogmas are only the partial products of a much more general tendency—*classical latinism*, which is hard to define exactly. It is a tendency toward uniformity, simplicity, and symmetry, an antipathy for all that is disparate, complex, unsymmetrical. Born of certain Roman and Judaic traditions, cultivated by the monarchy, it became a mental habit in France, a hereditary ideal, and one of the principal characteristics of the race. It begat the genius of the French language, as it did later the metric system. By contrast, in creating an exaggerated need for simple and sole formulas, it substituted principle for experience, theory for practice, fiction for a sense of reality. It has engendered the extreme centralization of the administration, as well as the polytechnic school, where engineers destined for the preparation of tobacco learn the same formulas as those who will operate mines. It has its advantages and its disadvantages. It is found, with minor differences, among all of the latin peoples, but nowhere more accentuated than in France.

By taking the form of a philosophic doctrine in the eighteenth century, it invaded the domain of politics and established a prodigious influence over the destinies of France. Thanks to its affinity to the mental characteristics of a whole race, that doctrine necessarily penetrated the masses rapidly and was not long in transforming itself into action. As always, it entered their dull consciousness only in the religious form of an undiscussed dogma. After having tried over several years to level the social order by dint of the guillotine and theoretical constitutions, the new religion found warfare to be the best use for the limitless devotion it had inspired. The cannon is the *ultima ratio* of dogmas as well as kings.

History has rarely seen an idea produce a comparable movement of grandiose expansion which, from Jemappes to Austerlitz, consecrated the triumph of the egalitarian dogma in military glory and sealed in blood its insoluble union with the nation which had given it birth.

But after the heroic period, dogmas which state terrestrial truths run into difficulties avoided by those which remain confined to the spiritual domain. The motto of the crusades, for example, "Dieu le veut," had a concrete object, the conquest of Jerusalem, and it assured the crusaders of providential assistance. It nevertheless took no less than three centuries and eight successive expeditions to make it lose its dogmatic quality. In the same way, the egalitarian fiction calls for a social and universal transformation, assured of providential assistance in conformity with the scheme and the laws of nature. As long as it is a matter of sustaining the cause by military force, all goes well. But when it comes to practical application, the difficulties are revealed and it would be necessary to make many experiments and suffer numerous failures before recognizing its essentially erroneous nature. It should be clear, then, to what degree political dogmatism has been disastrous for France, in what a harmful position of inferiority it must place her in the face of England, her implacable rival. Disillusionment has already begun: the American Anglo-Saxons, whom we take to have accepted our doctrine, do not hide the racial antipathy they profess for theoretical and centralizing latinism. And our experiments with native policy are just as disillusioning for our missionary zeal.

It is, unfortunately, all too certain that such a general and inveterate tendency can only be modified by slow evolution. I have not set out to find ways of hastening the process. Before trying to create a shift of opinion, those who are free of the surrounding dogmatism must first of all come to understand the situation. Most of them probably having little knowledge of colonies, it is for their consideration that I have written this study. However imperfect it may be, it will give them a general outline, which they can fill in from their own observation.

As for the partisans of assimilation, whose convictions I have sought to analyze, they should keep in mind that they have not hitherto met with any opposition, and that it is dangerous for a policy not to have any alternative, especially when it may not lead to brilliant results. Besides, they can afford to be generous toward their opponents, for they are assured of uncontested popularity for a long time to come, and they will triumph at the Colonial Congress of 1900 as they did at that of 1899.

11. Charles Temple on Relations
Between Dominant and Dependent Races

Charles Lindsay Temple (1871–1929) was a practicing imperialist, rather than a theorist of empire. After an early career in the foreign service, principally in Brazil, he served in Nigeria under Lugard and rose to the post of Lieutenant-Governor in 1914–17, after which he retired because of ill health.

It was during the first two decades of this century in Nigeria that the idea of Indirect Rule was developed into a theory of "native administration" to be widely imitated in British Africa. The idea and practice of ruling through traditional authorities was as old as the first European conquests in sixteenth-century Mexico and Peru, but now it was invested with layers of additional meaning and justification. Some administrators went further than others in the ideal of keeping Africa African (though under British command), and Temple was one of the extreme examples, with an enthusiasm for Indirect Rule exceeding that of Lugard himself.

His most thoroughgoing statements about the significance of race are not included in this selection, though they are implicit throughout. Here Temple states an amateur version of social-Darwinism theory to defend his suggestion that "native communities" be allowed to manage their own affairs. Elsewhere he makes it clear that he does not advocate bringing Western-educated Africans into the administration, much less that of electoral politics. His intent was rather to allow some circulation into and out of the élite of traditional authorities who were to rule for the British.

The selection is from Temple's book *The Native Races and Their Rulers* (Cape Town, 1918), where it forms the whole of the second chapter, pp. 15–27.

The Relations Existing Between Dominant
and Dependent Races. Quo Vadis?

THERE ARE few political officers to whom sometime in their careers, probably earlier than later, certain awkward problems relating to the destinies, in the extreme future, of the subject native races among whom they work will not have presented themselves. I say probably earlier because later in life the trammels of official routine have often gained such a mastery over the mind that in many cases the administrative eye-sight becomes, as it were,

shortened, and though seeing clearly and with microscopic distinctness matters connected with daily routine and the immediate
future (so that detectable mistakes may be avoided), is liable to
lose in a great measure the power of viewing the larger questions,
which, like the peaks of a great mountain range, must be looked at
from afar, or they will be obscured by the foot-hills at their base.
In early life every political officer will surely have asked himself
some such question as this: "What will be the final upshot of my
work amongst these natives? I suppose that I am influencing their
destinies; but what are those destinies? Will fifty years, a hundred
years, three hundred years hence the village head and his elders,
who have just left my office, still be telling—possibly my great-
great-great-grandson—that the crops will surely be good this year
owing to the great virtues of the white man; that the stock sheep,
goats, etc., have all increased greatly, thanks to the white man and
Allah! that the neighbouring villagers have encroached on fallow
lands and will the white man be so good as to go into the matter;
that the fathers of families in the village find great difficulty in
disciplining their wives and children, and the white man, being the
father, the mother, and the elder brother combined of everybody
in the district, will he put this little difficulty straight? Can it be
that the state of affairs that I see around me will last for ever? And
if it does change, in what way will the change take place, and what
form will it adopt?"

"But," it may be said, "why should these young officials in their
self-sufficiency boldly glance towards heights which their superiors
know very well to exist, but wisely and with true statecraft avoid
mentioning, far less thinking about? Such young men must surely
be youthful enthusiasts fresh from the Universities. Would it not
be better to discourage such idle flights of unguided, uncontrolled,
and possibly conceited imaginations? The young man in a public
office in England does not worry his head for a moment as to what
is going to happen to the great-grandson of the grocer whom he
deals with, of the boy who blacks his boots, or indeed with the
succeeding generations of all those with whom his daily work
brings him into contact. He very wisely leaves that to older heads,
and they in a fashion even more wise know that they are better
employed performing their daily duties efficiently than dreaming
over such idle theories. Some would even think that to do so is
showing an undue desire to foresee and possibly interfere with the

decrees of an all-seeing Providence, and would be deeply offended at the idea. Why, even Cabinet Ministers do not often worry their heads about such matters. Moreover, such speculations are the recognised preserves of philosophic writers with well-established reputations, and it would be a breach of the accepted rules of the game should others poach on these preserves." I freely admit that it is difficult to find any reply to such cogent arguments and reasoning based on established practice in so far as the official whose work lies amongst his fellow-country men in England is concerned. But there is a fundamental difference between the position that he occupies working amongst his fellows, and that of the political officer whose work lies amongst individuals belonging to that vast and dusky mass of humanity which can only be described as Native Subject Races. The first is working in normal conditions amongst people who are living in normal conditions. The white man whose administrative work lies among native races is placed in abnormal conditions, and the people amongst whom he works are living under abnormal conditions.

In the case of a community living in normal conditions there is a continual circulation, a process of natural selection going on, which alters the relative positions in the social scale of individuals to each other or of class to class. Nations are like a thronging crowd following each a road bordered by two deep and impassable ditches. Those in the front rank are able to control the rate of progress of the mass. Nature has planted in the minds of a large minority of the individuals of every race a desire to participate in this control over the actions of others. It is this instinct which predominates in the characters of those individuals whom we generally describe as ambitious. Without modification of the prime motive the outward manifestation of its existence is yet liable to assume two radically different forms. One of these may be termed social and the other anti-social.

To take examples where the existence of both the underlying motive and the form which it assumes can be readily followed. Of two oriental despots, to each of whom the one and only pleasure in life is to gloat over his power over others, one may be possessed of the ambitious instinct in a social form, the other in an anti-social form. The first will not rest content unless his people are visibly flourishing, increasing in numbers and in wealth; he will extend the borders of his empire; he will in short be a benevolent despot. The other, equally possessed of the ambitious instinct, and quite as jealous of his power to control the actions of others, but in whom the manifestation takes an anti-social form, will, so long as he is able to exert his power, be content whether his people be prosperous or not. It is the wielding of power which his nature requires, and he is equally satisfied be that power exerted in the direction of making others discontented and unhappy, or of making them prosperous and contented. Every ambitious individual, if successful, in proportion to the extent of his success occupies a position similar in kind, though possibly very different in degree, to that of one of the oriental despots described.

The presence of individuals possessed of the ambitious and social instinct is a necessary condition for the welfare and progress, nay for the very existence, of the race.

The ambitious instinct affects the individual in various ways. It may drive one to labour to acquire vast wealth in order to control his fellows (the miser who desires to obtain gold with the simple purpose of hoarding it is so rare that he may be left out of consideration). Another, on the contrary, may show the completest disregard for wealth, and yet exhibit this instinct in an even more pronounced degree by grasping at power through other means. The successful statesman, general, philosopher, poet, millionaire, all these are men in whom this ambitious instinct is developed to a marked extent. It may take the social or the anti-social form in every case. The millionaire may take pleasure in promoting free exchange of commodities, in philanthropic actions, and in rendering others happier generally; or he may actually employ the power which his wealth gives to him to establish privileges or monopolies, to "corner" the necessities of life, and thus drive down the rate of wages and render life more difficult for those around. The successful statesman may be really anxious to promote the welfare of the country (he must always pretend to be), or he may be actuated by motives purely selfish, such as the gratification of his pride attendant on the fact that a great deal of attention is paid to his doings and sayings. All successful ambitious men are actuated either by the social or by the anti-social instinct. As the proportion of ambitious individuals possessed of the social instinct increases or decreases, so does the nation become vital, great and powerful, or dwindle and finally die or lose its identity, as the case may be.

This struggle to get into the first rank and to control the actions of the mass causes a continual circulation in the body politic. The more active is this circulation the more opportunity there is for the leader imbued with the social ambitious instinct to grasp the reins of power. Where it is sluggish, the more likelihood is there that the race will fall under the control of unscrupulous, or even worse, incompetent leaders. In the struggle some of those who have been in the front rank are swept away, while the strong man may, if the circulation be free, force his way from the last to the first rank. The more freely this circulation takes place the more vital the race, and the more rapid its progress. The road along which the race is travelling is bordered by ditches which we may describe as those forces which are anti-social, all of which are based on and derive their strength from one great static influence which we term ignorance. The more the collective knowledge of the race increases the wider becomes the road, the more free the circulation, the more rapid the progress, and the greater the vital powers of the race.

Just as no perfectly healthy living body exists but each contains within itself the seeds of disease and death, so with races in no case has the national organisation been so perfected as to ensure that every individual endowed by nature with the requisite ability and the ambitious social instinct shall be in a position to influence the destinies of his fellow-men; nor, what is more important still, that the inefficient and those possessed of the anti-social instinct shall be deprived of such control. Nevertheless, during past decades, great strides have doubtless been made among the nations which constitute what may be called the civilisation of Western Europe (which may be said to include America and Japan), with the result that those nations have become so powerful that they have been able to seize a controlling hold over the affairs of the teeming millions of Asia and Africa.

In proportion as modes of Government have become established permitting of a free, or at all events freer, circulation in the body politic, and the static forces of ignorance, which permitted the actions of the individual to be controlled by either incompetent or anti-social leaders, have been overcome, so the European civilisations have progressed and their national ambitions have increased. The introduction of freer institutions which permit of a successful employment of the social ambitious instinct in the individual have a double effect: they not only call out and stimulate the growth of the social instinct but they starve and wither the anti-social instinct. The ambitious individual whose natural craving is to control others at any cost, even at the cost of their disadvantage or extinction, must, of necessity, restrict the circulation to a certain degree. It is evident that the masses will not knowingly permit themselves to be controlled to their own disadvantage. A certain measure of unhealthiness in the body politic, *i.e.* ignorance in the masses, is necessary to enable the anti-social leader to flourish. So we find in history that the forces which are ambitious and at the same time anti-social invariably combine to restrict the spread of knowledge beyond a certain point, or, where the growth is too strong to be controlled, at all events to impede its advance. As stated above, it is necessary that the anti-social leader should at all events masquerade in the guise of the social leader, and his actions combined with the ignorance of the masses reacting on each other cause the progress of knowledge to be slow. But an individual, however ignorant, is liable to know, to use a colloquialism, "on which side his bread is buttered," and gradually the world is advancing in civilisation, which really means that the masses are falling under social leadership, that is to say the leadership of men possessed by the social ambitions.

It may be said that this statement is open to objection and that the masses are moving in the direction of governing themselves. I submit that the phrase "Government by the masses" is meaningless, however admirable may be the ideal which it is intended to convey. It is an obvious truth that the actions of weaker individuals are controlled by the stronger individual. Whether the force of the latter is exerted indirectly through recognised "laws" affecting a large group, in which case it is termed "Government," or directly, in which case it is termed "personal influence," is immaterial to the argument. Since nature has endowed mankind unequally, it is unavoidable that the weaker should be controlled by the stronger. It is a truism to say that the stronger must be in a minority. However high the general standard is raised those who are the stronger (it is logical deduction) must be in the minority. The masses, therefore, I submit, never can rule themselves; it is a contradiction in terms to say that they can. The less competent majority is and must always be controlled by the more competent minority. This control may be for the benefit of the majority (in which case it is also good for the controlling minority), or it may lead to their detriment; in the latter case it is also in the long run unavoidably detrimental to the controlling minority also. The race or group of individuals increases in power and prosperity, or dwindles, dies out, or falls under the control of another more powerful race, as it comes under the influence of social or anti-social leaders.

Though the masses can never govern themselves, yet conditions may be created which render it more likely that they will fall under the control of the really social leader. In the case of a race living under normal conditions (by this I mean a race which has not fallen *en masse* under the domination of another race and thus become a subject race living under abnormal conditions) the general character of the masses has doubtless some reaction on the characters of its leaders. An intelligent mass is liable to resist the guidance of the unscrupulous ambitious leader of its own initiative; but far oftener it is rescued therefrom by other leaders possessed of the social ambitious instinct. In this respect the nations which constitute the civilisation of Western Europe have been so favoured by Providence in the immediate past that they occupy today a dominating position among the races of the world. Among these nations none has probably been so favoured as Great Britain. Thanks to the existence of the social ambitious instinct in the controlling minority of past generations, institutions have been established which facilitate circulation in the body politic, that is to say facilitate the advance of the social leader and hasten the degradation of the anti-social leader, probably more than has ever been the case amongst any other of the peoples of the world. Not that I claim perfect health for our body politic, but the relative health is good compared to that of other nations. No doubt it contains within itself the seeds of decay and death, and a constant watch and guard, not only to maintain our free institutions but also to ensure their growth, is doubtless necessary, if we, like other world powers in the history of the earth, are not to fall from the high place which under Providence we now occupy.

The destiny of nations has placed under our control during the immediately preceding generations so great a teeming mass of dusky humanity that history furnishes no parallel to the weight of national responsibility which we carry, and on our proper discharge of those responsibilities doubtless depends, not only the maintenance of the position which we now occupy, but our very existence as a distinct race.

As succeeding generations pass two clearly marked tendencies of fundamental importance are appearing which affect the relative positions of the conquered and conquering races. First the groups conquering and conquered have become immensely larger; secondly, they have become more and more divergent in their natures, and consequently the process of amalgamation between the individuals becomes more and more difficult. Not only has Nature decreed that certain races shall differ greatly in physique to others, that some, for instance, shall be dark-skinned and some light-skinned, but the appearance of great leaders of thought whose mentalities, differing greatly, have impressed themselves on large blocks of the human race, has caused, and is daily causing, a great and increasing divergence of the mental outlook. This again by varying the standard of ethics in the different groups has so acted on the physical natures of the individuals that the impossibility of fusion of certain groups with other groups is now, at this stage of the world's history, not a question of conjecture but of fact. I hazard that it might be possible for the Japanese and Chinese to become amalgamated, but that it is not possible for the European races to amalgamate with even such cognate races as those inhabiting the Indian Peninsula. Fusion between the European and the dark-skinned races of Africa is entirely out of the question. I submit this as a postulate confidently to any European whose work has carried him into close contact with African natives.

Groups of individuals have probably been conquering other groups of individuals since the very earliest dawn of man's appearance on this planet; certainly history is but one long succession of records of such conquests. The examples of the past all go to show, and, if we assume the truth of the maxim that history repeats itself, we must foresee that the same will happen in the future, that one of three destinies awaits the conquered group or race. It either fuses with, *i.e.*, becomes absorbed in or absorbs the conquering race, and this is the usual result; or it recaptures its liberty; or, less often, it dies out. In the first two cases the conquered race reverts from abnormal conditions to normal conditions, and will grow or decay as it falls under good or bad leadership. But so long as a race remains under the domination of another race it cannot be said to be living under normal conditions. Not only is the circulation in the body politic hindered, it is stopped. The organisation is in a state of suspended animation, which, I submit, cannot go on indefinitely; one of two things must happen, extinction or recovery.

There is at all events no parallel in history to warrant our assuming that what appears to be a natural law will not operate in the future as it has in the past. We may, I think, confidently predict that the future, however remote, will not see a complete fusion of the European conquering with the coloured conquered races, and a return to normality through that channel cannot be looked for. We may likewise set aside as inconceivable the supposition that the native coloured races, to-day under our rule propagating to an ever-increasing extent, will die out.

What then is to be their future?

Historical analogies lead us to one conclusion only, *i.e.*, that they will some day recapture their liberty.

Have we any reason to suppose that yet another solution of the problem is to be found, and that we can introduce a precedent so that the native subject races may remain in existence, unfused with ours, and yet in subjection? If the term subjection be used in its extreme sense I do not for a moment believe that any such solution exists. But if the term be used to designate those relations which I have described as existing between the masses and the leaders, the relations which exist between a more competent man and a less competent, by virtue of which the more competent can control the actions of the less competent for the advantage of both, then I think that a solution can be found, and that a return to normality in the case of the conquered race sufficient to render existence bearable, honourable, and even enjoyable, can be secured. It depends, however, as I shall try to show, entirely on the attitude which we as conquerors adopt towards the conquered, whether we stop the free circulation in the body politic by our institutions or so organise the dependent races as to leave open opportunities for a proper exercise of the social ambitious instinct on the part of the individual native leaders so endowed.

In the dawn of history it is probable that the conquering community did not worry its head about justifying its action in any way. It had to live and that was sufficient. As we have become more civilised, however, and the great leaders of human thought have taught us that each is to a certain extent responsible for his brother, and that nations as well as individuals have responsibilities towards each other, and as it has become more and more plain to all that the natural resources of this planet are, if employed to their full extent, amply large enough to support a population incalculably larger than that now existing upon it, it has become felt that some other justification than that of mere material necessity is required to warrant one race in grasping the reins of power over another.

Different conquering races have dealt with the conquered in various manners. In the early pre-historic days it is probable that the conquering race fused with or exterminated the conquered in every case. It may be said that they enslaved them and that this is not fusion. I contest this point. Without exception the women of such enslaved races became the concubines of the conquered, and so fusion gradually took place. In innumerable cases individuals of the conquered race were granted their freedom and the same privileges as were enjoyed by individuals of the conquering race. In many notable cases male slaves rose to the front or governing ranks of the community in which they lived. Thus fusion took place. In the sixteenth century the Spaniards and Portuguese to a great extent exterminated the Red Indians of South America, though even in this case considerable fusion took place, and sexual relations and even inter-marriage occurred between Spanish and Portuguese males and Indian females. We ourselves, although it was certainly not an avowed policy and probably one which public opinion in England or amongst the colonists themselves would not have tolerated had they been able to foresee the result, by introducing our own system of land-tenure quietly but surely exterminated the North American Indian. Indeed, the process was even more complete than in the case of Spain, for the mental and physical nature of the British differed more from that of the Indian than did that of the Spaniard. This is a statement of fact, I hasten to add, not in any way derogatory to the many splendid qualities of the band of conquerors which is headed by the names of Cortes and Pizarro. It is a physiological fact, for which we deserve neither credit nor blame, that fusion between ourselves and native races is perhaps more difficult than that between any other European and native races.

Vae Victis was for long an accepted principle and it was not until comparatively recent times that the idea that the conqueror had assumed any responsibilities towards the conquered came to be seriously considered, or even considered at all. Such clemency as was exerted was the outcome of purely utilitarian motives. At best the wise conqueror did not damage the conquered race more than was necessary to reduce it to subjection, because, by so doing, he would be damaging his own property. Motives of compassion would also restrain in some cases the conqueror from inflicting extreme cruelty on the conquered, just as he would be restrained from inflicting cruelty on a captured herd of stock. The idea that the conqueror had every right to exploit the conquered to any extent for his own benefit was universally entertained until very recent times, and indeed has not yet altogether disappeared. The more advanced idea that the conqueror has assumed responsibilities towards the conquered, that he has taken up "the white man's burden," is of even more recent date.

As Christianity has spread, Christian races have generally, in theory at least, placed conversion before their eyes as justifying their action as conquerors. The Spaniards gave the Indian the option of conversion or extermination in repeated instances, and the same may be said of the Muhammadan conquerors. Within quite recent times this plea of conversion as justification has been frankly ignored. We ourselves, particularly, place in the forefront of our policy an abnegation of any proselytizing intention; while we assume the responsibility of the economic welfare of the individual in this life we disclaim any responsibility as to his hereafter. The justification of conversion has to a great extent given way to the justification of "the humanitarian ideal." "We must assume control over the affairs of such a group because the leading men of that group are bullying and oppressing the rank and file. They are impeding healthy circulation in the body politic, and this is interfering with the normal exchange of commodities, so that not only will they be better off if we look after them but so shall we. We owe it to ourselves and to them to establish a better state of affairs." Thus we argue.

Acting on this principle the stronger groups have in this day of grace brought to a state of subjection all those weaker groups inhabiting the earth which it is possible so to control. A large proportion of mankind is living under conditions which cannot be described as normal. History has, I think, no exact parallel to this state of affairs.

Is it conceivable that masses of humanity should continue to exist indefinitely under conditions that are abnormal? The whole tendency of modern civilisation amongst the conquering races themselves is in an opposite direction. The institutions of every country

are being modified in the direction of breaking down those ob-
tacles which prevent the control of a nation's destinies from
passing out of the hands of any particular class. The preserves
created by kings, aristocratic classes, religious denominations—by
means of which the control of a nation's destinies remained, for
better or for worse, in the hands of a privileged few—have all been
increasingly broken into during recent generations; the nations
being impelled no doubt thereto by the instinct that the group of
individuals which was free from such drawbacks would have the
advantage over other groups still weighed down by those disadvantages.

These tendencies have disturbed the consciences of many individuals amongst the ruling races regarding their responsibilities
towards the conquered. They are daily more and more asking
themselves whether it can be right to establish amongst subject
races those very forces of bureaucratic Government which we
have been at so much pains to abolish in our own? The idea that
we have the right if we have the power to exterminate the conquered has long passed away. We have even got beyond the idea
that we may, if again we have the power, exploit the conquered.
"Have we," many are now asking themselves, "any right to interfere at all with these people?" And not without good reason. It is
not enough to say that we carry the *Pax Britannica* and economic
prosperity wherever we go. The Japanese may be quoted as an
Asiatic race which has prospered amazingly during the generations
immediately passed without the assistance of a European conqueror, indeed the advance there has far outrun that to be found in
any conquered group in the same time.

It may be said that had William the Conqueror been possessed of
Maxim guns, typewriters, and a few modern inventions, he would
have occupied Britain with a diminutive force; he would have
established a bureaucratic form of Government with a few District
Commissioners scattered over the land. Doubtless he would have
built railways for us, encouraged our trade, improved our economic position, in short he could and no doubt would have done
for us all that we do for the conquered native races. In that case we
should have avoided the Wars of the Roses, King Charles would
not have lost his head, countless evils we should have escaped. But
should we, had we been under such conditions for the past nine
centuries, even to-day be contented? During all those generations

should we not have kept the day of independence fresh in our memories? So it is, it may be said, with the native races living under our rule.

Whether such arguments are valid or fallacious depends, I submit, on the orientation given to the policy adopted by our Government toward the native races, for whose welfare we have made ourselves responsible. If we content ourselves with securing for the native peace and plenty, and nothing more, that is much, but it is not all; it is not enough to avert from us, in the long run, the effects of a growing desire for freedom on the part of the conquered on the one hand, and the throes of an unquiet conscience amongst ourselves on the other hand. We must, I submit, do more than that. We must give scope to the higher yearnings of human nature. We must open up channels and opportunities for the exercise of what I have described as the social ambitious instinct. We must permit, within certain limits and the more they can be gradually extended the better, the native communities to manage their own affairs; we must impede as little as possible the circulation in the body politic and allow the native leader endowed with a legitimate and useful ambition to enjoy to a reasonable extent opportunities for the exertion of his talent. The means by which the course towards this end can be followed and by what means it can be, and is being, deflected, I propose to discuss in another chapter.

12. Sydney Olivier on Race and Empire

One curious feature of the British Empire in the imperial era was the fact that the Colonial Office attracted a number of outstanding men who were very much interested in social reform and chose imperial administration as the institution through which they would work. The tradition goes back to James Stephen, who was permanent Under-Secretary of State for the Colonies from 1836 to 1847, and used his position to see that the emancipation act was carried out as intended and not distorted by administrative orders or colonial legislation. In the early twentieth century, Sidney Webb, one of the founders of Fabian socialism, also worked in the Colonial Office and sought to use the empire as an instrument of social reform. Still later, during the Second World War and the liquidation of empire that followed, Andrew Cohen played a similar role.

Sydney Haldane, Lord Olivier (1859–1943), belonged to the circle of Sidney and Beatrice Webb and George Bernard Shaw and was

Secretary of the Fabian Society from 1886 to 1890. He entered the
Colonial Office in 1882 and served in a number of posts in Britain and
overseas, particularly in the West Indies. He was especially noted for
his Governorship of Jamaica, in 1907–13, where he worked to improve
the position of the small settlers, descendants of slaves who had taken
to the hills to avoid being pulled into the rural proletariat of plantation
workers. Among his writings were two books about Jamaica, one of
them, *The Myth of Governor Eyre* (1933), being an attack on the
record and performance of one of his predecessors. The present selection is from the second edition of *White Capital and Coloured
Labour* (London, 1929), pp. 19–48. Reprinted by permission of the
author's Literary Estate and The Hogarth Press Ltd.

Chapter I. Introductory

THE GENERAL aim of this book is to discuss the effects of association between white people, commonly spoken of as representing
European or "Western" civilisation, but viewed especially in their
economic activities as traders, planters, industrial organisers, employers and masters, and people of those races (in the scope of the
book chiefly African) that are popularly described as "coloured,"
when the latter are brought, by contact with white men, into the
position of employees, wage-workers and labourers, labour tenants
or contact-bondsmen, used or sought to be used as assistants in the
white men's economic activity. What is the White man going to
make of the Black, or the Black of the White in industry? The
question is one of very rapidly growing importance.

Much has been written bearing upon this topic under the stimulus of the increasing interests of white men in tropical countries,
since the principal European Governments, now nearly fifty years
ago, were scrambling for the Partition of Africa. One view of its
significance was idealised for popular currency by Mr. Rudyard
Kipling in the phrase "The White Man's Burden," which British
Imperial patriotism was invited to shoulder. Mr. Benjamin Kidd
wrote his well-known books on *The Control of the Tropics* and
The Government of Tropical Dependencies. A doctrine was thus
popularised, not essentially at all inhumane or ignoble, but liable to
be accepted in somewhat crude interpretations by the colonising
individuals whose activities and enterprise created in practice the
situation that was developing, and certainly very influential in the
minds of some of the statesmen and administrators who had to
handle that situation—a doctrine which might be briefly sum-

marised thus: Tropical countries are not suited for settled habitation by whites. Europeans cannot work in their climate or rear their children there. The native can prosper and labour under good government, but is incapable of developinig his own country's resources. He is barbarian, benighted, and unprogressive. One of the principal reasons for this arrested development is that his livelihood has been made so easy for him by natural conditions that he has not been obliged to work, at any rate not to work steadily and in a proper and workmanlike manner. The European therefore must, in the interests of human progress, make arrangements to enable and to induce the black man to work productively under his direction and training. To him the economic profit, which the black cannot either create or wisely use; to the black man peace and protection, relief from disease and famine, moral and social improvement and elevation and the blessings of European culture in general. To effect these uplifting developments is "The White Man's Burden"; in this spirit must we control the tropics; along these lines alone can the problem of racial relations in our new possessions be solved.

It is pertinent to observe that this philosophy, which the idealism of Mr. Kipling and Mr. Kidd undoubtedly did a great deal to popularise, was primarily conceived and elaborated with special reference to tropical countries in which white men were not expected to make their own permanent racial homes. It was manifestly prepared for by admiration of the character of the administrative, organising, directing, and executive work done by the British in India and Egypt, and by confidence about what similar work could effect if applied to the problems of the much wider fields for similar work which were opening out in Africa. These were the examples appealed to by the poets and prophets who invested with popular glamour the imperialism of their generation. Sympathetically conceived, the philosophy invited a programme of administrative and engineering efficiency rather than one of industrial and profiteering exploitation. And, speaking very broadly and generally, it may be claimed that the ideas of high-minded men who accepted it with disinterested goodwill have been applied, with advantage to Africans, over extensive areas added in Africa to the British Empire. But at the time when its political vogue was being established few of those who accepted it in this country were thinking of the conditions of what is called "white man's country" in Africa, or were intimate with the problems characteristic of mixed societies already established in areas so described. Fifty years ago the limits of established "white man's country" in colonised Africa lay within the boundaries of the South African Republic and the Orange Free State. The British settlement of Rhodesia had not been imagined. The highlands of Kenya and Tanganyika had not been prospected as the future homes of European communities. And when the genuine colonisation of these areas began to attract attention they were not advertised as countries in which the white man could take up his burden, but as profitable and delightful places of residence for young Englishmen with a little capital. And they are still being so advertised—in our daily Press—as offering all the advantages of the pleasantest life on earth, that of an English country landowner or gentleman farmer in a good sporting country. Whatever may prove to be the future fate of equatorial Africa, the comparatively recent white settlement in such countries has contributed to the problem of the relations between white capital and coloured labour a great deal of matter for thought which was not in evidence when first the new imperialism was being preached and when the first edition of this book was composed. The subject of "white men's countries," predominantly inhabited by black men, in Africa, now invites much more detailed consideration than at that time it appeared to do.

I have referred to the philosophy of "The White Man's Burden" theory without criticising its premises. But these demand some scrutiny, for the problems arising contain some elements of which that theory takes commonly too little account. "Half devil and half child" was the lyrical description applied by Mr. Kipling to the human material to be dealt with. We need not entirely scout it as inappropriate. But doubts, or at least a disposition to cautious consideration, begin to make themselves felt as soon as we approach the inquiry what kind of a saint is expected to be made of the devil and what kind of a man of the child? The savage, we say, is not "civilised." Is he capable of being taught to adapt himself to the characteristic industrial forms of our own civilisation? Are we satisfied that it is desirable that he should do so? Are the operations and methods in which white capital does actually engage coloured labour attractively representative of the essentials of European civilisation? Are the agents employed in them typically well qualified to promote its appreciation? These are not ironical questions. Many responsible people whose intelligence and the humanity of whose disposition command respect apparently take it for granted that the answers must be "Yes!" What, indeed, do we understand by "civilisation" and what or which are the characteristics, whether spiritual or utilitarian, of our own civilization which we should soberly think it desirable to impart to African native races? Stress is laid, particularly in some areas of intermixture, on "racial" characteristics. What is race? Have distinctions of race any bearing on the relations of capital and labour? Granted racial distinctions, how deep do racial characteristics go? And what common characteristics of human nature are there more fundamental and more important to be regarded because they are in the long run more powerful than race and racial peculiarities? Is it not, to detached reflection, sometimes apparent that some parts of what, according to our customary habits of thinking, is devilish or childish in savage peoples, are the embodiment or manifestation of ingredients in human nature that may act as a wholesome solvent of some limitations of our own racial and conventional civilisation? It needed a Zulu's unbiassed intelligence to enable Bishop Colenso to recognise certain obvious critical difficulties in the Pentateuch. That record is typical. It is useful to bear it in mind when the doings or sayings of savages startle or shock one. Like those of children and lunatics, they frequently compel one to review what it is that one really does feel and think oneself.

The African peoples, which include a great variety and intermixture of distinguishable racial strains and of which the two principal groupings are commonly distinguished as the negro and the Bantu, make up the most important "uncivilised" mass of humanity. I shall not deal in this survey with the brown or the dark white peoples of the Mediterranean area or the "Semitic" strains that have filtered into Africa from the north and north-east. Both these, especially the brown "Hamitics," have impinged on and interbred with the Negro, Hottentot, and Bushman stocks. In North Central and West Africa the resulting populations make up the so-called Negro mass: southward and through East Africa, the tribes, also racially mixed, described as "Bantu," because their languages are akin or of common origin. Both these divisions are "negroid," incorporating the curly-woolled, ebony-skinned, broad-nosed, long-headed typical black man whose hypothetical primitive common stock is distinguished as one of the three or four great racial divisions of human kind.

The negro more than any of these African peoples has been brought into intimate and influential contact with Europeans by the process of slavery. With negroes white capital has experimented protractedly in the West Indies and in both continents of America, under varying social and economic conditions. The Asiatic peoples, negroid, brown or white, racially in some cases much nearer akin to Europeans than any Africans are, have attained far earlier maturity in their civilisations, in which they long forestalled Europe, and offer far less tractable material than the African for economic and social development and specialisation. Their territories, moreover, are fully occupied. European permeation and exploitation of China are inconceivable in the sense in which we are witnessing such permeation and exploitation of Africa, in which there may still be room for the evolution of completely new types of productive communities. The populations of India are now unlikely to become in any important degree more amenable than they are to the operations of European capital. Capitalist Industrialism is indeed growing up there, and Indians, having long ago developed outstanding skill and taste in handicrafts, are perhaps more constitutionally adapted to capitalist industrial methods of wealth production than are Africans; but the problems of such developments in India seem likely to arise increasingly between Indians and Indians. The North American Indian races in general are a dwindling and ineffectual survival very recalcitrant to capitalist civilisation; the Pacific negroid races do not display the expansive fertility and the colonising vigour of the African negroids in their principal strains.

Some preliminary discussion of the difficult topic of race seems to be necessary, in order to clear the ground as far as possible of some prepossessions and almost axiomatic assumptions entertained by a good many people about unalterable limitations of racial faculty, which are constantly reflected in doctrines as to the attitude necessary or appropriate in the industrial relations between white and black. It is, doubtless, indisputable that the social conventions and assumptions of one race may fail to find sympathetic response in another, whose own special racial temperament and prejudices may offer a stubborn resistance to appeals which to the former seem to express the perfection of human reason, quite independently of difference of language. The grammar of interracial intercourse is still imperfect. At present the satisfactory carrying on of such intercourse is largely a temperamental matter, a practical art; but its methods not really a mystery. The faculty of dealing with alien or uncivilised races, untrained in the assumptions of our civilisation, like that of dealing with children likewise untrained, may be more or less a personal gift, but essentially it is merely an application of common human intelligence, perspicacity, sympathy, and good temper.

It is important to attempt to do justice to the more markedly distinguishable psychological and temperamental characteristics of African racials and to realise the conditions of life under which apparent peculiarities have been evolved. It is sometimes hastily said that "the native mind" of the African is "inscrutable"; but much of its working is unaccountable only to the commentator who considers it exclusively from the standpoint of his own pursuits and interests.

In this connection I have myself found it very enlightening and instructive, and an exceedingly useful corrective of prepossessions and prejudices still mischievously and disastrously prevalent, to examine the phenomena manifested among populations of African origin which have been transplanted from their native environments and kept under the continuous influence of the white man—first in slavery, and, subsequently, either as members of a labouring proletariat or as a free peasantry. The materials for such a survey lie principally in the British West Indies and in the United States of America, and I propose to examine their aspect in these lands with some fulness. Returning thence to Africa I shall review the conditions prevailing in territories of the British connection there both in colonised and colonisable regions and in those in which residential white colonisation is not attempted, and the problem taken in hand has been simply that of the opening and control of tropical countries for the profit of Europeans, both as consumers of the exports they can be made to yield and as exporters of the goods they can be induced to consume.

Under all these diverse conditions one complaint on the part of the white man is found to be common—that the black man is lazy. And at the back of the black man's mind there persists (not, as a rule, expressed—sometimes most deeply dissembled) a profound and unquestioned conviction that the white man is there for the purpose of getting the better—of "taking advantage," to use a constant phrase—of the black. Both impressions have justification, and neither is completely and finally just.

It should be recognised and borne in mind that in this country the public opinion that supports European, or perhaps I should only say British, Imperialism in Africa is, on the whole, a humane and liberally disposed sentiment, and that there is a good deal of justification for satisfaction with the results of our interventions there, fully allowing for all that must be confessed of injustice and detriment to large numbers of the natives. White intervention has generally started by taking in hand what native government in African communities had never succeeded in doing with any permanence; maintaining peace and establishing a basis for social development. There have been extremely able and very powerful native rulers, some recklessly bloody, like Chaka, some pacifically statesmanlike, as was Moshesh, but their dynasties have generally been shortlived. It would hardly, however, be reasonable for any European nation seriously to claim for itself moral credit for any such good results, where they can be shown, as though the desire to effect them had been the incentive of its colonisations. For although our public opinion is liberal and philanthropic, and, if informed and aroused, as it was a hundred years ago in regard to the slave-trade and slavery, may be relied upon to condemn and restrain oppression, and even to make sacrifices for what it feels to be right, its cognizance of the operations of African exploitation or processes of development lags generally far in the rear of the practical activities of their operative promoters, and receives very incomplete information about them through the Press or the libraries. "There is no money," editors and publishers tell us, "in circumstances as to serve, when examined, merely as proofs of the general rule (as in the cases of the Protectorates established in Basutoland and Bechuanaland), no nation has ever colonised, annexed, or established a sphere of influence from motives of disinterested philanthropy towards a native people. Bechuanaland itself was first "protected" merely in order to block Boer expansion. That part of it which was required for British Imperial purposes (namely, to keep the road to the North open for Mr. Rhodes' Cape to Cairo railway) was annexed to the Cape Colony, and has since been incorporated in the Union of South Africa, by no means in the interests or to the satisfaction of the native inhabitants, but much the reverse, as the history of the Langberg "Rebellion" testifies. Only what lay on the west side of this "corridor" remained a "protected," not incorporated, native territory. In order to maintain an unsophisticated and unprejudiced habit of judgment in regard to Imperial expansion, it is necessary always to bear in mind the historical truth that the motive of almost all such expansions has always been the interest, immediate or anticipated, of European traders, treasure seekers, investors, or colonists, or to punish or restrain cattle-stealing or attacks upon white missionaries or explorers. It should also be remembered that where such restraint or punishment alone has been the object, or even where allegiance has been tendered by native chiefs for the purpose of getting protection, the extension of sovereignty was repeatedly in times past refused, notwithstanding all the benefits that European rule might presumably have brought to the natives, so long as no white man's economic interest backed the demand. Historically, the Partition of Africa was not engaged in in order to take up the White Man's Burden or for any philanthropic or humanitarian motive, but in order to ensure that the productive resources and the consuming markets of the distributed territories should be kept open to the several national Powers that appropriated them, or, in some cases, to guarantee from encroachment the boundaries of previous appropriations. The agreeable belief that Europe in the Partition of Africa "took up the White Man's Burden" has produced a good deal of soporific illusion which has kept the British nation complacently unaware of much that has been done in its name which, if realised, would have profoundly disturbed it.

I do not wish to lay stress on what has been objectionable in the results, but it is essential that these topics should be approached with an intelligence purged of cant. It is ignorant and perverse to denounce the Partition of Africa and the intercourse of the white with the black as unmixed evils for Africans; it is unjust comprehensively to talk about European administrators and officials as merely parasites on the countries they govern, whether India or others; but we must set out with a clear recognition of the fact that when the European colonises or annexes tropical countries the force that actually sets him in motion is a desire for his own commercial or industrial profit or possibly to secure some position necessary for the defence of Imperial communications or other national advantage, and not a desire to benefit coloured people. When he really wants to go to Africa for the sake of the natives he becomes a missionary. There is no disparagement of the colonising European in recognising and bearing in mind this fundamental fact. He has, in my opinion, an incontestable human right to go and inoffensively to seek his fortune in any part of the world he may choose without molestation.

The European only begins to become obnoxious when he seeks to entrap, constrain, or coerce uncivilised natives into subservience to his personal interest under the pretext of doing them good. In hardly any country except England and the United States, however, is it possible, or assumed to be necessary, that there should be any public profession of disinterested philanthropy in connection with Imperial expansion. Such a pretence was deliberately diffused in the United States to justify the Americo-Spanish War of 1898, the annexation of Porto Rico and the Philippine Islands, and the commercial incorporation of Cuba into the sphere of American exploitation. (I myself was at Washington during the period of that enthusiasm, and remember its glowing atmosphere.) Nicaragua and Central America generally are now experiencing the attentions of a kindred benevolence. Philanthropic motive is almost always advertised to the public of England whenever we have similar exploits on foot. Our own electorate is, in fact, still so liberal minded and so humane in its disposition towards native African peoples and, in parts, still so traditionally suspicious of the designs of exploiting capitalism, where natives of Africa are concerned, that in order to commend to it policies of Imperial expansion it has generally been deemed necessary to appeal to its benevolent interests. The establishment of our power over Uganda and the building of the Uganda railway, for which there were substantial Imperial and commercial motives, were urgently (and sincerely enough) appealed for as a means of killing the slave trade. The invasion of Rhodesia and the appropriation of all its land by the British South Africa Chartered Company, which were prompted by precisely similar imperialist and commercial motives, were engineered and accomplished under pretext of suppressing the atrocities of the Matabele.

If, when we have come into contact with backward races through such pursuit of our interests, we so order our dealings that benefits, on the whole, accrue to them (which is far from being entirely or always the case), if it may actually be to the native's interest (as is often the case, and he finds it so) that the white man should employ him at wages, that is no reason at all for claiming moral credit for ourselves for the colonisation. The native (bear this always well in mind) is not deceived in this matter. He may recognise and appreciate the immediate advantage of being relieved from molestation by martial tribes or slave raiders, and, if he is part of a conquered and overrun population, he may appreciate deliverance from exacting overlords, but his memory of the relief will be short, and for the most part he remains, or quickly becomes, in his relations with his new white governors, devoid of any lively feeling of obligation conferred, or reason for gratitude on these accounts towards their local representatives. He sees that what they do they do for their own purposes and not for his. Hence, often, arises that fundamental suspiciousness in his mind which offends us as uncharitable and ungracious. Hence, sometimes, what we denounce as his treacheries and his rebellions. Moreover, no more than the farming or trading or mining colonists do the men who go to these colonies to take part in the Government go there, generally speaking, from philanthropy. They go, as a rule, primarily to earn salaries, and, though they may display the spirit of a devoted public service, it must always be remembered that to the native they and their dependents are merely a set of rulers, making a living out of his country and out of the taxes they make him pay, because they cannot make it at home, and interfering with his affairs as a pretext for doing so, even if the taxation levied is not, as it often is, still more obviously imposed for the purpose of making him work for white employers. We must austerely disenchant the facts and dispel the glamour which our conviction as to our own moral standards, our consciousness of our own altruistic purposes, and our desire to think the best of ourselves, may hang about them for us, before we can hope to form any accurate judgment of the aspect in which those facts appear to the African.

In short, in any survey of questions of colonisation and conquest the moral or philosophical justification follows after, and is quite secondary in importance to the facts of the will and interest. These lead,—the white man's purpose of making his living or his desire of increased wealth determine expansion. No colony can be made by a benevolent theory of Imperialism; it can only be made by acts of Imperial policy, and these are in practice chiefly dictated by efficient practical interest and by the operations of people who want to colonise and are capable of maintaining themselves as colonists. And it is between these parties—between Capitalist-Imperialism and its agents and the coloured populations of colonised countries—that the questions this book has to deal with arise. The problems and details of annexationist policy, of conquest and invasion—the topics of native wars and rebellions—are antecedent to those of industrial relations in the established colony, and, although rebellions have repeatedly arisen from crude methods of attempting economic exploitation, I do not desire to devote space to their criticism. It may be impossible to ignore them entirely, because, although in some communities the industrial relations between Capital and Labour have grown up independently of such conflicts, in others they have not. For example, such factors have nothing whatever to do with the relations between white capital and coloured labour in the United States, the West Indies, our West African colonies and Nigeria, in Uganda, or theoretically in Kenya, but they have something to do with them still in the Cape Colony, more in Natal, a great deal in the Northern Provinces of the Union of South Africa, something in Rhodesia and Nyasaland, something for a quite different set of reasons in Tanganyika, and something, by a kind of induction or infection of Boer tradition, in Kenya. We are, in fact, witnessing as I write a remarkable manifestation of reactive influence by the attitude towards natives characteristic of the Northern Provinces of the South African Union upon the different traditions of the Cape Colony, subsidiarily of Natal, and more remotely, but not with less importance, in British East Africa.

Chapter II. Race

What constitutes race? It is still possible, apparently, for many people to think of "races" as though they had originated generally in special creations, of the individuals that compose them as specially contoured characters entering life on earth in suitably appointed or chosen environment, and of some races as intended by their Creator to serve and some to dominate. But we are, I think, in Europe (though not yet in the United States of America), entitled to deal with the moulding causes of race from the point of view of evolutionary biology, to believe, that is, that the physical and temperamental distinctions of races have been shaped and stereo- typed by the conditions of their environment during the course of their respective natural histories. I take it that the distinctions (I do not say the human identities) exhibited by races can be to a very great extent validly explained on Darwinian principles of selection, and that whatever may be deemed essentially human (or essentially divine, if you will) in man, it is certainly not his distinctions in the category of race. There are endowments common to all races, in greater or less degree, about which great controversy has indeci- sively raged, as to how they could have been produced by natural selection; the musical sense, for example (in regard to which Darwin's own hypothetical biological explanation was extremely absurd); and still more remarkably and puzzlingly, we find in dis- tinct races, remote in time and place, exhibitions of very specialised and elaborate human faculty and achievement in Art, Science, Philosophy, and Religion, for the emergence of which it appears quite impossible to assign any plausible explanation in parallel biological causes arising out of identity in physical environment.

But special differentiating characteristics of races may confi- dently be said to be, in great measure at any rate, reactions of the physical environment of a stock realising its will-to-live continu- ously and progressively under special controlling, but not over- powering, conditions, little altered through long periods of time. We may even go so far as to say that the special race characteristics which such protracted process will evolve, although they may be, for the race concerned, a necessary condition of its best-adapted existence in its environment, are probably, at any rate are often, limitations, excrescences, or shortcomings of humanity. It is pos- sible to hold this judgment, both as to the savage and the civilised, without implying the dogmatic assertion of any essential or final human type.

Moreover, as a further preliminary caution, one salient, ubiqui- tous reality must also be borne in mind: the infinite, inexhaustible distinctness of personality between individuals, so much a funda- mental fact of life that one almost would say that the assimilating race characteristics are merely incrustations concealing this spar- kling variety. It is common enough, indeed, for hasty observers, whose faculties of perception and sympathy are baffled by their racial limitations, to tell us that the people of some foreign tribe or nation are all precisely alike, both in face and character: intelligent and sympathetic insight, however, will always disclose, under every human complexion and civilisation, the same independent definition of each individual that every one imputes unhesitatingly to the persons of his own intimate circle. Not even "two peas" are really alike: and no closely observant gardener would use the vulgar adage. Yet, again, notwithstanding all this variety amongst individuals—far wider than the variety among races—we meet, so far as race does not preclude us from seeing it, in every human being an ultimate, unmistakable likeness to every other, transcending Family, Race, and Nation alike, yet in no wise overbearing, or transcending, or neutralising his own individuality, but rather establishing and completing it, and at the same time knitting it up with our own.

What circumstances produce a distinct race, the race that the Greek poets spoke of as "autochthonous"—sprung from the soil? Apparently, first and chiefly the Earth—long settlement in the same country and climate. These influences having done their work, a racial type will obstinately persist in even a race become nomadic and cosmopolitan, as the Jews and the Gipsies. The strain remains recognisable even though it may be modified by a new domicile and by intermarriage. The Jews of different countries are not difficult to discriminate at sight to an accustomed observer. The ancient race-theory—the myth of earth-parentage—appears to be a true account of the greater part of the matter. Whatever may be the cause or creative force of humanity, the distinguishing and moulding force of race appears as local environment. It is necessary, perhaps, to emphasise this, because, to a mongrel town-dwelling population it tends to present itself as merely a poetical figure of speech. Towns do not produce physical races, they obliterate them. Towns, doubtless, produce social types, as London the cockney, but that is a different thing. Such types vary rapidly. The town-dweller who has not himself undergone the moulding and nourishing power of Earth in natural surroundings is likely and prone to suppose that the city may do what the country does, which is not the case. The evolution of the Boer people, one of well-marked physical and mental characteristics, notwithstanding that it is of mixed immigrant origin, Dutch, French, and in some degree British, is an instance of the development of something very like race, within modern record, by the conditions of the South African veldt, a witness of the race-making power of the Earth still at work in her uncocknified regions.

When a race has established and maintained itself for generations in a consistent environment—a primitive race not reaching as yet a very high degree of civilisation—and has staved off the disadvantageous effects of excess of population by means of birth control, infanticide, organised emigration, or moderate chronic war with its neighbours, it will have fitted all its bodily adaptation and the processes of its daily life so intimately and so fully into the mould of its natural surroundings that it will not be conscious of itself as other than a part of nature. Such a race, in the vigour of its maturity, is a full cup; its form is saturated to the skin with the energy that has forced it into the natural mould of its life; it is sensitive at the surface, reacting immediately according to its own native impulse, not critical of its motives and instincts, not hesitant between feeling and action, thought and word, not sceptical where it believes. It is very fully aware of the things of its own world; it is not aware of, and does not imagine, things outside of it. The invisible, for that race, abuts entirely upon, and is concerned only with, its own visible world. The habitual religiosity of the pagan resulting from this condition is unimaginable, unintelligible, to the faculties of the European normal invader, who at best is conscious in himself of a duality, a "war in his members," and for whom, in general, religion is in great part an auxiliary and detachable equipment for certain purposes, a matter of clergy and Sundays, perhaps of "salvation," but certainly not of "business." The only forces the primitive race knows are those that mould, impel, and attack it: its spiritual world is the community of its own ancestors: its gods and devils are all concerned with itself; and thus it comes about that each natural race, when it comes to personify the invisible, no matter whether its god-ery be singular or plural, its devils one or legion, believes and feels and knows itself to be a "chosen people." I say "knows itself," because its knowledge, like the rest of its life, will have followed the mould of its biological evolution, and because it will have developed only such associations of theory and understanding as its environment has permitted. And accordingly when, confronted with other tribal god-eries, it enters upon theological criticism, it lays down unhesitatingly (if it has any sufficient self-respect) that all those gods are but idols, but that it is its Lord that made the heavens.

Moreover, it will, from precisely similar causes, develop the belief that it is itself the crown of Creation, free Man, and itself only, and that all other nations are outer barbarians, Gentiles, savages, and by nature designed to be slaves, which it, the chosen people, will never, never be. This has constantly been the expressed doctrine of patriotic philosophers in more or less primitive peoples, when they have passed into a self-conscious critical stage. Even Aristotle could not transcend this universal illusion. In this country, even among our confusedly blended people (easily distinguishable to the eye of a field anthropologist into at least a dozen long-domiciled, distinct racial types), it had come, not many years ago, to be so unquestioningly and universally held, that Mr. Kipling's "Recessional," which expressed some post-Jubilee qualms in regard to it, was hailed by our popular critics as an achievement of superhuman inspiration, almost blasphemous in the audacity of its humility.

Because of their evolution in different environments and their differences in physical adaptation and social heritage, all races are likely to differ one from another in their capacities, their knowledge, and their powers; and each race, so far as it works by the light of its own formulated conscious knowledge and critical and logical habits, is constitutionally unprepared for understanding or even imagining the existence of much that enters into the life of each of all other races and that may be either the most sacred or the most commonplace thing in that life. Further, it is noticeable that more than one of the races of which we habitually speak as inferior, and which appear to be effete or decaying, are far in advance of the average Anglo-Saxon who is deemed to be our own type and standard, not only in some of the most desirable and attractive human qualities, but in artistic, poetical, and other of the higher spiritual forms of genius or faculty. When, therefore, individuals of different races are confronted, each of them is largely deficient in mental equipment for even apprehending the existence, far more so for understanding the significance of much that is vividly alive and permanently important in the consciousness of the alien. The one cannot recognise that the other is a full cup; he shapes for himself a ridiculous patchwork caricature of a few conspicuous characteristics as a hypothesis of the foreign creature's nature, and fills out the figure with the attributes of the children, the imbeciles, and the criminals of his own nationality. I could not refer to a better corrective of this style of illusion in relation to savage races than the late Miss Mary Kingsley's books on West Africa, in which, with a fine, direct sympathy, the insight of the straightforward woman of genius, she analysed and appreciated the psychology of the native tribes of the "Coast"; quite seriously taking them as rational human beings to be weighed in the same scales as the white races.

The criticism, therefore, which one race may pass on another will almost always be impertinent and provincial. Complete apprehension of the racial point of view, complete recognition of what it really is that the alien means by his formulas, is hardly to be attained. In many cases a meaning common to both races is disguised by different modes of expression; in many the two need considerable education before they can even be capable of meaning quite the same thing. A clear understanding is essential between those who are to be fused into one organic community. What avenues have we towards interracial understanding?

We encounter, in the United States, in South Africa, in India, and elsewhere, a conviction on the part of the majority of the racially white inhabitants that the white and the coloured can blend no more than oil and water. Whatever be the explanations of race prejudice, and whatever our judgment of its significance, its existence must be recognised as a fact of very influential importance in regard to mixed societies. On the other hand, it is evident that in countries with a vigorous black population no stable mixed community can grow up so long as colour prejudice, distinction of privileges between white and black, and race antagonism maintain their supremacy. Such relations between white and coloured in a white-governed State are only compatible with the institution of slavery or with modified analogous forms of domination. Whether the white man likes it or not, the fact must be faced that, under the capitalist system of industry, which deals with the coloured man as an independent wage-earner, and in a society in which he has the stimulus of the white man's ideals of education, the coloured man must advance, and he visibly does advance, to a level of understanding and self-reliance in which he will not accept the negrophobist theory of exclusion. Especially will this be the case if the elements of the Christian religion are communicated to the coloured people and the New Testament placed in their hands, even if they are not otherwise educated; as the feudalism of Europe discovered when the same revolutionary matter got into the heads and hands of its peasantries. The condition of the society in which this process is taking place grows increasingly unstable, unless race prejudice and race discrimination are modified.

In the history of the world assimilation has in fact come about to a vast extent by interbreeding and mixture of races. And though the idea of this method may be scouted as out of the range of practical consideration or influence in connection with modern colour problems, and though I should admit that it may tend to decrease in importance as compared with direct mental conjunctions, yet I consider that the habit of opinion and sentiment at present in the ascendant unduly undervalues its real importance, and I propose to mention some reasons for judging that where it takes place it is advantageous. We should at least give full credit to its possibilities before passing to consider other methods of fusion.

The question of the relations between white and coloured races is obscured by a mass of prejudice, ignorance, and lack of perception, proportional to the isolating differences in their evolved constitutions. These barriers are not different in kind or in strength from those which once separated neighbouring European tribes. What has happened as between these we can trace and recognise, and this recognition will help us to approach the contemporary problem.

What happens when two persons of different race intermarry? Each race, we have argued, has produced its own specialised body, adapted to a limited exercise of human capacities. In neither case, one may say in no possible case, is the average race-body (including the brain and nervous system) anything approaching to a competent vehicle of all the qualities and powers that we imply by humanity. Of course, we have had very splendid and comprehensive human types among those races of whose activities and productions records remain, and I think there can be no doubt that there have been others equally capable, of which there is only fragmentary and inferential record; but none that we can judge of come near to satisfying us as being completely and immediately capable of all the human apprehensions and activities known to us. I do not wish to overweight this idea of the limitation or specialisation of racial faculty, which not only can be enlarged, more or less, by educational influences, but is staggeringly transcended by men of what we call "genius." The truly great men of all races are impressively near akin. Each race, too, on the premises thus suggested, is likely to exhibit habitually a good deal of human faculty that is absent in others. So far, then, as there survives in a mixed race the racial body of each of its parents, so far it is a superior human being, or rather, I would say, potentially a more competent vehicle of humanity. I say this with reservation, because there are certain sets-off to the recognised advantages of hybridisation which must be taken into account and to which I shall return later. To people who suffer from the complex of a horror of "colour," which is a specialised and localised form of race prejudice, and not more universal, stronger, or more "natural" than are similar prejudices between persons distinguished by other accidents, I would here observe that I am thinking not only of mulattoes or crosses between white and "coloured" races, but equally of the interbreedings have produced the most progressive of "white" nations, including our own, and of blends of coloured races.

The human body, we gather (at this stage of microscope manufacture), originates from a selective combination out of two sets of cells. Each set, theoretically (so I read), can build up a whole new body by itself. (This is called Parthenogenesis.) In practice it habitually combines for the work with another set, supplied by a parent of opposite sex. Unless the qualities or potentialities resident in both sets of cells are precisely identical, or unless the differing qualities are eliminated in the shuffle, which according to the experiments is by no means what happens, though some may emerge dominant and some lie recessively latent until evoked by a fresh combination, it would appear that the power that employs itself in the making of life (which is evidently omniscient but apparently limited in effective command of materials) obtains by hybridisation at any rate a more widely ranging instrument to use for its purposes. How far it will be a superior, and how far, as it often is in some respects, a less reliable instrument, depends on conditions of which nobody knows anything safe to assert dogmatically. But in the course of a number of generations of interbreeding of hybrids of two original strains there comes to be established something like a real new race, combining in a stable amalgam a particular selection of the qualities of both. This stabilisation of new varieties has long been a practical art in plant and animal breeding. The observations and generalisations founded on the studies of Mendel have added a good deal to the practical science of these operations.

The development of the physical constitution follows the guidance provided in the inheritance of the body-building chromosomes, and it cannot be doubted that the capacity of exhibiting and exercising mental qualities follows like conditions.

But the most arresting fact that appears to be emerging from recent studies of evolutionary anatomy is that the brains of the higher species appear to have developed in advance and, it is tempting to say, in anticipation of the necessary, common, or even possible exercise by the mass of the species of the faculties thus provided for.

The distinction between the different sets of cells often persists for many generations, notwithstanding the modifying influence of environment, which presumably tends to overcome the immigrant type, or both types if the home of the hybrid race is different from that of either parent. And at first, in many cases, the hybrid will really be obviously and conspicuously two kinds of man. When cells of Race A and cells of Race B have done their parts side by side they will be conscious of and internally criticise one another, each claiming to do the job in his own way. This very often spoils the hybrid's digestion. Quite often, of course, the joint work is more efficient. And sometimes, when the A cell has done work unfamiliar to the B cell or the B to the A, the one may have been unable to maintain any balance with the other, and will probably be quite unable to control its proceedings when its primitive instincts are strongly aroused.

Indeed it would appear, not only that certain qualities of cells are chronically recessive and others dominant, but that in occasional crises the whole vitality, power, and consciousness may transfer itself to one side of the combination, as occurs in cases of multiple personality under hypnotic influence. And this transference is by no means always to the side of the race reputed inferior. If the mulatto may "go Fantee," he may also, at times, entirely transcend his more barbarous instincts and consciousness.

Such cases, however, are rare: for the most part there appears to be a mingling of character with a good deal of double consciousness, so that to a fortunately constituted hybrid his ancestors are a perpetual feast; he knows them from inside, and he sees them from outside simultaneously. I do not go so far as to say that a man to be a good critic must be a hybrid, but I think it would be found to be pretty generally true. Foreigners constantly make the mistake of thinking that Englishmen and Scotsmen are hypocrites. Only one who is both an Englishman and an alien—whether British, Irish, Welsh, Cornish, French, Spaniard, German, or Jew on his alien side—can really appreciate and enjoy to the full the rich feast of contemporary English psychology. Its most humorous, because most sympathetic, satirists are Englishmen of mixed race. And the same, of course, may be said of all the literature of satire in any society.

A further characteristic in the hybrid as distinguished from the man of pure race may appropriately be noted. Whereas the pure race in its prime knows one Man only, itself, and one God, its own Will, which has created it in its own image, the hybrid is incapable of this exclusive racial pride, and inevitably becomes aware that there is something, the something that we call the Human, which is greater than the one race or the other, and something in the quality of creative power that is stronger than national God of Will. What were, for each specialised race, final forms of truth, become, when competing in the field of our human consciousness, mutually destructive, and each recognisably insufficient. Yet the hybrid finds himself still very much alive, and not at all extinguished by the loss of conviction as to the paramountcy of either of his confronted racial dogmas.

An experience somewhat similar occurs to a race whose racial God is defeated and deposed by conquest: and where a conquered race has not, as the Jews and several other nomad races have done, transcended the usual domiciliary and settled habits of permanent races, has not spiritualised and mobilised its God and moved conquering among its nominal conquerors, we have seen either a practically atheistic philosophy adopted, of renunciation of the Will, or a second new God set up, as among the mixed broken peoples of the Roman Empire—the God of the human and the conquered, who knows himself something more than his conqueror. Even Imperial Rome, which went further in its deification of its own will than any great people on earth, by making its Commander-in-Chief, its Caesar, its national God, was captured by the reaction of the culture of the nations whom it overran. The flood of Oriental mysticism drowned the old tribal fetichism of Rome, and thus prepared the way for much of what grew into Christianity.

But it is not only cultured and civilised races that may know themselves in some respects greater than the beef-witted race that conquers them. I pass from the case of hybridised peoples and deal with that of the survivors of an ancient conquered race. If they avoid physical degeneration (as, retaining their old habitat, there is no presumption that they will not) they do remain to a great extent invincible. So long as they remain a race, their God, their Will, their pride of place as the chosen people survives; and they see often that the conqueror is only a heavy-fisted brute, to whom they know themselves to be superior, not, indeed, in all effectual qualities, but in many of those which mankind most values and which are most distinctively human. We need not speak yet of the African, or even of the Hindu. Irishmen, doubtless, recognise that the English have great qualities, and yet it has not been possible for the Irish to accept English rule. All other nations of the world do Irishmen the justice of perceiving that they have an endowment of qualities the absence of which in the typical Englishman has rendered him somewhat imperfectly loved, and when not feared, disliked, as lacking in essential humanities. Now not only the Irish under the English, but every conquered race that remains unmixed, retains in itself this seed of invincibility, this treasure that it has and its conqueror has not, which makes it the superior of its conqueror, so long as he treats it not as human but as alien and inferior. Every race (not hybridised), however much it may respect its conqueror for respectable human qualities, also despises him for his shortage in others, just as woman, treated likewise by man, has despised him to the full as much as he in his claim to the lordship of creation has disparaged her.

In fact, the lack of mutual understanding that arises from race is strikingly analogous to that which arises from difference of sex, both in its origins and in its manifestations. The origin is bound up with differences of bodily adaptation and function. How common it is for each sex, in moments of irritation, to charge the other with perfidy and lack of straightforwardness. How universal is this same accusation between different races. But the fact is that the truth is really different for different races and for the two sexes. They live to some extent in different worlds. A conquered race that speaks two languages will tell the truth in its own language, and will lie in that of its conquerors—very often from an honest desire to tell what it supposes to be the conqueror's truth, namely, what he desires, which is what, in fact, is real for him through expressing his will. This phenomenon is widely familiar from the Groves of Blarney to the haunts of the Heathen Chinee.

Sir Harry Johnston in his little book, *The Backward Races*, and D. Norman Leys in *Kenya*, explain very lucidly the principal reasons in their environment why few African peoples have yet succeeded in developing civilisations. Isolation from the great streams of civilisation which have diffused true human culture from the homes of its early development has no doubt been paramount among these causes: but the conflict with parasitic diseases, the vagaries of African rainfall, intertribal warfare, raiding and pillage, and, more than anything else, the incessant slave-taking promoted during three centuries by Christian and Moslem peoples, have been the principal factors of their repressive environment.

The negro is progressing, and that disposes of all the arguments in the world that he is incapable of progress.

"When I am discouraged and disheartened, I have this to fall back on. If there is a principle of right in the world which finally prevails: and I believe that there is: if there is a merciful but justice-loving God: and I believe that there is: we shall win: for we have right on our side: while those who oppose us can defend themselves by nothing in the moral law, nor even by anything in the enlightened thought of the age.

"The main difficulty of the race question does not lie so much in the actual condition of the blacks as it does in the mental attitude of the whites: and a mental attitude, especially one not based on truth, can be changed more easily than actual conditions . . . the difficulty of the problem is not so much due to the facts presented as to the hypothesis assumed for its solution.

"When the white race assumes as a hypothesis that it is the main object of creation and that all things else are merely subsidiary to its well-being, sophisms, subterfuge, perversion of conscience, arrogance, injustice, oppression, cruelty, sacrifice of human blood are all required to maintain the position, and its dealings with other races become indeed a problem, a problem which, if based on a hypothesis of common humanity could be solved by the simple rules of justice."—J. W. Johnson in *Autobiography of an Ex-Coloured Man*.

"We are ranged on the side of civilisation. Our interests are intertwined with civilised interests. We would not like to go back naked to the kraals and live a barbarous life. We have renounced

that life once and for all. If to-day there were a war between barbarism and civilisation we would be on the side of civilisation. The
Europeans regard us as a solid block of undifferentiated barbarism
and the Europeans as a solid block of innate capacity to govern;
whereas the division is not on these lines. The division is between
civilisation and ignorance, which may be found in both blocks.
There are many Europeans not capable of governing, just as there
may be a few black men who are so far removed from their native
conditions that they would not make a mess of civilised interests.
The fact is, we are growing and developing under civilisation, and
we shall be more and more a power on the side of civilisation."—
Dr. J. J. T. Jabavu, Professor of Bantu Languages in the South
African Native University, Fort Hare.

Chapter III.
The Industrial Factor in Race Prejudice

It is an unhappy but undeniable fact of experience, and it is the
basis of democratic conviction and method in politics and industry,
that if circumstances give one average man uncontrolled command
over the services of another for his own personal purposes, he will
in most cases abuse it to the latter's disadvantage. The presumption
that a white man will do this if he is given command of black men
to work for him is not disposed of by protesting that our countrymen in the colonies are as humane as ourselves in this country. For
the most part, indeed, it is positively not the fact that the men who
find occupation in the colonies as employers or overseers of native
labour are as considerate in their disposition, or as circumspect in
their methods of discipline, as the average of British employers in
this country: it would be illusory to pretend that they are so; and
they certainly do not as a class claim any such qualification, rather
shunning the imputation of stay-at-home squeamishness, or, as Mr.
Rhodes phrased it, "unctuous rectitude." And in the population of
a new exploiting settlement such diamonds of the rougher type
predominate. Even in a democratic white community—for example, the United States—the attitude of organised white capital
towards organised white labour, determined only by economic
motives, is frankly ruthless. Nothing is gained by pretending that a
labour driver is more considerate when he is dealing with black
men: on the contrary, the danger of injustice is greater where there
is racial distinction. This, at best, interposes a barrier to understanding of the employee's feeling, and baffles the operation of sympathy: but, where this disadvantage is aggravated by a positive

doctrine of racial incompatibility and inferiority, race prejudice reinforces the tendency to take advantage of the subordinate class in exploitation. The equitable claims that are recognised in the fellow white man are not recognised or are expressly denied to exist in the black. That this doctrine is prevalent, if not absolutely predominant, in the industrial communities that are springing up on a basis of coloured labour, no well-informed observer will for a moment deny.

It is preached unhesitatingly as an axiom of public policy in America and in South Africa that the safety of the State depends upon the maintenance of this doctrine. The distinction in sensibility, in physical needs, in industrial standard between African native races and the white was spoken of by such an authority as Lord Milner as a providential dispensation. I do not suggest that Lord Milner was one of those who regard such distinctions as permanent: he took active steps to provide higher education for Africans; but the authoritative promulgation of such a doctrine reacts upon the temper and attitude of the employer in industry and upon his conceptions of suitable methods for dealing with coloured workmen. That the doctrine is itself rather a product of the industrial relation than a cause of its deficiency in humanity and intelligence is evident from a consideration of the enormous degree to which it has gained ground during the recent extension of capitalist industrial enterprise in territories with coloured proletariats.

The reactions in the United States of the Great War in creating an increased demand in the Middle States for coloured factory labour to take the place of white workers enlisted have considerably, but only temporarily, modified the increase of colour prejudice which was manifesting itself before the War in the Southern States. This increase was due to the development of capitalist manufacturing industry in the South. Industrial antagonism was being stimulated by the competition between white and black labour. White labour was calling in racial prejudice to its aid, as it had been called in in politics; and the white men's Unions were determined to exclude that labour from the factories where they worked. The interlude of the War, which rendered it necessary for employers to fill up their labour vacancies by employing negroes even at the white man's standard of wages, abated this exclusiveness for a time, and negroes or negro Unions were admitted to the white man's industrial organisations on a footing of equal conditions. But when self-interest impels one race of men to do injustice to another they will find a moral or religious excuse for it. I have already referred to how this affects colour prejudice in America. In South Africa the coincidence is more ostentatious. The phenomena of the Congo Free State, where the native was denied any kind of human right, were purely and directly the expression of exploiting greed.

The closest and most intimate contacts between white men and Africans in Africa have been that of missionaries, who settled among them, devoting themselves to their education. They took with them, and under the practical and personal intercourse have seen no ground for abandoning, the conviction of fundamental humanity of the races, expressed in the religious formula of sonship of a common Father. But when it becomes possible for white men to get into industrial relations with the same native the white man's social theory suffers a change, the secular creed asserts itself, and the spiritual doctrine, in the faith of which chattel slavery was abolished, becomes a laughing-stock. The sentiment that the black man is only fit for slavery is heard quite frequently now; it has become common within our own memory. It is notable that in a country like Nigeria, where there has as yet been little invasion of capital seeking labour for direct employment (notwithstanding the late Lord Leverhulme's benevolent projects), we are still priding ourselves on following the old British theory in practice and eschewing slavery. We still justify our claims to be there on our practical propaganda of freedom. But where that imported demand for productive labour, of which I have spoken above, is becoming the paramount interest in the community, the tendency of local political theory is in the contrary direction.

The "negrophilist," to use that question-begging term which in such countries habitually carries so much odium and disparagement, is one whose judgment is not yet warped by the influence of the economic demands of the capitalist industrial system. He takes men as he finds them upon their general qualities, and has no more prejudice either against them or in their favour than he has under the influence of the snobbishness created by our property system at home with regard to the qualities of the "working man." His most common type has been the Evangelical missionary, but he is common enough in those of our own classes which are not influenced by any distorting interest towards putting material pressure upon the native, or keeping him, as the phrase is, in his place.

The "negrophilist" missionary does not consider that the black man has nothing to learn from the white; he considers that he has an immense deal to learn, and that much of his nature is still exceedingly brutish in departments of character in which civilisation has in greater measure, though very far from completely, humanised and refined the white. But he cannot accept the superficial deductions which race prejudice makes from these differences. All over the world, where white men mix with coloured, very many will be found filled with acute race prejudice. It is rampant among English people in India. But in the same collocations many people will also be found who discern and feel that the race distinctions are superficial, and, so far as being absolute and insuperable, are really, compared with the dominant facts, unimportant. These men have enjoyed personal friendships with persons of the alien race, and they know that such friendship is of precisely the same quality as is their friendship for men and women of their own race or for men and women of France, Germany, or any other nation that may from time to time have been patriotically regarded as "alien" and as the natural foe of their country. But this appreciation of equality is attained in a region of human relations quite distinct from the sphere of economic self-interest; and the man who comes in contact with other races under the stimulus of economic motive or purpose is not favourably placed to discover it. Quite the reverse. In the simplest form of such confrontation he may, if he enter the aliens' country, have to fight for his life before he can even think of peaceably producing his own living, much more of getting the alien in helping to do it. In South Africa the Boer migrations into unoccupied territories where they had every right to settle had actually in some instances to compete with a simultaneous counter-immigration of military Bantu tribes. The resulting conflicts and mutual cattle-stealing activities permanently affected the whole social theory and interracial balance of the Northern territories of the South African Union. We must recognise that the contacts of human races seeking subsistence have always for the most part begun with war, and that if Britons are hostile to any European nation to-day it is chiefly through economic jealousy. And even of those who assert the inferiority of the alien many admit an essential human equality; only they allege the necessity of making the alien behave himself by processes that involve the practical denial of it.

IV

The Economics of Empire

THE ROLE of economic motives behind the European drive for empire is still one of the most hotly debated of all historical problems concerning imperialism. But that problem belongs to the historical analysis of imperialism, not to the history of imperial thought. Whatever his underlying motives, every advocate of imperial expansion argued that the conquest he proposed would be profitable to his country—at least that it would pay its own way out of local revenue. No European legislature could be expected to vote willingly for a long-term financial drain on the taxpaying voters. Imperialists were therefore concerned about economic development, and they looked to the body of economic theory available in nineteenth-century Europe.

The core of this theory was classical economics, going back to Adam Smith and coming down to the neoclassical school of the early twentieth century. It carried the expectation that price would be fixed by the interaction of demand and supply, that government should refrain from undue interference in economic affairs, that business firms would be controlled by those who invested capital in them, and that workers would be forced by the competition of their fellows to accept a wage near the cost of their subsistence.

These ideas were all very well for dealing with Europe, but imperialists tended to see a wide area of exceptionalism overseas. Few denied the truth of "economic law" as it seemed to apply in Europe, but other environments and other peoples seemed to require special adaptations. One exception to allow for was the climate of the wet tropics. From the sixteenth-century explorers onward, Europeans reported the luxuriant vegetation and imagined a vast and untapped potential for agricultural production. In fact, most tropical soils are poor in comparison to those of Europe, luxuriant vegetation notwithstanding, but the myth of tropical exuberance lived far into the twentieth century. It raised the expected level of profitability from future acquisitions in the tropics. More important still, it led imperial theorists to believe that tropical peoples lived a life of plenty with little labor. Carlyle's picture of Quashee, the happy West Indian, sitting under his pumpkin tree and supplying his wants without effort is only an exaggerated version of the common belief.

The myth of tropical exuberance could be extended to support a number of other expectations. If the workers' wants were few and subsistence cheap, they could hardly be expected to compete with one another on the labor market like the European working class. Instead, they could earn enough to satisfy their economic demand—or so the myth went—in a very short time. Once that point had been reached, they would prefer leisure to income. Whereas European precedent suggested that increasing wages would increase the supply of labor, imperial economic thought tended to the opposite belief—that higher wage rates would satisfy the workers more quickly and thus decrease the amount of labor offered. This expectation is sometimes called the backward-leaning supply curve for labor.

The myth of tropical exuberance also led to the expectation of chronic underemployment. European observers tended to look on the self-sufficient village of the tropics as a miniature economy with a tragic misuse of its human resources. Especially where women did the kind of field work customarily done by men in Europe, they assumed that the men were simply idle. If so, here was a resource that could easily be diverted to productive work on the European-owned mines and plantations.

On any of these bases, the key problem for economic development was to break into the traditional economy and divert the underemployed manpower, thus producing goods for export to the world in place of leisure for the "natives." All three of the imperialists in this section were concerned about the labor problem. One solution, suggested here by Vignon, was simply to use the powers of government to recruit workers. Village chiefs could "persuade" men to sign contracts for a period of time, and the contract could be enforced by penal sanctions. A second solution was to manipulate the tax structure so as to produce artificial demands that could only be met through wage labor. This idea first came into prominence as a scheme to assure a labor supply after the West Indian slaves were emancipated. It was taken up on a large scale in the

British Empire when the third Earl Grey became Secretary of State for the Colonies in 1846. He announced and explained it in his famous dispatch to Lord Torrington, Governor of Ceylon, and this dispatch was copied and enclosed with instructions to a variety of colonial governors—to Natal, the Gold Coast, Sierra Leone, and Trinidad, among others.

By the twentieth century, some form of regressive direct taxation was used in many other European colonies in the wet tropics, usually in the form of a hut tax or poll tax. If the rate of taxation was low, it was merely a revenue measure, but rate of taxation was often set intentionally at the value of one or two months' labor, with the aim of forcing every male to work during that length of time each year for a European employer in order to find the cash to meet his obligation.

A third way to meet the labor problem was a form of inter-market arbitrage in labor. When planters in a particular colony needed more labor than was available at the wages they were willing to pay, they could sometimes arrange government assistance in hiring labor from a distance—often from India, where money wages were low. The wage rate was written into a long-term contract, enforceable by penal sanctions, and the workers were shipped *en masse* to new homes where price levels and wages on the open market were often much higher.

Other forms of assisted immigration avoided the penal contracts but sought to produce the same result. Economic theorists since the days of Adam Smith had held that wages were high in developing countries with plenty of land but few people. In effect, the prime economic factors of land and labor were in disequilibrium. One way to correct the disequilibrium would be to move people from places where land was scarce and labor cheap to places where land was cheap and labor scarce. In the 1830's and 40's, this idea was important in British discussion of land and labor policy for true colonies like Australia. It was an easy step to think of doing the same in the West Indies, filling up the country with immigrants and creating scarcity so that people would be forced to work—and it was this possibility that Carlyle denounced in the selection below.

These administrative devices and suggestions were only a few among many. They were prominent in the French and British empires, but other imperial powers tried other schemes. In Spanish America, debt peonage became the most common device for labor control from the seventeenth century, and it remained dominant in nineteenth-century Latin America. In Indonesia, the Dutch experimented with a variety of expedients, including the forced delivery of exportable crops. Whatever the means, European empires in the tropics rarely depended solely on the "cash nexus" between employer and employed to assure a supply of labor.

13. Thomas Carlyle on the Nigger Question

Carlyle (1795–1881) was not principally interested in imperial questions, but rather in English politics and in historical writing with political overtones such as his *French Revolution* (1837), which founded his reputation. He was deeply concerned about the Irish question, however, and from time to time with the West Indies. His "Occasional Discourse on the Nigger Question" was one sally, originally published in *Fraser's Magazine* in December, 1849. Again in the 1860's, Carlyle was a leader of those who defended the conduct of Governor Eyre of Jamaica, whose career was to be re-examined much later by Lord Olivier. A reading of Carlyle's "Nigger Question" alongside Olivier's discussion of race leaves no doubt as to why the two men were on opposite sides on that issue.

In its original form, this essay was published anonymously, allowing the author to speak in hyperbole rather than giving a reasoned discussion. It was also written at a moment of crisis in many of the sectors of life that interested Carlyle. The Irish potato famine was still in progress. The Chartist movement was one center of English political controversy, while the Revolutions of 1848 on the Continent had brought a new phase to the delayed aftermath of the French Revolution of 1789. While all of these elements enter the picture, the essay is chiefly famous as one of the most vitriolic pieces of racist writing in nineteenth-century England, and the most prominent statement of the conclusions that might be drawn from the myth of tropical exuberance.

The version reprinted here is from Thomas Carlyle, *Critical and Miscellaneous Essays, The Works of Thomas Carlyle* (London, 1905), pp. 348–383.

Occasional Discourse
on the Nigger Question*

THE FOLLOWING Occasional Discourse, delivered by we know not whom, and of date seemingly above a year back, may perhaps be

---

* First printed in *Fraser's Magazine*, December 1849; reprinted in the form of a separate Pamphlet, London, 1853.

welcome to here and there a speculative reader. It comes to us,—no speaker named, no time or place assigned, no commentary of any sort given,—in the handwriting of the so-called "Doctor," properly "Absconded Reporter," Dr. Phelim M'Quirk, whose singular powers of reporting, and also whose debts, extravagancies and sorrowful insidious finance-operations, now winded-up by a sudden disappearance, to the grief of many poor tradespeople, are making too much noise in the police-offices at present! Of M'Quirk's composition we by no means suppose it to be; but from M'Quirk, as the last traceable source, it comes to us;—offered, in fact, by his respectable unfortunate landlady, desirous to make-up part of her losses in this way.

To absconded reporters who bilk their lodgings, we have of course no account to give; but if the Speaker be of any eminence or substantiality, and feel himself aggrieved by the transaction, let him understand that such, and such only, is our connection with him or his affairs. As the Colonial and Negro Question is still alive, and likely to grow livelier for some time, we have accepted the Article, at a cheap market-rate; and give it publicity, without in the least committing ourselves to the strange doctrines and notions shadowed forth in it. Doctrines and notions which, we rather suspect, are pretty much in a "minority of one," in the present era of the world! Here, sure enough, are peculiar views of the Rights of Negroes; involving, it is probable, peculiar ditto of innumerable other rights, duties, expectations, wrongs and disappointments, much argued of, by logic and by grape-shot, in these emancipated epochs of the human mind!—Silence now, however; and let the Speaker himself enter.

MY PHILANTHROPIC FRIENDS,—It is my painful duty to address some words to you, this evening, on the Rights of Negroes. Taking, as we hope we do, an extensive survey of social affairs, which we find all in a state of the frightfulest embroilment, and as it were of inextricable final bankruptcy, just at present; and being desirous to adjust ourselves in that huge upbreak, and unutterable welter of tumbling ruins, and to see well that our grand proposed Association of Associations, the UNIVERSAL ABOLITION-OF-PAIN ASSOCIATION, which is meant to be the consummate golden flower and summary of modern Philanthropisms all in one, do *not* issue as a universal "Sluggard-and-Scoundrel Protection Society,"—we have judged that, before constituting ourselves, it would be very proper to commune earnestly with one another, and discourse together on the leading elements of our great Problem, which surely is one of the greatest. With this view the Council has decided, both that the Negro Question, as lying at the bottom, was to be the first handled, and if possible the first settled; and then also, what was of much more questionable wisdom, that—that, in short, I was to be Speaker on the occasion. An honourable duty; yet, as I said, a painful one!—Well, you shall hear what I have to say on the matter; and probably you will not in the least like it.

West-Indian affairs, as we all know, and as some of us know to our cost, are in a rather troublous condition this good while. In regard to West-Indian affairs, however, Lord John Russell is able to comfort us with one fact, indisputable where so many are dubious, That the Negroes are all very happy and doing well. A fact very comfortable indeed. West-Indian Whites, it is admitted, are far enough from happy; West-Indian Colonies not unlike sinking wholly into ruin: at home too, the British Whites are rather badly off; several millions of them hanging on the verge of continual famine; and in single towns, many thousands of them very sore put to it, at this time, not to live "well" or as a man should, in any sense temporal or spiritual, but to live at all:—these, again, are uncomfortable facts; and they are extremely extensive and important ones. But, thank Heaven, our interesting Black population,—equalling almost in number of heads one of the Ridings of Yorkshire, and in *worth* (in quantity of intellect, faculty, docility, energy, and available human valour and value) perhaps one of the streets of Seven Dials,—are all doing remarkably well. "Sweet blighted lilies,"—as the American epitaph on the Nigger child has it,—sweet blighted lilies, they are holding-up their heads again! How pleasant, in the universal bankruptcy abroad, and dim dreary stagnancy at home, as if for England too there remained nothing but to suppress Chartist riots, banish united Irishmen, vote the supplies, and *wait* with arms crossed till black Anarchy and Social Death devoured us also, as it has done the others; how pleasant to have always this fact to fall-back upon: Our beautiful Black darlings are at last happy; with little labour except to the teeth, *which* surely, in those excellent horse-jaws of theirs, will not fail!

Exeter Hall, my philanthropic friends, has had its way in this matter. The Twenty Millions, a mere trifle despatched with a single dash of the pen, are paid; and far over the sea, we have a few black persons rendered extremely "free" indeed. Sitting yonder with their beautiful muzzles up to the ears in pumpkins, imbibing sweet pulps and juices; the grinder and incisor teeth ready for ever new work, and the pumpkins cheap as grass in those rich climates: while the sugar-crops rot round them uncut, because labour cannot be hired, so cheap are the pumpkins;—and at home we are but required to rasp from the breakfast-loaves of our own English labourers some slight "differential sugar-duties," and lend a poor half-million or a few poor millions now and then, to keep that beautiful state of matters going on. A state of matters lovely to contemplate, in these emancipated epochs of the human mind; which has earned us not only the praises of Exeter Hall, and loud long-eared hallelujahs of laudatory psalmody from the Friends of Freedom everywhere, but lasting favour (it is hoped) from the Heavenly Powers themselves;—and which may, at least, justly appeal to the Heavenly Powers, and ask them, If ever in terrestrial procedure they saw the match of it? Certainly in the past history of the human species it has no parallel: nor, one hopes, will it have in the future. [*Some emotion in the audience; which the Chairman suppressed.*]

Sunk in deep froth-oceans of "Benevolence," "Fraternity," "Emancipation-principle," "Christian Philanthropy," and other most amiable-looking, but most baseless, and in the end baleful and all bewildering jargon,—sad product of a sceptical Eighteenth Century, and of poor human hearts left *destitute* of any earnest guidance, and disbelieving that there ever was any, Christian or Heathen, and reduced to believe in rose-pink Sentimentalism alone, and to cultivate the same under its Christian, Anti-christian, Broad-brimmed, Brutus-headed, and other forms,—has not the human species gone strange roads, during that period? And poor Exeter Hall, cultivating the Broad-brimmed form of Christian Senti-mentalism, and long talking and bleating and braying in that strain, has it not worked-out results? Our West-Indian Legislatings, with their spoutings, anti-spoutings, and interminable jangle and babble; our Twenty millions down on the nail for Blacks of our own; Thirty gradual millions more, and many brave British lives to boot, in watching Blacks of other people's; and now at last our ruined sugar-estates, differential sugar-duties, "immigration loan," and beautiful Blacks sitting there up to the ears in pumpkins, and doleful Whites sitting here without potatoes to eat: never till now, I think, did the sun look-down on such a jumble of human non-senses;—of which, with the two hot nights of the Missing-Despatch Debate,* God grant that the measure might now at last be full! But no, it is not yet full; we have a long way to travel back, and terrible flounderings to make, and in fact an immense load of nonsense to dislodge from our poor heads, and manifold cobwebs to rend from our poor eyes, before we get into the road again, and can begin to act as serious men that have work to do in this Uni-verse, and no longer as windy sentimentalists that merely have speeches to deliver and despatches to write. O Heaven, in West-Indian matters, and in all manner of matters, it is so with us: the more is the sorrow!—

The West Indies, it appears, are short of labour; as indeed is very conceivable in those circumstances. Where a Black man, by work-ing about half-an-hour a-day (such is the calculation), can supply himself, by aid of sun and soil, with as much pumpkin as will suffice, he is likely to be a little stiff to raise into hard work! Supply and demand, which, science says, should be brought to bear on him, have an uphill task of it with such a man. Strong sun supplies itself gratis, rich soil in those unpeopled or half-peopled regions almost gratis; these are *his* "supply"; and half-an-hour a-day, di-rected upon these, will produce pumpkin, which is his "demand." The fortunate Black man, very swiftly does he settle *his* account with supply and demand:—not so swiftly the less fortunate White man of those tropical localities. A bad case, his, just now. He him-self cannot work; and his black neighbour, rich in pumpkin, is in no haste to help him. Sunk to the ears in pumpkin, imbibing sac-charine juices, and much at his ease in the Creation, he can listen to the less fortunate white man's "demand," and take his own time in supplying it. Higer wages, massa; higher, for your cane-crop cannot wait; still higher,—till no conceivable opulence of cane-crop will cover such wages. In Demerara, as I read in the Blue-book of last year, the cane-crop, far and wide, stands rotting; the fortunate black gentlemen, strong in their pumpkins, having all

* Does any reader now remember it? A cloudy reminiscence of some such thing, and of noise in the Newspapers upon it, remains with us,—fast hastening to abolition for everybody. (*Note of* 1849.)—This Missing-Des-patch Debate, what on earth was it? (*Note of* 1853.)

struck till the "demand" rise a little. Sweet blighted lilies, now getting-up their heads again!

Science, however, has a remedy still. Since the demand is so pressing, and the supply so inadequate (equal in fact to *nothing* in some places, as appears), increase the supply; bring more Blacks into the labour-market, then will the rate fall, says science. Not the least surprising part of our West-Indian policy is this recipe of "immigration"; of keeping-down the labour-market in those islands by importing new Africans to labour and live there. If the Africans that are already there could be made to lay-down their pumpkins, and labour for their living, there are already Africans enough. If the new Africans, after labouring a little, take to pumpkins like the others, what remedy is there? To bring-in new and ever new Africans, say you, till pumpkins themselves grow dear; till the country is crowded with Africans; and black men there, like white men here, are forced by hunger to labour for their living? That will be a consummation. To have "emancipated" the West Indies into a *Black Ireland;* "free" indeed, but an Ireland, and Black! The world may yet see prodigies; and reality be stranger than a nightmare dream.

Our own white or sallow Ireland, sluttishly starving from age to age on its act-of-parliament "freedom," was hitherto the flower of mismanagement among the nations: but what will this be to a Negro Ireland, with pumpkins themselves fallen scarce like potatoes! Imagination cannot fathom such an object; the belly of Chaos never held the like. The human mind, in its wide wanderings, has not dreamt yet of such a "freedom" as that will be. Towards that, if Exeter Hall and science of supply-and-demand are to continue our guides in the matter, we are daily travelling, and even struggling, with loans of half-a-million and suchlike, to accelerate ourselves.

Truly, my philanthropic friends, Exeter-Hall Philanthropy is wonderful. And the Social Science,—not a "gay science," but a rueful,—which finds the secret of this Universe in "supply and demand," and reduces the duty of human governors to that of letting men alone, is also wonderful. Not a "gay science," I should say, like some we have heard of; no, a dreary, desolate, and indeed quite abject and distressing one; what we might call, by way of eminence, the *dismal science.* These two, Exeter-Hall Philanthropy and the Dismal Science, led by any sacred cause of Black Emancipation, or the like, to fall in love and make a wedding of it,—will give birth to progenies and prodigies; dark extensive moon-calves, unnamable abortions, wide-coiled monstrosities, such as the world has not seen hitherto! [*Increased emotion, again suppressed by the Chairman.*]

In fact, it will behove us of this English nation to overhaul our West-Indian procedure from top to bottom, and ascertain a little better what it is that Fact and Nature demand of us, and what only Exeter Hall wedded to the Dismal Science demands. To the former set of demands we will endeavour, at our peril,—and worse peril than our purse's, at our soul's peril,—to give all obedience. To the latter we will very frequently demur, and try if we cannot stop short where they contradict the former,—and especially *before* arriving at the black throat of ruin, whither they appear to be leading us. Alas, in many other provinces besides the West Indian, that unhappy wedlock of Philanthropic Liberalism and the Dismal Science has engendered such all-enveloping delusions, of the moon-calf sort, and wrought huge woe for us, and for the poor civilised world, in these days! And sore will be the battle with said moon-calves; and terrible the struggle to return out of our delusions, floating rapidly on which, not the West Indies alone, but Europe generally, is nearing the Niagara Falls. [*Here various persons, in an agitated manner, with an air of indignation, left the room; especially one very tall gentleman in white trousers, whose boots creaked much. The President, in a resolved voice, with a look of official rigour, whatever his own private feelings might be, enjoined "Silence, Silence!" The meeting again sat motionless.*]

My philanthropic friends, can you discern no fixed headlands in this wide-weltering deluge, of benevolent twaddle and revolutionary grape-shot, that has burst-forth on us; no sure bearings at all? Fact and Nature, it seems to me, say a few words to us, if happily we have still an ear for Fact and Nature. Let us listen a little and try.

And first, with regard to the West Indies, it may be laid-down as a principle, which no eloquence in Exeter Hall, or Westminster all, or elsewhere, can invalidate or hide, except for a short time only, That no Black man who will not work according to what ability the gods have given him for working, has the smallest right to eat pumpkin, or to any fraction of land that will grow pumpkin, however plentiful such land may be; but has an indisputable and perpetual *right* to be compelled, by the real proprietors of said land, to do competent work for his living. This is the everlasting duty of all men, black or white, who are born into this world. To do competent work, to labour honestly according to the ability given them; for that and for no other purpose was each one of us sent into this world; and woe is to every man who, by friend or by foe, is prevented from fulfilling this the end of his being. That is the "unhappy" lot: lot equally unhappy cannot otherwise be provided for man. Whatsoever prohibits or prevents a man from this his sacred appointment to labour while he lives on earth,—that, I say, is the man's deadliest enemy; and all men are called upon to do what is in their power or opportunity towards delivering him from that. If it be his own indolence that prevents and prohibits him, then his own indolence is the enemy he must be delivered from: and the first "right" he has,—poor indolent blockhead, black or white,—is, That every *un*prohibited man, whatsoever wiser, more industrious person may be passing that way, shall endeavour to "emancipate" him from his indolence, and by some wise means, as I said, compel him, since inducing will not serve, to do the work he is fit for. Induce him, if you can: yes, sure enough, by all means try what inducement will do; and indeed every coachman and carman knows that secret, without our preaching, and applies it to his very horses as the true method:—but if your Nigger will not be induced? In that case, it is full certain, he must be compelled; should and must; and the tacit prayer he makes (unconsciously he, poor blockhead), to you, and to me, and to all the world who are wiser than himself, is, "Compel me!" For indeed he *must*, or else do and suffer worse,—he as well as we. It were better the work did come out of him! It was the meaning of the gods with him and with us, that his gift should turn to use in this Creation, and not lie poisoning the thoroughfares, as a rotten mass of idleness, agreeable to neither heaven nor earth. For idleness does, in all cases, inevitably *rot*, and become putrescent;—and I say deliberately, the very Devil is in *it*.

None of you, my friends, have been in Demerara lately, I apprehend? May none of you go till matters mend there a little! Under the sky there are uglier sights than perhaps were seen hitherto! Dead corpses, the rotting body of a brother man, whom fate or unjust men have killed, this is not a pleasant spectacle; but what say

you to the dead soul of a man,—in a body which still pretends to
be vigorously alive, and can drink rum? An idle White gentleman
is not pleasant to me; though I confess the real work for him is not
easy to find, in these our epochs; and perhaps he is seeking, poor
soul, and may find at last. But what say you to an idle Black
gentleman, with his rum-bottle in his hand (for a little additional
pumpkin you can have red-herrings and rum, in Demerara),—rum-
bottle in his hand, no breeches on his body, pumpkin at discretion,
and the fruitfulest region of the earth going back to jungle round
him? Such things the sun looks-down upon in our fine times; and I,
for one, would rather have no hand in them.

Yes, this is the eternal law of Nature for a man, my beneficent
Exeter-Hall friends; this, that he shall be permitted, encouraged,
and if need be, compelled to do what work the Maker of him has
intended by the making of him for this world! Not that he should
eat pumpkin with never such felicity in the West-India Islands is,
or can be, the blessedness of our Black friend; but that he should
do useful work there, according as the gifts have been bestowed on
him for that. And his own happiness, and that of others round him,
will alone be possible by his and their getting into such a relation
that this can be permitted him, and in case of need, that this can be
compelled him. I beg you to understand this; for you seem to have
a little forgotten it, and there lie a thousand inferences in it, not
quite useless for Exeter Hall, at present. The idle Black man in the
West Indies had, not long since, the right, and will again under
better form, if it please Heaven, have the right (actually the first
"right of man" for an indolent person) to be *compelled* to work as
he was fit, and to *do* the Maker's will who had constructed him
with such and such capabilities, and prefigurements of capability.
And I incessantly pray Heaven, all men, the whitest alike and the
blackest, the richest and the poorest, in other regions of the world,
had attained precisely the same right, the divine right of being
compelled (if "permitted" will not answer) to do what work they
are appointed for, and not to go idle another minute, in a life which
is so short, and where idleness so soon runs to putrescence! Alas,
we had then a perfect world; and the Millennium, and true "Organisation of Labour," and reign of complete blessedness, for all
workers and men, had then arrived,—which in these our own
poor districts of the Planet, as we all lament to know, it is very far

from having yet done. [*More withdrawals; but the rest sitting with increased attention.*]

Do I, then, hate the Negro? No; except when the soul is killed out of him, I decidedly like poor Quashee; and find him a pretty kind of man. With a pennyworth of oil, you can make a handsome glossy thing of Quashee, when the soul is not killed in him! A swift, supple fellow; a merry-hearted, grinning, dancing, singing, affectionate kind of creature, with a great deal of melody and amenability in his composition. This certainly is a notable fact: The black African, alone of wild-men, can live among men civilised. While all manner of Caribs and others pine into annihilation in presence of the pale faces, he contrives to continue; does not die of sullen irreconcilable rage, of rum, of brutish laziness and darkness, and fated incompatibility with his new place; but lives and multiplies, and evidently means to abide among us, if we can find the right regulation for him. We shall have to find it; we are now engaged in the search; and have at least discovered that of two methods, the old Demerara method, and the new Demerara method, neither will answer.

Alas, my friends, I understand well your rage against the poor Negro's slavery; what said rage proceeds from; and have a perfect sympathy with it, and even know it by experience. Can the oppressor of my black fellow-man be of any use to me in particular? Am I gratified in my mind by the ill-usage of any two- or four-legged thing; of any horse or any dog? Not so, I assure you. In me too the natural sources of human rage exist more or less, and the capability of flying out into "fiery wrath against oppression," and of signing petitions; both of which things can be done very cheap. Good heavens, if signing petitions would do it, if hopping to Rome on one leg would do it, think you it were long undone!

Frightful things are continually told us of Negro slavery, of the hardships, bodily and spiritual, suffered by slaves. Much exaggerated, and mere exceptional cases, say the opponents. Exceptional cases, I answer; yes, and universal ones! On the whole, hardships, and even oppressions and injustices are not unknown in this world; I myself have suffered such, and have not you? It is said, Man, of whatever colour, is born to such, even as the sparks fly upwards. For in fact labour, and this is properly what we call hardship, misery, etc. (meaning mere ugly labour not yet done), labour is not joyous but grievous; and we have a good deal of it to do among us here. We have, simply, to carry the whole world and its businesses upon our backs, we poor united Human Species; to carry it, and shove it forward, from day to day, somehow or other, among us, or else be ground to powder under it, one and all. No light task, let me tell you, even if each did his part honestly, which each doesn't by any means. No, only the noble lift willingly with their whole strength, at the general burden; and in such a crowd, after all your drillings, regulatings, and attempts at equitable distribution, and compulsion, what deceptions are still practicable, what errors are inevitable! Many cunning ignoble fellows shirk the labour altogether; and instead of faithfully lifting at the immeasurable universal handbarrow with its thousand-million handles, contrive to get on some ledge of it, and be lifted!

What a story we have heard about all that, not from vague rumour since yesterday, but from inspired prophets, speakers and seers, ever since speech began! How the giant willing spirit, among white masters, and in the best-regulated families, is so often not loaded only but overloaded, crushed-down like an Enceladus; and, all his life, has to have armies of pigmies building tabernacles on his chest; marching composedly over his neck, as if it were a highway; and much amazed if, when they run their straw spear into his nostril, he is betrayed into sudden sneezing, and oversets some of them. [*Some laughter, the speaker himself looking terribly serious.*] My friends, I have come to the sad conclusion that SLAVERY, whether established by law, or by law abrogated, exists very extensively in this world, in and out of the West Indies; and, in fact, that you cannot abolish slavery by act of parliament, but can only abolish the *name* of it, which is very little!

In the West Indies itself, if you chance to abolish Slavery to Men, and in return establish Slavery to the Devil (as we see in Demerara), what good is it? To save men's bodies, and fill them with pumpkins and rum, is a poor task for human benevolence, if you have to kill their soul, what soul there was, in the business! Slavery is not so easy to be abolished; it will long continue, in spite of acts of parliament. And shall I tell you which is the one intolerable sort of slavery; the slavery over which the very gods weep? That sort is not rifest in the West Indies; but, with all its sad fruits, prevails in nobler countries. It is the slavery of the strong to the weak; of the great and noble-minded to the small and mean! The slavery of Wisdom to Folly. When Folly all "emancipated," and become supreme, armed with ballot-boxes, universal suffrages, and appealing to what Dismal Sciences, Statistics, Constitutional Philosophies, and other Fool Gospels it has got devised for itself, can say to Wisdom: "Be silent, or thou shalt repent it! Suppress thyself, I advise thee; canst thou not contrive to cease, then?" That also, in some anarchic-constitutional epochs, has been seen. When, of high and noble objects, there remained, in the market-place of human things, at length none; and he that could not make guineas his pursuit, and the applause of flunkies his reward, found himself in such a minority as seldom was before.

Minority, I know, there always was: but there are degrees of it, down to minority of one,—down to suppression of the unfortunate minority, and reducing it to zero, that the flunky-world may have peace from it henceforth. The flunky-world has peace; and descends, manipulating its ballot-boxes, Coppock suffrages, and divine constitutional apparatus; quoting its Dismal Sciences, Statistics, and other satisfactory Gospels and Talmuds,—into the throat of the Devil; not bothered by the importunate minority on the road. Did you never hear of "Crucify him! Crucify him!" That was a considerable feat in the suppressing of minorities; and is still talked-of on Sundays,—with very little understanding, when I last heard of it. My friends, my friends, I fear we are a stupid people; and stuffed with such delusions, above all with such immense hypocrisies and self-delusions, from our birth upwards, as no people were before; God help us!—Emancipated? Yes, indeed, we are emancipated out of several things, and into several things. No man, wise or foolish, any longer can control you for good or for evil. Foolish Tomkins, foolish Jobson, cannot now singly oppress you: but if the Universal Company of the Tomkinses and Jobsons, as by law established, can more than ever? If, on all highways and byways, that lead to other than a Tomkins-Jobson winning-post, you meet, at the second step, the big, dumb, universal genius of Chaos, and are so placidly yet peremptorily taught, "Halt here!" There is properly but one slavery in the world. One slavery, in which all other slaveries and miseries that afflict the earth are included; compared with which the worst West-Indian, white, or black, or yellow slaveries are a small matter. One slavery over which the very gods weep. Other slaveries, women and children and stump-orators weep over; but this is for men and gods! [*Sensation; some, however, took snuff.*]

If precisely the Wisest Man were at the top of society, and the next-wisest next, and so on till we reached the Demerara Nigger (from whom downwards, through the horse, etc., there is no question hitherto), then were this a perfect world, the extreme *maximum* of wisdom produced in it. That is how you might produce your maximum, would some god assist. And I can tell you also how the *minimum* were producible. Let no man in particular be put at the top; let all men be accounted equally wise and worthy, and the notion get abroad that anybody or nobody will do well enough at the top; that money (to which may be added success in stump-oratory) is the real symbol of wisdom, and supply-and-demand the all-sufficient substitute for command and obedience among two-legged animals of the unfeathered class: accomplish all those remarkable convictions in your thinking department; and then in your practical, as is fit, decide by count of heads, the vote of a Demerara Nigger equal and no more to that of a Chancellor Bacon: this, I perceive, will (so soon as it is fairly under way, and *all* obstructions left behind) give the *minimum* of wisdom in your proceedings. Thus were your minimum producible,—with no God needed to assist, nor any Demon even, except the general Demon of *Ignavia* (Unvalour), lazy Indifference to the production or non-production of such things, which runs in our own blood. Were it beautiful, think you? Folly in such million-fold majority, at length peaceably supreme in this earth. Advancing on you as the huge buffalo-phalanx does in the Western Deserts; or as, on a smaller scale, those bristly creatures did in the Country of the Gadarenes. Rushing, namely, in wild *stampede* (the Devil being in them, some small fly having stung them), boundless,—one wing on that edge of your horizon, the other wing on that, and rearward whole tides and oceans of them :—so could Folly rush; the enlightened public one huge Gadareness-swinery, tail cocked, snout in air, with joyful animating short squeak; fast and ever faster; down steep places,—to the sea of Tiberias, and the bottomless cloacas of Nature: quenched there, since nowhere sooner. My friends, such sight is *too* sublime, if you are out in it, and are not of it!—

* * *

Well, *except* by Mastership and Servantship, there is no conceivable deliverance from Tyranny and Slavery. Cosmos is not Chaos, even approximately, can contrive to govern, all is right, or is ever striving to become so; where folly is "emancipated," and gets to govern, as it soon will, all is wrong. That is the sad fact; and in other places than Demerara, and in regard to other interests than those of sugar-making, we sorrowfully experience the same.

I have to complain that, in these days, the relation of master to servant, and of superior to inferior, in all stages of it, is fallen sadly out of joint. As may well be, when the very highest stage and form of it, which should be the summary of all and the keystone of all, is got to such a pass. Kings themselves are grown sham-kings; and their subjects very naturally are sham-subjects; with mere lip-homage, insincere to their sham-kings;—sincere chiefly when they get into the streets (as is now our desperate case generally in Europe) to shoot them down as nuisances. Royalty is terribly gone; and loyalty in consequence has had to go. No man reverences another; at the best, each man slaps the other good-humouredly on the shoulder, with, "Hail, fellow; well met":—at the worst (which is sure enough to *follow* such unreasonable good-humour, in a world like ours), clutches him by the throat, with "Tyrannous son of perdition, shall I endure thee, then, and thy injustices forever?" We are not yet got to the worst extreme, we here in these Isles; but we are well half-way towards it, I often think.

Certainly, by any ballot-box, Jesus Christ goes just as far as Judas Iscariot; and with reason, according to the New Gospels, Talmuds and Dismal Sciences of these days. Judas looks him in the face; asks proudly, "Am not I as good as thou? Better, perhaps!" slapping his breeches-pocket, in which is audible the cheerful jingle of thirty pieces of silver. "Thirty of them here, thou cowering pauper!" My philanthropic friends, if there be a state of matters under the stars which deserves the name of damnable and damned, this I perceive is it! Alas, I know well whence it came, and how it could not help coming;—and I continually pray the gods its errand were done, and it had begun to go its ways again. Vain hope, at least for a century to come! And there will be such a sediment of Egyptian mud to sweep away, and to fish all human things out of again, once this most sad though salutary deluge is well over, as the human species seldom had before. Patience, patience!—

In fact, without real masters you cannot have servants; and a master is not made by thirty pieces or thirty-million pieces of silver; only a sham-master is so made. The Dismal Science of this epoch defines him to be master good enough; but he is not such: you can see what kind of master he proves, what kind of servants he manages to have. Accordingly, the state of British servantship, of American helpship—I confess to you, my friends, if looking out for what was *least* human and heroic, least lovely to the Supreme Powers, I should not go to Carolina at this time; I should sorrowfully stay at home! Austere philosophers, possessed even of cash, have talked to me about the possibility of doing without servants; of trying somehow to serve yourself (boot-cleaning, etc., done by contract), and so escaping from a never-ending welter, dirtier for your mind than boot-cleaning itself. Of which the perpetual *fluctuation*, and change from month to month, is probably the most inhuman element; the fruitful parent of all else that is evil, unendurable and inhuman. A poor Negro overworked on the Cuba sugar-grounds, he is sad to look upon; yet he inspires me with sacred pity, and a kind of human respect is not denied him; him, the hapless brother mortal, performing something useful in his day, and only suffering inhumanity, not doing it or being it. But with what feelings can I look upon an overfed White Flunky, if I know his ways? Disloyal, unheroic, this one; *in*human in his character, and his work, and his position; more so no creature ever was. Pity is not for him, or not a soft kind of it; nor is any remedy visible, except abolition at no distant date! He is the flower of *nomadic* servitude, proceeding by month's warning, and free supply-and-demand; if obedience is not in his heart, if chiefly gluttony and mutiny are in his heart, and he has to be bribed by high feeding to do the shows of obedience,—what can await him, or be prayed for him, among men, except even "abolition"?

The Duke of Trumps, who sometimes does me the honour of a little conversation, owned that the state of his domestic service was by no means satisfactory to the human mind. "Five-and-forty of them," said his Grace; "really, I suppose, the cleverest in the market, for there is no limit to the wages: I often think how many quiet families, all down to the basis of society, I have disturbed, in attracting gradually, by higher and higher offers, that set of fellows to me; and what the use of them is when here! I feed them like aldermen, pay them as if they were sages and heroes:—Samuel

Johnson's wages, at the very last and best, as I have heard you say, were 300*l*. or 500*l*. a year; and Jellysnob, my butler, who indeed is clever, gets, I believe, more than the highest of these sums. And, shall I own it to you? In my young days, with one valet, I had more trouble saved me, more help afforded me to live,—actually more of my will accomplished,—than from these forty-five I now get, or ever shall. It is all a serious comedy; what you call a melancholy sham. Most civil, obsequious, and indeed expert fellows these; but bid one of them step-out of his regulated sphere on your behalf! An iron law presses on us all here; on them and on me. In my own house, how much of my will can I have done, dare I propose to have done? Prudence, on my side, is prescribed by a jealous and ridiculous point-of-honour attitude on theirs. They lie here more like a troop of foreign soldiers that had invaded me, than a body of servants I had hired. At free quarters; we have strict laws of war established between us; they make their salutes, and do certain bits of specified work, with many becks and scrapings; but as to *service*, properly so-called—!—I lead the life of a servant, sir; it is I that am a slave; and often I think of packing the whole brotherhood of them out of doors one good day, and retiring to furnished lodgings; but have never done it yet!"—Such was the confession of his Grace.

For, indeed, in the long-run, it is not possible to buy *obedience* with money. You may buy work done with money: from cleaning boots to building houses, and to far higher functions, there is much work bought with money, and got done in a supportable manner. But, mark withal, that is only from a class of supportably wise human creatures: from a huge and ever-increasing insupportably foolish class of human creatures you cannot buy work in that way; and the attempt in London itself, much more in Demerara, turns out a very "serious comedy" indeed! Who has not heard of the Distressed Needlewomen in these days? We have thirty-thousand Distressed Neddlewomen,—the most of whom cannot sew a reasonable stitch; for they are, in fact, Mutinous Serving-maids, who, instead of learning to work and to obey, learned to give warning: "Then suit yourself, Ma'am!" Hapless enfranchised White Women, who took the "freedom" to serve the Devil with their faculties, instead of serving God or man; hapless souls, they were "enfranchised" to a most high degree, and had not the wisdom for so ticklish a predicament,—"Then suit yourself, Ma'am";—and so have tumbled from one stage of folly to the other stage; and at last are on the street, with five hungry senses, and no available faculty whatever. Having finger and thumb, they do procure a needle, and call themselves Distressed Needlewomen, but cannot sew at all. I have inquired in the proper places, and find a quite passionate demand for women that can sew,—such being unattainable just now. "As well call them Distressed Astronomers as Distressed Needlewomen!" said a lady to me: "I myself will take three *sewing* Needlewomen, if you can get them for me today." Is not that a sight to set before the curious?

Distressed enough, God knows;—but it will require quite other remedies to get at the bottom of *their* complaint, I am afraid. O Brothers! O Sisters! It is for these White Women that my heart bleeds and my soul is heavy; it is for the sight of such mad notions and such unblessed doings now all-prevalent among mankind,— alas, it is for such life-theories and such life-practices, and ghastly clearstarched life-hypocrisies, playing their part under high Heaven, as render these inevitable and unaidable,—that the world of today looks black and vile to me, and with all its guineas, in the nostril smells badly! It is not to the West Indies that I run first of all; and not thither with "enfranchisement" first of all, when I discern what "enfranchisement" has led to in hopefuler localities. I tell you again and again, he or she that will not work, and in the anger of the gods cannot be compelled to work, shall die! And not he or she only: alas, alas, were it the guilty only!— But as yet we cannot help it; as yet, for a long while, we must be patient, and let the Exeter-Hallery and other tragic Tomfoolery rave itself out. [*Deep silence in the small remnant of audience;— the gentleman in white trousers came in again, his creaking painfully audible in spite of efforts.*]

My friends, it is not good to be without a servant in this world; but to be without master, it appears, is a still fataler predicament for some. Without a master, in certain cases, you become a Distressed Needlewoman, and cannot so much as live. Happy he who has found his master, I will say; if not a good master, then some supportable approximation to a good one; for the worst, it appears, in some cases, is preferable to none!

Happy he who has found a master;—and now, farther I will say, having found, let him well keep him. In all human relations *permanency* is what I advocate; *nomadism*, continual change, is what I perceive to be prohibitory of any good whatsoever. Two men that have got to coöperate will do well not to quarrel at the first cause of offence, and throw-up the concern in disgust, hoping to suit themselves better elsewhere. For the most part such hope is fallacious; and they will, on the average, not suit themselves better, but only about as well,—and have to begin again *bare*, which loss often repeated becomes immense, and is finally the loss of everything, and of their joint enterprise itself. For no mutual relation while it continues "bare," is yet a human one, or can bring blessedness but is only waiting to become such,—mere new-piled crags, which, if you leave them, *will* at last "gather moss," and yield some verdure and pasture. O my friends, what a remedy is this we have fallen upon, for everything that goes wrong between one man and another: "Go, then; I give you a month's warning!" What would you think of a sacrament of marriage constructed on such principles? Marriage by the month,—why this too has been tried, and is still extensively practised in spite of Law and Gospel; but it is not found to do! The legislator, the preacher, all rational mortals, answer, "No, no!" You must marry for longer than a month, and the contract not so easily revocable, even should mistakes occur, as they sometimes do.

I am prepared to maintain against all comers, That in every human relation, from that of husband and wife down to that of master and servant, *nomadism* is the bad plan, and continuance the good. A thousand times, since I first had servants, it has occurred to me, How much better had I servants that were bound to me, and to whom I were bound! Doubtless it were not easy; doubtless it is now impossible: but if it could be done! I say, if the Black gentleman is born to be a servant, and, in fact, is useful in God's creation only as a servant, then let him hire not by the month, but by a very much longer term. That he be "hired for life,"—really here is the essence of the position he now holds! Consider that matter. All else is abuse in it, and this only is essence;—and the abuses must be cleared away. They must and shall! Yes; and the thing itself seems to offer (its abuses once cleared away) a possibility of the most precious kind for the Black man and for us. Servants hired for life, or by a contract for a long period, and not easily dissoluble; so and not otherwise would all reasonable mortals, Black and White, wish to hire and to be hired! I invite you to reflect on that; for you will find it true. And if true, it is important for us, in reference to this Negro Question and some others. The Germans say, "you must empty-out the bathing-tub, but not the baby along with it." Fling-out your dirty water with all zeal, and set it careering down the kennels; but try if you can keep the little child!

How to abolish the abuses of slavery, and save the precious thing in it, alas, I do not pretend that this is easy, that it can be done in a day, or a single generation, or a single century: but I do surmise or perceive that it will, by straight methods or by circuitous, need to be done (not in the West-Indian regions alone); and that the one way of helping the Negro at present (Distressed Needlewoman etc. being quite out of reach) were by piously and strenuously beginning it. Begun it must be, I perceive; and carried on in all regions where servants are born and masters; and are *not* prepared to become Distressed Needlewomen, or Demerara Niggers, but to live in some human manner with one another. And truly, my friends, with regard to this world-famous Nigger Question,— which perhaps is louder than it is big, after all,—I would advise you to attack it on that side. Try against the dirty water, with an eye to *save* the baby! That will be a quite new point of attack; where, it seems to me, some real benefit and victory for the poor Negro, might before long be accomplished; and something else than Demerara freedom (with its rum-bottle and no breeches,— "baby" quite *gone* down into the kennels!), or than American stump-oratory, with mutual exasperation fast rising to the desperate pitch, might be possible for philanthropic men and women of the Anglo-Saxon type. Try this; perhaps the very Carolina planter will coöperate with you; he will, if he has any wisdom left in this exasperation! If he do not, he will do worse; and go a strange road with those Niggers of his.

By one means or another these enormities we hear of from the Slave States,—though I think they are hardly so hideous, any of them, as the sight our own Demerara now offers,—must be heard of no more. Men will and must summon "indignation-meetings" about them; and simple persons,—like Wilhelm Meister's Felix flying at the cook's throat for plucking pigeons, yet himself seen shortly after pelting frogs to death with pebbles that lay handy,— will agitate their caucuses, ballot-boxes, dissever the Union, and, in short, play the very devil, if these things are not abated, and do not go on abating more and more towards perfect abolition. *Unjust* master over servant *hired for life* is, once for all, and shall be, unendurable to human souls. To *cut* the tie, and "fling Farmer Hodge's horses quite loose" upon the supply-and-demand principle: that, I will believe, is not the method! But by some method, by hundredfold restrictions, responsibilities, laws, conditions, cunning methods, Hodge must be got to treat his horses *justly*, for we cannot stand it longer. And let Hodge think well of it,—I mean the American two-footed Hodge,—for there is no other salvation for him. And if he would avoid a consummation like our Demerara one, I would advise him to know this secret; which our poor Hodge did not know, or would not practise, and so is come to such a pass!—Here is part of my answer to the Hon. Hickory Buckskin, a senator in those Southern States, and man of really respectable attainments and dimensions, who in his despair appears to be entertaining very violent projects now and then, as to uniting with our West Indies (under a *New Downing Street*), forming a West-Indian empire, etc., etc.

"The *New Downing Street*, I take it, is at a great distance here; and we shall wait yet a while for it, and run good risk of losing all our Colonies before we can discover the way of managing them. On that side do not reckon upon help. At the same time, I can well understand you should 'publicly discuss the propriety of severing the Union,' and that the resolution should be general, 'you will rather die,' etc. A man, having certified himself about his trade and post under the sun, is actually called upon to 'die' in vindication of it, if needful; in defending the possibilities he has of carrying it on, and eschewing with it the belly of Perdition, when extraneous Insanity is pushing it thither. All this I presuppose of you, of men born of your lineage; and have not a word to say against it.

"Meanwhile suffer me to say this other thing. You will not find Negro Slavery defensible by the mere resolution, never so extensive, to defend it. No, there is another condition wanted: That your relation to the Negroes, in this thing called slavery (with such an emphasis upon the word) be actually fair, just and according to the facts;—fair, I say, not in the sight of New-England platforms, but of God Almighty the Maker of both Negroes and you. That is the one ground on which men can take their stand; in the long-run all human causes, and this cause too, will come to be settled *there*. Forgive me for saying that I do not think you have yet got to that point of perfection with your Negro relations; that there is probably much in them *not* fair, nor agreeable to the Maker of us, and to the eternal laws of fact as written in the Negro's being and in ours.

"The advice of advices, therefore, to men so circumstanced were, With all diligence make them so! Otherwise than *so*, they are doomed by Earth and by Heaven. Demerara may be the maddest remedy, as I think it is a very mad one: but some remedy we must have; or if none, then destruction and annihilation, by the Demerara or a worse method. These things it would behove you of the Southern States, above all men, to be now thinking of. How to make the Negro's position among his White fellow-creatures a just one,—the real and genuine expression of what *commandment* the Maker has given to both of you, by making the one of you thus and the other so, and putting you in juxtaposition on this Earth of His? That you should *cut* the ligature, and say, 'He has made us equal,' would be saying a palpable falsity, big with hideous ruin for all concerned in it: I hope and believe, you, with our example before you, will say something much better than that. But something, very many things, do not hide from yourselves, will require to be said! And I do not pretend that it will be easy or soon done, to get a proper code of laws (and still more difficult, a proper system of habits, ways of thinking, for a basis to such 'code') on the rights of Negroes and Whites. But that also, you may depend upon it, has fallen to White men as a duty;—to you now in the first place, after our sad failure. And unless you can do it, be certain, neither will you be able to keep your Negroes; your portion too will be the Demerara or a worse one. This seems to me indubitable.

"Or perhaps you have already begun? Persist diligently, if so; but at all events, begin! For example, ought there not to be in every Slave State, a fixed legal sum, on paying which, any Black man was entitled to demand his freedom? Settle a fair sum; and let it stand fixed by law. If the poor Black can, by forethought, industry, self-denial, accumulate this sum, has he not proved the actual 'freedom' of his soul, to a fair extent: in God's name, why will you keep his body captive? It seems to me a well-considered law of this kind might do you invaluable service,—might it not be a real *safety-valve*, and ever-open *chimney*, for that down-pressed Slave-world with whatever injustices are still in it; whereby all the stronger and really worthier elements would escape peaceably, as they arose, instead of accumulating there, and convulsing you, as

now? Or again, look at the Serfs of the Middle Ages: they married
and gave in marriage, nay, they could not even be *divorced* from
their natal soil; had home, family, and a treatment that was human.
Many laws, and gradually a whole code of laws, on this matter
could be made! And will have to be made; if you would avoid the
ugly Demerara issue, or even uglier which may be in store. I can
see no other road for you. This new question has arisen, million-
voiced: 'What *are* the wages of a Black servant, hired for life by
White men?' This question must be answered, in some not insupportably erroneous way: gods and men are warning you that you
must answer it, if you would continue there!'—The Hon, Kickory
never acknowledged my letter; but I hope he is getting on with the
advice I gave him, all the same!

For the rest, I never thought the "rights of Negroes" worth
much discussing, nor the rights of men in any form; the grand
point, as I once said, is the *mights* of men,—what portion of their
"rights" they have a chance of getting sorted out, and realised, in
this confused world. We will not go deep into the question here
about the Negro's rights. We will give a single glance into it, and
see, for one thing, how complex it is.

West-India Islands, still full of waste fertility, produce abundant
pumpkins: pumpkins, however, you will observe, are not the sole
requisite for human well-being. No; for a pig they are the one
thing needful: but for a man they are only the first of several
things needful. The first is here; but the second and remaining,
how are they to be got? The answer is wide as human society
itself. Society at large, as instituted in each country of the world, is
the answer such country has been able to give: Here, in this poor
country, the rights of man and the mights of man are—such and
such! An approximate answer to a question capable only of better
and better solutions, never of any perfect, or absolutely good one.
Nay, if we inquire, with much narrower scope, as to the right of
chief management in cultivating those West-India lands: as to the
"right of property" so-called, and of doing what you like with
your own? Even this question is abstruse enough. Who it may be
that has a right to raise pumpkins and other produce on those
Islands, perhaps none can, except temporarily, decide. The Islands
are good withal for pepper, for sugar, for sago, arrow-root, for
coffee, perhaps for cinnamon and precious spices; things far nobler

than pumpkins; and leading towards Commerces, Arts, Politics and Social Developments, which alone are the noble product, where men (and not pigs with pumpkins) are the parties concerned! Well, all this fruit too, fruit spicy and commercial, fruit spiritual and celestial, so far beyond the merely pumpkinish and grossly terrene, lies in the West-India lands: and the ultimate "proprietor-ship" of them,—why, I suppose, it will vest in him who can the *best* educe from them whatever of noble produce they were created fit for yielding. He, I compute, is the real "Vicegerent of the Maker" there; in him, better and better chosen, and not in another, is the "property" vested by decree of Heaven's chancery itself!

Up to this time it is the Saxon British mainly; they hitherto have cultivated with some manfulness: and when a manfuler class of cultivators, stronger, worthier to have such land, abler to bring fruit from it, shall make their appearance,—they, doubt it not, by fortune of war, and other confused negotiation and vicissitude, will be declared by Nature and Fact to *be* the worthier, and will become proprietors,—perhaps also only for a time. That is the law, I take it; ultimate, supreme, for all lands in all countries under this sky. The one perfect eternal proprietor is the Maker who created them: the temporary better or worse proprietor is he whom the Maker has sent on that mission; he who the best hitherto can educe from said lands the beneficent gifts the Maker endowed them with; or, which is but another definition of the same person, he who leads hitherto the manfulest life on that bit of soil, doing, better than another yet found can do, the Eternal Purpose and Supreme Will there.

And now observe, my friends, it was not Black Quashee, or those he represents, that made those West-India Islands what they are, or can, by any hypothesis, be considered to have the right of growing pumpkins there. For countless ages, since they first mounted oozy, on the back of earthquakes, from their dark bed in the Ocean deeps, and reeking saluted the tropical Sun, and ever onwards till the European white man first saw them some three short centuries ago, those Islands had produced mere jungle, savagery, poison-reptiles and swamp-malaria: till the white European first saw them, they were as if not yet created,—their noble elements of cinnamon, sugar, coffee, pepper black and grey, lying all asleep, waiting the white enchanter who should say to them,

Awake! Till the end of human history and the sounding of the Trump of Doom, they might have lain so, had Quashee and the like of him been the only artists in the game. Swamps, fever-jungles, man-eating Caribs, rattlesnakes, and reeking waste and putrefaction, this had been the produce of them under the incompetent Caribal (what we call Cannibal) possessors, till that time; and Quashee knows, himself, whether ever he could have introduced an improvement. Him, had he by a miraculous chance been wafted thither, the Caribals would have eaten, rolling him as a fat morsel under their tongue; for him, till the sounding of the Trump of Doom, the rattlesnakes and savageries would have held-on their way. It was not he, then; it was another than he! Never by art of his could one pumpkin have grown there to solace any human throat; nothing but savagery and reeking putrefaction could have grown there. These plentiful pumpkins, I say therefore, are not his: no, they are another's; they are his only under conditions. Conditions which Exeter Hall, for the present, has forgotten; but which Nature and the Eternal Powers have by no manner of means forgotten, but do at all moments keep in mind; and, at the right moment, will, with the due impressiveness, perhaps in a rather terrible manner, bring again to our mind also!

If Quashee will not honestly aid in bringing-out those sugars, cinnamons and nobler products of the West-Indian Islands, for the benefit of all mankind, then I say neither will the Powers permit Quashee to continue growing pumpkins there for his own lazy benefit; but will shear him out, by and by, like a lazy gourd overshadowing rich ground; him and all that partake with him,—perhaps in a very terrible manner. For, under favour of Exeter Hall, the "terrible manner" is not yet quite extinct with the Destinies in this Universe; nor will it quite cease, I apprehend, for soft sawder or philanthropic stump-oratory now or henceforth. No; the gods wish besides pumpkins, that spices and valuable products be grown in their West Indies; thus much they have declared in so making the West Indies:—infinitely more they wish, that manful industrious men occupy their West Indies, not indolent two-legged cattle, however "happy" over their abundant pumpkins! Both these things, we may be assured, the immortal gods have decided upon, passed their eternal Act of Parliament for: and both of them, though all terrestrial Parliaments and entities oppose it to the death, shall be done. Quashee, if he will not help in bringing-out the spices, will get himself made a slave again (which state will be a little less ugly than his present one), and with beneficent whip, since other methods avail not, will be compelled to work.

Or, alas, let him look across to Haiti, and trace a far sterner prophecy! Let him, by his ugliness, idleness, rebellion, banish all White men from the West Indies, and make it all one Haiti,—with little or no sugar growing, black Peter exterminating black Paul, and where a garden of the Hesperides might be, nothing but a tropical dog-kennel and pestiferous jungle,—does he think that will forever continue pleasant to gods and men? I see men, the rose-pink cant all peeled away from them, land one day on those black coasts; men *sent* by the Laws of this Universe, and inexorable Course of Things; men hungry for gold, remorseless, fierce as the old Buccaneers were;—and a doom for Quashee which I had rather not contemplate! The gods are long-suffering; but the law from the beginning was, He that will not work shall perish from the earth; and the patience of the gods has limits!

Before the West Indies could grow a pumpkin for any Negro, how much European heroism had to spend itself in obscure battle; to sink, in mortal agony, before the jungles, the putrescences and waste savageries could become arable, and the Devils be in some measure chained there! The West Indies grow pine-apples, and sweet fruits, and spices; we hope they will one day grow beautiful Heroic Human Lives too, which is surely the ultimate object they were made for: beautiful souls and brave; sages, poets, what not; making the Earth nobler round them, as their kindred from of old have been doing; true "splinters of the old Harz Rock"; heroic white men, worthy to be called old Saxons, browned with a mahogany tint in those new climates and conditions. But under the soil of Jamaica, before it could even produce spices or any pump-kin, the bones of many thousand British men had to be laid. Brave Colonel Fortescue, brave Colonel Sedgwick, brave Colonel Brayne, —the dust of many thousand strong old English hearts lies there; worn-down swiftly in frightful travail, chaining the Devils, which were manifold. Heroic Blake contributed a bit of his life to that Jamaica. A bit of the great Protector's own life lies there; beneath those pumpkins lies a bit of the life that was Oliver Cromwell's. How the great Protector would have rejoiced to think, that all this was to issue in growing pumpkins to keep Quashee in a com-fortably idle condition! No; that is not the ultimate issue; not that.

The West-Indian Whites, so soon as this bewilderment of phi-lanthropic and other jargon abates from them, and their poor eyes get to discern a little what the Facts are and what the Laws are, will strike into another course, I apprehend! I apprehend they will, as a preliminary, resolutely *refuse* to permit the Black man any privilege whatever of pumpkins till he agree for work in return. Not a square inch of soil in those fruitful Isles, purchased by British blood, shall any Black man hold to grow pumpkins for him, except on terms that are fair towards Britain. Fair; see that they be not unfair, not towards ourselves, and still more, not towards him. For injustice is *forever* accursed: and precisely our unfairness towards the enslaved Black man has,—by inevitable revulsion and fated turn of the wheel,—brought about these present confusions.

Fair towards Britain it will be, that Quashee give work for priv-ilege to grow pumpkins. Not a pumpkin, Quashee, not a square yard of soil, till you agree to do the State so many days of service. Annually that soil will grow you pumpkins; but annually also, without fail, shall you, for the owner thereof, do your appointed days of labour. The State has plenty of waste soil; but the State will religiously give you none of it on other terms. The State wants sugar from these Islands and means to have it; wants virtuous industry in these Islands, and must have it. The State demands of you such service as will bring these results, this latter result which includes all. Not a Black Ireland, by immigration, and boundless black supply for the demand;—not that, may the gods forbid!—but a regulated West Indies, with black working population in adequate numbers; all "happy," if they find it possible; and *not* entirely unbeautiful to gods and men, which latter result they *must* find possible! All "happy," enough; that is to say, all working according to the faculty they have got, making a little more divine this Earth which the gods have given them. Is there any other "happiness,"—if it be not that of pigs fattening daily to the slaugh-ter? So will the State speak by and by.

Any poor idle Black man, any idle White man, rich or poor, is a mere eye-sorrow to the State; a perpetual blister on the skin of the State. The State is taking measures, some of them rather extensive, in Europe at this very time, and already, as in Paris, Berlin and elsewhere, rather tremendous measures, to *get* its rich white men set to work; for alas, they also have long sat Negro-like up to the ears in pumpkin, regardless of "work," and of a world all going to waste for their idleness! Extensive measures, I say; and already (as, in all European lands, this scandalous Year of street-barricades and fugitive sham-kings exhibits) *tremendous* measures; for the thing is urgent to be done.

The thing must be done everywhere; *must* is the word. Only it is so terribly difficult to do; and will take generations yet, this of getting our rich European white men "set to work!" But yours in the West Indies, may obscure Black friends, your work, and the getting of you set to it, is a simple affair; and by diligence, the West-Indian legislatures, and Royal governors, setting their faces fairly to the problem, will get it done. You are not "slaves" now; nor do I wish, if it can be avoided, to see you slaves again: but decidedly you have to be servants to those that are born *wiser* than you, that are born lords of you; servants to the Whites, if they *are* (as what mortal can doubt they are?) born wiser than you. That, you may depend on it, my obscure Black friends, is and was always the Law of the World, for you and for all men: To *be* servants, the more foolish of us to the more wise; and only sorrow, futility and disappointment will betide both, till both in some approximate degree get to conform to the same. Heaven's laws are not repealable by Earth, however Earth may try,—and it has been trying hard, in some directions, of late! I say, no well-being, and in the end no being at all, will be possible for you or us, if the law of Heaven is not complied with. And if "slave" mean essentially "servant hired for life,"—for life, or by a contract of long continuance and not easily dissoluble,—I ask once more, Whether, in all human things, the "contract of long continuance" is not precisely the contract to be desired, were the right terms once found for it? Servant hired for life, were the right terms once found, which I do not pretend they are, seems to me much preferable to servant hired for the month, or by contract dissoluble in a day. What that amounts to, we have known, and our thirty-thousand Distressed Astronomers have known; and we don't want that! [*Some assent in the small remnant of an audience. "Silence!" from the Chair.*]

To state articulately, and put into practical Lawbooks, what on all sides is *fair* from the West-Indian White to the West-Indian Black; what relations the Eternal Maker *has* established between these two creatures of His; what He has written down with intricate but ineffaceable record, legible to candid human insight, in the respective qualities, strengths, necessities and capabilities of each of the two: this, as I told the Hon. Hickory my Carolina correspondent, will be a long problem; only to be solved by continuous human endeavour, and earnest effort gradually perfecting itself as experience successively yields new light to it. This will be to "*find the right terms*"; terms of a contract that will endure, and be sanctioned by Heaven, and obtain prosperity on Earth, between the two. A long problem, terribly neglected hitherto;—whence these West-Indian sorrows, and Exeter-Hall monstrosities, just now! But a problem which must be entered upon, and by degrees be completed. A problem which, I think, the English People also, if they mean to retain human Colonies, and not Black Irelands in addition to the White, cannot begin too soon. What are the true relations between Negro and White, their mutual duties under the sight of the Maker of them both; what human laws will assist both to comply more and more with these? The solution, only to be gained by honest endeavour, and sincere reading of experience, such as have never yet been bestowed on it, is not yet here; the solution is perhaps still distant. But some approximation to it, various real approximations, could be made, and must be made:—this of declaring that Negro and White are *un*related, loose from one another, on a footing of perfect equality, and subject to no law but that of supply-and-demand according to the Dismal Science; this, which contradicts the palpablest facts, is clearly no solution, but a cutting of the knot asunder; and every hour we persist in this is leading us towards *dis*solution instead of solution!

What, then, is practically to be done by us poor English with our Demerara and other blacks? Well, in such a mess as we have made there, it is not easy saying what is first to be done! But all this of perfect equality, of cutting quite loose from one another; all this, with "immigration loan," "happiness of black peasantry," and the other melancholy stuff that has followed from it, will first of all require to be *un*done, and the ground cleared of it, by way of preliminary to "doing!" After that there may several things be possible.

Already one hears of Black *Adscripti glebae;* which seems a promising arrangement, one of the first to suggest itself in such a complicacy. It appears the Dutch Blacks, in Java, are already a kind of *Adscripts*, after the manner of the old European serfs; bound, by royal authority, to give so many days of work a year. Is not this something like a real approximation; the first step towards all manner of such? Wherever, in British territory, there exists a Black man, and needful work to the just extent is not to be got out of him, such a law, in defect of better, should be brought to bear upon said Black man! How many laws of like purport, conceivable some of them, might be brought to bear upon the Black man and the White, with all despatch by way of solution instead of dissolution to their complicated case just now! On the whole, it ought to be rendered possible, ought it not, for White men to live beside Black men, and in some just manner to command Black men, and produce West-Indian fruitfulness by means of them? West-Indian fruitfulness will need to be produced. If the English cannot find the method for that, they may rest assured there will another come (Brother Jonathan or still another) who can. He it is whom the gods will bid continue in the West Indies; bidding us ignominiously, "Depart, ye quack-ridden, incompetent!"—

One other remark, as to the present Trade in Slaves, and to our suppression of the same. If buying of Black war-captives in Africa, and bringing them over to the Sugar Islands for sale again be, as I think it is, a contradiction of the Laws of this Universe, let us heartily pray Heaven to end the practice; let us ourselves help Heaven to end it, wherever the opportunity is given. If it be the most flagrant and alarming contradiction to the said Laws which is now witnessed on this Earth; so flagrant and alarming that a just man cannot exist, and follow his affairs, in the same Planet with it; why, then indeed—— But is it, quite certainly, such? Alas, look at that group of *un*sold, unbought, unmarketable Irish "free" citizens, dying there in the ditch, whither my Lord of Rackrent and the constitutional sheriffs have evicted them; or at those "divine missionaries," of the same free country, now traversing, with rags on back, and child on each arm, the principal thoroughfares of London, to tell men what "freedom" really is;—and admit that there may be doubts on that point! But if it *is*, I say, the most alarming contradiction to the said Laws which is now witnessed on this earth; so flagrant a contradiction that a just man cannot exist, and follow his affairs, in the same Planet with it, then, sure enough, let us, in God's name, fling-aside all our affairs, and hasten out to put an end to it, as the first thing the Heavens want us to do. By all manner of means. This thing done, the Heavens will prosper all other things with us! Not a doubt of it,—provided your premiss be not doubtful.

But now, furthermore, give me leave to ask, Whether the way of doing it is this somewhat surprising one, of trying to blockade the continent of Africa itself, and to watch slave-ships along that extremely extensive and unwholesome coast? The enterprise is very gigantic; and proves hitherto as futile as any enterprise has lately done. Certain wise men once, before this, set about confining the cuckoo by a big circular wall; but they could not manage it!—Watch the coast of Africa? That is a very long Coast; good part of the Coast of the terraqueous Globe! And the living centres of this slave mischief, the live coals that produce all this world-wide smoke, it appears, lie simply in two points, Cuba and Brazil, which *are* perfectly accessible and manageable.

If the Laws of Heaven do authorise you to keep the whole world in a pother about this question; if you really can appeal to the Almighty God upon it, and set common interests, and ter-restrial considerations, and common sense, at defiance in behalf of it,—why, in Heaven's name, not go to Cuba and Brazil with a sufficiency of Seventy-fours; and signify to those nefarious coun-tries: "Nefarious countries, your procedure on the Negro Ques-tion is too bad; see, of all the solecisms now submitted to on Earth, it is the most alarming and transcendent, and, in fact, is such that a just man cannot follow his affairs any longer in the same Planet with it. You clearly will not, you nefarious populations, for love or fear, watching or entreaty, respect the rights of the Negro enough; —wherefore we here, with our Seventy-fours, are come to be King over you, and will on the spot henceforth see for ourselves that you do it!"

Why not, if Heaven do send us? The thing can be done; easily, if you are sure of that proviso. It can be done: it is the way to "suppress the Slave-trade"; and so far as yet appears, the one way.

Most thinking people,—if hen-stealing prevail to a plainly un-endurable extent, will you station police-officers at every hen-roost; and keep them watching and cruising incessantly to and fro over the Parish, in the unwholesome dark, at enormous expense, with almost no effect? Or will you not try rather to discover where the fox's den is, and kill the fox! Which of those two things will you do? Most thinking people, you know the fox and his den; there he is,—kill him, and discharge your cruisers and police-watchers!—[*Laughter.*]

O my friends, I feel there is an immense fund of Human Stupidity circulating among us, and much clogging our affairs for some time past! A certain man has called us, "of all peoples the wisest in action"; but he added, "the stupidest in speech":—and it is a sore thing, in these constitutional times, times mainly of universal Parliamentary and other Eloquence, that the "speakers" have all first to emit, in such tumultuous volumes, their human stupor, as the indispensable preliminary, and everywhere we must first see that and its results *out*, before beginning any business.—(*Explicit MS.*)

14. Earl Grey and Regressive Taxation for Tropical Colonies

Henry George Grey, Viscount Howick and third Earl Grey (1802–94), was one of the most outstanding British Secretaries of State for the Colonies. He served as Under-Secretary for the Colonies in 1830–33, when the act for the emancipation of slaves in the British Empire was being prepared. In 1846–52 he was Secretary in Lord John Russell's administration, a crucial period in many parts of the empire, and he later defended his tenure in office in a volume entitled *The Colonial Policy of Lord John Russell's Administration,* where his suggestions for increasing the labor supplied in tropical territories were spelled out in detail.

The selection below is from his dispatch to Lord Torrington, Governor of Ceylon, No. 22, October 24, 1848, as printed in the Parliamentary Sessional Papers, 1849, xxxvi (1018), pp. 342–345.

Downing-street, October 24, 1848

My Lord,

1. In more than one of the other Despatches which will reach you by the present opportunity, I have expressed the satisfaction which I have felt at your prompt and successful efforts to put an immediate end to the insurrection which, unhappily, has recently occurred in Ceylon. But considering that so much objection has been taken on this occasion to your financial measures, and that memorials have been transmitted to me to ascribing the outbreak to the just discontent these measures are said to have created, I con-

sider it due to you to record more fully than I have yet done some of the general grounds on which I approve of those measures, and on which they still appear to me to be deserving of approval.

2. In the first place, it must be borne in mind that a review of the whole financial system of Ceylon had become absolutely indispensable. I need not recapitulate at any length the circumstances which created this necessity, for they are sufficiently adverted to in the outset of the Despatch I wrote to you on the 17th of July last, No. 252. Within the last few years Ceylon had, for the first time, become a field for the skill and enterprise of British settlers, and by that means acquired a prospect of the numerous social advantages which must follow from the residence amidst a rude population of persons having the habits and acquirements of civilization. The methods, however, of raising a revenue which had grown up concurrently with the obsolete system of Government monopolies, were quite unsuited to the spirit of commerce, and even had it been otherwise, the fact came to light, not merely that the surplus which had been believed to have accumulated in former years was much smaller than had been supposed, but also that a large proportion of the revenue, which had been depended upon in settling the former financial arrangements of the colony, had been derived either from sources of an extraordinary kind, the continuance of which could not be calculated upon, or from taxes which could not be maintained, and that thus, under these arrangements, the revenue from the close of 1845, had fallen so far short of the annual expenditure that the previous surplus had been absorbed, and there was a very large deficiency to be provided for when the Colonial Budget of the present year came under your consideration. The alterations, therefore, in the previous system of taxation which, with the concurrence of the Legislative Council you introduced, far from having been rash and uncalled-for, were dictated by the most imperious necessity.

3. Your Lordship is aware that in laying down the principles on which it appeared to me that the task of revising the financial arrangements of the colony should be undertaken by those on whom, as resident upon the spot and having the fullest information, I felt that the principal charge of performing it must devolve, I impressed upon you the plain and obvious policy of trusting for a restoration of the finances of the colony, not to any measures it might be in your power to adopt in order to obtain a larger

revenue, but, on the contrary, to the reductions of expenditure which must be affected in order to bring down its amount within that of the income on which you might fairly calculate. It was impossible for me to convey in language more emphatic than in the Despatch to which I have above referred, the injunctions of Her Majesty's Government that no practicable retrenchments should be spared until this paramount object was effected; and I am satisfied that these instructions will be acted upon by yourself and the principal officers of your Government, and by the Legislative Council, with the requisite union of vigour and of regard for existing rights and for the wants of the public service. It has not, therefore, been for the purpose of upholding an excessive amount of establishments that the new taxes in Ceylon have been approved, but they were sanctioned for the sake of the same object which led your Lordship to propose them, namely, the improvement of trade and encouragement of industry by the reduction of other taxes calculated to retard the progress of the colony.

4. The real question which, perhaps, would be found to lie at the bottom of any fair and impartial discussion of this subject, is a comparison between the merits of direct and indirect taxation, as the means of obtaining from the humbler and most numerous classes of the population the contributions towards the exigencies of the public service which in some form must be required from them. That in one shape or another these classes must contribute their share of the taxes, in order to afford that public revenue which is essential to the first objects of society, is a truth which I believe will not be denied. It has again and again been demonstrated that the largest fortunes in a community, even though they were entirely sacrificed, would prove but small, compared with the wants of the whole society. It is only by the aid of contributions which, whilst rendered as little burthensome and as equitable as possible, are yet, directly or indirectly, paid by those whose only income is derived from their labour, and who form the great majority of every community, that it is possible to derive an adequate public revenue. Assuming this point to be conceded, the only question can be, whether it is most for the advantage of the humbler classes, and for the good of society, that their contributions should be made directly or indirectly?

5. Now I believe that in this respect there is a great difference between European and Asiatic communities. In a more advanced

state of society, such as exists in our own country, the habits of even the humblest of the people are such that they pay their full share of the taxes imposed on articles of consumption, and it admits of doubt whether, owing to the competition for obtaining employment in a densely-peopled country, where there is no other resource to the poor man than labour for wages, some of those taxes which are apparently charged upon property do not really fall upon the labourers. In such a country it would neither be fair nor politic to subject them likewise to a taxation falling directly upon their own class. But in such countries as Ceylon the case is very different. The disposition of the natives is to be content with the subsistence which they can obtain, almost without labour, from a fertile soil; their climate renders very little clothing necessary; they purchase very few luxuries, or articles of importation; and they can rarely be induced to labour for hire, considering the indulgence of idleness preferable to any luxury which they could purchase by means of their industry.

6. By such a people comparatively little can be contributed to the Customs revenue, because their consumption is so limited, both in its nature and amount. Neither could taxes laid on any particular branch of industry, as, for instance, coffee planting, reach them, for they do not generally work for hire. Their habits, fortunately, are temperate, but for this very reason the revenue which can be derived from an excise upon liquors, or from licences for their sale, is necessarily limited in amount. It appears quite obvious, therefore, that either some direct impost must be laid upon them, or else that the great bulk of the population cannot be made to contribute such an amount to the public revenue as is absolutely necessary if those institutions and that machinery of government are to be kept up which are essential to the progress, and even to the maintenance of civilized society.

7. It is probably for some such reasons as these that, from the earliest ages of which we have a record, the people of India and of Ceylon have been subject to direct taxation in some shape or other, principally by requiring either gratuitous service or the contribution of a proportion of the produce of their labour from the cultivators of land. The methods adopted of imposing this burthen on the population may have been objectionable, and it is my own opinion that, both in India and under the native Governments in Ceylon, they were generally either extremely objectionable in

themselves or were much abused; but the practice of requiring direct contributions from the mass of the people appears to me to have arisen from a necessity, inherent in the character, circumstances, and habits of the people, which must continue equally to be felt by their present rulers. But, further, it appears to me to be a mistake to regard the imposition of direct taxation to a moderate amount, upon a population in such circumstances, as really injurious to them. I am persuaded that it may, on the contrary, be conducive to their true welfare. The view of this subject which I conceive to be erroneous has probably been adopted from applying to a very different state of society a judgment founded upon that to which we are accustomed in Europe. In all European countries the necessity of supplying their daily wants is, to the labouring classes, a sufficient motive to exertion; indeed, the difficulty which they experience in obtaining the means of comfortable subsistence is so great that it has generally been considered (as it always ought to be) the great object of the Governments of these countries, in their financial arrangements, to avoid aggravating this difficulty by the imposition of taxes calculated to enhance the cost of subsistence. But the case is very different in tropical climates, where the population is very scanty in proportion to the extent of territory; where the soil, as I have already observed, readily yields a subsistence in return for very little labour; and where clothing, fuel, and lodging, such as are there required, are obtained very easily. In such circumstances there can be but little motive to exertion to men satisfied with an abundant supply of their mere physical wants, and accordingly experience proves that it is the disposition of the races of men by which these countries are generally inhabited to sink into an easy and listless mode of life quite incompatible with the attainment of any high degree of civilization. But if it be admitted, as I think it must, that the real welfare of mankind consists, not alone in the enjoying an abundance of the necessaries of life, but in their being also placed in a situation favourable to their moral improvement, and to their advance in civilization, it follows that, in such countries as I have adverted to, it may be for the true interest of the working classes that the contributions demanded from them towards the wants of the State should somewhat increase the amount of exertion required for procuring a subsistence.

8. The greater progress which civilization has made in temperate

as compared to tropical climates, has always, and I believe justly, been attributed to the power with which necessity, which is proverbially the mother of invention, and the mainspring of human exertion, has operated in the former as compared to the latter; hence the obvious policy of giving additional force to this stimulus in those cases in which it is found to be deficient.

9. Nor is it to be lost sight of that while direct taxation is, in such circumstances, calculated to promote the progress of society, indirect taxation has the very opposite effect. To create and to foster a taste for the habits of civilized life in a rude population, it is requisite that they should have before them the example of civilized men, and that the gratification of the wants of civilized life should be rendered as easy to them as possible; but with this view imported articles should be rendered cheap, and those branches of trade and industry which require the direction of civilized and educated men, such as the production of sugar and coffee, should be encouraged. Hence the peculiar importance of avoiding the imposition of any taxes which can interfere with trade and the expediency of adopting the very opposite policy to that which would be proper in Europe, by endeavouring, in the imposition of taxes, to make them press, so far as prudence will admit, rather upon those who are content with a mere subsistence than upon the possessors of property and the purchasers of luxuries. I cannot forbear remarking that what is now taking place in the West Indian colonies, and the difficulties which are there experienced from the deficiency of adequate motives for industry, afford a striking illustration of the justice of the views I have thus explained to you.

10. I have dwelt longer on these general topics than I should otherwise have done, because I have been anxious to explain my reasons for believing that, quite independently of any immediate exigency in the affairs of Ceylon, there were wider and more permanent causes which rendered the kind of taxation you suggested the most natural and the best adapted to the country for which it was designed. It only remains for me now to say a few words on the question how far the particular measures themselves were well chosen and properly adapted to their purpose. . . .

I have, &c.,

(Signed)   GREY.

15. Louis Vignon on the Exploitation of Empire

Born in 1859, Louis Valéry Vignon belonged to the generation that came to maturity and prominence in the great age of imperialism that preceded the First World War. An economist by training, he occupied a succession of official posts in the French government at a professional rather than a political level. Most of his voluminous writings were concerned with the French Empire, especially with the economics of empire and the French role in North Africa.

The two selections translated below are from his book *L'exploitation de notre empire colonial* (Paris, 1900), pp. 56–60 and 146–151. Both illustrate the common belief that overseas conditions are such that economic policy there is exempt from the usual rules and practices of the metropolitan economy.

In labor policy, he held that the government was responsible for assuring a supply of labor that would be disciplined, cheap, and abundant enough to meet all French needs. Government intervention was also expected to secure capital for colonial development by granting privileges and monopolies to private firms. French capitalists may well have wanted this same combination of privilege and tight control over the working class at home, but they had little hope of getting it—and they rarely asked for it quite so blatantly as this.

Colonial Labor

OUR SUBJECT is so vast that we make no pretense of fully discussing any part of it. Nevertheless one cannot pass over the question of colonial labor in silence.

What will become of a colonist having land to clear or plant, forests or mines to exploit, if he lacks men?

It is therefore a duty of the administration to bestir itself to assure the colonists of the necessary workers, and this duty will be called upon from now on in all of our possessions with the exception of Algeria-Tunisia. The question is also complex. On one hand, in effect, labor can be supplied either by the inhabitants of the country themselves, or, if they are too few or incapable of regular work, by "immigrants" recruited elsewhere—in India, Java, or China—under set conditions and under agreements between the colonial administration and the exporting government. It is important, as well, in both cases that the labor be abundant enough to supply all existing needs, especially at seasonal peaks; susceptible enough to discipline for the colonists not to be at the mercy of caprice or demands which might compromise the outcome of their enterprise; cheap, so that employers will not find themselves at a disadvantage compared to competing countries.

One can sense the difficulties of the problem. Without going into detail, they can be briefly stated.

In Tonkin, while the population is numerous in the delta, it is, to the contrary, sparce in the highlands. Thus the capitalist who has received a concession of vacant lands situated in the mountainous region must negotiate with families on the lower Song Coi [Red River delta] to get them to follow him. To succeed, he needs the support of the local administrators. In Madagascar, General Gallieni has several times made wise-appearing decisions in regard to native labor contracts. Nevertheless he has not been able to satisfy the legitimate needs of the colonists. In black Africa, labor is generally scarce and defective. Over the centuries, slavery, wars, and massacres have depopulated immense regions. Thus the natives, being without wants, did not feel obliged to work. In the interior, they only kept up the cultivation that surrounded their villages, and that carelessly. On the coast, in contact with the Europeans, they devoted themselves to the export trade but neglected to work the soil. Therefore, even the ingenuity of the labor contractors and the high wages they agreed to were often not enough to keep the natives on the plantations, or at work in mine and forest. It is therefore proper that the colonists make sure of the good will of the village chiefs while at the same time the administrators intervene to facilitate the recruitment of the blacks, to assure their respect of contracts, and to prescribe penal sanctions if necessary.

In the Antilles, Guiana, Réunion, New Caledonia, and Tahiti, the planters and mine operators ceaselessly beg the local authorities for help in procuring the work they need. Another aspect of the problem arises in these colonies, different from the former group. Because the inhabitants either refuse to work regularly or are too few, the administration finds itself obliged to find labor abroad; that is, to recruit Indian, Chinese, Javanese, Annamite, or black "immigrants." The suppression of slavery in 1848 has posed a problem in our oldest colonies, which is not yet resolved. The blacks and mulattoes being unwilling to stay on the plantations after the act of emancipation, in order to save the whites from ruin, the imperial government had to conclude a convention with England in 1861, which authorized the French administration to recruit and sign contracts in India, with laborers for the Antilles, Réunion, and Guiana. But today that convention, without having been specifically ended, has no effect. Hindu recruitment is suspended, so that our colonies find themselves in a serious crisis. In Guiana, the plantations have disappeared, and there are not enough men at the placer workings. In the Antilles, the proprietors complain of the lack of workers. "If labor were not lacking," wrote the Chamber of Agriculture at Pointe-à-Pitre to the Minister, "the area of Guadeloupe under cultivation could be doubled."

Finally, in Réunion, the situation is the worst of all. The planters have the use of only 20,000 to 25,000 Indian coolies, while their neighbors on Mauritius have 150,000. In their inferior position, they lose part of their crops. Labor is so short that some days it is necessary to use convicts to load ships in the harbor. In the face of such problems, the government is asked daily in all four colonies either to negotiate with England to re-establish Indian immigration, to deal with the Dutch administration on Java, or else to recruit workers in Indo-China. Is it necessary to add that the colonists on New Caledonia and Tahiti also demand "immigrants" to work their lands and mines?

It is not necessary to insist further on the importance of the labor question to the colonies. It is manifest that here too the local administration and the central government have grave responsibilities. . . .

Colonial Capital

The colonial debt is not the only outlet which our overseas establishments offer to capitalists. Colonial bonds have, it is true, an advantage which will make them desirable to heads of families, and this is the fact that they assure a fixed return. But there are other enterprises which beg for brains and money, and, though promising only a variable return, may nevertheless give a greater profit. Companies in shipping, commerce, agriculture, plantations, industry, banks, the exploitation of mines and forests will little by little be asking for billions. The future of our colonial empire will depend on the number and prosperity of these firms, small, medium, and large.

It is not my intention to study in succession each form of metropolitan activity in the colonies. In the first part of this work, for that matter, the settlement of colonists in our different possessions was discussed—land grants, cultivation, experimental farms, and industry. Later on, the influence of customs regulations on the development of commerce will be taken up. But banks, and most of all the great commercial and development companies, have a special importance; they can only be founded with government aid; they must have grants of privilege or monopoly. For these reasons, they deserve our attention.

The Great Colonial Companies in This Century

Twenty years ago, it was allowed that the role of the great colonial companies in the world was finished. Most had liquidated their business, rather unhappily for that matter, in the last part of the eighteenth century. The last, the East India Company—"the old lady of London"—had disappeared in 1858. About 1880, it was thought that, at a time when public wealth had enormously increased, when steam navigation and electricity had greatly increased the ease and rapidity of communication, the free association of capitals under individual initiative would suffice for the economic development of distant lands. But the discovery of the interior of the African continent, where European commerce had heretofore exploited only the coasts, the seizure and partition of Oceania with widely scattered islands—these events soon brought about a modification of our ideas.

The chiefs of state in the sixteenth and seventeenth centuries, learning of the existence of America, the West Indies, the coasts of Africa, of India, Java, China, and Japan, and wishing to asure their countries of a share in the lands or commerce of the new regions, judged that such large and distant enterprises were beyond the strength of a few merchants and could only be conducted by powerful associations. They therefore favored the establishment of great companies for colonization, commerce, and even for conquest, to which, in order to attract the large capitals needed, they granted privileges and monopolies. The chiefs of state at the end of the nineteenth century, learning of the existence of lands ignored up to that point, of new worlds that could be acquired, where trade could be conducted, also judged that individual initiative, however bold and enterprising, was not sufficient for such a task. Thus it was that in the past twenty years England, Germany, the Congo state, and Portugal, beginning all over again, have created various kinds of privileged companies, which have been given orders, in a manner of speaking, to explore the new territories, conquer them, establish the first commercial relations, experiment with the first cultivation, and open the indispensable communications.

If the details, the tasks, the difficulties inherent in the system itself are set aside, this borrowing from the past has already brought about some valuable results. It was likely, furthermore, that this was a necessity.

In the old colonies like the Antilles, or countries significantly similar to Europe, such as Australia or Algeria, or even the great developing colonies, long open to the commerce and activity of the colonizing people, crisscrossed with arteries of communication, pacified, administered, like India or Java, the individual action of the farmer, the planter, or the merchant is easily conceivable. If companies with several hundreds of thousands of francs, or better still with several millions, have a greater chance for success in these countries (and they do everywhere), private individuals can still carry on many enterprises proportional to their capital and talents. On the other hand, individual action is too weak to take in hand the exploitation of an unknown country, almost inaccessible, located in the center of a continent whose shores themselves are inhospitable—regions as difficult to reach at the end of the nineteenth century as the Indies, China, or Japan were a century ago. Here a more powerful force is necessary, with a larger capital than individual enterprise can bring together.

But special difficulties immediately appear. In effect, it is a matter of raising a considerable capital—not 5,000,000 or 10,000,000 but 25, 50, 100, or more—the sum required for the fleets, the storehouses, the merchandise, the postal service, the miltia, and the personnel needed for an enterprise of a very special character. For the founders of such a powerful company to be able to promise the investors they are trying to attract that the enterprise, being well managed, will triumph over the foreseeable dangers and stumbling blocks and will pay dividends, it is not enough for them to show the calculations and the general probabilities that capitalists are usually content with in ordinary business. It is necessary for them to be able to give the shareholder assurance that the company in which he is about to invest his money will be the sole beneficiary from its initial establishment expenses—from the prospecting costs, in a manner of speaking—which is to say that they must offer guarantees for the future, after having first obtained them from the government. Without such precautions, it is possible that once the enterprise was under way a new company would spring up suddenly, taking advantage of the studies made by the first, profiting from its experience, from its work in taking over, and would set itself up alongside the first without great expense. Having thus to pay dividends on a much smaller capital than its predecessor, it would be able to buy dearer and sell cheaper and thus put the "discoverers" of the country in a position of being unable to regain their expenses and realize the profits they could legitimately expect.

These are the considerations—without neglecting political conditions, which must not be forgotten—which led governments to consent for the time being and under certain restrictions to grant special facilities, privileges, and partial monopolies to the capitalists joined together with an eye to the exploitation of those newly discovered worlds.

Besides, it can be seen that this procedure, this exception to the principle of free enterprise, is not as exceptional as it seems to certain people. When a state wants to build or open a railroad, when a city wants to assure itself of public transportation or the provision of water, gas, or electricity, it must promise various privileges to the companies who take on these expensive enterprises, in order to prevent competition and thus allow them to recover within a certain period of years the interest and the capital on the sums committed.

V

The "Civilizing Mission"

NOTHING IN the whole imperial effort had as great an impact on the world as the introduction of Western education. All of Africa and half of Asia are now ruled by élite groups who use Western languages for business and administration. However firm individual imperialists may have been in their belief that subject peoples could not and should not be converted to the Western way of life, it was essential in all empires to develop cadres of local people to carry out subordinate tasks of administration. This called for at least some education—enough to produce a literate class capable of staffing the lower ranks of the bureaucracy.

This need in turn raised a number of questions for decision. Education has a fundamental place in the formation of any society, and imperialist thought about education carried at least implicit concern for social goals. These goals were not always carefully watched when it came to educational planning; educational plans were not always carried out; and the results were not always those intended. Imperial thought about education is nevertheless one touchstone for examining what the imperialists thought they were doing.

Among the many problems to be solved was that of finance— what part of a limited colonial budget should go to education of any kind? This was followed by other questions. Should the government concentrate on educating the working class to be more useful? Or should it use the schools as a route of social mobility for the most intelligent? Should education follow the patterns of the local intellectual culture and tradition, or should it be entirely Western in concept and language of instruction? Should it be "industrial" or "literary"?

Nor was the "civilizing mission" entirely a matter of governmental effort. A large part of the educational establishment in Asian and African empires was actually in the hands of the missionary societies, and the missions' primary aim of religious conversion was itself a form of education. A body of mission theory therefore grew up alongside the educational theory, with a similar gap between intent and achievement. And the missions had special problems of their own, analogous to some of the political problems of empire. What was to happen, for example, when an overseas population had been converted to Christianity? Should it go its own way with its own ecclesiastical regime, or should it remain indefinitely under the tutelage of the mother church in Europe or America?

The range of problems in either the education or the mission field is too wide for a fully representative set of selections, but those that follow illustrate at least a few of the common imperialist views.

16. Thomas Babington Macaulay on Education for India

In spite of his greater reputation as author of a *History of England* and a career in English politics, Thomas Babington Macaulay (1800–59) also had a long-standing interest in the British Empire. His father, Zachary Macaulay, had been Governor of Sierra Leone, and he himself served as a member of the Supreme Council of India from 1834 to 1838. While he was in India, the Committee of Public Instruction was deeply divided over the government's policy of supporting education in Arabic and Sanskrit, and the issue was passed up to higher authority. On this occasion, Macaulay wrote his famous "Minute," an opinion for consideration by the Governor-General in Council, dated February 2, 1835, quoted here in full from H. Sharp (Ed.), *Selections from the Educational Records of the Government of India, Part I, 1781–1839* (Calcutta, 1920), pp. 107–117. Macaulay's conversionist views were accepted by Lord Bentinck, the Governor-General, and the issue was closed for the time being.

It was not closed in the long run, however, neither in India nor anywhere else in the non-Western world. The question of how much to preserve from the past, how much and what can be usefully borrowed from the West, is still widely debated. But this recent debate involves an internal decision for each non-Western society; Macaulay's judgment as an outsider has little relevance.

As it seems to be the opinion of some of the gentlemen who compose the Committee of Public Instruction that the course which they have hitherto pursued was strictly prescribed by the British Parliament in 1813 and as, if that opinion be correct, a legislative act will be necessary to warrant a change, I have thought it right to refrian from taking any part in the preparation of the adverse statements which are now before us, and to reserve what I had to say on the subject till it should come before me as a Member of the Council of India.

It does not appear to me that the Act of Parliament can by any art of construction be made to bear the meaning which has been assigned to it. It contains nothing about the particular languages or sciences which are to be studied. A sum is set apart "for the revival and promotion of literature, and the encouragement of the learned natives of India, and for the introduction and promotion of a knowledge of the sciences among the inhabitants of the British territories." It is argued, or rather taken for granted, that by literature the Parliament can have meant only Arabic and Sanscrit literature; that they never would have given the honourable appellation of "a learned native" to a native who was familiar with the poetry of Milton, the metaphysics of Locke, and the physics of Newton; but that they meant to designate by that name only such persons as might have studied in the sacred books of the Hindoos all the uses of cusa-grass, and all the mysteries of absorption into the Deity. This does not appear to be a very satisfactory interpretation. To take a parallel case: Suppose that the Pacha of Egypt, a country once superior in knowledge to the nations of Europe, but now sunk far below them, were to appropriate a sum for the purpose "of reviving and promoting literature, and encouraging learned natives of Egypt," would any body infer that he meant the youth of his Pachalik to give years to the study of hieroglyphics, to search into all the doctrines disguised under the fable of Osiris, and to ascertain with all possible accuracy the ritual with which cats and onions were anciently adored? Would he be justly charged with inconsistency if, instead of employing his young subjects in decyphering obelisks, he were to order them to be instructed in the English and French languages, and in all the sciences to which those languages are the chief keys?

The words on which the supporters of the old system rely do not bear them out, and other words follow which seem to be quite decisive on the other side. This lakh of rupees is set apart not only for "reviving literature in India," the phrase on which their whole interpretation is founded, but also "for the introduction and promotion of a knowledge of the sciences among the inhabitants of the British territories"—words which are alone sufficient to authorise all the changes for which I contend.

If the Council agree in my construction, no legislative act will be necessary. If they differ from me, I will propose a short act rescinding that clause of the Charter of 1813 from which the difficulty arises.

The argument which I have been considering affects only the form of proceeding. But the admirers of the oriental system of education have used another argument, which, if we admit it to be valid, is decisive against all change. They conceive that the public faith is pledged to the present system, and that to alter the appropriation of any of the funds which have hitherto been spent in encouraging the study of Arabic and Sanscrit would be downright spoliation. It is not easy to understand by what process of reasoning they can have arrived at this conclusion. The grants which are made from the public purse for the encouragement of literature differ in no respect from the grants which are made from the same purse for other objects of real or supposed utility. We found a sanitarium on a spot which we suppose to be healthy. Do we thereby pledge ourselves to keep a sanitarium there if the result should not answer our expectations? We commence the erection of a pier. Is it a violation of the public faith to stop the works, if we afterwards see reason to believe that the building will be useless? The rights of property are undoubtedly sacred. But nothing endangers those rights so much as the practice, now unhappily too common, of attributing them to things to which they do not belong. Those who would impart to abuses the sanctity of property are in truth imparting to the institution of property the unpopularity and the fragility of abuses. If the Government has given to any person a formal assurance—nay, if the Government has excited in any person's mind a reasonable expectation—that he shall receive a certain income as a teacher or a learner of Sanscrit or Arabic, I would respect that person's pecuniary interests. I would rather err on the side of liberality to individuals than suffer the public faith to be called in question. But to talk of a Government pledging itself to teach certain languages and certain sciences, though those languages may become useless, though those sciences may be exploded, seems to me quite unmeaning. There is not a single word in any public instrument from which it can be inferred that the Indian Government ever intended to give any pledge on this subject, or ever considered the destination of these funds as unalterably fixed. But, had it been otherwise, I should have denied the competence of our predecessors to bind us by any pledge on such a subject. Suppose that a Government had in the last century enacted in the most solemn manner that all its subjects should, to the end of time, be inoculated for the small pox, would that Government be bound to persist in the practice after Jenner's discovery? These promises of which nobody claims the performance, and from which nobody can grant a release, these vested rights which vest in nobody, this property without proprietors, this robbery which makes nobody poorer, may be comprehended by persons of higher faculties than mine. I consider this plea merely as a set form of words, regularly used both in England and in India, in defence of every abuse for which no other plea can be set up.

I hold this lakh of rupees to be quite at the disposal of the Governor-General in Council for the purpose of promoting learning in India in any way which may be thought most advisable. I hold his Lordship to be quite as free to direct that it shall no longer be employed in encouraging Arabic and Sanscrit, as he is to direct that the reward for killing tigers in Mysore shall be diminished, or that no more public money shall be expended on the chaunting at the cathedral.

We now come to the gist of the matter. We have a fund to be employed as Government shall direct for the intellectual improvement of the people of this country. The simple question is, what is the most useful way of employing it?

All parties seem to be agreed on one point, that the dialects commonly spoken among the natives of this part of India contain neither literary nor scientific information, and are moreover so poor and rude that, until they are enriched from some other quarter, it will not be easy to translate any valuable work into them. It seems to be admitted on all sides, that the intellectual improvement of those classes of the people who have the means of pursuing higher studies can at present be effected only by means of some language not vernacular amongst them.

What then shall that language be? One-half of the committee

maintain that it should be the English. The other half strongly recommend the Arabic and Sanscrit. The whole question seems to me to be—which language is the best worth knowing?

I have no knowledge of either Sanscrit or Arabic. But I have done what I could to form a correct estimate of their value. I have read translations of the most celebrated Arabic and Sanscrit works. I have conversed, both here and at home, with men distinguished by their proficiency in the Eastern tongues. I am quite ready to take the oriental learning at the valuation of the orientalists themselves. I have never found one among them who could deny that a single shelf of a good European library was worth the whole native literature of India and Arabia. The intrinsic superiority of the Western literature is indeed fully admitted by those members of the committee who support the oriental plan of education.

It will hardly be disputed, I suppose, that the department of literature in which the Eastern writers stand highest is poetry. And I certainly never met with any orientalist who ventured to maintain that the Arabic and Sanscrit poetry could be compared to that of the great European nations. But when we pass from works of imagination to works in which facts are recorded and general principles investigated, the superiority of the Europeans becomes absolutely immeasureable. It is, I believe, no exaggeration to say that all the historical information which has been collected from all the books written in the Sanscrit language is less valuable than what may be found in the most paltry abridgments used at preparatory schools in England. In every branch of physical or moral philosophy, the relative position of the two nations is nearly the same.

How then stands the case? We have to educate a people who cannot at present be educated by means of their mother-tongue. We must teach them some foreign language. The claims of our own language it is hardly necessary to recapitulate. It stands pre-eminent even among the languages of the West. It abounds with works of imagination not inferior to the noblest which Greece has bequeathed to us—with models of every species of eloquence,—with historical compositions which, considered merely as narratives, have seldom been surpassed, and which, considered as vehicles of ethical and political instruction, have never been equalled, —with just and lively representations of human life and human nature,—with the most profound speculations on metaphysics, morals, government, jurisprudence, trade,—with full and correct information respecting every experimental science which tends to preserve the health, to increase the comfort, or to expand the intellect of man. Whoever knows that language has ready access to all the vast intellectual wealth which all the wisest nations of the earth have created and hoarded in the course of ninety generations. It may safely be said that the literature now extant in that language is of greater value than all the literature which three hundred years ago was extant in all the languages of the world together. Nor is this all. In India, English is the language spoken by the ruling class. It is spoken by the higher class of natives at the seats of Government. It is likely to become the language of commerce throughout the seas of the East. It is the language of two great European communities which are rising, the one in the south of Africa, the other in Australasia,—communities which are every year becoming more important and more closely connected with our Indian empire. Whether we look at the intrinsic value of our literature, or at the particular situation of this country, we shall see the strongest reason to think that, of all foreign tongues, the English tongue is that which would be the most useful to our native subjects.

The question now before us is simply whether, when it is in our power to teach this language, we shall teach languages in which, by universal confession, there are no books on any subject which deserve to be compared to our own, whether, when we can teach European science, we shall teach systems which, by universal confession, wherever they differ from those of Europe differ for the worse, and whether, when we can patronize sound philosophy and true history, we shall countenance, at the public expense, medical doctrines which would disgrace an English farrier, astronomy which would move laughter in girls at an English boarding school, history abounding with kings thirty feet high and reigns thirty thousand years long, and geography made of seas of treacle and seas of butter.

We are not without experience to guide us. History furnishes several analogous cases, and they all teach the same lesson. There are, in modern times, to go no further, two memorable instances of a great impulse given to the mind of a whole society, of prejudices overthrown, of knowledge diffused, of taste purified, of arts and sciences planted in countries which had recently been ignorant and barbarous.

The first instance to which I refer is the great revival of letters among the Western nations at the close of the fifteenth and the beginning of the sixteenth century. At that time almost everything that was worth reading was contained in the writings of the ancient Greeks and Romans. Had our ancestors acted as the Committee of Public Instruction has hitherto acted,—had they neglected the language of Thucydides and Plato, and the language of Cicero and Tacitus, had they confined their attention to the old dialects of our own island, had they printed nothing and taught nothing at the universities but chronicles in Anglo-Saxon and romances in Norman French,—would England ever have been what she now is? What the Greek and Latin were to the contemporaries of More and Ascham, our tongue is to the people of India. The literature of England is now more valuable than that of classical antiquity. I doubt whether the Sanscrit literature be as valuable as that of our Saxon and Norman progenitors. In some departments—in history for example—I am certain that it is much less so.

Another instance may be said to be still before our eyes. Within the last hundred and twenty years, a nation which had previously been in a state as barbarous as that in which our ancestors were before the Crusades has gradually emerged from the ignorance in which it was sunk, and has taken its place among civilised communities. I speak of Russia. There is now in that country a large educated class abounding with persons fit to serve the State in the highest functions, and in nowise inferior to the most accomplished men who adorn the best circles of Paris and London. There is reason to hope that this vast empire which, in the time of our grandfathers, was probably behind the Punjab, may in the time of our grand-children, be pressing close on France and Britain in the career of improvement. And how was this change effected? Not by flattering national prejudices; not by feeding the mind of the young Muscovite with the old women's stories which his rude fathers had believed; not by filling his head with lying legends about St. Nicholas; not by encouraging him to study the great question, whether the world was or not created on the 13th of September; not by calling him "a learned native" when he had mastered all these points of knowledge; but by teaching him those foreign languages in which the greatest mass of information had been laid up, and thus putting all that information within his reach. The languages of western Europe civilised Russia. I cannot doubt that they will do for the Hindoo what they have done for the Tartar.

And what are the arguments against that course which seems to be alike recommended by theory and by experience? It is said that we ought to secure the co-operation of the native public, and that we can do this only by teaching Sanscrit and Arabic.

I can by no means admit that, when a nation of high intellectual attainments undertakes to superintend the education of a nation comparatively ignorant, the learners are absolutely to prescribe the course which is to be taken by the teachers. It is not necessary however to say anything on this subject. For it is proved by unanswerable evidence, that we are not at present securing the co-operation of the natives. It would be bad enough to consult their intellectual taste at the expense of their intellectual health. But we are consulting neither. We are withholding from them the learning which is palatable to them. We are forcing on them the mock learning which they nauseate.

This is proved by the fact that we are forced to pay our Arabic and Sanscrit students while those who learn English are willing to pay us. All the declamations in the world about the love and reverence of the natives for their sacred dialects will never, in the mind of any impartial person, outweigh this undisputed fact, that we cannot find in all our vast empire a single student who will let us teach him those dialects, unless we will pay him.

I have now before me the accounts of the Mudrassa for one month, the month of December, 1833. The Arabic students appear to have been seventy-seven in number. All receive stipends from the public. The whole amount paid to them is above 500 rupees a month. On the other side of the account stands the following item:

Deduct amount realized from the out-students of English for the months of May, June, and July last—103 rupees.

I have been told that it is merely from want of local experience that I am surprised at these phoenomena, and that it is not the fashion for students in India to study at their own charges. This only confirms me in my opinions. Nothing is more certain than that it never can in any part of the world be necessary to pay men for doing what they think pleasant or profitable. India is no exception to this rule. The people of India do not require to be paid for

eating rice when they are hungry, or for wearing woollen cloth in
the cold season. To come nearer to the case before us:— The
children who learn their letters and a little elementary arithmetic
from the village schoolmaster are not paid by him. He is paid for
teaching them. Why then is it necessary to pay people to learn
Sanscrit and Arabic? Evidently because it is universally felt that
the Sanscrit and Arabic are languages the knowledge of which does
not compensate for the trouble of acquiring them. On all such
subjects the state of the market is the decisive test.

Other evidence is not wanting, if other evidence were required.
A petition was presented last year to the committee by several ex-
students of the Sanscrit College.. The petitioners stated that they
had studied in the college ten or twelve years, that they had made
themselves acquainted with Hindoo literature and science, that
they had received certificates of proficiency. And what is the fruit
of all this? "Notwithstanding such testimonials," they say, "we
have but little prospect of bettering our condition without the kind
assistance of your honourable committee, the indifference with
which we are generally looked upon by our countrymen leaving
no hope of encouragement and assistance from them." They therefore beg that they may be recommended to the Governor-General
for places under the Government—not places of high dignity or
emolument, but such as may just enable them to exist. "We want
means," they say, "for a decent living, and for our progressive
improvement, which, however, we cannot obtain without the
assistance of Government, by whom we have been educated and
maintained from childhood." They conclude by representing very
pathetically that they are sure that it was never the intention of
Government, after behaving so liberally to them during their
education, to abandon them to destitution and neglect.

I have been used to see petitions to Government for compensation. All those petitions, even the most unreasonable of them,
proceeded on the supposition that some loss had been sustained,
that some wrong had been inflicted. These are surely the first
petitioners who ever demanded compensation for having been
educated gratis, for having been supported by the public during
twelve years, and then sent forth into the world well furnished
with literature and science. They represent their education as an
injury which gives them a claim on the Government for redress, as
an injury for which the stipends paid to them during the infliction

were a very inadequate compensation. And I doubt not that they are in the right. They have wasted the best years of life in learning what procures for them neither bread nor respect. Surely we might with advantage have saved the cost of making these persons useless and miserable. Surely, men may be brought up to be burdens to the public and objects of contempt to their neighbours at a somewhat smaller charge to the State. But such is our policy. We do not even stand neuter in the contest between truth and falsehood. We are not content to leave the natives to the influence of their own hereditary prejudices. To the natural difficulties which obstruct the progress of sound science in the East, we add great difficulties of our own making. Bounties and premiums, such as ought not to be given even for the propagation of truth, we lavish on false texts and false philosophy.

By acting thus we create the very evil which we fear. We are making that opposition which we do not find. What we spend on the Arabic and Sanscrit Colleges is not merely a dead loss to the cause of truth. It is bounty-money paid to raise up champions of error. It goes to form a nest not merely of helpless place-hunters but of bigots prompted alike by passion and by interest to raise a cry against every useful scheme of education. If there should be any opposition among the natives to the change which I recommend, that opposition will be the effect of our own system. It will be headed by persons supported by our stipends and trained in our colleges. The longer we persevere in our present course, the more formidable will that opposition be. It will be every year reinforced by recruits whom we are paying. From the native society, left to itself, we have no difficulties to apprehend. All the murmuring will come from that oriental interest which we have, by artificial means, called into being and nursed into strength.

There is yet another fact which is alone sufficient to prove that the feeling of the native public, when left to itself, is not such as the supporters of the old system represent it to be. The committee have thought fit to lay out above a lakh of rupees in printing Arabic and Sanscrit books. Those books find no purchasers. It is very rarely that a single copy is disposed of. Twenty-three thousand volumes, most of them folios and quartos, fill the libraries or rather the lumber-rooms of this body. The committee contrive to get rid of some portion of their vast stock of oriental literature by giving books away. But they cannot give so fast as they print.

About twenty thousand rupees a year are spent in adding fresh masses of waste paper to a hoard which, one should think, is already sufficiently ample. During the last three years about sixty thousand rupees have been expended in this manner. The sale of Arabic and Sanscric books during those three years has not yielded quite one thousand rupees. In the meantime, the School Book Society is selling seven or eight thousand English volumes every year, and not only pays the expenses of printing but realizes a profit of twenty per cent. on its outlay.

The fact that the Hindoo law is to be learned chiefly from Sanscrit books, and the Mahometan law from Arabic books, has been much insisted on, but seems not to bear at all on the question. We are commanded by Parliament to ascertain and digest the laws of India. The assistance of a Law Commission has been given to us for that purpose. As soon as the Code is promulgated the Shasters and the Hedaya will be useless to a moonsiff or a Sudder Ameen. I hope and trust that, before the boys who are now entering at the Mudrassa and the Sanscrit College have completed their studies, this great work will be finished. It would be manifestly absurd to educate the rising generation with a view to a state of things which we mean to alter before they reach manhood.

But there is yet another argument which seems even more untenable. It is said that the Sanscrit and the Arabic are the languages in which the sacred books of a hundred millions of people are written, and that they are on that account entitled to peculiar encouragement. Assuredly it is the duty of the British Government in India to be not only tolerant but neutral on all religious questions. But to encourage the study of a literature, admitted to be of small intrinsic value, only because that literature inculcates the most serious errors on the most important subjects, is a course hardly reconcilable with reason, with morality, or even with that very neutrality which ought, as we all agree, to be sacredly preserved. It is confessed that a language is barren of useful knowledge. We are to teach it because it is fruitful of monstrous superstitions. We are to teach false history, false astronomy, false medicine, because we find them in company with a false religion. We abstain, and I trust shall always abstain, from giving any public encouragement to those who are engaged in the work of converting the natives to Christianity. And while we act thus, can we reasonably or decently bribe men, out of the revenues of the State, to waste their youth in learning how they are to purify themselves after touching an ass or what texts of the Vedas they are to repeat to expiate the crime of killing a goat?

It is taken for granted by the advocates of oriental learning that no native of this country can possibly attain more than a mere smattering of English. They do not attempt to prove this. But they perpetually insinuate it. They designate the education which their opponents recommend as a mere spelling-book education. They assume it as undeniable that the question is between a profound knowledge of Hindoo and Arabian literature and science on the one side, and superficial knowledge of the rudiments of English on the other. This is not merely an assumption, but an assumption contrary to all reason and experience. We know that foreigners of all nations do learn our language sufficiently to have access to all the most abstruse knowledge which it contains sufficiently to relish even the more delicate graces of our most idiomatic writers. There are in this very town natives who are quite competent to discuss political or scientific questions with fluency and precision in the English language. I have heard the very question on which I am now writing discussed by native gentlemen with a liberality and an intelligence which would do credit to any member of the Committee of Public Instruction. Indeed it is unusual to find, even in the literary circles of the Continent, any foreigner who can express himself in English with so much facility and correctness as we find in many Hindoos. Nobody, I suppose, will contend that English is so difficult to a Hindoo as Greek to an Englishman. Yet an intelligent English youth, in a much smaller number of years than our unfortunate pupils pass at the Sanscrit College, becomes able to read, to enjoy, and even to imitate not unhappily the compositions of the best Greek authors. Less than half the time which enables an English youth to read Herodotus and Sophocles ought to enable a Hindoo to read Hume and Milton.

To sum up what I have said. I think it clear that we are not fettered by the Act of Parliament of 1813, that we are not fettered by any pledge expressed or implied, that we are free to employ our funds as we choose, that we ought to employ them in teaching what is best worth knowing, that English is better worth knowing than Sanscrit or Arabic, that the natives are desirous to be taught English, and are not desirous to be taught Sanscrit or Arabic, that neither as the languages of law nor as the languages of religion have the Sanscrit and Arabic any peculiar claim to our encouragement, that it is possible to make natives of this country thoroughly good English scholars, and that to this end our efforts ought to be directed.

In one point I fully agree with the gentlemen to whose general views I am opposed. I feel with them that it is impossible for us, with our limited means, to attempt to educate the body of the people. We must at present do our best to form a class who may be interpreters between us and the millions whom we govern—a class of persons Indian in blood and colour, but English in tastes, in opinions, in morals and in intellect. To that class we may leave it to refine the vernacular dialects of the country, to enrich those dialects with terms of science borrowed from the Western nomenclature, and to render them by degrees fit vehicles for conveying knowledge to the great mass of the population.

I would strictly respect all existing interests. I would deal even generously with all individuals who have had fair reason to expect a pecuniary provision. But I would strike at the root of the bad system which has hitherto been fostered by us. I would at once stop the printing of Arabic and Sanscrit books. I would abolish the Mudrassa and the Sanscrit College at Calcutta. Benares is the great seat of Brahminical learning; Delhi of Arabic learning. If we retain the Sanscrit College at Benares and the Mahometan College at Delhi we do enough, and much more than enough in my opinion, for the Eastern languages. If the Benares and Delhi Colleges should be retained, I would at least recommend that no stipends shall be given to any students who may hereafter repair thither, but that the people shall be left to make their own choice between the rival systems of education without being bribed by us to learn what they have no desire to know. The funds which would thus be placed at our disposal would enable us to give larger encouragement to the Hindoo College at Calcutta, and establish in the principal cities throughout the Presidencies of Fort William and Agra schools in which the English language might be well and thoroughly taught.

If the decision of His Lordship in Council should be such as I anticipate, I shall enter on the performance of my duties with the greatest zeal and alacrity. If, on the other hand, it be the opinion of the Government that the present system ought to remain unchanged, I beg that I may be permitted to retire from the chair of the committee. I feel that I could not be of the smallest use there. I feel also that I should be lending my countenance to what I firmly believe to be a mere delusion. I believe that the present system tends not to accelerate the progress of truth but to delay the natural death of expiring errors. I conceive that we have at present no right to the respectable name of a Board of Public Instruction. We are a Board for wasting the public money, for printing books which are of less value than the paper on which they are printed was while it was blank—for giving artificial encouragement to absurd history, absurd metaphysics, absurd physics, absurd theology—for raising up a breed of scholars who find their scholarship an incumbrance and blemish, who live on the public while they are receiving their education, and whose education is so utterly useless to them that, when they have received it, they must either starve or live on the public all the rest of their lives. Entertaining these opinions, I am naturally desirous to decline all share in the responsibility of a body which, unless it alters its whole mode of proceedings, I must consider, not merely as useless, but as positively noxious.

2nd February 1835.

T. B. MACAULAY.

I give my entire concurrence to the sentiments expressed in this Minute.

W. C. BENTINCK.

17. The British Privy Council Considers Negro Education

During the 1840's, a good deal of attention in British imperial circles turned to the West Indies, formerly the most valuable of all overseas colonies but then passing through a period of social and economic crisis following the emancipation of the slaves in 1838—a crisis made still deeper by the technological obsolescence of outmoded British plantations in contrast to the new establishments in Cuba. The problem of choosing an appropriate form of education for children of the former slaves was referred to the Privy Council's Committee on Education. Its recommendations were just as conversionist as Macaulay's Minute, with no suggestion that the West Indians had a culture worth preserving. But neither was there a suggestion that West Indian children might profit from reading the great works of English literature and science. The aim was strictly that of creating a docile and semi-skilled working class, through an educational system heavily biased toward "industrial education." The report was entitled "Brief Practical Suggestions on the Mode of Organizing and Conducting Day-Schools of Industry, Model Farm-Schools, and Normal Schools, as Part of a System of Education for the Coloured Races of the British Colonies," and was dated January 6, 1847. It is quoted here from Parliamentary Sessional Papers, 1847, xlv, [787], pp. 30–37.

Privy Council Office, Whitehall, January 6, 1847.

SIR,

THE letter which, by the direction of Earl Grey, was transmitted to this office on the 30th of November, together with the despatches from Governors of the West Indian Colonies which accompanied it, have been under the consideration of the Lord President of the Council.

Under his Lordship's directions a short and simple account is now submitted of the mode in which the Committee of Council on Education consider that Industrial Schools for the coloured races may be conducted in the Colonies, so as to combine intellectual and industrial education, and to render the labour of the children available towards meeting some part of the expense of their education.

From this account will be purposely excluded any description of *the methods* of intellectual instruction, and all minute details of the organization of schools. Whatever suggestions respecting discipline may be offered will be condensed into brief hints, or confined to those general indications which are universally applicable.

It would be presumptuous to attempt to describe those varieties in discipline which might be suggested by a better knowledge of the peculiarities of a race which readily abandons itself to excitement, and perhaps needs amusements which would seem unsuitable for the peasantry of a civilized community.

While endeavouring to suggest the mode by which the labour of negro children may be mingled with instruction fitted to develop their intelligence, it would be advantageous to know more of the details of Colonial culture, and of the peculiarities of household life in this class, and thus to descend from the general description into a closer adaptation of the plans of the school to the wants of the coloured races. This, however, cannot now be attempted.

In describing the mode in which the instruction may be interwoven with the labour of the school, so as to render the connection as intimate as possible, it will however be necessary to repeat the illustrations in various forms, which may appear trivial. But this mutual dependence of the moral and physical training, of the intellectual and industrial teaching, and even of the religious education and the instruction of the scholars in the practical duties of life, requires a detailed illustration. Christian civilization comprehends this complex development of all the faculties, and the school of a semi-barbarous class should be established on the conviction that these several forms of training and instruction mutually assist each other.

Instead of setting forth this principle more fully, it is considered expedient to furnish numerous though brief practical details of its application, which may with local knowledge be easily expanded into a manual for schools of industry for the coloured races.

Even within the limits which will be assigned to the instruction of the children of these races in this paper, it may be conceived that, bearing in mind the present state of the negro population, and taking into account the means at present at the disposal of the Colonial legislatures in the different dependencies, a too sanguine view has been adopted of the amount of instruction which may be hoped to be imparted.

Certainly it is true that some time must elapse before the limits assigned in this paper to such instruction, even in the day-schools, can be reached; but less, that what is described could not be regarded as a transforming agency, by which the negro could be led, within a generation, materially to improve his habits. If we would have him rest satisfied with the meagre subsistence and privation of comfort consequent on his habits of listless contentment with the almost spontaneous gifts of a tropical climate, a less efficient system may be adopted; but if the native labour of the West Indian Colonies is to be made generally available for the cultivation of the soil by a settled and industrious peasantry, no agent can be so surely depended upon as the influence of a system of combined intellectual and industrial instruction, carried to a higher degree of efficiency than any example which now exists in the Colonies.

Nor will a wise Colonial Government neglect any means which affords even a remote prospect of gradually creating a native middle class among the negro population, and thus, ultimately, of completing the institutions of freedom, by rearing a body of men interested in the protection of property, and with intelligence enough to take part in that humbler machinery of local affairs which ministers to social order.

With these remarks, I proceed at once to enter on the practical suggestions which I am directed to offer.

The objects of education for the coloured races of the Colonial dependencies of Great Britain may be thus described: —

To inculcate the principles and promote the influences of Christianity, by such instruction as can be given in elementary schools.

To accustom the children of these races to habits of self-control and moral discipline.

To diffuse a grammatical knowledge of the English language, as the most important agent of civilization for the coloured population of the Colonies.

To make the school the means of improving the condition of the peasantry, by teaching them how health may be preserved by proper diet, cleanliness, ventilation, and clothing, and by the structure of their dwellings.

To give them a practical training in household economy, and in the cultivation of a cottage garden, as well as in those common handicrafts by which a labourer may improve his domestic comfort.

To communicate such a knowledge of writing and arithmetic, and of their application to his wants and duties, as may enable a peasant to economize his means, and give the small farmer the power to enter into calculations and agreements.

An improved agriculture is required in certain of the Colonies to replace the system of exhausting the virgin soils, and then leaving to natural influences alone the work of reparation. The education of the coloured races would not, therefore, be complete for the children of small farmers unless it included this object.

The lesson-books of Colonial schools should also teach the mutual interests of the mother-country and her dependencies; the rational basis of their connection, and the domestic and social duties of the coloured races.

These lesson-books should also simply set forth the relation of wages, capital, labour, and the influence of local and general government on personal security, independence, and order.

For the attainment of these objects, the following classes of institutions are required.

Day-schools of industry and model farm-schools.

A training-school for the instruction of the masters and mistresses of day-schools.

The order in which these institutions are enumerated is that in which they may be most conveniently described.

A day-school of industry might, in the tropical climates, with the exception of a mode-rate salary for the schoolmaster, be made self-supporting. The school should be regarded as a large Christian family, assembled for mutual benefit, and conducted by a well-ordered domestic economy.

For this purpose, the children, having breakfasted, should be at school at a very early period after sunrise.

At this hour they should be assembled for morning prayer. The utmost reverence should pervade this religious exercise.

The work of the day would then commence. The scholars would have their dinner at the school, and in the evening would return to their homes immediately before sunset. The school would close, as it began, with prayer.

From sunrise until sunset their life would be under the training and instruction of the master and mistress of the school. Their labour would be principally devoted to the business of the household and of the school-garden. Their instruction would be such as would prepare them for the duties of their station in life.

To this end the school premises should comprise—

1. A house for the master and for the mistress.
2. A school-room for the boys, and another for the girls, each convertible into a dining-room.
3. A class-room for undisturbed religious instruction.
4. A large garden-plot, sufficient to provide garden-stuff for the dinners of the school during the whole year.
5. A tool-house and carpenter's shop.
6. A kitchen, store-room, larder, and scullery.
7. A wash-house and laundry.

The training of the scholars in industry and in cottage economy would, under these arrangements, be regarded as second only to their instruction from the Holy Scriptures, and their training in the duties of a religious life.

In a race emerging from barbarism, the training of children in obedience and cheerful industry, in mutual forbearance and good will, and in that respect for property and care to use the blessings of Providence without abusing them, for which a school of industry affords an opportunity closely resembling the training of children in a Christian family, would greatly promote the success of the religious instruction.

Immediately after prayers the master would divide the boys into working parties under the charge of apprenticed monitors or pupil-teachers. The schedule of the school routine would describe the duty of each party, and the time allotted to it.

The garden should be divided into two principal plots. The school-plot should be cultivated by the whole school, in common, for the production of all those vegetables which would be required in considerable quantities for the school-kitchen.

These crops should be so adapted to the seasons as to afford a constant supply, either in store or to be daily gathered from the ground.

In the labour and practical instruction of the garden they would learn the theory and practice of its culture, and the use of the crops of the different seasons in supplying the wants of a family.

The scholars' plot should be divided into allotments proportioned to the strength of the scholars. The sense of personal interest and responsibility would here be developed, and the pupil would cultivate habits of self-reliance, neatness, and perseverance.

In the large school-plot the combination of individual efforts for a common object, and the advantages of order, method, harmony, and subordination, would be exemplified.

For the management of the garden two or three parties could therefore be detached, according to the work appropriated to the season.

The repairs of the tool-house and of the implements of gardening, as well as the fencing of the garden, would sometimes employ a party in the carpenter's shop.

In the Colonies in which the slave population has recently been emancipated, and in those very recently settled, it might also be desirable to have at hand, as a part of the school stock, a quantity of the rough material of which labourers' dwellings are constructed. With this material a cottage might be built on an improved plan, with a due regard to ventilation, to drainage, to the means provided for the escape of smoke, to the nature of the floor, the provision of rude but substantial furniture, and the most healthy bedding, together with the out-buildings required for domestic animals and the family.

Such a cottage, when built, might be again altered, enlarged, or pulled down and rebuilt, as a part of the industrial instruction, important in its civilizing influences.

The master would superintend, direct, and explain the garden operations.

While in the field or workshed, he would have an opportunity of improving the manners and habits of his scholars, not by the rigidity of a military discipline, exacting an enforced order, but by the cheerful acquiescence of a sense of duty and convenience arising from his patient superintendence. The harmony, industry, and skill of his scholars should be promoted by his vigilance, and encouraged by his example.

The garden operations of the month would form a subject of oral instruction in the school.

In these oral lessons would be explained the reasons for the succession of crops; for the breadth sown; for the nature of the manure selected; for the mode of managing the crop; and the uses to which it was to be devoted.

The accidents to which the crop is liable, and the means of providing against them, might even lead the teacher into a familiar account of the habits of various insects; their mode of propagation; the peculiarities of season which favour their development; and the mode of detecting and destroying them, before their ravages are extensively injurious or fatal to the crop.

Familiar lessons on the effects of night and day, of heat and light, of dew and rain, of drainage and irrigation, and the various kinds of manure, and of the succession of the seasons on vegetation, would not only inform the minds of the scholars, but give them a more intelligent interest in the common events of the natural world.

In the school also would be kept an account of the expenses incurred on the garden. To this end the reception of all articles on which outlay had been incurred—as, for example, tools, manure, wood, seeds, &c.—should be attended with some formality; and the boys should be practised in examining or weighing them, and entering them in the account. In like manner the garden produce should be weighed before delivered at the kitchen, and an account kept of the quantity gathered daily, and of its market value.

The objects of outlay and the results of labour should be brought into one balance-sheet, showing the profits of the garden at the close of the year.

As a preparation for this general account-keeping, each boy might also enter, in a subordinate account, the outlay and produce of his own allotment.

In both cases the amount of labour should be daily registered, and its value fixed, as an element to be ultimately entered in the balance-sheet.

Once or twice in the week the girls and boys would bring from home early in the morning a bundle of clothes to be washed at the school.

The wash-house should be fitted up with the utensils commonly found in the best labourers' cottages, or which, with frugality and industry, could be purchased by a field-workman; and the girls should be employed in successive parties in washing, drying, and ironing their clothes.

They should likewise bring from home clothes requiring to be mended, and cloth to be made into shirts and dresses for their families, and the mistress should teach them to cut it out, and make it up, and to mend their clothes.

The employments of the girls would co-operate with those of the boys as respects instruction in cottage economy, by the connection of the garden with the kitchen.

In the kitchen, the vegetables received from the garden would be prepared for cooking, and the girls would be instructed in the preparation of the cheap food which a labourer could afford to purchase, or could grow in his own garden.

For the sake of convenience and despatch, a large part of this cooking must be conducted in a wholesale manner for the school dinner, but, in order to give instruction in the preparation of a cottage meal, a separate dinner should daily be provided for the superintendents of working parties. This should be cooked with the utensils commonly found in cottages.

The employments of the girls should be accompanied by suitable instruction in the school. Thus an account should be kept of the clothes received from each scholar's family to be washed, and of their return to the boy or girl by whom they were brought.

The amount of garden-stuff and stores daily consumed in the school dinner should be entered, and the value estimated.

The purchase of utensils, stores, &c., should be recorded by the scholars.

Among the topics of oral instruction, cottage economy should be second only to religious instruction. The duties of a skilful housewife would be exemplified in the training in industry, but these practical arts should be accompanied with familiar lessons on the best mode of husbanding the means of the family, on the prices and comparative nutritious qualities of various articles of food; and on simple recipes for preparing them. Each girl should write in a book, to be taken with her from the school, the recipes of the cottage meals she had learned to prepare; and the familiar maxims of domestic economy which had been inculcated at school.

Such instruction might profitably extend to domestic and personal cleanliness, the management of children in infancy, and general rules as to the preservation of health.

On the subject of cottage economy, it would be well that a class-book should be prepared, containing at least the following heads: —

1. *Means of preserving Health*
A. Cleanliness.   B. Ventilation.   C. Drainage.   D. Clothing.
E. Exercise.   F. Management of children.
2. *Means of procuring Comfort.*
A. The cottage garden.   B. The piggery.   C. The cottage kitchen.   D. The dairy.   E. The market.   F. Household maxims.

The various industrial employment of the scholars would curtail the ordinary hours of school. Certainly, all that has been described might be accomplished, and at least two or three hours daily reserved for religious and other instruction.

The Holy Scriptures should be used only as a medium of religious teaching. They should not be employed as a hornbook, associated in the mind of the child with the drudgery of mastering the almost mechanical difficulty of learning to read, at an age when it cannot understand language too often left unexplained. On the contrary, the Holy Scriptures should only be put into the hands of those children who have learned to read with fluency.

To the younger children a short portion of the Scripture should be daily read, and made the subject of an oral lesson.

Those of riper age should be taught to receive and read the Scriptures with reverence.

The art of reading should be acquired from class-books appropriate to an industrial school. Besides the class-book for the more advanced scholars on cottage economy, the earlier reading lessons might contribute instruction adapted to the condition of a class emerging from slavery or barbarism.

The lessons on writing and arithmetic, as has been before observed, ought to be brought into daily practical use in the employment of the scholars. Nothing is learned so soon or retained so surely as knowledge the practical relation of which is perceived.

The scholar should *thus* be taught to write from dictation, as an exercise of memory, and of spelling and punctuation, as well as of writing.

They should be gradually trained in the composition of simple letters on the business of the school, the garden, or kitchen; and exercised in writing abstracts of oral lessons from memory. The power of writing on the actual events and business of their future lives would thus be acquired.

Within these limits the instruction of the coloured races, combined with a systematic training in industry, cannot fail to raise the population to a condition of improved comfort; but it will also give such habits of steady industry to a settled and thriving peasantry as may in time develop the elements of a native middle class. This would probably be a consequence of an education within these limits; but if this were accomplished, and time permitted further instruction, an acquaintance might be sought with the art of drawing plans, and those of land-surveying and levelling. Some instruction in geography also would enable them better to understand the Scriptures, and the connection of the colony with the mother country.

The master and mistress should be assisted by apprentices, whose number should be proportioned to the size of the schools. These apprentices should be chosen from the most proficient and best conducted scholars, who are also likely to have an example set them by their parents in harmony with their education. At the age of thirteen they should be bound by agreement for six years, and might receive in *lieu* of stipend a quantity of the garden produce sufficient to induce their parents cheerfully to consent to their employment in the school. Careful separate instruction should be given them by the master, at a period daily set apart for the purpose, and they should be furnished with books, as means of self-education.

With the aid of such apprenticed assistants, the school might be divided into classes varying in size, according to the skill and age of the apprentices, and the number of the scholars. In the early stage of their apprenticeship, it may not be expedient to intrust these youths with the management of a class containing more than twelve children. At the age of sixteen, they might teach sixteen children; and at the age of eighteen, probably twenty children. The master would instruct twenty-four, or thirty, or more children in a class, according to circumstances.

The school, therefore, will be divided into classes of twelve, sixteen, twenty, and twenty-four children.

The Model Farm-School may be described with greater brevity, because much that has been said respecting the *Day-School of Industry* is applicable to it.

The Model Farm-School is intended for the class of labourers who have accumulated sufficient money to become small farmers, and for the small farmers who, with more knowledge and skill, would be enabled to employ their capital to greater advantage. Its object is to create a thriving, loyal, and religious middle class among the agricultural population. As the process of culture must differ in the various Colonies, it is not possible to give more than general indications respecting it.

As it would be improbable that a sufficient number of scholars could be collected from one neighbourhood, they should be boarders, and the cost of their lodging, maintenance, and in some Colonies also of their instruction, should be defrayed by their parents. The buildings therefore should provide—

> A lofty dormitory divided by partitions, six feet high, into separate compartments, each containing one bed, and affording the master the means of overlooking the room from his own apartment.
> A refectory.
> Class-rooms.

A kitchen, &c. &c.
Store-rooms.
Apartments for the master and his assistants.

To these school buildings should be added—

Farm buildings, comprising all the arrangements necessary in each climate for the shelter of the produce of the farm, and when necessary for its preparation for exportation; for the housing of stock; for the dairy; for the preparation of manures, and of food for the cattle; and for the shelter of agricultural machines and implements.

The industrial occupations of the scholars would be those of farm-servants.

In the field, the draining or irrigation of the land; ploughing, harrowing, and the preparation of the soil by various manures adapted to its chemical character; the sowing of the different crops with machines or by the hand; the expedients for preserving the seed thus sown; the weeding, hoeing, or drill-ploughing of the growing crop. The gathering in of the harvest would either be done solely by the labour of the scholars or with such assistance as might be required by the climate.

In the homestead, with a similar reservation, they would conduct the management of the stock; of the manures and composts; the housing of the crop, and its preparation for exportation; and the economy of the dairy.

Besides these purely farm occupations, it would be well to have on the premises a wheelwright's and blacksmith's shop, in which they might learn to mend the carts, waggons, and farming machines and implements, to repair the farming premises, and to shoe the horses.

The domestic services of the household should have in view the establishment of religious exercises, such as could be properly continued in a farmer's family.

Besides a thorough instruction in the Holy Scriptures, the course of teaching would comprise the following subjects:—

Probably the scholars on their admission into the school would be able to read and write with ease. They should also learn English grammar, as previously explained in relation to the day-school.

They would proceed to acquire arithmetic, in connection with keeping accounts of the management of a farm, and with practice in all farming calculations. Mensuration, land-surveying and level-ling, and plan-drawing would be taught, and their practical appli-cation constantly exemplified in the measurement of timber or of labourers' work; in estimates for drainage, irrigation, and other agricultural purposes; and in preparing plans from actual survey.

As soon as the rudiments of chemical knowledge were acquired, further instruction should proceed, in connection with the practi-cal application of these elements, to the actual operations of the farm (all of which should be explained with their aid), and after-wards to practical illustrations which the farm itself did not afford.

The pupils should, by frequent practice, acquire expertness in the use of tests of the quality of soils.

The chief characteristics of soils should be understood, and their relation to different forms of vegetation, together with the ex-pedients by which, under varying circumstances, soils naturally of a low degree of fertility may be cultivated, so as to produce abundant crops.

In like manner practical lessons should be given on the influence of various soils; of different kinds of manure; of the natural influ-ences of light, heat, rain, dew, night and day, and of the seasons on vegetable life; on the effects of drainage, and of the various modes of working and of cultivating the soil, and managing different crops.

On such knowledge should be grounded instruction in the most improved methods of cropping a farm; the use of the best imple-ments and machines; on composts and manures; and the best mode of procuring seeds.

Time would also probably be found to impart some acquain-tance with veterinary medicine, as far, at least, as a general knowl-edge of the structure of the horse, cow, sheep, and other common domestic animals; of the methods of preparing their food; of the best means of preserving them in health by appropriate food, warmth, ventilation, and cleanliness; the precautions to be em-ployed in peculiar localities and under special circumstances of climate.

Under the head of *arts of construction* falls the mode of plan-ning farm buildings so as to ensure an economy of labour with the utmost convenience and security; and with arrangements for promoting the health of the stock; the best plans for constructing roofs; the proper strength required for timbers of different bearings, and the best method of economizing materials, with a due regard to permanence of structure.

Wherever peculiar processes are required for the preparation of the crop for exportation, the object of them, whether mechanical or chemical, should be explained to the pupils.

Some knowledge of the laws of natural phenomena would enable them to comprehend the use of the thermometer, barometer, and other common instruments, and would free them from vulgar errors and popular superstitions.

The head master of the farming-school should be competent by experience and skill to superintend the farm, as well as to give the combined practical and theoretical agricultural knowledge of the course proposed to be taught.

He would require assistant-masters, according to the size of the school, to teach the rudiments, and thus prepare every class for his instruction.

Each class should be taught in a separate room. The assistant masters would probably be promoted to these offices from the charge of day-schools of industry, and might there be deemed to be in training as candidates for the head mastership of farm-schools.

A matron or house-steward would manage all the domestic duties, with the aid of some servants.

It is not necessary here to repeat the general indications given respecting discipline, which have been set forth in relation to the day-school. The same principles are applicable to the model farm-school.

The course of study should extend, if possible, from the age of 14 or 15 to that of 18 or 19. There would not be the same need of apprentices in these schools as in the day-schools, because the scholars would be of a riper age, and might be more fitly intrusted, as monitors, with the superintendence of working parties. The whole of the instruction in classes would be conducted by the head master and his assistants.

The *day-school of industry*, and the *model farm-school*, having thus been described, it is now convenient to set forth the arrangements for the *training of the masters of such schools*.

The apprenticeship of scholars from 13 to 19 years of age in the day-school of industry must be regarded as a preliminary training in all the duties of the masters of such a school. It would be expedient that the pupil-teacher should be the child of parents who would set him a good example; that he should be bound by indentures which should specify his work, his remuneration, the knowledge he was to gain in each year under the instruction of the master; the nature of the annual examination which he should pass before some competent officer; the persons from whom certificates of conduct should be annually required; the test of his practical skill in gardening and field-work, and in the art of teaching and governing a class.

When the indenture was fulfilled, the pupil-teacher should be admitted to a competition of bursaries or exhibitions to the normal school, to be held annually. The most proficient, skilful, and best conducted should be selected for these rewards, and sent with a bursary, which would defray the chief part of the expense of their further training, to the *normal school.*

If the day-schools of industry were efficient, the residence in the normal school might be limited to a year or a year and a half; but if these schools were not in an efficient state, the period of training in the normal school would have to be proportionately extended.

The *normal school* would adjoin a *model day-school of industry.* The students of the normal school would thus have an opportunity of witnessing a good example of the management of such a day-school, and of acquiring the art of teaching. They would here improve the processes of instruction and the modes of discipline which they had acquired in schools of inferior efficiency, and make practical trial of the principles of school management, which would be taught in the normal school.

A principal master and assistant-masters in the proportion of one master to every 30 or 40 candidate-teachers would be required in the normal school.

All the subjects of instruction pursued, either in the model farm-schools or in the day-schools of industry, should be here resumed.

The masters should here lead the candidates through a systematic course of instruction on each subject, revising their previous acquirements; rendering them more precise, accurate, and rational; and developing them beyond the limits within which their future duties as teachers would be confined.

The group of subjects from which the pursuits of the candidates in the normal school might be selected can be more properly described than the exact limits to be placed on such studies in each colony.

The course of the normal school would comprise certain of the following subjects:—

1. Biblical instruction and the Evidences of Christianity.
2. English Grammar and Composition.
3. English History.
4. Geography.
5. Chemistry, and its applications to Agriculture.
6. The Theory of Natural Phenomena in their relation to Agriculture.
7. The rudiments of Mechanics.
8. Arithmetic and Book-keeping.
9. The art of Land Surveying and Levelling, and practical Mensuration.
10. Drawing from Models and Plan Drawing.
11. The Theory and Practice of Agriculture and Gardening.
12. The Management of Farming Stock, including the Treatment of their Diseases.
13. The art of organizing and conducting an Elementary School.
14. Vocal Music.

It is unnecessary to enter into minute details as to the daily routine of the normal school: some general indication of principles only is required.

The principal object to be kept in view throughout the training of the apprentice and candidate teacher is the *formation of character*.

The prolonged training in the day-school, followed by the residence in the normal school, cannot fail to make them acquainted with the details of the school-keeping, with the management of a garden, and the art of teaching a class.

As only the most advanced of the pupil-teachers would be selected for the normal school, the revision of their studies in that school would give them a considerable command of the elementary knowledge required in schools of industry. In these respects much confidence may be expressed as to the results of their training. The dispositions with which they approach their duties as schoolmasters and mistresses are still more important.

The discipline of the apprentice and student should afford no encouragement to the presumption and pedantry which often accompany an education, necessarily incomplete, yet raised above the level of the class from which the pupil-teachers are taken; yet it should not be such as to weaken the spring of the natural energies, or to subdue the force of individual character. No form of training is less capable of establishing sound moral sentiments than that which exacts an unreasoning obedience. The discipline which thus subdues the will, makes the pupil feebler for all virtuous actions.

To train the student in simplicity, humility, and truth, and at the same time to strengthen his mental powers, to inform his intelligence, to elevate his principles, and to invigorate his intellect, are the objects of his education.

On this account, the domestic life of the apprentice with his own parents, under the best influences of his own class in society, might, if his family were a religious household, usefully alternate with the discipline and duties of the day-school. He would understand, from experience, the wants, the cares, and hopes of the labouring class whose children he would have to educate. Instead of being repelled by their coarseness and poverty, and thus unfitted for daily contact with them, he would have a sympathy with their condition, which the training of the school would direct to proper objects.

He ought to enter and to leave the training-school, attracted by preference to the education of the labouring poor.

While in the day-school, the pupil-teacher would partake the common work of the garden, &c. This labour should be during some hours daily continued in the normal school. He should still feel that his origin and his future employment were in harmony.

With this view, his dress should have no distinction but that of greater simplicity and cleanliness. Any pretension beyond the ordinary peasant's dress, which his parents could provide, should be discouraged. He should strive to teach by his example how that common dress could be worn with frugality and neatness.

In like manner, in the normal school a peculiar dress is undesirable. The candidate-teacher should continue, during three hours daily, to partake the rudest toils of the field and garden. Out-door labour should alternate with mental cultivation, both to enable the student to conduct a school of industry with success, and also to build all his intellectual acquirements on the experience of the life of those supported by manual industry. No alteration in the dress of the student should appear to suggest, that with his entrance into the normal school commences the separation between the candidate and his own class in society. Few things could be more injurious than to do anything which might tend to sever such sympathies, or to take the example of an educated peasant out of his own sphere in life.

The apprentice should not exchange the fare of the peasant's cottage and the simple dinner of the day-school for a better diet in the normal school. His meals should be such only as he might certainly hope to procure by his vocation as schoolmaster. In like manner, while, in his bed-room, provision was made for privacy, every arrangement should be marked by a severe simplicity. More abundant comfort, approaching to luxury, would make it difficult to the candidate in after life to encounter the inevitable privations of his profession as a teacher of the poor.

The household life of the normal school should be marked by reverential attention to religious exercises and duties.

At an early period in the morning the school should be assembled for prayers. After prayers, the principal would speak to the students on subjects connected with the moral discipline of the school. He would endeavour to lead them to feel under what influences their life could enable them to fulfil the highest aims of their calling. Whatever had happened incompatible with such a view of their duties, and which was not rather a subject for private personal admonition, might become, after prayers, a source of instruction, in which should mingle no element of rebuke. In like manner the pursuits of the day should close.

No part of the discipline of the establishment should contradict such instruction. In everything an appeal should be made to the reason and the conscience. Vigilance, to be wisely exerted, should wear no appearance of distrust or suspicion, but it should also be incessant.

The intercourse between the principal and the candidate-teachers should be frank and confiding.

Whenever concealment and evasion commence, even in slight

matters, the authority and influence of the principal are in danger. It would become him then to reflect on the grounds of his regulations; to explain them fully to his students, and to endeavour to establish in their minds a conviction of their value. On some occasions it may be wise to make some relaxations in his rules, in a matter not essential to principle, and which is found to be galling in practice. In this way, and not by any system of "espionage," the whole life of the students should constantly pass in review before him. The advice of the principal should be open to his scholars as that of a friend.

Their time should be as fully occupied as possible. Relaxation should be found in change of employment and exercise in the duties of the field and garden. If the sense of life in a family were maintained, and a filial subordination characterized the discipline, the most wholesome results would ensue.

With these brief indications, I am directed to solicit your attention to those portions of the Minutes of the Committee of Council on Education which relate to the establishment and support of normal schools, and to the reports presented by Her Majesty's Inspectors on the condition of the normal and model schools now existing in Great Britain, in which will be found further details of the principles on which these institutions are conducted.

I have the honour to be,

Sir,

Your obedient Servant,

J. P. Kay Shuttleworth,

Benj. Hawes, jun., Esq., M.P.,
Under-Secretary of State for the Colonies.

18. Rufus Anderson and the Theory of Missions

Although the United States carried out its nineteenth-century conquests against sparsely settled Indians in its own hinterland and participated very little in overseas imperialism until the very end of the century, it was far more active in the missionary effort that paralleled imperialism in many parts of the world. American missionaries operated within the empires of the other Western powers, and American missionary societies were in close touch with their European counterparts.

Rufus Anderson (1796–1872) was one of the American missionary leaders who had a considerable influence in Europe as well, especially through Henry Venn, the mid-century secretary of the Church Missionary Society in England.[1] Both Anderson and Venn were concerned with the relationship between Christianity and Western civilization in general—should Christianity be taught alone, or as a part of a broader program of Westernization? Both were concerned with the proper role of the missionary. Anderson argues here that the missionary's obligation is to teach Christianity and move on, rather than staying as pastor over the new congregation he has founded, and Venn later laid out the goal of new churches overseas which would be self-supporting, self-controlling, and self-propagating.

This view had its parallel in the imperialism of free trade,[2] which also reached its greatest popularity as an ideal in the 1850's and 60's, with the expectation that economic development and growing world trade would take place under Western influence, but without the need for direct European imperial control. When the voluntary conversionist view began to weaken in European imperial thought toward the end of the century, an equivalent change took place in missionary theory. The tough-minded theory of trusteeship in secular circles helped to shift the missionary expectation of free churches overseas to a sterner paternalism with racist overtones and the insistence that European missionaries keep the upper hand in the churches they had founded.

Anderson's career was focused on the American Board of Foreign Missions, which he served from 1822 to 1866 in many different capacities. After his retirement from active work, he turned historian and published *A History of the Missions of the American Board of Foreign Missions*, in five volumes, in 1872. The selection that follows is his pamphlet *The Theory of Missions to the Heathen, a Sermon on the Ordination of Mr. Edward Webb as a Missionary to the Heathen* (Boston, 1845), quoted in full.

Sermon.

COMPARING THE present period of the church with the apostolical, we come to two very different results respecting our own age. One is, that the facilities enjoyed by us for propagating the gospel throughout the world, are vastly greater than those enjoyed by the apostles. The other is, that it is far more difficult now, than it was then, to impart a purely spiritual character to missions among the heathen.

1. See J. F. A. Ajayi, "Henry Venn and the Policy of Development," *Journal of the Historical Society of Nigeria*, 1:331–342 (1959).

2. J. Gallagher and R. Robinson, "The Imperialism of Free Trade," *Economic History Review*, 6 (2nd ser.):1–15 (1953).

As to facilities, we have the advantage of the apostles in all respects, except the gift of tongues. The world, as a whole, was never so open to the preacher of the gospel since the introduction of the Christian dispensation. The civilization, too, that is connected with modern science, is all connected also with Christianity in some of its forms. I should add, that the civilization which the gospel has conferred upon our own New England is the highest and best, in a religious point of view, the world has yet seen.

But, on the other hand, this very perfection of our own social religious state becomes a formidable hindrance to establishing such purely spiritual missions among heathen nations, as were those of the apostolical times. Not that this is the only hindrance to this result; there are many others, but this is an important one. For, the Christian religion is identified, in all our conceptions of it from our earliest years, with the almost universal diffusion among its professors of the blessings of education, industry, civil liberty, family government, social order, the means of a respectable livelihood, and a well ordered community. Hence *our* idea of piety in converts among the heathen very generally involves the acquisition and possession, to a great extent, of these blessings; and *our* idea of the propagation of the gospel by means of missions is, to an equal extent, *the creation among heathen tribes and nations of a highly improved state of society, such as we ourselves enjoy.* And for this vast intellectual, moral and social transformation we allow but a short time. We expect the first generation of converts to Christianity, even among savages, to come into all our fundamental ideas of morals, manners, political economy, social organization, right, justice, equity; although many of these are ideas which our own community has been ages in acquiring. If we discover that converts under the torrid zone go but half clothed, that they are idle on a soil where a small amount of labor will supply their wants, that they sometimes forget the apostle's cautions to his converts, not to lie one to another, and to steal no more, in communities where the grossest vice scarcely affects the reputation, and that they are slow to adopt our ideas of the rights of man; we at once doubt the genuineness of their conversion, and the faithfulness of their missionary instructors. Nor is it surprising that this feeling is strongest, as it appears to be, in the most enlightened and favored portions of our country; since it is among those whose privilege it is to dwell upon the heights of Zion, that we have the most reason to expect this feeling, until they shall have reflected maturely on the difference there is between their own circumstances and states of mind, and those of a heathen and barbarous people.

Now the prevalence of these sentiments at home has exerted an influence on all the missions. Nor is the influence new. You see it in the extent to which farmers and mechanics—pious but secular men—were sent, many years ago, along with the missionaries, to assist in reclaiming the savages of the wilderness from the chase and settling them in communities like our own—a practice now nearly discontinued, except where the expense is borne by the national government.

Unless this influence is guarded against by missionaries and their directors, the result is that the missions have *a two-fold object of pursuit;* the one, that simple and sublime spiritual object of the ambassador for Christ mentioned in the text, "persuading men to be reconciled to God"; the other, the reorganizing, by various direct means, of the structure of that social system, of which the converts form a part. Thus the object of the missions becomes more or less complicated, leading to a complicated, burdensome, and perhaps expensive course of measures for its attainment.

I may be allowed, therefore, to invite attention to what is conceived to be *our true and only office and work in missions to the heathen.* "Now then we are ambassadors for Christ; as though God did beseech you by us, we pray you, in Christ's stead, be ye reconciled to God." The ambassadors here spoken of were missionaries—missionaries to the heathen, for such were Paul and his associates; sent, instead of Christ the Mediator, on a ministry withheld from angels, to plead with rebellious men to become reconciled to God. They are ambassadors sent on the same general errand that brought the Lord Jesus from heaven, and their commission is to proclaim abroad the fact, history, design and effect of his atonement, and bring its renovating power to bear as widely as possible upon the human race.

It will be necessary to dwell a short time on the leading aspects of this enterprise. And,

1. The vocation of the missionary who is sent to the heathen, is not the same with that of the settled pastor.

The work of human salvation is one of vast extent, whether we regard the time it is to occupy, the objects upon which it operates, the agents it employs, or the results which are to be accomplished. And it is performed with that regard for order and gradual development, which generally characterizes the works of God. Upon the Lord Jesus it devolved to make the atonement, thus preparing the way, as none else could do, for reconciling man to his Maker; and then He returned to the heaven whence he came. Upon his immediate disciples it then devolved to make proclamation of the atonement, and its kindred and dependent doctrines, throughout the world, the whole of which world, excepting Judea, was then heathen. This they were to do as his representatives and ambassadors; and to expedite the work, they were furnished with the gift of tongues, and an extraordinary divine influence attended their preaching. Their commission embraced only the proclamation of the gospel and planting its institutions. As soon as the gospel by their means had gained a footing in any one district of country, they left the work in charge to others, called elders and also bishops or overseers of the flock and church of God, whom they ordained for the purpose. Sometimes they did not remain even long enough to provide spiritual guides for the churches they had planted. "For this cause," says Paul to Titus, "left I thee in Crete, that thou shouldest set in order the things that are wanting, and ordain elders in every city, as I had appointed thee." The elders were the pastors of the new churches. Elsewhere the apostle speaks of different departments of labor and influence assigned to the ministers of Christ. He says that when Christ ascended up on high he gave gifts unto men; to some apostles, to some prophets, to some evangelists, to some pastors and teachers. Whatever was the peculiar office of "prophets" and "teachers," none can doubt that "evangelists" were fellow-laborers of the apostles in the missionary work, and that "pastors" had the stated care and instruction of particular churches. Now missionaries are the true and proper successors of the apostles and evangelists, and their sphere of duty is not the same with that of pastors, who are successors, in their sacred functions, not so much of the apostles and evangelists, as of the elders and bishops. It enters into the nature of the pastor's relation, that he remain or be intended to remain long the spiritual instructor of some one people. It is indeed as really his business to call sinners to repentance, as it is that of the missionary; but, owing to his more permanent relations, and to the fact that he is constituted the religious guide and instructor of his converts during the whole period of their earthly pilgrimage, his range of duty in respect to them is more comprehensive than that of the missionary in respect to his converts. The pastor is charged, in common with the missionary, with reconciling men to God; and he has also an additional charge, arising from the peculiar circumstances of his relation, with respect to their growth in grace and sanctification. But the missionary's *great* business in his personal labors, is with the unconverted. His embassy is to the rebellious, to beseech them, in Christ's stead, to be reconciled to God. His vocation, as a soldier of the cross, is to make conquests, and to go on, in the name of his divine Master, "conquering and to conquer"; committing the security and permanency of his conquests to another class of men created expressly for the purpose. The idea of *continued conquest* is fundamental in missions to the heathen, and is vital to their spiritual life and efficiency. It will doubtless be found on inquiry, that missions among the heathen have always ceased to be healthful and efficient, have ceased to evince the true missionary spirit in its strength, whenever they have ceased to be actively aggressive upon the kingdom of darkness.

In a word, the missionary prepares new fields for pastors; and when they are thus prepared, and competent pastors are upon the ground, he ought himself to move onward,—the pioneer in effect of a Christian civilization—but in office, work and spirit, an ambassador for Christ, to preach the gospel where it has not been preached. And, whatever may be said with respect to pastors, it is true of the missionary, that he is to keep himself as free as possible from entanglements with literature, science and commerce, and with questions of church government, politics and social order. For,

2. The object and work of the missionary are preëminently spiritual.

His embassy and message are as really from the other world, as if he were an angel from heaven. He who devotes himself to the work of foreign missions, comes thereby under peculiar engagements and obligations. His situation is in some important respects peculiar, compared with that of all others. His sphere of action lies beyond the bounds of his native land, beyond the bounds of Christendom, where society and the family and human nature lie all in ruins. As the great Originator and Lord of the enterprise came from the realms of heavenly blessedness to this world when it was one universal moral waste, so his representatives and ambassadors have now to go from those portions of the earth that have been illuminated by his gospel to regions that are as yet unvisited by these benign influences. They are therefore required prëeminently to renounce the world. From the nature of the case they make a greater sacrifice of worldly blessings, than their brethren at home can do, however much disposed. They forsake their native land and the loved scenes of their youthful days. Oceans separate them from their relatives and friends. They encounter torrid heats and strange diseases. They traverse pathless wilds, and are exposed to burning suns and chilling night-damps, to rain or snow. Yet these things, when in their most repulsive forms, are reckoned by missionaries as the least of the trials appertaining to their vocation. The foreign missionary's greatest sacrifices and trials are *social* and *religious*. It is here that he has a severity of trial, which even the domestic missionary ordinarily cannot have. Whatever the devoted servant of Christ upon the frontiers may endure for the present, he sees the waves of a Christian civilization not far distant rolling onward, and knows that there will soon be all around him gospel institutions and a Christian community. But it is not so with the foreign missionary. It requires great strength of faith in Christ for him to look at his rising family, and then with unruffled feelings towards the future. True, he sees the gospel taking hold of minds and hearts in consequence of his ministry, and souls converted and reconciled to God; he gathers churches; he sees around him the germs of a future Christian civilization. But then, owing to the imperfect and disordered state of society in heathen communities, he dares not anticipate so much social advancement for two or three generations to come, as would make it pleasant to think of leaving his children among the people for whose spiritual well-being he delights to spend his own strength and years. And then his heart yearns ofttimes to be braced and cheered by social Christian fellowship of a higher order than he finds among his converts from heathenism. It is not the "flesh-pots of Egypt" he looks back upon, nor any of the pleasant things that used to gratify his *senses* in his native land; but he does sometimes think of the kindred spirits he would find in that land, and of the high intellectual and spiritual fellowship he would enjoy in their society, and how it would refresh and strengthen his own mind and heart. Often there is a feeling of weakness and faintness arising from the want of such fellowship, which is the most painful part of his sufferings. The foreign missionary is obliged, indeed, to act prëeminently upon the doctrine of a future life, and of God's supreme and universal government, and to make a deliberate sacrifice of time for eternity, and of earth for heaven. And this he does as an act of duty to his Redeemer, for the sake of extending the influence of his redemption, and bringing its reconciling and saving power to bear upon the myriads of immortal souls dwelling beyond the utmost verge of the Christian church.

And thus the foreign missionary is driven, as it were, by the very circumstances of his position, as well as led by his commission and his convictions of duty, to concentrate his attention and energies upon the SOUL, ruined though immortal. And truly it is a vast and mighty ruin he beholds—more affecting to look upon in the light of its own proper eternity, than would be the desolation of all the cities in the world. It is too vast a ruin for a feeble band to attempt the restoration of every part at once. As Nehemiah concentrated his energies upon rebuilding the walls of the city of his fathers, rightly concluding that if the walls were rebuilt and threw their encouraging protection around, the other portions of the city would rise of course; so the missionary, as a thoughtful and wise man, sets himself to reconcile the alienated heart to God, believing that that point being gained, and the principle of obedience implanted, and a highly spiritual religion introduced, a social renovation will be sure to follow. He considers not, therefore, so much the relations of man to man, as of man to God; not so much the relations and interests of time, as those of eternity; not so much the intellectual and social degradation and debasement, the result of barbarism or of iron-handed oppression, as the alienation and estrangement of the heart of man from his Maker, and the deadly influence of hateful and destroying passions upon his soul. As when a house is burning in the dead of night, our first and great concern is not for the house, but for the sleeping dwellers within; so the missionary's first and great concern is for the *soul*, to save it from impending wrath.

And the *means* he employs in this ministry of reconciliation, are as single and spiritual as the end he has in view. He *preaches the cross of Christ*. The apostle Paul declares that this was his grand theme. And it is remarkable how experience is bringing modern missionaries to the same result. Their grand agent is oral instruction; their grand theme is the cross. And now, perhaps not less than in the days of the apostles, the Holy Spirit appears to restrict his *converting* influences among the heathen chiefly to this species of agency, and to this grand theme. Excepting in the schools, the usefulness of books is chiefly with those whose hearts have been in some measure moved and roused by the preached word. It appears to be the will of the great Redeemer, who came in person to begin the work, that his salvation shall everywhere be proclaimed in person by his ambassadors, and that his message of grace shall have all the impressiveness of look and voice and manner, which they are able to give it. After the manner of their illustrious predecessor, they must teach publicly, and from house to house, and warn every one night and day with tears. The necessity of this in order to reconcile rebellious men to God, has not been diminished by the multiplication of books through the press. Well-authenticated cases of *conversion* among pagans, by means of books alone, not excepting even the Scriptures, are exceedingly rare. By the divine appointment, there must also be the living preacher; and his preaching must not be "with the wisdom of words, lest the cross of Christ should be made of none effect."

You see, then, Brethren, the high spiritual calling of the missionary. At the very threshold of his work, he is required, in a prëeminent degree, to renounce the world. His message, wherein lies his duty and all his hope of success, is concerning the cross of Christ; and the object of it is to restore the lost spiritual relation between man and God. The impression he is designing to make is directly upon the soul. And his work lies so altogether out of the common range of worldly ideas, and even of the ideas of many professed Christians, that multitudes have no faith in it; it is to them like a root out of a dry ground, and they see no form nor comeliness in it, and nothing that should lead them to desire it. Nor is it until the civilizing results come out, that these unsanctified or very partially sanctified persons can give the missionary work any degree of their respect.

The necessity of connecting a system of *education* with modern missions, is not inconsistent with the view we have taken of the true theory of missions to the heathen. The apostles had greatly the advantage of us in procuring elders, or pastors for their churches.

In their day the most civilized portions of the world were heathen—as if to show the weakness of mere human learning and wisdom; and the missionary labors of the apostles and their associates, so far as we have authentic accounts of them, were in the best educated and in some respects highly educated portions of the earth. Wherever they went, therefore, they found mind in comparatively an erect, intelligent, reasoning posture; and it would seem that men could easily have been found among their converts, who, with some special but brief instruction concerning the gospel, would be fitted to take the pastoral care of churches. But it appears that, until schools expressly for training pastors were in operation,—as ere long they were at Alexandria, Caesarea, Antioch, Edessa, and elsewhere,—it pleased God essentially to aid in qualifying men for the office of pastors by a miraculous agency; the Holy Ghost exerting upon them a supernatural influence, by which their understandings were strengthened and spiritually illuminated, and they gifted with powers of utterance.

But, at the present time, the whole civilized world is at least nominally Christian, and modern missions must be prosecuted among uncivilized, or at least partially civilized tribes and nations, from which useful ideas have in great measure perished. Even in those heathen nations which make the greatest pretensions to learning, as in India, we find but little truth existing on any subject. Their history, chronology, geography, astronomy, their notions of matter and mind, and their views of creation and providence, religion and morals, are exceedingly destitute of truth. And yet it is not so much a *vacuity* of mind here that we have to contend with, as it is *plenitude of error*—the unrestrained accumulations and perversions of depraved intellect for three thousand years. But among savage heathens, it is *vacuity* of mind, and not a *plenitude*, we have to operate upon. For, the savage has few ideas, sees only the objects just about him, perceives nothing of the relations of things, and occupies his thoughts only about his physical experiences and wants. He knows nothing of geography, astronomy, history, nothing of his own spiritual nature and destiny, and nothing of God.

In these circumstances and without the power of conferring miraculous gifts, modern missionaries are constrained to resort to education in order to procure pastors for their churches. They select the most promising candidates, and take the usual methods to train them to stand alone and firm in the gospel ministry, and to be

competent spiritual guides to others. This creates, it will be perceived, a necessity for a system of education of greater or less
extent in each of the missions, embracing even a considerable
number of elementary schools. The whole is designed to secure,
through the divine blessing, a competent native ministry, who shall
aid missionaries in their work, and at length take their places. The
schools, moreover, of every grade, are, or ought to be so many
preaching places, so many congregations of youth, to whom, often
with parents and friends attending, the gospel is more or less
formally proclaimed.

I have thus endeavored, my Brethren, to set before you the
foreign missionary enterprise in what I conceive to be its true scrip-
tural character; as an enterprise, the object of which, and the sole
object, is the reconciling of rebellious men in heathen lands to
God.

And what is true of the individual missionary, is of course
equally true of the Missionary Society, which directs his labors and
is the medium of his support. The Society sends forth men to be
evangelists, rather than permanent pastors; and when pastors are
required by the progress and success of the work, it seeks them
among native converts on the ground. And herein it differs from
the appropriate usages of the Home Missionary Society, which,
operating on feeble churches within Christian communities, or in
districts that are soon to be covered with a Christian civilization of
some sort, sends forth its preachers all to become settled pastors as
soon as possible. The foreign missionary work is in fact a vast
evangelism; with conquest, in order to extend the bounds of the
Redeemer's kingdom, for its object; having as little to do with the
relations of this life and the things of the world and sense, and as
few relations to the kingdoms of this world, as is consistent with the
successful prosecution of its one grand object—the restoring, in the
immortal soul of man, of that blessed attraction to the Centre of
the Spiritual Universe which was lost at the fall.

This method of conducting foreign missions, besides its evident
conformity to Scripture, is supported by various weighty considerations.

1. It is the only method that, as a system of measures, will
commend itself strongly to the consciences and respect of mankind.

The first mission sent forth under the care of the American Board, was such a mission. And it was sent to the subjects of a nation, with which our country was then unhappily at war. But the missionaries were regarded on all hands as belonging prëeminently to a kingdom not of this world, and having an object of a purely spiritual nature. And when, notwithstanding this, the policy of the East Indian government would have sent them away, it was this that gave convincing and overwhelming force to the following appeal made by our brethren to the governor of Bombay:

> We entreat you by the spiritual miseries of the heathen, who are daily perishing before your eyes, and under your Excellency's government, not to prevent us from preaching Christ to them. We entreat you by the blood of Jesus which he shed to redeem them, —as ministers of Him, who has all power in heaven and earth, and who with his farewell and ascending voice commanded his ministers to go and teach all nations, we entreat you not to prohibit us from teaching these heathens. By all the principles of our holy religion, by which you hope to be saved, we entreat you not to hinder us from preaching the same religion to these perishing idolaters. By all the solemnities of the judgment day, when your Excellency must meet your heathen subjects before God's tribunal, we entreat you not to hinder us from preaching to them that gospel, which is able to prepare them, as well as you, for that awful day.

Nothing but a consciousness of the high spirituality of their object and the impossibility of connecting it with questions of a secular nature, imparted boldness to our brethren to make this appeal, and gave it favor and efficacy in the high places of power. And it is this, which lately preserved our brethren on Mount Lebanon harmless amid the fury and carnage of a civil war. And this it is that imparts a degree of inviolability to the persons and efforts of Protestant heralds of the cross among all the nations which respect their religion. It is the grand predominance of the *spiritual* in their characters and pursuits, showing that they really do belong to a kingdom not of this world, and are not to be involved in the conflicting relations and interests of earthly communities. English statesmen in India acknowledge, that the general prevalence of Christianity in that country would at length make it impossible for their nation to hold the country in subjection, and yet they encourage the labors of the missionary. This they do because the missionary's *object*, whatever be the known *tendency* of his labors, is not to change the civil relations of the people, but to give them the gospel and save their souls; and because these statesmen are convinced in their consciences, that this is an object of unquestionable benevolence and obligation, for which Christ died, for which the ministry was instituted, which at this day is to be countenanced and encouraged at all events by every man claiming the name of a Christian; and which, however humbling it shall prove in its results to avaricious and ambitious nations, cannot be otherwise than beneficial on the broad scale of the world and to the great family of men.

2. This method of conducting missions is the only one, on which missionaries can be obtained in large numbers, and kept cheerfully in the field.

For objects that are not spiritual and eternal, men will seldom renounce the world for themselves and their families, as missionaries must do. Mere philosophers have never gone as missionaries; and seldom do mere philanthropists go into the heathen world, nor would they remain long, should they happen to go. Nor will a merely impulsive, unreflecting piety ever bring about a steady, persevering, laborious, self-denying mission. It generally gives out before the day for embarkation, or retires from the field before the language is acquired and the battle fairly commenced. Nothing but the grand object of reconciling men to God, with a view to their eternal salvation, and the happiness and glory thus resulting to Christ's kingdom, will call any considerable number of missionaries into the foreign field, and keep them cheerfully there. And it is necessary that this object be made to stand out alone, in its greatness and majesty, towering above all other objects, as the hoary-headed monarch of the Alps towers above the inferior mountains around him. It is not fine conceptions of the beautiful and orderly in human society that will fire the zeal of a missionary; it is not rich and glowing conceptions of the life and duties of a pastor; it is not broad and elevated views of theological truth, nor precise and comprehensive views of the relations of that truth to moral subjects. It is something more than all this, often the result of a different cast of mind and combination of ideas. The true missionary character indeed is based upon a single sublime conception— that of *reconciling immortal souls to God*. To gain this with an effective practical power, the missionary needs himself to have passed from death unto life, and to have had deep experience of his own enmity to God and hell-desert, and of the vast transforming agency of the reconciling grace of God in Christ. As this conception has more of moral greatness and sublimity in it than any other that ever entered the mind of man, no missionary can attain to the highest elevation and dignity of his calling, unless he have strong mental power and a taste for the morally sublime. This the apostle Paul had. What conceptions of his office and work and of spiritual things animated the great soul of that apostle! "Now, then, we are ambassadors for Christ; as though God did beseech you by us, we pray you, in Christ's stead, be ye reconciled to God."—"Eye hath not seen, nor ear heard, neither have entered into the heart of man the things which God hath prepared for them that love him."— "Oh the depth of the riches both of the wisdom and knowledge of God."—"Able to comprehend with all saints what is the breadth and length and depth and height, and to know the love of Christ, which passeth knowledge."

To make persevering and useful missionaries, however, it is not necessary that the power of thought and of spiritual apprehension should come nearly up to that of the apostle Paul. But there should be a similar cast of mind, similar views and feelings, and a similar character. There should be a steady and sober, but real enthusiasm, sustained by a strongly spiritualized doctrinal experience, and by the "powers of the world to come," intent upon reconciling men to God from a conviction of its transcendent importance.

Such men must compose the great body of every mission, or it will not be worth supporting in the field; and the only way such men can be induced to engage in the work, is by having the idea of spiritual conquest, through the cross of Christ, the predominant and characteristic idea of the enterprise. That will attract their attention while they are preparing for the ministry; that will enlist their consciences and draw their hearts; that will constrain them to refuse every call to settle at home, however inviting; and if they have learning and eloquence, that will lead them the more to desire to go where Christ has not been preached, where useful talent of every kind will find the widest scope for exercise.

Nor will any other scheme of missions, that was ever devised, keep missionaries cheerfully in the field. It is only by having the eye intent on the relations the heathen sustain to God, and on their reconciliation to him, and by cultivating the spirit of dependence on God and the habit of looking to him for success, that the piety of a mission can be kept flourishing, its bond of union perfect, its active powers all in full, harmonious and happy exercise. And unless these results are secured, missionaries, like the soldiers of a disorganized army, will lose their courage, their energy and zeal, their serenity and health, and will leave the field. Alas for a mission, where the absorbing object of attention with any of its members is any thing else, than how Christ crucified shall be preached to the heathen so as most effectually to persuade them to be reconciled to God.

3. This method of conducting missions is the only one, that will subjugate the heathen world to God.

No other will be found mighty to pull down the strong holds of the god of this world. The weapons of our warfare must be spiritual. The enemy will laugh at the shaking of a spear, at diplomatic skill, at commerce, learning, philanthropy, and every scheme of social order and refinement. He stands in fear of nothing but the cross of Christ, and therefore we must rely on nothing else. With that we may boldly pass all his outworks and entrenchments, and assail his very citadel. So did Philip, when he preached Jesus as the way of reconciliation to the eunuch; so did Peter, when preaching to the centurion; so did Apollos, when preaching to the Greeks; so did Paul, through his whole missionary career. It is wonderful what faith those ancient worthies had in the power of a simple statement of the doctrine of salvation through the blood of Christ. But they had felt its power in their own hearts, they saw it on the hearts of others, and they found reason to rely on nothing else. And the experience of modern missions has done much to teach the inefficacy of all things else, separate from this. Who does not know, that the only cure for the deep-seated disorders of mankind must be wrought in the heart, and that nothing operates there like the doctrine of salvation by the cross of Christ? This is true in the most highly civilized communities; but perhaps it is specially true among benighted heathens. In their deplorable moral degradation, they need just such an argument, striking even the very senses, and convincing of sin, of their own lost state, and of the love of God. Nothing else will be found like that to bridge the mighty gulf which separates their thoughts from God and the spiritual world. Nothing else will concentrate, like that, the rays of divine truth and grace upon their frozen affections. With the truth, that God so loved the world as to give his only begotten Son that whosoever believeth on him should not perish but have everlasting life, we go forth through the heathen world; and, with any thing like the faith in its efficacy through the Holy Spirit which the apostles had, we shall be blessed with much of their success. Yes, my Brethren, this is the only effectual way of prosecuting missions among the heathen—*holding up* CHRIST AS THE ONLY SAVIOR OF LOST SINNERS. It requires the fewest men, the least expense, the shortest time. It makes the least demand for learning in the great body of the laborers. It involves the least complication in means and measures. It is the only course that has the absolute promise of the Presence of Christ, or that may certainly look for the aid of the Holy Spirit. It keeps Christ constantly before the missionary's own soul, as an object of intensest interest and desire, with a vast sanctifying, sustaining, animating influence on his own mind and preaching. It furnishes him with a power transcending all that human wisdom ever contrived, for rousing and elevating the soul of man and drawing it heavenward—the idea of LOVE, infinite and infinitely disinterested, personified in the Lord Jesus, and suffering to the death to save rebellious and ruined man! And if the doctrine comes glowing from our own experience, we shall not fail to get the attention of the heathen, and our success among them will far exceed what we might expect among gospel-hardened sinners here at home. I might dwell long on the history of missions, ancient and modern, in the most satisfactory illustration of this point, did the time permit; but it is not necessary.

Let me add, that there is no way so direct and effectual as this, to remove the social disorders and evils that afflict the heathen world; indeed, there is no other way. Every specific evil and sin does not need and cannot have a separate remedy, for they are all streams from one fountain, having a common origin in a depraved and rebellious heart. Urge home, then, the divinely appointed remedy for a wicked heart; purify the fountain; let love to God and man fill the soul; and soon its influence will appear in every department and relation of life. If reforms in religion and morals are not laid deep in the heart, they will be deceptive, and at all events transient. The evil spirit will return in some form, and with seven-fold power. New England owes her strong repugnance to slavery, and her universal rejection of that monstrous evil, to the highly evangelical nature of her preaching. And were the whole southern section of our own land, or even a considerable portion of it, favored with such highly evangelical preaching, slavery could not there long exist. But in heathen lands especially, an effective public sentiment against sin, in any of its outward forms, can be created no where, except in the church; and it can be there created only by preaching Christ in his offices and works of love and mercy, with the aid of the ordinances he has given for the benefit of his disciples, especially the sacrament of his supper. Thus at length, even in barbarous heathen lands, the force of piety in the hearts of the individual members of the church will be raised above that of ignorance, prejudice, the power of custom and usage, the blinding influence of self-interest falsely apprehended, and the ridicule and frowns of an ungodly and perverse world. Indeed, if we would make any thing of converts in pagan lands, we must bring them to the ordinances of the gospel, and into the church, as soon as they give satisfactory evidence of regeneration; for they are too child-like, too weak, too ignorant to be left exposed to the dangers that exist out of the fold, even until they shall have learned all fundamental truths. And besides, the school of Christ for young converts from heathenism, *stands within the fold,* and *there,* certainly, the compassionate Savior would have them all gathered, and carried in the arms, and cherished "even as a nurse cherisheth her children."

Finally; This method of conducting missions is the only one, that will unite in this work the energies of the churches at home.

Well understood, this will unite the energies of the churches—so far as Christians can be induced to prosecute missions for the purpose of reconciling men to God. Making this the grand aim of missions, and pressing the love of Christ home upon the hearts and consciences of men, as the grand means of effecting this, will certainly commend itself to the understandings and feelings of all intelligent Christians. Not only will a large number of good and faithful missionaries be obtained, but they will be supported, and prayed for, and made the objects of daily interest and concern. And how delightful it is to think, that the Head of the church has been pleased to make the object and work of missions so entirely simple, so spiritual, and so beyond the possibility of exception, that evangelical Christians of every nation and name can unite in its promotion. But if we change the form of the work, and extend the range of its objects of direct pursuit, and of course multiply the measures and influences by which it is to be advanced, we then open the door for honest and invincible diversities of opinion among the best of men, and render it impossible that there should be united effort, on a scale at all commensurate with the work, and for a long period. The church militant becomes divided and weak, and is easily paralized and thwarted in its movements by the combined and united legions of the Prince of darkness.

It would seem, therefore, that missions to the heathen must have a highly spiritual nature and development, or prove utterly impracticable and abortive. Such, it is believed, are the convictions of all who have had much experience in such enterprises. Unless missions have this nature and development in a very high degree, they will not commend themselves strongly to the consciences and respect of mankind; they will neither command the requisite number of laborers, nor keep them cheerfully in the field; they will prove inadequate to the subjugation of the heathen world to God; nor will they unite in this great enterprise the energies and prayers of the churches. In a word, they will not continue long to exist, unless Christ the Lamb of God be in them, reconciling the world unto himself, and causing his servants to make the salvation of the souls of men their all-commanding end and aim. Men may *resolve* that it shall be otherwise; but their purposes, however decided, will be in vain against the unalterable laws, which God has given the work of missions to the heathen.

BELOVED BROTHER,—In the system of missions, with which you are soon to be connected, the aim has been, and is more and more, as experience is acquired, to prosecute the work on the principles advocated in this discourse. So far as your own influence is concerned, see that the system be rendered still more spiritual in its temper, objects, and measures. See, too, that your own renunciation of the world is entire before you enter upon your self-denying work, and that it be your determination to know nothing among the heathen but Christ and him crucified. Only by looking constantly unto Jesus, will you be able to run with patience the race set before you. As an ambassador of Christ, sent to plead with men in his stead to be reconciled to God, see that you are true to your vocation, and faithful to your trust, and that you never descend from the elevated ground you occupy. Whatever oscillations in public sentiment there may be from time to time in the Christian mind at home, you need not fear, if your character, preaching and influence are formed on the New Testament, that you will be forgotten in the contributions and prayers of God's people. At all events, be faithful unto death, and whatever be your lot here below, the result in eternity will be more blessed to you, than it is possible for your mind now to conceive, or your heart to desire.

FATHERS AND BRETHREN,—Let it be our prayer, that God will be pleased to strengthen our own faith in the realities of the unseen world. Then shall we be better able to pray as we ought for our missionary brethren, that they may be intent on their single but great object of winning souls to Christ, and be so imbued with the spirit of Christ, that his image shall be fully stamped on all their converts. Let us urge upon our brethren among the heathen the imperative duty of making full proof of their ministry as *missionaries*, rather than as *pastors;* and let us lay upon them "no greater burden," than the "necessary things" appertaining to their high and peculiar vocation. We must indeed hold them to the principle, that they shall treat those only as loyal subjects of our infinite Sovereign, who give evidence of hearty submission and reconciliation; but we will leave it to their better-informed judgments to determine,—in the remote, vast and varied, and to us almost unknown fields of their labors,—what is and what ought to be satisfactory evidence of actual reconciliation. Then will our brethren rejoice in having a simple, well-sustained, and glorious enterprise before them, and also "for the consolation" of the liberty conceded to them by the "elders" and the "whole church." In this good old way, marked with the footsteps of the apostles, there is hope for the world, for the whole world, that it may be reconciled to God. And when the principles of love and obedience are once restored to men, and men are at peace with God, and united to Him, then will they be at peace with one another. Then wars will cease, and all oppression. Then the crooked in human affairs shall be made straight and the rough places plain, the valleys shall be exalted and the mountains and hills made low, and the glory of the Lord shall be revealed, and all flesh see it together.

19. Joost Van Vollenhoven
and Educational Planning for French West Africa

Joost Van Vollenhoven (1877–1918) was among the most able of the
French governors of the period just before the First World War. Born
in Algeria to a *colon* family of Dutch descent, he entered the colonial
service by way of the *École coloniale* and served in the central administration in Paris, then in West Africa and Brazzaville, before his
appointment as Governor in Hanoi in 1912. He rose to be Governor-
General of Indo-China in 1914, but then resigned and volunteered for
active service at the front. After a military career as an officer of the
Moroccan infantry, he was again recalled to the colonial service in
1917 and sent as Governor-General of French West Africa. Early in
1918, he came into conflict with his superiors in Paris over the policy
of recruiting still more black Africans for service in France, and
especially over the special role assigned in this recruitment to Blaise
Diagne, the first African elected to represent the coastal cities of
Senegal in the French National Assembly. He again resigned and requested transfer to his old unit at the front, where he was killed in
action on July 20, 1918.

   Van Vollenhoven is best remembered in West Africa for his efforts
in the field of education, and for his ideas on the proper use of traditional authorities in the French administration. As an active administrator, he did not write widely for publication, but a number of his
administrative circulars were gathered together and published after
his death in a book entitled *Une âme de chef* (Paris, 1920). Although
Van Vollenhoven had many of the Associationist attitudes of his time,
the importance he placed on education—however little he was actually
able to accomplish—suggests the survival of Assimilationist policies
which were to continue as an undertone in French imperial thought
into the 1950's. The selection is from Van Vollenhoven's "Circular
on Educational Planning," dated October 5, 1917, and directed to the
commandants de cercle throughout French West Africa. It is quoted
from *Une âme de chef*, pp. 178–81, and 186–189.

Circular on Educational Planning

October 5, 1917

I WILL not waste time with customary generalizations. I will not
boast of the benefits of education, after so many others have done
so, and I will not show once again that it should be the cornerstone
of our colonial policy. I will also refrain from attacking the out-

moded adages which would no longer be current if people did not discuss them so much. It is not true that the natives are hostile to education; to be convinced, it is only necessary to visit our schools, insufficient though they be. It is not true that the native who has learned to read and write in French and who knows arithmetic necessarily becomes a declassed unfortunate and malcontent, as though this tiny load were too heavy for him. He is a man who is conscious of his dignity, who has broken with the barbarism of ancestral prejudices, who has come to understand that education is the best protection and the sole road toward progress; he will no longer surprise anyone when he becomes the rule rather than the exception. I will abstain, finally, from reopening the eternal discussion of programs, and I will not quarrel over the advantage or disadvantage of excluding Louis XIV or the tributaries of the Loire from our textbooks. My preoccupation is simpler, and my ambition is nevertheless greater. I have made a calculation which torments me and will torment all who will make it with me. There are in French West Africa 1,800,000 children of school age. At the present moment, only 20,000 of them receive instruction. After a French occupation which has lasted for a half century in most of French West Africa, such a tiny proportion of school attendance is inadmissible. Ninety-nine per cent of our children are excluded from our schools; for these little ones there are neither classes, nor teachers, nor books. Some years from now—only a few years from now—we must be able to show other figures, other proportions, more in conformity with what France usually does in a country which flies her flag and is enlightened by her genius.

What effort should be made to attain this result? What method must be followed? How are we to get the necessary teachers and classes? What should our educational plan be? I will tell you. . . .

For the moment, I will not speak of secondary education, of the various forms of technical or professional education, or even of education for girls. It is not that these questions do not interest me, but their study would take me too far afield, and, besides, I will have an opportunity to return to them. I will limit myself for the moment to common-law education; that is, to primary education.

In French West Africa, this kind of instruction is given in regional schools and in village schools. In the first of these, as in the second, the goal pursued is the same: to develop the mind of the pupils without denationalizing them or uprooting them. In the first, as in the second, they are taught French, arithmetic, the metric system, and the usual hygiene. Finally, in regional as in village schools, the tendency is completely practical. There is manual training, varying according to the region, and an important role is reserved for practical agricultural instruction. Taking note of the program of May 1, 1914, it seems that the difference between the two educational establishments is more one of degree than of kind. In the regional schools, the things which can be no more than outlined and skimmed over in the village schools are completed and studied at greater depth. But even to understand the form of instruction, it is not enough to glance through the program; it has to be seen in reality, and then the difference between the regional and village schools can be seen before one's own eyes. The regional school, located in the principal town of the colony or the *cercle*, is generally a little better outfitted. It is directed by an educated and experienced teacher, with the aid of several assistants. The village schools, on the other hand, are too often assigned to young local teachers, whose pedagogical attainments consist mainly of good will, if indeed the school is not in charge of monitors better qualified to sit on the benches than to take the teacher's chair. With rare exceptions, the village schools, badly outfitted, badly run, badly attended, are only nurseries where the children learn to speak French. The best of them, those who are ambitious or whose parents hold a higher position, go directly to the regional school. The latter thus benefit from a quality of recruitment that both explains and justifies their authority; the blacks know as well as the whites how to distinguish a good education from a bad one.

I believe that we should take this lesson into account, and since we are on the eve of a great effort, ask ourselves in which direction we wish it to go.

Should we increase the number of village schools and wait until the first level is better attended, both quantitatively and qualitatively, before multiplying the number of regional schools, or would it be better to reverse the proposition? Would it not be wiser to set up a strong regional school in the principal town of each *cercle* as rapidly as possible, well located, well run by a competent director, with assistants who will learn from the example of the director? One would try to recruit the best elements of the *cercle* for this school, and the solid instruction given to these children would be the best of advertising. I think it is enough to describe the two methods, and the choice will be clear. Half programs, half measures, progress in appearances only—these are all dangerous to colonies. It is necessary to do the job well once and for all and avoid camouflage which fools no one. Since it is understood that our means are insufficient and will remain so for some years to come, it is necessary to avoid waste; it is necessary, indeed, to concentrate effort in order to obtain the highest returns. Regional schools will be set up first; village schools will follow and benefit from the example and the results. They will be the accessory, the indispensable complement, but they cannot live and prosper in the absence of the principal organ—first the tree, then the foliage! . . .

The teacher problem dominates the educational problem; it has a quite different importance from that of programs. Pupils will always profit from the lessons of a good teacher.

But immediately after the teacher problem comes that of the physical plant. It is indispensable that the schools be well outfitted, that they do honor to the town, and that, by the importance we give to the building, we mark in the eys of the natives the importance we attach to the work that goes on within. The budgetary considerations, which have been so often brought forward to retard progress and slow the necessary development of education, have operated with a special effectiveness in this respect. I will not go into the sad impressions I have had in visiting the schools of French West Africa. At Porto Novo, I found a model scholarly grouping. In some other places, I found decent places, but too often I have seen schools miserable in appearance, so disgusting that their closing and demolition is called for as a sanitary measure. One certainly feels that this state of affairs cannot continue, and that it is bitterly derisory to speak of work, of progress, of civilization, in dirty huts, without air, without light, and sometimes without a roof.

I certainly understand that it is necessary to guard against vague recommendations, and to give orders only to the extent that they can and must be carried out. I have recommended the development of regional schools, and I have said that I would see to the recruitment in France of teachers necessary to assure the operation of these schools. How will these schools be set up?

A regional school of middling importance should be composed of three classes, each planned for thirty pupils. It should include, besides, lodging for a director belonging to the French educational system, and lodging for two teachers of local origin. That is the problem to solve. It has been solved—when it has been solved—in a rather strange way, and in general it seems to me that the usual concern has been to lodge the masters and place the classrooms in a single building. Most often, a vast two-story building has been constructed, which costs 75,000 to 100,000 francs, at the least. In the three or four upstairs rooms, the masters are lodged. In the three or four rooms on the ground floor, the classes are held. This system, which seems especially favored in French West Africa, is deplorable, for it is evident that everyone is quite ill at ease in such a situation. In a country where everything is open, it can be imagined what the life of an ill or tired teacher must be, living above his class, and, on the other hand, what teaching must be like in contiguous rooms, weakly partitioned, with all the doors and windows open. Lessons are taught in a continual hubbub. It defies good sense; it defies hygiene; and it is astonishing that we have not yet broken away from such detestable mistakes. The remedy is nevertheless simple and easy to carry out in these countries where space is available. It is necessary to spread out. It is necessary to build a scholastic camp exactly like an army camp. It is necessary to choose a vast plot of land and set up competely independent buildings. Each class will have its own building; according to the resources available, this building will be either in masonry roofed with tile or in adobe roofed with thatch. The walls need be raised to only half the height of the doors, and the windows in the majority of cases can be nothing but large openings. Lodging for the staff should be isolated in the same way as the classes. The classic three-room house must be built in the camp for the director of the school, and less imposing lodging provided for the assistants. It goes without saying that these prescriptions cannot be applied in cities, but in bush they must be scrupulously followed. The center of the plot will serve simultaneously as a playing field and a garden, provided for in the instructions of August 5, 1916.

If the sum of 50,000 to 100,000 francs, which is now spent to build a masonry school complex, is devoted to this camp, something quite good will result and we will have model scholastic

groupings without difficulty. It will be necessary to build at least
five of these scholastic camps each year. Thus, in three years, all of
our *cercles* will be provided for and the educational plan laid down
by the present circular can be finished with the least delay, both in
staff and in physical plant. Need I add that, since the regional
schools will be ahead of the village schools, it can be foreseen that
most of the pupils attending will be boarders, and their food should
be provided; there is no objection, on the other hand, if most of
this food comes from the harvest of the pupils' own crops. In fact,
agriculture does not require daily work in this country; all crops
are seasonal.

In sum, the goal that I pursue is simple. I would like there to be a
three-class regional school in each *cercle* of French West Africa,
well built, well run, and well attended, and in no more than three
years from now. To obtain this result, I will put at least five new
teachers from the French system at your disposal each year. That
calls for an initial expense of 50,000 francs a year, or 150,000 at the
end of three years, and this expense will continue. In addition, it
will be necessary to add to this figure the salaries of the native
assistants, which will represent an expense of 50,000 to 75,000
francs. Then, the construction of the schools will require an effort
on your part, which will come to 300,000 to 500,000 francs per
year, or 900,000 to 1,500,000 francs in three years, but this expense
will disappear from your budgets as soon as the program is completed. The total effort to be made by your colony will vary from
1.5 million to 2.5 million francs for each of the first three years,
and will then stabilize at between 500,000 and 600,000 francs a
year.

I believe that this sacrifice is in no way excessive, neither in
comparison with the goal to be attained nor with the means which
will be ours. As I have in fact explained in my circular of September 20th, French West Africa cannot continue to vegetate as it has
done, and we cannot continue to administer with the stinginess that
has characterized our administration up to this time. It is necessary
to make an effort, and this effort must be considerable. At the base
of this effort is the quantitative and qualitative improvement of the
race, for man is the principal resource of this country. Medical
assistance on one hand, public instruction on the other, must now
find the place in our achievements which they have occupied up to

now only in our projects. You understand this; your support will
not fail me in assuring the execution of this part of my program.
Nothing is more important.

20. Lord Lugard on Educational Planning for Nigeria

Frederick D. Lugard (1858–1945) had a career that ranged over an
immense field of imperial activity, beginning as a soldier in the Anglo-
Afghan War of 1879–80 and ending as Governor-General of Nigeria
in 1914–19. He was too independent in his judgments to be considered
a typical pro-consul of the British Empire at its height; but he played
a crucial personal role in the conquest of Uganda and Northern Nigeria, and he was articulate in expressing his theories about the empire. The school of Indirect Rule, of which Temple (see above, pp.
93–105) was the most prominent other spokesman, was first formed during Lugard's administration as High Commissioner of Northern Nigeria in 1900–06.
    In the field of education, Lugard held views that were common in
his time. He believed that education of the "natives" was essential to
the progress of the empire, but he also had a marked distrust of educated Africans and a preference for the gentlemanly manners of the
Nigerian emirs. His plan for increasing education without producing a
class of educated rebels against British rule is the subject of the passage
that follows, drawn from Chapters XXI and XXII of his major work,
The Dual Mandate in British Tropical Africa, 4th ed. (London, 1929),
pp. 425–430, 432, 442–450, 457–460. Some of the original footnotes
have been omitted.

IF A life happy and progressive so far as the individual is concerned,
useful, sympathetic, and stimulating in its relations with the community, may be said to constitute a worthy ideal, the object which
education in Africa must have in view must be to fit the ordinary
individual to fill a useful part in his environment, with happiness to
himself, and to ensure that the exceptional individual shall use his
abilities for the advancement of the community and not to its detriment, or to the subversion of constituted authority.

    Its results should be manifest in the adaptation of the people to
the existing conditions of life, and in enabling them to effect some
betterment and progress in those conditions. It should train a generation able to achieve ideals of its own, without a slavish imitation
of Europeans, capable and willing to assume its own definite sphere
of public and civic work, and to shape its own future. The educa-

tion afforded to that section of the population who intend to lead the lives which their forefathers led should enlarge their outlook, increase their efficiency and standard of comfort, and bring them into closer sympathy with the Government, instead of making them unsuited to and ill-contented with their mode of life. It should produce a new generation of native chiefs of higher integrity, a truer sense of justice, and appreciation of responsibility for the welfare of the community. As regards that smaller section who desire to take part in public or municipal duties, or to enter the service of Government or of commercial firms, education should make them efficient, loyal, reliable and contented—a race of self-respecting native gentlemen. Finally, the policy should popularise education, should extend it to the ignorant masses instead of confining it to the few, and should increase the output of youths well qualified to meet the demand, whether clerical, professional, or industrial.

The diffusion of education throughout the country, and especially the education of the sons of native rulers, is particularly desirable in order to avoid the present danger of a separate educated class (in West Africa chiefly confined to the coast cities) in rivalry with the accepted rulers of the people.

The impact of European civilisation on tropical races has indeed a tendency to undermine that respect for authority which is the basis of social order. The authority of the head, whether of the tribe, the village, or the family, is decreased, and parental discipline is weakened—tendencies which, as Lord Macdonnell observed, are probably inseparable from that emancipation of thought which results from our educational system and needs the control of scholastic discipline. These tendencies are no doubt largely due to the fact that each generation is advancing intellectually beyond its predecessor, so that "the younger men view with increasing impatience the habits, traditions, and ideas of their elders."* From this standpoint we may even regard this restlessness as a measure of progress.

These tendencies became very marked in India towards the close of the nineteenth century. The failure of the system of Indian education is graphically described by Sir V. Chirol, and appears now to be very generally admitted. "A purely literary type of

---

* Selected Records of Indian Government, 265, p. 11.

education was the only one generally provided by Government,"
says the Industrial Report of 1919, and the intellectual classes
eagerly grasped at the prospect of Government, professional, and
clerical employment, with the result that a disproportionate number of persons with a purely literary education were created, and
industrial development was arrested.

Prosperity would seem to be a contributory cause—as in Egypt
and Ireland,—for, as the special correspondent of the "Times,"
writing in 1913, observes: "The people of India have never been so
well off, never so wisely cared for, never so secure as they are to-
day." Yet the undermining of all authority is rapidly proceeding.
Parents complain of the intractability of their boys. The local press
preaches sedition, and racial strife is stirred up by misrepresentation
and false reports. If "the influence of education for good depends
on the qualities of character it is able to evoke," it must be judged
to have failed. Its aim, it is alleged, has been to train the intellect,
and to gauge the product of the schools by the ability to pass tests
in prescribed fields of knowledge, to the neglect of moral discipline
and standards of duty. Positive knowledge as tested by competitive
examinations has constituted the key to success.

As long ago as December 1887 the Government of India drew
the attention of the local Governments to "the growth of tendencies unfavourable to discipline in the rising generation," and
various suggestions were made to counteract this tendency. They
included the establishment of hostels and boarding-houses, the appointment of British headmasters and of school monitors, the
recognition of field sports as a part of the school training, the
adoption of disciplinary punishments which should fall more directly on the offender than fines, and of prizes for good conduct,
together with moral instruction based on the fundamental principles of natural religion, and having a direct bearing on personal
conduct. The suggestions were favourably received, and the replies
of the local Governors and of educational experts were published
in the Blue-book from which I have quoted, under the title, "Discipline and Moral Training in the Schools and Colleges of India"
(255 pages). It is a volume so full of ripe experience and suggestion
that the Colonial Office would do well to place it in the hands of
the Director of Education in every colony.

On 18th June of the following year a resolution was passed
which recognised the necessity for abandoning the purely literary

scope of education, and it was followed in 1889 by a still wider recognition of the defects of the system. The results were, however, small, though they led the way to Lord Curzon's Educational Conference, and the very important resolution of March 1904.

The system which had proved so disastrous in India had its counterpart in the Crown colonies and dependencies, and its results were similar. The lessons of India were ignored. I have already quoted the opinion of a French writer that a literary education on European lines has mischievous results, and only produces hostility and ingratitude. The results achieved by Holland, and to a lesser degree by Germany, in their Eastern colonies are contrasted to our disadvantage. In South Africa General Smuts has recently described the existing system as "wholly unsuited to native needs, and positively pernicious, leading the native to a dead wall, over which he is unable to rise, and becomes a ready prey to the agitator."

The results in West Africa were described by the Secretary of State (Mr. Harcourt) in 1916 as "very unsatisfactory," a verdict endorsed by Dr. Blyden and by many other leading Africans, including the (native) Acting Director of Education in Nigeria (Mr. Carr). The output of the schools is described as unreliable, lacking in integrity, self-control, and discipline, and without respect for authority of any kind. The vanity of the young men produced by the schools had (said the senior native councillor in Lagos) become intolerable, and something, he urged, must be done to rescue the rising generation from these evils. It is only to be expected that the result of the present system should be to create a prejudice against education, since, as a Sierra Leone chief remarked, "it teaches youths to despise their elders," while others ascribed the increased cost of food to the unwillingness of youths from school to work on the land. Provincial reports speak of the contempt for manual work shown by boys from schools.

Education has brought to such men only discontent, suspicion of others, and bitterness, which masquerades as racial patriotism, and the vindication of rights unjustly withheld. As citizens they are unfitted to hold posts of trust and responsibility where integrity and loyalty are essential, or to become leaders of their own community in the path of progress. They have lost touch, as I said in chapter iv, with their own people. Fortunately there are many and brilliant exceptions.

Since education has in the past been largely in the hands of the

Missions, to whom moral training would naturally be of the first importance, how are these results to be explained? Was there no means by which the disruptive forces of education could be minimised in a country like Africa, where the problem is comparatively simple? The lack of discipline among Mission converts has indeed occasionally led to political disturbances, both in Nigeria and in Ashanti.

The fault has, I think, lain primarily on the Governments, for the grant on which the aided schools depend has been based on a purely intellectual test. Great as are the results achieved by the Missions in Africa—and they are great indeed in Uganda, Nyasaland, and West Africa—they too must bear their share of the blame in having set too slight a value on discipline, and concentrated too much on the acquisition of such knowledge as would enable their pupils to do creditably in the Government examinations, and the training of a specialised class for evangelical work. . . .

I have placed the formation of character in the foreground of African education, for if this be recognised as a primary function of education in communities whose standards have been moulded by centuries of Christian ethics, whose youth even in its most squalid surroundings is subjected, however unconsciously, to the influence of those standards, whether in the board school or the picture palace, how much more necessary is it in Africa, where, as a rule, such influences are absent? Among the primitive tribes ethical standards must be created—among few are they a vital and potent force. If, for instance, in his village home the African boy perceives that self-indulgence and lack of self-control excite no reprobation; that thrift, ambition, and initiative are conceptions as foreign to his associates as an alien tongue, for which his language has no appropriate terms; if justice, fair-play, truthfulness, and mutual obligation have no influence in guiding the actions of those around him,—then these conceptions must be created and built up. I do not for a moment mean to infer that there is a complete lack of such qualities among Africans who have not been brought into contact with the higher standards, for I profoundly believe that these conceptions are all innate in humanity, and are exhibited in a greater or less degree, even in the primitive savage, but they are generally undeveloped, and are not enforced by the public opinion of the community, and lack the sanction of local custom.

If, then, it is admitted that it is inevitable that education should produce a ferment of new and progressive ideas, subversive of the old order, the function of a sound system must be to guide these tendencies so that they may conduce to the betterment of the body politic and not to its disintegration. . . .

Assuming, then, that the Government takes the lead in the task of education, let us consider the nature of the problem which it has to solve, so far as class-room instruction is concerned. There may be said to be three objects which educational agencies have in view—viz., (*a*) the literary training required for posts in which a good knowledge of English and accounting is necessary; (*b*) the technical training of mechanics and artisans employed with power-driven plant and other technical work; and (*c*) the teaching of crafts and agriculture and the very elementary schooling suitable to village life.

We sometimes hear the opinion that it would be better if the African confined himself to agriculture and artisan work, and left literary education alone. We read that in India the output of the schools and universities is in excess of the demand, and creates an unemployable class which becomes a prey to the agitator. In tropical Africa, on the contrary, there is an unlimited demand, not only for subordinates but for doctors and for the Civil Staff, if men with the proper qualifications both of education and of character were available.

The progress made in the development of Africa would have been impossible were it not for the enormous number of Africans who fill posts in which a knowledge of English, of reading, writing, and arithmetic, and, to a lesser degree, of book-keeping and accountancy, is required. Those who are employed in the technical departments, such as surveyors, telegraphists, printers, and skilled men in the workshops, require the same initial training. With the extension of railways and the expansion of Government departments and of private enterprise, the demand for such men has become very large indeed.

The result in West Africa is that boys who have only half completed their education are tempted to leave school, and are able to obtain posts which demand much higher qualifications than they possess, so that two or three may be necessary to do the work, with ill success, which one efficient man should perform. Thus the standard of efficiency is lowered, and wages, as compared with the cost of living and the value of the work done, increase beyond the scale paid in England and elsewhere for similar work. The wages paid to clerks react on the technical departments, and it becomes increasingly difficult to secure an adequate number of apprentices with elementary schooling, or of teachers for the schools. The latter deficiency tends further to restrict the supply at its source. So difficult has the situation become in Nigeria that the Acting Director of Education—himself a native African of great distinction—urged the necessity of importing clerical subordinates in large numbers from the East.

It is clear that in dependencies so situated the Government cannot rely on the output of the Mission schools only—much as the British African tropics are indebted to them in the past,—and the creation of an adequate number of Government primary and secondary schools is a matter which must not be left (as it has too often been) until the deficiency has already caused grave injury to the country. Schools are required at every provincial and at many divisional headquarters. Whenever it is possible, the boys should be boarders, for the reasons already given, and the school should not be nearer than one or two miles from a native city. An age limit should be fixed for each class or standard.

The medium of instruction, except in the lower standards, should be English, and as many scholarships as possible should be provided. In the northern provinces of Nigeria the cost of buildings and native staff is borne by the native administrations (42 per cent in 1913), that of the British staff and inspectorate by general revenue. Each school would, of course, have its "normal class" for the training of teachers, and its continuation classes. Uniformity in the "standards" of the various schools is of importance, so that the degree of proficiency of any boy, who is certified as having passed a certain standard, may be known to his prospective employer.

The chief function of Government primary and secondary schools among primitive communities is to train the more promising boys from the village schools as teachers for those schools, as clerks for the local native courts, and as interpreters. For these the higher standards are not required.

The village schools must depend on these primary and secondary Government schools for their supply of teachers; and since the teaching in the village schools is chiefly industrial, each of the "literary" schools should have a class in which native crafts and industries (especially agriculture) are taught, so that boys who desire to become teachers in village schools may be properly qualified.

Village schools should, in my opinion, be adapted to the requirements of the peasantry, who do not seek either a literary education to qualify them as clerks, &c., or a technical training for power-driven workshops. Their object is to improve the village craftsmen and agriculturists, to raise the standard of life, comfort, and intelligence in the village community, and to teach habits of discipline, industry, and truthfulness. At these schools trades should be taught (carpentry, blacksmithing, agriculture, &c.), together with some rudimentary schooling in elementary hygiene, colloquial English, and such moral and religious instruction, whether Christian or Mohamedan, as may help to free the peasant from the cruel domination of superstitious and inhuman practices. To this may usefully be added simple explanations of British aims—the advantages of railways, roads, currency, and free labour, the reasons for taxation, &c. In the higher classes some small knowledge of "the 3 R's" may be included, which shall render the pupil—and through him the village—less liable to be the victim of misrepresentation and fraud.

These schools would not be intended to qualify a boy for Government employment, or to develop into literary schools. They would be affiliated to the nearest Government primary or secondary school. In non-Moslem districts Mohamedan teachers would not be employed, and in practice no doubt these schools would be largely in the hands of the Missions. They would be conducted by a carefully-selected native teacher, and would not be boarding-schools. The medium of instruction would be the vernacular—in the higher classes English or a local *lingua franca*—such as Arabic, Swaheli, or Hausa. The boys would at first spend about half their time in elementary education, and later practically the whole time in learning some craft. The instruction imparted would be very simple, and given from the most practical standpoint, special attention being devoted to the introduction of better appliances, in order to improve the quality and increase the quantity of the output.

The instruction given at each school should be especially adapted to the occupations most suited to, or traditional in, the village. In some weaving, in others smelting, dyeing, or tanning may be time-honoured crafts. Similarly in regard to agriculture, the care of those crops which are chiefly cultivated in the district would receive special attention—cotton in one, cocoa in another, and so on.

The Indian Industrial Report—published since these instructions were issued in Nigeria—recommends practically identical methods in regard to the "cottage industries" of India, which, it is suggested, may be assisted by peripatetic instructors, teaching improved processes, and introducing new patterns and designs and labour-saving devices. The report emphasises the difference in training needed for these cottage industries, and the class-room study and apprenticeship necessary to produce skilled mechanics.

The teaching of the village school may be carried to a higher stage in the agricultural classes on the one hand, or in a Central Industrial School on the other. In the latter native arts and crafts would be taught by skilled native craftsmen, under the supervision of a British foreman. The object would be to preserve all that is best in native design and art, while introducing better methods, appliances, and tools. Carpentry and wood-carving, metal-work and engraving on brass and copper, blacksmith's work, smelting and casting, leather-work and tanning, weaving and embroidery on cloth and leather, and other native industries, would be taught. To these might be added such new crafts as are suitable for cottage industry, such as brickmaking and the construction of country carts and wheels. There would be no class-room instruction—though pupils would be encouraged to attend the evening classes at the provincial school,—and no attempt to train boys for wage-earning employment.

It is very desirable that provincial schools—and essential that all village schools—should possess a good school garden, in which boys can acquire a knowledge of the various plants under cultivation, and of the use of garden tools and agricultural implements.

Before passing to technical education, I have a very tentative suggestion to offer, to which I have already referred in chapter iv. Parents deplore the tendency of young men to embark prematurely on an independent career, which in such circumstances can offer little prospect of success, and exposes them to temptation, and to the cost of maintaining a separate establishment beyond their means. In order to check this tendency and to maintain parental discipline, it may perhaps be feasible to institute a scheme of clerical apprentices somewhat on the following lines. Youths between the ages of seventeen and twenty, recommended not merely for intellectual ability but for sterling character, would be selected from among the seniors at the best schools for employment on progressive salaries during four or five years. They would reside during this apprenticeship with their parents, and be attached to the Secretariat or Treasury, but in order to acquire proficiency and fluency in English and thorough qualifications for their duties, they would continue to attend school for certain hours. They might be called "student clerks" or "cadets," and if they pass the required tests at the end of their term, they would have received a much better and more prolonged education than the ordinary clerk. They would be bound to enter the Government service, if wanted, for a period of, say, five years, and would be eligible for accelerated promotion. Eventually the cadets might become a *corps d'élite*, and aspire to high posts.

We have dealt with two of the great classes for whom educational facilities are required—viz., the literary (clerical) class, and the rural (industrial) class. The third group consists of the artisans and mechanics employed in Government and commercial workshops—by the railway, marine, public works, and printing departments,—most of whom are engaged in handling power-driven machinery. For these a primary education is a necessary preliminary, but the "manual training," which has found favour both in Government and in Mission schools, is of little or no use. The workshop staff reports that not only is a training in box- and chair-making useless for a boy who desires to become a trained mechanic, but that he must unlearn much of what he has learnt, and begin all over again. Much valuable time is also lost in giving such teaching to boys whose intention it is to become clerks, and have no need of it.

The Indian Industrial Report (as I have already said) endorses this view, and emphasises the necessity of discriminating between the industrial training needed for cottage industries and the class-room study, and the apprenticeship necessary to produce skilled mechanics.

As soon as the youth has passed the required standard he should become an apprentice in the department which he desires to adopt. It is of the utmost importance that every technical department should train a large number of apprentices. Their training must be conducted by a special instructor, and not left (as used to be the case) to the chance assistance of men engaged in work themselves. In other words, each technical department should have a technical class attached to it for the training of apprentices. The instructor would also hold classes for special instruction in theory and drawing, &c., for those who show special aptitude—not in night-schools, when they are too tired to learn, but during working hours,—and they could improve their general education by attending continuation classes at the provincial school. The aim should be to put the apprentices on the same level as the clerical branch, in pay, housing, opportunities for recreation, and general status, so as to attract to it an equally good class. During his five years' indenture an apprentice is, of course, paid a progressive wage.

The aptitude of the African as a skilled worker is abundantly in evidence in the railway, printing, and other workshops. In West Africa, as an "engineer correspondent" testifies, he has replaced Europeans in many departments of skilled work, and he does not require an undue amount of European supervision. Even in such highly technical work as acetylene welding and cutting, in pattern-making from dimensioned drawings, and in the use of the lathe and of modern machine tools, he bears witness to his efficiency.

If the African does not yet aspire to the position of foreman, it is because he has hitherto lacked sufficient general education, and has not entered the shops at a sufficiently early age. When boys of sixteen or seventeen, having passed the fifth or sixth standard so that they can make accurate calculations and correctly interpret plans and drawings, can acquire in the shops from a special instructor some knowledge of the theoretical side of the work and the reasons for the various processes, there is no reason why they should not become efficient managers and shop-foremen. The weak point of the qualified African engineer who holds a technical degree is that his ability to memorise enables him to fill his head with formulae of which he does not appreciate the full meaning. He must also acquire the ability to control men, and a greater sense of responsibility in his work.

In the Sudan the Gordon College provides an extra departmental institute for technical training. A similar institution is in course of erection in the northern provinces of Nigeria, a considerable part of the funds having been provided by a bequest of the late Sir

Alfred Jones. Such an institute supplements, but cannot supersede, the value of the training acquired by apprentices in workshops, but it has a special value in Nigeria, since it provides an opportunity of training Mohamedan youths who do not readily mix with the artisans from the coast.

It has also an additional value in providing a means of showing that the skilled workman occupies no inferior status to that of the clerk, and of promoting healthy rivalry in sports between the two classes. By these various means the tropical African dependencies should be able to produce competent native foremen of works instead of being dependent on British artisans, who are very costly, and of whom the supply is strictly limited. . . .

The Governments of our Crown colonies and dependencies have, I think, been too ready to leave the burden of education to be borne by the Missions. In most of the African dependencies the proportion of revenue devoted to this all-important object might well be doubled or even trebled. Regarding our task from either of the two standpoints which I have emphasised in this volume—viz., our duty to the natives, and our responsibility to civilisation—the obligation is insistent. It is from the natives that the bulk of the revenue is ultimately derived, and it is our duty to train them so that they may take that share in municipal and governmental work for which they prove themselves to be qualified; that they may fill the posts, both clerical and technical, for which good salaries are offered; that they may learn to adopt scientific methods in business and agriculture, so as to make the best of their opportunities, their labour, and the resources of their country, and hold their own in the world's competition.

The merchant, the miner, and the trader need the help of educated natives, whether as clerks and accountants or as artisans, to assist in the development of the country—a development in which Africans are themselves taking an increasingly prominent part. It is useless to build railways if you have no clerks, accountants, telegraphists, or signalmen, and no artisans for the workshops—and the same may be said of every other department. The employment of natives of the country by Government and commercial firms not only benefits the country by keeping the money in it, but saves the passage-money of aliens, and promotes continuity, which is sacrificed by employing Europeans, who have constantly to go on leave. Alike, therefore, from motives of moral obligation or material progress, there can be no way in which the revenue can be better applied than in promoting education.

Though little material reduction in the cost of education can be expected from school fees, it is, I think, important that they should be imposed, however nominal in amount. . . . The African is not singular in regarding as of little value what costs him nothing. The primitive savage is indeed apt to think that he should rather be paid for allowing his children to attend school, since he loses their household labour.

The time has not yet come for compulsory education in Africa, if for no other reasons than the paucity of qualified teachers, and the enormous cost. When, however, a boy receives his education free of cost, it would seem desirable that he should be compelled to remain and complete the school course. In most of the African dependencies there is an eager demand, both on the part of the parents and children—a demand which may be expected to continue unless the results of education are such as to create a prejudice against it. But although universal education is as yet a distant ideal, it should, I think, be a primary object of British policy to disseminate education throughout the country, with a view to breaking down the distinction between the educated and Europeanised class in the capital cities, and the bulk of the population in the interior. Each provincial capital to begin with should become a centre from which educational progress may radiate.

So important in my view are the main considerations in regard to education, which it has been the purpose of this and the preceding chapter to present to my readers, that I will venture briefly to recapitulate them, lest they should be obscured by the minor matters of detail referred to. I have emphasised the fact that not only as trustees for their advancement are we pledged to afford to the races of the tropics the best education we can give to fit them for an increasing share in governmental and municipal duties, but that the irresistible material progress of the country demands an ever-increasing supply of Africans with both a literary and a technical education—a demand which we ourselves have created, and one which may be the greatest and most potent factor for good if rightly used; for evil, and ultimate disaster, if the basis of our structure be founded on wrong principles. Moreover, great as are the claims of the minority, from whose ranks the demands of Govern-

ment and commerce are supplied, they must not obscure those of
the great majority who are content to live the life their fathers
have lived in their villages.

The coloured races of the world are awakening to self-con-
sciousness under Western influences. In Africa tribal rule is dis-
integrating. On the form which the new aspirations take will
depend the future relations of these peoples with the white races of
the world. Are the foundations being truly laid? Is the education
provided by our schools such as to guide those aspirations into the
channels best adapted for the evolution of individual character and
racial progress? This is the great problem upon which incalculable
results may—nay, must—depend.

My aim has been to urge that these results may best be achieved
by placing the formation of character before the training of the
intellect, and to make some few suggestions as to how this may be
done—by boarding-schools; by an adequate British staff; by so
framing the grant code and regulations as to enlist the co-operation
of the Mission Societies, and extend the control of Government
over all educational agencies; and finally, by the encouragement of
moral and religious instruction. And by this I do not mean any
particular system of philosophy or of creeds. "I speak of the controlling force and guiding principle which ministers through creeds
and systems of philosophy to spiritual needs—the force which inspires a man to a sense of duty, to unswerving integrity and
loyalty, whether in the public or the private relations of life. It is
additional to and greater than the secular and utilitarian education
of the class-room. It is founded generally on religious sanctions,
and finds its highest expression in the noblest of creeds. It is an
essential part of the environment and atmosphere of any institution
fit to train and educate a nation."*

* Speech at the opening of the Hong-Kong University, 11th March 1912.

VI

The Exercise of Imperium

The imperialists were very much concerned about the proper way to rule an empire, even though their ideas were sometimes confined to administrative reports and memoranda for the internal use of the governments themselves. The nineteenth century was, also, the period when administration became far more complex in Europe itself, and each European government passed through phases of administrative consolidation and reform. In this process, European countries borrowed ideas from one another, and all arrived at a structure of bureaucracy sharing many common features, though each country retained its own administrative style. The imperial administrations took this bureaucratic tradition overseas, often simplifying and making it more uniform in the process, and some improvements in the technology of administration originated over-seas—as in British India—only later being applied in the home country.

As a result, the formal structures of imperial administration had much in common, regardless of the metropolitan power. The chain of command in political administration ran from a central ministry in charge of colonies to a governor, from the governor to one or two levels of provincial administration, and from provincial admin-istration to a local district which was normally the point where orders were actually turned into practice. Each empire also devel-oped its own organs of ancillary administration, following the common divisions of ministerial function in Europe—justice, army, health, education, and the like.

But under the broad uniformity, all kinds of deviations were possible, even within a single empire. For the French, Algeria was normally dominated by the army, while the old colonies in the

Antilles and the new ones in tropical Africa were ruled by naval officers. Tunisia and Morocco were "protectorates," under the Foreign Ministry. Three different ministries in Paris were therefore involved, and the British Empire was equally fragmented, with parts controlled from the India Office, the Colonial Office, and the Foreign Office.

Even greater deviation from uniformity was introduced as the Europeans responded to local diversity. All of the great empires of the nineteenth century depended on some form of local staff, either traditional rulers kept in power under the new empire, or else a locally recruited staff of subordinate officials. Local agency inevitably introduced local factors to which the Europeans had to adjust. Even within a single culture area, the adjustment might not be identical: the British ruled through the sultans of Malaya in a very different way from the Dutch use of Javanese Regents; and the French adapted themselves still differently to the Chinese style of administration in Vietnam.

The two selections printed here illustrate British and French ideas about administration for West Africa. A dichotomy is sometimes drawn for that area between the British practice of Indirect Rule and the French direct administration, but it has frequently been overdrawn. Theorists in Europe might write about administrative systems designed to be generally practiced, but administrators in the field warped them to suit local conditions or personal predilections.

Even the theoretical aspects of Indirect Rule grew out of the special conditions Lugard encountered in Northern Nigeria. Forced to govern a large and populous region with few men, he learned to economize on European manpower and then went on to write about Indirect Rule as a theoretically desirable system of government. The French often wrote about the advantages of direct administration through an administrative hierarchy, but the district officer, or *commandant de cercle*, still found that he had to rule too many people through too few Europeans. His actual rule might therefore be as indirect in actuality as that of his British counterpart—as the passage from Delavignette indicates.

Neither of the two selections should be read as an accurate picture of colonial rule as it was actually carried out. Both are rather glorified pictures of imperial administration as it was supposed to be, and historians are only now beginning to dig out the diverse reality of the imperial era. They do, however, give a sense of what the men who ruled Africa thought they were doing, and how they went about it.

21. Lord Lugard on Indirect Rule

The following passage is the whole of Chapter X of Lugard's *Dual Mandate in British Tropical Africa*, pp. 193–213, entitled "Methods of Ruling Native Races," with only the footnotes omitted. In this chapter, more than in those on education, he shows the racist underpinning of his own thought about colonial government, and his design of an administrative structure that would allow Africa to develop "in its own way." Reprinted by permission of William Blackwood & Sons Ltd.

IF CONTINUITY and decentralisation are, as I have said, the first and most important conditions in maintaining an effective administration, co-operation is the key-note of success in its application—continuous co-operation between every link in the chain, from the head of the administration to its most junior member,—co-operation between the Government and the commercial community, and, above all, between the provincial staff and the native rulers. Every individual adds his share not only to the accomplishment of the ideal, but to the ideal itself. Its principles are fashioned by his quota of experience, its results are achieved by his patient and loyal application of these principles, with as little interference as possible with native customs and modes of thought.

Principles do not change, but their mode of application may and should vary with the customs, the traditions, and the prejudices of each unit. The task of the administrative officer is to clothe his principles in the garb of evolution, not of revolution; to make it apparent alike to the educated native, the conservative Moslem, and the primitive pagan, each in his own degree, that the policy of the Government is not antagonistic but progressive—sympathetic to his aspirations and the guardian of his natural rights. The Governor looks to the administrative staff to keep in touch with native thought and feeling, and to report fully to himself, in order that he in turn may be able to support them and recognise their work.

When describing the machinery of Government in an African dependency in chapter vi, I spoke of the supervision and guidance exercised by the Lieut.-Governor, the Residents, and the District Officers over the native chiefs. In this chapter I propose to discuss how those functions should be exercised.

Lord Milner's declaration that the British policy is to rule subject races through their own chiefs is generally applauded, but the manner in which the principle should be translated into practice admits of wide differences of opinion and method. Obviously the extent to which native races are capable of controlling their own affairs must vary in proportion to their degree of development and progress in social organisation, but this is a question of adaptation and not of principle. Broadly speaking, the divergent opinions in regard to the application of the principle may be found to originate in three different conceptions.

The first is that the ideal of self-government can only be realised by the methods of evolution which have produced the democracies of Europe and America—viz., be representative institutions in which a comparatively small educated class shall be recognised as the natural spokesmen for the many. This method is naturally in favour with the educated African. Whether it is adapted to peoples accustomed by their own institutions to autocracy—albeit modified by a substantial expression of the popular will and circumscribed by custom—is naturally a matter on which opinions differ. The fundamental essential, however, in such a form of Government is that the educated few shall at least be representative of the feelings and desires of the many—well known to them, speaking their language, and versed in their customs and prejudices.

In present conditions in Africa the numerous separate tribes, speaking different languages, and in different stages of evolution, cannot produce representative men of education. Even were they available, the number of communities which could claim separate representation would make any central and really representative Council very unwieldy. The authority vested in the representatives would be antagonistic (as the Indian Progressives realise) to that of the native rulers and their councils,—which are the product of the natural tendencies of tribal evolution,—and would run counter to the customs and institutions of the people.

An attempt to adapt these principles of Western representative Government to tropical races is now being made in India. It is at present an Eastern rather than an African problem, but as a great experiment in the method of Government in tropical countries, the outcome of which "many other native races in other parts of the world are watching with strained attention," it demands at least a passing reference here.

Though the powers entrusted to the elected representatives of the people are at first restricted under the dyarchical system (which reserves certain subjects for the Central Authority), the principle of government by an educated minority, as opposed to government by native rulers, is fully accepted. It must be admitted that there is a considerable body of well-informed opinion in India and England—voiced here by the India Association, Lord Syden-ham (who speaks with the authority of an ex-Governor of Bombay), and others—which expresses much misgiving as to the wisdom of placing all political power "in the hands of a disaffected minority unrepresentative of India," and regards it as "an attempt to govern India by the narrowest of oligarchies, whose interests often conflict with those of the millions."

The experiment has so far shown much promise of success, but the real test is not merely whether the native councillors show moderation and restraint as against extremists of their own class, but whether, when legislation has to be enacted which is unpopular with the illiterate masses and the martial races of India, there may be a reluctance to accept what will be called "Babu-made law," though it would have been accepted without demur as the order of "the Sirkar"—the British Raj.

It is, of course, now too late to adopt to any large extent the alternative of gradually transforming the greater part of British India into native States governed by their own hereditary dynasties, whose representatives in many cases still exist, and extending to them the principles which have so successfully guided our relations with the native States in India itself, and in Malaya in the past. It is one thing to excite an ignorant peasantry against an alien usurper, but quite another thing to challenge a native ruler.

Such a system does not exclude the educated native from participation in the government of the State to which he belongs, as a councillor to the native ruler, but it substitutes for direct British rule, not an elected oligarchy but a form of government more in accord with racial instincts and inherited traditions. It may be that while dyarchy and representative government may prove suitable to Bengal, and perhaps to some other provinces, the alternative system may be found to be best adapted to Mohamedan States, and

to other of the warlike races of India, where representatives of the
ancient dynasties still survive. Time alone will show. I shall recur
to this subject in the next chapter.

The second conception is that every advanced community
should be given the widest possible powers of self-government
under its own ruler, and that these powers should be rapidly increased with the object of complete independence at the earliest
possible date in the not distant future. Those who hold this view
generally, I think, also consider that attempts to train primitive
tribes in any form of self-government are futile, and the administration must be wholly conducted by British officials. This in the
past has been the principle adopted in many dependencies. It
recognised no alternative between a status of independence, like
the Sultans of Malaya, or the native princes of India, and the direct
rule of the district commissioner.

But the attempt to create such independent States in Africa has
been full of anomalies. In the case of Egbaland, where the status
had been formally recognised by treaty, the extent to which the
Crown had jurisdiction was uncertain, yet, as we have seen, international conventions, including even that relating to the protection
of wild animals, which was wholly opposed to native customary
rights, were applied without the consent of the "Independent"
State, and powers quite incompatible with independence were exercised by the Suzerain.

The paramount chief might receive ceremonial visits from time
to time from the Governor, and even perhaps be addressed as
"Your Royal Highness," and vested with titular dignity and the
tinsel insignia of office. His right to impose tolls on trade, and to
exact whatever oppressive taxes he chose from his peasantry, was
admitted, but his authority was subject to constant interference.
The last-joined District Officer, or any other official, might issue
orders, if not to him, at any rate to any of his subordinate chiefs,
and the native ruler had no legal and recognised means of enforc-
ing his commands. He was necessarily forbidden to raise armed
forces—on which in the last resort the authority of the law must
depend—and could not therefore maintain order.

The third conception is that of rule by native chiefs, unfettered
in their control of their people as regards all those matters which
are to them the most important attributes of rule, with scope for
initiative and responsibility, but admittedly—so far as the visible

horizon is concerned—subordinate to the control of the protecting Power in certain well-defined directions. It recognises, in the words of the Versailles Treaty, that the subject races of Africa are not yet able to stand alone, and that it would not conduce to the happiness of the vast bulk of the people—for whose welfare the controlling Power is trustee—that the attempt should be made.

The verdict of students of history and sociology of different nationalities, such as Dr. Kidd, Dr. Stoddard, M. Beaulieu, Meredith Townsend[1] and others is, as I have shown, unanimous that the era of complete independence is not as yet visible on the horizon of time. Practical administrators (among whom I may include my successor, Sir P. Girouard, in Northern Nigeria) have arrived at the same conclusion.

The danger of going too fast with native races is even more likely to lead to disappointment, if not to disaster, than the danger of not going fast enough. The pace can best be gauged by those who have intimate acquaintance alike with the strong points and the limitations of the native peoples and rulers with whom they have to deal.

The Fulani of Northern Nigeria are, as I have said, more capable of rule than the indigenous races, but in proportion as we consider them an alien race, we are denying self-government to the people over whom they rule, and supporting an alien caste—albeit closer and more akin to the native races than a European can be. Yet capable as they are, it requires the ceaseless vigilance of the British staff to maintain a high standard of administrative integrity, and to prevent oppression of the peasantry. We are dealing with the same generation, and in many cases with the identical rulers, who were responsible for the misrule and tyranny which we found in 1902. The subject races near the capital were then serfs, and the victims of constant extortion. Those dwelling at a distance were raided for slaves, and could not count their women, their cattle, or their crops their own. Punishments were most barbarous, and included im-

1. These "students of history and sociology" are an interesting collection of publicists, not social scientists. For Kidd, see above, pp. 33–40. Lothrop Stoddard was a prominent American racist of the period before the First World War. The title of his best-known book, *The Rising Tide of Color*, accurately suggests his point of view. The other prominent figure in the list is Paul Leroy-Beaulieu, a French geographer and one of the chief leaders in the late-nineteenth-century French movement for imperial expansion.

palements, mutilation, and burying alive. Many generations have passed since British rule was established among the more intellectual people of India—the inheritors of centuries of Eastern civilisation—yet only to-day are we tentatively seeking to confer on them a measure of self-government. "Festina lente" is a motto which the Colonial Office will do well to remember in its dealings with Africa.

That the principle of ruling through the native chiefs is adopted by several of the governments of British Tropical Africa can be seen from recent local pronouncements. The Governor of Sierra Leone, in his address to the Legislative Council last December (1920), remarks that "nine-tenths of the people enjoy autonomy under their own elected chiefs. . . . European officers are the technical advisers, and helpers of the tribal authority." The Governor of the Gold Coast on a similar occasion observed: "The chiefs are keenly appreciative of our policy of indirect rule, and of the full powers they retain under their native institutions." The powers retained by the Kabaka of Uganda and his Council are very wide indeed.

The system adopted in Nigeria is therefore only a particular method of the application of these principles—more especially as regards "advanced communities,"—and since I am familiar with it I will use it as illustrative of the methods which in my opinion should characterise the dealings of the controlling Power with subject races.

The object in view is to make each "Emir" or paramount chief, assisted by his judicial Council, an effective ruler over his own people. He presides over a "Native Administration" organised throughout as a unit of local government. The area over which he exercises jurisdiction is divided into districts under the control of "Headmen," who collect the taxes in the name of the ruler, and pay them into the "Native Treasury," conducted by a native treasurer and staff under the supervision of the chief at his capital. Here, too, is the prison for native court prisoners, and probably the school, which I shall describe more fully in the chapter on education. Large cities are divided into wards for purposes of control and taxation.

The district headman, usually a territorial magnate with local connections, is the chief executive officer in the area under his charge. He controls the village headmen, and is responsible for the assessment of the tax, which he collects through their agency. He must reside in his district and not at the capital. He is not allowed to pose as a chief with a retinue of his own and duplicate officials, and is summoned from time to time to report to his chief. If, as is the case with some of the ancient Emirates, the community is a small one but independent of any other native rule, the chief may be his own district headman.

A province under a Resident may contain several separate "Native Administrations," whether they be Moslem Emirates or pagan communities. A "division" under a British District Officer may include one or more headmen's districts, or more than one small Emirate or independent pagan tribe, but as a rule no Emirate is partly in one division and partly in another. The Resident acts as sympathetic adviser and counsellor to the native chief, being careful not to interfere so as to lower his prestige, or cause him to lose interest in his work. His advice on matters of general policy must be followed, but the native ruler issues his own instructions to his subordinate chiefs and district heads—not as the orders of the Resident but as his own,—and he is encouraged to work through them, instead of centralising everything in himself—a system which in the past had produced such great abuses. The British District Officers supervise and assist the native district headmen, through whom they convey any instructions to village heads, and make any arrangements necessary for carrying on the work of the Government departments, but all important orders emanate from the Emir, whose messenger usually accompanies and acts as mouthpiece of a District Officer.

The tax—which supersedes all former "tribute," irregular imposts, and forced labour—is, in a sense, the basis of the whole system, since it supplies the means to pay the Emir and all his officials. The district and village heads are effectively supervised and assisted in its assessment by the British staff. The native treasury retains the proportion assigned to it (in advanced communities a half), and pays the remainder into Colonial Revenue.

There are fifty such treasuries in the northern provinces of Nigeria, and every independent chief, however small, is encouraged to have his own. The appropriation by the native administration of market dues, slaughter-house fees, forest licences, &c., is authorised by ordinance, and the native administration receives also the fines and fees of native courts. From these funds are paid the salaries of the Emir and his council, the native court judges, the district and village heads, police, prison warders, and other employees. The surplus is devoted to the construction and maintenance of dispensaries, leper settlements, schools, roads, courthouses, and other buildings. Such works may be carried out wholly or in part by a Government department, if the native administration requires technical assistance, the cost being borne by the native treasury.

The native treasurer keeps all accounts of receipts and expenditure, and the Emir, with the assistance of the Resident, annually prepares a budget, which is formally approved by the Lieut.-Governor.

In these advanced communities the judges of the native courts—which I shall describe in a later chapter—administer native law and custom, and exercise their jurisdiction independently of the native executive, but under the supervision of the British staff, and subject to the general control of the Emir, whose "Judicial Council" consists of his principal officers of State, and is vested with executive as well as judicial powers. No punishment may be inflicted by a native authority, except through a regular tribunal. The ordinances of government are operative everywhere, but the native authority may make by-laws in modification of native custom—e.g., on matters of sanitation, &c.,—and these, when approved by the Governor, are enforced by the native courts.

The authority of the Emir over his own people is absolute, and the profession of an alien creed does not absolve a native from the obligation to obey his lawful orders; but aliens—other than natives domiciled in the Emirate and accepting the jurisdiction of the native authority and courts—are under the direct control of the British staff. Townships are excluded from the native jurisdiction.

The village is the administrative unit. It is not always easy to define, since the security to life and property which has followed the British administration has caused an exodus from the cities and large villages, and the creation of innumerable hamlets, sometimes only of one or two huts, on the agricultural lands. The peasantry of the advanced communities, though ignorant, yet differs from that of the backward tribes in that they recognise the authority of the Emir, and are more ready to listen to the village head and the Council of Elders, on which the Nigerian system is based.

Subject, therefore, to the limitations which I shall presently discuss, the native authority is thus *de facto* and *de jure* ruler over his own people. He appoints and dismisses his subordinate chiefs and officials. He exercises the power of allocation of lands, and with the aid of the native courts, of adjudication in land disputes and expropriation for offences against the community; these are the essential functions upon which, in the opinion of the West African Lands Committee, the prestige of the native authority depends. The lawful orders which he may give are carefully defined by ordinance, and in the last resort are enforced by Government.

Since native authority, especially if exercised by alien conquerors, is inevitably weakened by the first impact of civilised rule, it is made clear to the elements of disorder, who regard force as conferring the only right to demand obedience, that government, by the use of force if necessary, intends to support the native chief. To enable him to maintain order he employs a body of unarmed police, and if the occasion demands the display of superior force he looks to the Government—as, for instance, if a community combines to break the law or shield criminals from justice,—a rare event in the advanced communities.

The native ruler derives his power from the Suzerain, and is responsible that it is not misused. He is equally with British officers amenable to the law, but his authority does not depend on the caprice of an executive officer. To intrigue against him is an offence punishable, if necessary, in a Provincial Court. Thus both British and native courts are invoked to uphold his authority.

The essential feature of the system (as I wrote at the time of its inauguration) is that the native chiefs are constituted "as an integral part of the machinery of the administration. There are not two sets of rulers—British and native—working either separately or in co-operation, but a single Government in which the native chiefs have well-defined duties and an acknowledged status equally with British officials. Their duties should never conflict, and should overlap as little as possible. They should be complementary to each other, and the chief himself must understand that he has no right to place and power unless he renders his proper services to the State."

The ruling classes are no longer either demi-gods, or parasites preying on the community. They must work for the stipends and position they enjoy. They are the trusted delegates of the Governor, exercising in the Moslem States the well-understood powers of "Wakils" in conformity with their own Islamic system, and recognising the King's representative as their acknowledged Suzerain.

There is here no need of "Dyarchy,"[2] for the lines of development of the native administration run parallel to, and do not intersect, those of the Central Government. It is the consistent aim of the British staff to maintain and increase the prestige of the native ruler, to encourage his initiative, and to support his authority. That the chiefs are satisfied with the autonomy they enjoy in the matters which really interest and concern them, may be judged by their loyalty and the prosperity of their country.

Comparatively little difficulty, it may be said, would be experienced in the application of such a system to Moslem States, for even if their rulers had deteriorated, they still profess the standards of Islam, with its system of taxation, and they possess a literate class capable of discharging the duties I have described. No doubt the alien immigrants in the northern tropical belt afford better material for social organisation, both racially and through the influence of their creed, than the advanced communities of negro stock which owe nothing to Islam, such as the Baganda, the Ashantis, the Yorubas, the Benis, and others. But the self-evolved progress in social organisation of these latter communities is in itself evidence that they possessed exceptional intelligence, probably more widely diffused among the peasantry than would be found among those over whom an alien race had acquired domination. They too had evolved systems of taxation and of land tenure, and had learnt to delegate authority. The teaching of missions through many decades had in most cases produced a class who, if their energies were rightly directed to the service of their communities instead of seeking foreign outlets, would form a very valuable aid in the building up of a "Native Administration." That these communities are fully capable of adopting such a system has been proved in recent years in South Nigeria.

They have not produced so definite a code of law, or such advanced methods of dispensing justice, as the Koran has introduced, and they lack the indigenous educational advantages which the use of Arabic and the religious schools have conferred on the Moslem.

2. A constitutional device in the government of India, where control over certain governmental departments was "reserved" to the control of imperial officials while others were "transferred to the responsibility of the locally-elected legislature.

On the other hand, many—especially the Baganda—have benefited greatly by the Christian schools, and a wider range of knowledge, including English. Some of their chiefs—notably Khama of Bechuana, and several of those in Uganda—have been remarkable men. Among many of these communities the chiefs exercise an influence different in its nature from that accorded to an alien ruler, and based on superstitious veneration.

The limitations to independence which are frankly inherent in this conception of native rule—not as temporary restraints to be removed as soon as may be, but as powers which rightly belong to the controlling Power as trustee for the welfare of the masses, and as being responsible for the defence of the country and the cost of its central administration—are such as do not involve interference with the authority of the chiefs or the social organisation of the people. They have been accepted by the Fulani Emirs as natural and proper to the controlling Power, and their reservation in the hands of the Governor has never interfered with the loyalty of the ruling chiefs, or, so far as I am aware, been resented by them. The limitations are as follows:—

(1) Native rulers are not permitted to raise and control armed forces, or to grant permission to carry arms. To this in principle Great Britain stands pledged under the Brussels Act. The evils which result in Africa from an armed population were evident in Uganda before it fell under British control, and are very evident in Abyssinia to-day. No one with experience will deny the necessity of maintaining the strictest military discipline over armed forces or police in Africa if misuse of power is to be avoided, and they are not to become a menace and a terror to the native population and a danger in case of religious excitement—a discipline which an African ruler is incapable of appreciating or applying. For this reason native levies should never be employed in substitution for or in aid of troops.

On the other hand, the Government armed police are never quartered in native towns, where their presence would interfere with the authority of the chiefs. Like the regular troops, they are employed as escorts and on duty in the townships. The native administration maintain a police, who wear a uniform but do not carry firearms.

(2) The sole right to impose taxation in any form is reserved to

the Suzerain power. This fulfils the bilateral understanding that the peasantry—provided they pay the authorised tax (the adjustment of which to all classes of the population is a responsibility which rests with the Central Government)—should be free of all other exactions whatsoever (including unpaid labour), while a sufficient proportion of the tax is assigned to the native treasuries to meet the expenditure of the native administration. Special sanction by ordinance—or "rule" approved by the Governor—is therefore required to enable the native authority to levy any special dues, &c.

(3) The right to legislate is reserved. That this should remain in the hands of the Central Government—itself limited by the control of the Colonial Office, as I have described—cannot be questioned. The native authority, however, exercises very considerable power in this regard. A native ruler, and the native courts, are empowered to enforce native law and custom, provided it is not repugnant to humanity, or in opposition to any ordinance. This practically meets all needs, but the native authority may also make rules on any subject, provided they are approved by the Governor.

(4) The right to appropriate land on equitable terms for public purposes and for commercial requirements is vested in the Governor. In the Northern Provinces of Nigeria (but not in the South) the right of disposing of native lands is reserved to the Governor by ordinance. In practice this does not interfere with the power of the native ruler(as the delegate of the Governor) to assign lands to the natives under his rule, in accordance with native law and custom, or restrict him or the native courts from adjudicating between natives regarding occupancy rights in land. No rents are levied on lands in occupation by indigenous natives. Leases to aliens are granted by the Central Government.

If the pressure of population in one community makes it necessary to assign it to a portion of the land belonging to a neighbour with a small and decreasing population, the Governor (to whom appeal may be made) would decide the matter. These reservations were set out in the formal letter of appointment given to each chief in Northern Nigeria.

(5) In order to maintain intact the control of the Central Government over all aliens, and to avoid friction and difficulties, it has been the recognised rule that the employees of the native administration should consist entirely of natives subject to the native authority. If aliens are required for any skilled work by the native

administration, Government servants may be employed and their salaries reimbursed by the native treasury. For a like reason, whenever possible, all non-natives and natives not subject to the local native jurisdiction live in the "township," from which natives subject to the native administration are as far as possible excluded. This exclusive control of aliens by the Central Government partakes rather of the nature of "extra-territorial jurisdiction" than of dualism.

(6) Finally, in the interests of good government, the right of confirming or otherwise the choice of the people of the successor to a chiefship, and of deposing any ruler for misrule or other adequate cause, is reserved to the Governor.

The revenue of a native administration consists, as I have said, not of an arbitrary sum assigned to it by the Governor, but of a fixed proportion of the statutory tax collected by its agency, together with the fines and fees from native courts, market dues, and similar receipts assigned by the Governor. Thus, though the Suzerain Power imposes the taxes (whether direct in the form of an income tax or indirect as customs dues, &c.), and the general *rate* of the former is fixed by the Governor, the acutal assessment is in the hands of the native ruler and his representatives—the district and village heads—guided and assisted by the British staff. It therefore appears to the taxpayer as a tax imposed by his own native ruler, though he knows that the vigilant eye of the District Officer will see that no unauthorised exactions are made, and that any injustice will be remedied. Since the salaries of the ruler and the officials of the "Native Administration" are paid out of their own native treasury funds, they cannot be regarded by him as officials paid by Government.

The proportion assigned to the native administration in advanced communities is a half of the general income and cattle tax, —the proportion is less in pagan communities. On the inauguration of the tax in Nigeria the proceeds were quite insufficient to meet even the necessary salaries of chiefs; but with improved assessment, a more honest collection, and increased prosperity, the sum, without additional burden, has become so large that in the more wealthy Emirates there is a considerable surplus, when all the salaries of the very largely-increased establishments of native officials, police and prison staff, &c., have been paid. From these funds native court-

houses, treasuries, schools, and prisons for native court prisoners
have been built, and the balance, invested in a reserve fund, totalled
in 1919 £486,654, exclusive of the large sums voted by the Emirs
towards the cost of the war. These reserve funds—originally
created to meet any emergency, such as famine or cattle disease,
when Northern Nigeria had no colonial reserve, and was dependent on a grant-in-aid—are now available for public works of
benefit to the people.

The revenues of the native administrations do not appear in the
colonial budget of revenue and expenditure, and are independent
of colonial treasury or audit control. The proper expenditure of
these large sums—obtained by taxes imposed and enforced by the
Suzerain Power—must obviously depend in part on the ability of
each native ruler, and in part on the Resident who advises him.
"Unfettered control" may in some cases mean that a Resident,
and not the ruling chief, disposes of large revenues independent of
the Lieut.-Governor; in other cases it may mean a tendency to
multiply offices and pay high salaries, which either overburden the
finances of other less wealthy treasuries, or cause discontent among
its employees, and ultimately enhance the cost of labour throughout the country—a result which is inimical to production and
progress, unless necessitated by economic causes. It is a tendency
which a Resident, however much he has identified himself in the
interests of the native administration, may not find it easy to resist,
though he sets his face against nepotism and the reckless exercise of
patronage and display—which are so apt to be regarded as the
symbol of power by a native ruler.

Pending the growth of a fuller sense of public responsibility and
of an enlightened public opinion, some check may be afforded by
the preparation of annual estimates of revenue and expenditure in a
very simple form. These should require the approval of the Governor (or of the Lieut.-Governor), as the colonial estimates require
that of the Secretary of State, and any subsequent alteration
should require the like sanction. While refraining as far as possible
from interference in detail, the Lieut.-Governor can, by suggestion
and comparison, effect some co-ordination and uniformity where
desirable, and can best discriminate between the scope which may
be allowed to an individual, and the grant of extended powers of
universal application.

The habits of a people are not changed in a decade, and when powerful despots are deprived of the pastime of war and slave-raiding, and when even the weak begin to forget their former sufferings, to grow weary of a life without excitement, and to resent the petty restrictions which have replaced the cruelties of the old despotism, it must be the aim of Government to provide new interests and rivalries in civilised progress, in education, in material prosperity and trade, and even in sport.

There were indeed many who, with the picture of Fulani mis-rule fresh in their memory, regarded this system when it was first inaugurated with much misgiving, and believed that though the hostility of the rulers to the British might be concealed, and their vices disguised, neither could be eradicated, and they would always remain hostile at heart. They thought that the Fulani as an alien race of conquerors, who had in turn been conquered, had not the same claims for consideration as those whom they had displaced, even though they had become so identified with the people that they could no longer be called aliens.

But there can be no doubt that such races form an invaluable medium between the British staff and the native peasantry. Nor can the difficulty of finding any one capable of taking their place, or the danger they would constitute to the State if ousted from their positions, be ignored. Their traditions of rule, their mono-theistic religion, and their intelligence enable them to appreciate more readily than the negro population the wider objects of British policy, while their close touch with the masses—with whom they live in daily intercourse—mark them out as destined to play an important part in the future, as they have done in the past, in the development of the tropics.

Both the Arabs in the east and the Fulani in the west are Mo-hamedans, and by supporting their rule we unavoidably encourage the spread of Islam, which from the purely administrative point of view has the disadvantage of being subject to waves of fanaticism, bounded by no political frontiers. In Nigeria it has been the rule that their power should not be re-established over tribes which had made good their independence, or imposed upon those who had successfully resisted domination.

On the other hand, the personal interests of the rulers must rapidly become identified with those of the controlling Power. The forces of disorder do not distinguish between them, and the rulers soon recognise that any upheaval against the British would equally make an end of them. Once this community of interest is established, the Central Government cannot be taken by surprise, for it is impossible that the native rulers should not be aware of any disaffection.

This identification of the ruling class with the Government accentuates the corresponding obligation to check malpractices on their part. The task of educating them in the duties of a ruler becomes more than ever insistent; of inculcating a sense of responsibility; of convincing their intelligence of the advantages which accrue from the material prosperity of the peasantry, from free labour and initiative; of the necessity of delegating powers to trusted subordinates; of the evils of favouritism and bribery; of the importance of education, especially for the ruling class, and for the filling of lucrative posts under Government; of the benefits of sanitation, vaccination, and isolation of infection in checking mortality; and finally, of impressing upon them how greatly they may benefit their country by personal interest in such matters, and by the application of labour-saving devices and of scientific methods in agriculture.

Unintentional misuse of the system of native administration must also be guarded against. It is not, for instance, the duty of a native administration to purchase supplies for native troops, or to enlist and pay labour for public works, though its agency within carefully defined limits may be useful in making known Government requirements, and seeing that markets are well supplied. Nor should it be directed to collect licences, fees, and rents due to Government, nor should its funds be used for any purpose not solely connected with and prompted by its own needs.

I have throughout these pages continually emphasised the necessity of recognising, as a cardinal principle of British policy in dealing with native races, that institutions and methods, in order to command success and promote the happiness and welfare of the people, must be deep-rooted in their traditions and prejudices. Obviously in no sphere of administration is this more essential than in that under discussion, and a slavish adherence to any particular type, however successful it may have proved elsewhere, may, if unadapted to the local environment, be as ill-suited and as foreign to its conceptions as direct British rule would be.

The type suited to a community which has long grown accustomed to the social organisation of the Moslem State may or may not be suitable to advanced pagan communities, which have evolved a social system of their own, such as the Yorubas, the Benis, the Egbas, or the Ashantis in the West, or the Waganda, the Wanyoro, the Watoro, and others in the East. The history, the traditions, the idiosyncracies, and the prejudices of each must be studied by the Resident and his staff, in order that the form adopted shall accord with natural evolution, and shall ensure the ready co-operation of the chiefs and people.

Before passing to the discussion of methods applicable to primitive tribes, it may be of interest to note briefly some of the details —as apart from general principles—adopted in Nigeria among the advanced communities.

Chiefs who are executive rulers are graded—those of the first three classes are installed by the Governor or Lieut.-Governor, and carry a staff of office surmounted for the first class by a silver, and for the others by a brass crown. Lower grades carry a baton, and are installed by the Resident, or by the Emir, if the chief is subordinate to him. These staves of office, which are greatly prized, symbolise to the peasantry the fact that the Emir derives his power from the Government, and will be supported in its exercise. The installation of an Emir is a ceremonial witnessed by a great concourse of his people, and dignified by a parade of troops. The native insignia of office, and a parchment scroll, setting out in the vernacular the conditions of his appointment, are presented to him. The alkali (native judge) administers the following oath on the Koran: "I swear in the name of God, well and truly to serve His Majesty King George V and his representative the Governor of Nigeria, to obey the laws of Nigeria and the lawful commands of the Governor, and of the Lieut.-Governor, provided that they are not contrary to my religion, and if they are so contrary I will at once inform the Governor through the Resident. I will cherish in my heart no treachery or disloyalty, and I will rule my people with justice and without partiality. And as I carry out this oath so may God judge me." Pagan chiefs are sworn according to their own customs on a sword.

Native etiquette and ceremonial must be carefully studied and observed in order that unintentional offence may be avoided. Great importance is attached to them, and a like observance in accordance with native custom is demanded towards British officers.

Chiefs are treated with respect and courtesy. Native races alike in India and Africa are quick to discriminate between natural dignity and assumed superiority. Vulgar familiarity is no more a passport to their friendship than an assumption of self-importance is to their respect. The English gentleman needs no prompting in such a matter—his instinct is never wrong. Native titles of rank are adopted, and only native dress is worn, whether by chiefs or by schoolboys. Principal chiefs accused of serious crimes are tried by a British court, and are not imprisoned before trial, unless in very exceptional circumstances. Minor chiefs and native officials appointed by an Emir may be tried by his Judicial Council. If the offence does not involve deprivation of office, the offender may be fined without public trial, if he prefers it, in order to avoid humiliation and loss of influence.

Succession is governed by native law and custom, subject in the case of important chiefs to the approval of the Governor, in order that the most capable claimant may be chosen. It is important to ascertain the customary law and to follow it when possible, for the appointment of a chief who is not the recognised heir, or who is disliked by the people, may give rise to trouble, and in any case the new chief would have much difficulty in asserting his authority, and would fear to check abuses lest he should alienate his supporters. In Moslem countries the law is fairly clearly defined, being a useful combination of the hereditary principle, tempered by selection, and in many cases in Nigeria the ingenious device is maintained of having two rival dynasties, from each of which the successor is selected alternately.

In pagan communities the method varies; but there is no rigid rule, and a margin for selection is allowed. The formal approval of the Governor after a short period of probation is a useful precaution, so that if the designated chief proves himself unsuitable, the selection may be revised without difficulty. Minor chiefs are usually selected by popular vote, subject to the approval of the paramount chief. It is a rule in Nigeria that no slave may be appointed as a chief or district headman. If one is nominated he must first be publicly freed.

Small and isolated communities, living within the jurisdiction of a chief, but owing allegiance to the chief of their place of origin—a common source of trouble in Africa—should gradually be absorbed into the territorial jurisdiction. Aliens who have settled in a district for their own purposes would be subject to the local jurisdiction.

22. Delavignette on French Administration in West Africa

Robert Delavignette (1897–   ) was a French colonial administrator who had himself been a *commandant de cercle*. He rose through the ranks of colonial administration to serve as governor of several colonies. In addition, he was at various times Director of the École Nationale de la France d'Outre-Mer, where officers in the French colonial service were trained, and a key civil servant within the Ministry of Colonies in Paris. Throughout his career, he represented the broadly liberal tendencies within the French colonial service, occupying a position roughly analogous to that of Lord Olivier in Britain. His best-known work is *Service africain* (Paris, 1946), which was translated into English as *Freedom and Authority in French West Africa* (London, 1950). This selection is the whole of Chapter V, "The Native Chiefs," pp. 71–84. It reflects conditions in French West Africa as they were just before the Second World War, while the preceding selection from Lord Lugard has to do with a period about two decades earlier. Reprinted by permission of International African Institute.

V. The Native Chiefs

STRAW CHIEFS AND CHIEFS OF THE LAND

WHEN I was head of a subdivision on the Upper Volta, I went on tour in the first months of my stay, and landed unexpectedly in a distant village, little visited. The Chief gave me a good reception. I came back there two years later, at the end of my tour, and had a still better reception. The Chief, however, did not seem to me to be the same man. I had before me an old man, while it was a young man who had received me the first time, and I recognized him, standing behind the old man. I asked the two of them why the chieftainship of the village had passed from the one to the other without my being told of it. The old man said to me: "He whom you see behind me was in front of me," and he explained, "It is I who am the Chief, to-day as the other time, and in front of this man, as behind him. But two years ago we did not know you, and he showed himself in my place." It is not unusual to fail to recognize the real chief right away, but it makes one stop and think. And I propose to analyse the machinery of our administration through the chiefs, bearing this incident in mind.

In all territorial administration the native chiefs act as cogwheels between the colonial authority and the native peoples. In French West Africa, which is a federation of colonies, the supreme authority in each colony is vested in the Governor. Within the colony, authority is exercised, in the name of the Governor and under his control, by the Commandants of districts (*cercles*); the *cercle* may be divided into subdivisions, but nevertheless it constitutes the administrative unit, and the Commandant of a *cercle* represents the administrative authority. How does the government, which is centered in the *cercle*, establish relations with the native peoples? This is precisely the function of the *cercle*. It is the motor mechanism which directly engages with the native machinery, the canton, which in turn sets in motion a certain number of villages. Colony and *cercle* on the one-hand, *cercle*, canton and village on the other, these are the interlocking parts of the administrative machinery. Commandants of *cercles* and heads of subdivisions belong to the Colonial Administrative Service,* and to the Civil Service of the Federation of French West Africa. Chiefs of cantons and villages are the native chiefs properly so-called, and by abbreviation "the Chiefs."

In French West Africa, which is eight times the area of France and comprises a population of fifteen millions, the territorial administration is like a power current passing from the 118 *cercles* to the 2,200 cantons and the 48,000 villages. The native policy that affects fifteen million men depends to a considerable degree on the character of the 118 *cercle*. Commandants and their collaborators and the 50,000 native chiefs.† Native policy is worth what they are worth. It is what their relations with each other and with the native peoples make it.

The importance of these relations must be thoroughly understood. The *cercle* is only a motor mechanism so long as it is a transformer of energy. The Commandant of the *cercle* is not truly

* In 1937 there were 385 Colonial Administrators in French West Africa, half of them posted to offices at headquarters in each colony.

† See table.

CHIEFTAINSHIPS IN THE COLONIES OF FRENCH WEST AFRICA

	Provincial chiefs, or chiefs of a group of cantons or tribes	Canton chiefs, or chiefs of tribes	Village chiefs or assimilated to that status:				
			Ordinary	Independent	Assimilated (Ward chiefs)	Dependent Divisions	Independent Divisions
SENEGAL	2	135 (auxiliary chiefs, temporary chiefs, deputy chiefs)	9,352				
Circonscription of DAKAR and dependencies		1	41		51		
MAURITANIA	3	50	819 village chiefs, or chiefs of divisions or subdivisions				
GUINEA		262	4,057	8	9 (mixed communes of Konakry and Kankan)		

SOUDAN	1 paramount chief, 8 provincial chiefs or chiefs of a group of tribes	719	10,907	132	15	622	40
NIGER	3	183	6,585	5			
DAHOMEY	5 (known as chefs supérieurs)	161	3,494		20		
IVORY COAST	10	516 canton chiefs, 62 tribal chiefs, 117 chiefs of groups of tribes	11,892				
Totals	32	2,206	47,147	145	95 48,049	622	40

a commander except in so far as he can understand the chiefs and get a hearing from them. If his authority is to be effective he has to work through the chiefs, in daily contact with them. And this brings me back to what happened to me: authority is like a force running to waste if it contacts a false chief instead of finding the real one. And among the hundred-odd villages of the dozen cantons of my subdivision, I had at least once lost my authority.

What, then, are the characteristics of a real native chief?

As a rule, the chiefs are studied according to the classification used by the administration: first of all the village chief, then the canton chief, sometimes a chief of a province, more rarely still a great chief whom we call king or emperor. But this is merely an account of the hierarchy of authority among the chiefs, and not a definition of the chiefly powers itself. But the power of a chief may be defined in relation to its quality rather than its extent; it may happen, for example, that an ordinary village headman wields more power in his village than a chief of a province in his province. Instead of considering chiefs in relation to the hierarchy in which we place them, let us consider their authority as it is exercised in relation to their own territory. And let us remember that the real chief does exist, though he may be concealed.

Chiefs like the one I saw the first time in the village where I learned my lesson are, so to speak, more or less men of straw. They play the part which, in certain big department stores, is assigned to the employé who has to receive the complaints of short-tempered customers. At any demand from the administration—tax, labour service, recruiting, census, new crops to be tried—the fake chief is put forward. On him will fall the wrath of a hoodwinked administration. The reason for this is that the Administration bothers the chiefs too much; it harasses them by perpetually summoning them for meetings; it hustles them with constant demands, exhausts them with requisitions, holds them responsible, on pain of forfeiting their property or even their liberty, for the carrying out of all the orders which it pours out at random. Is it any wonder that the chiefs take refuge in tricks and stratagems? Or else it disconcerts them by issuing directives which it has not succeeded in making plain to them; which means that it is a bad transformer of energy. The inadequacy or the faults of an administration may be measured by the number of "straw chiefs" which come between it and the real chiefs.

There are other reasons also, which go deep into the heart of African affairs. There are cases where custom decrees that relations with strangers outside the tribe should be regulated by special functionaries, lower in rank than the chief. Thus traders, whether travelling or resident, are the concern of a special minister known as Chief of the market or Chief of strangers. In some parts of Africa, colonials are regarded in the same way as the merchants in the market, strangers who pitch their camp to-day and are gone to-morrow. This in itself shows that only material transactions can be carried out with them.

In the social function of the true chief, at the core of his authority, is a spiritual quality which a stranger cannot apprehend and may not touch. The very life of the country is dependent on the chief. If the Administration fails to understand him, that life withdraws itself; if he is humiliated, it is wounded; if he is overthrown, it is extinguished. To let the chief be seen is rashly and immodestly to expose that holy part where the body social can be mortally wounded.

Canton chiefs rarely have "straw chiefs." Obviously it is more difficult for them than for village chiefs to hide themselves and mislead the Administration. But, more than this, it seems that after fifty years of colonization, the spiritual quality of native power has left the big chiefs to take refuge with the small ones, who have not been so much affected by European influence.

It is often said that the colonial administration was wrong in breaking the power of African potentates, and that it is now necessary to restore their traditional authority. But where were these great chiefs? With a few exceptions—such as the Mogho-Naba of Ouagadougou among the Mossi—the countries that were conquered at the end of the last century had lost their sovereigns during the slave-trading epoch. And many of the natural chiefs had been more or less detached from their traditional functions through the influence of Moslem proselytizing, long before the French colonial era.

Certainly some of the appointments made were open to criticism: cases where the chiefdom was created at the same time as the chief, or where a man was appointed to a chiefdom to which he had no right. Thus some of the chiefs appointed were the personal employés of the Administration, or even slaves, while the old families of the country were passed over. Here again the villages, which

seemed unimportant, were left undisturbed and it was mainly
chiefs of cantons whom we appointed. These things, in fact, did
not encroach on custom as much as has been supposed. For most of
the great chiefs who were displaced by our nominees were themselves feudatories who held their fiefs from the slave-trader for
whom they rounded up the game, or they were the soldiers of a
Moslem war lord who handed over the pagan cultivators to them
as serfs. They did not express, they rather oppressed the old Africa
of the land and the villages. And in replacing them by our chiefs of
cantons, we have most often merely substituted for a usurper a sort
of functionary.

The canton is in most cases a former feudal province turned into
an administrative district. *The village, on the other hand, is not an
administrative creation. It is still a living entity.* And, in spite of
appearances, it is the *village* chief who retains the ancient, intrin-
sically African authority.

In former times, the chieftainship everywhere had the same simplicity of structure as in the village, whether it concerned a
province or the suzerainty over an aggregate of provinces. The
words "kingdom" or "empire" give an inaccurate idea of it. If we
examine the derivation of the generic names of the big chiefs who
still exist—the Amenokhall of the Tuareg; the Ardo, the Rouga or
the Mani of the Fulani; the Mogho-Naba of the Mossi; the Damel
of the Wolof; and many others whose names ring in the chronicles
of the earliest travellers, we find an original philological flowering.
Our appellation, "great chief," is as summary and superficial in
negro Africa as it would be in Europe to-day, where the Germanic
Führer was not the Latin Duce.

The great African chiefdoms were, in their essential character,
identical with the smallest ones. Empires and kingdoms had the
same political organization and were of the same social essence as
the village. The Soudanese Empire of Soundiata Keita issued from
the village of Kangaba and spread over all the regions of the
Soudan, to shrink back later to the village that gave it birth. While
it lasted it raised a gigantic pyramid which reproduced at the apex
the same arrangement as at the base. Or rather it was the village of
Kangaba itself stretched out to an empire. Just as in our own day
the habitation of the biggest chief only differs from that of his
humblest subject by the number of huts put side by side—the same
huts for everyone—so the structure of an empire was only made

up of a collection of villages. He who knows the village knows the eternal Africa.

We are incapable of such simplicity. There is no differentiation of powers—the chief possesses them all. At one and the same time, and generation after generation, he has been leader of the army, judge, political sovereign and master of home affairs. We think he mixes everything together; we cannot get used to the idea that he *is* everything together. If he delegates his powers he does so *en bloc* and often to a slave. We notice that he has Ministers around him, but they seem to be dignitaries with no clearly regulated functions: the chief of the horsemen, for instance, does not concern himself only with the cavalry—he also has strange religious prerogatives.

We speak of restoring the traditional authority of these sovereigns of the past, without understanding that by introducing our notion of differentiation of powers we have in fact shaken the community more profoundly than if we had shown lack of consideration for its chief. Of what use is it to respect a symbol if we empty it of its meaning?

The chieftainship had a unity derived from the solidarity of the community. The chief led the same kind of life as his people. An Emir of the Moors to-day, who lives in a house on St. Louis-in-Senegal, who gets into his car to go and visit the tribe, is no longer a chief in the native sense of the word. He may well be a progressive man, but in fact he leaves the people without a chief. It is not from a house that he can govern tents; it is not in a car that he can be understood by a community of camel drivers.

The secret of this simplicity, unity, solidarity, is still to be found in the village. It is that the chief's power is the religious bond which unites all the members of the community. *This is a much older religion than Islam,* and it comes from the earth rather than from heaven. It is the communion of a human group with the earth to which it prays in order to cultivate it. The chief is the descendant of the first cultivators of the land. He perpetuates that family and distributes to the living the fields of the earliest dead; in the name of the original family, he hands on the knowledge he has received—knowledge of the soil and of the animals, some of them hostile, some protectors. In 1923, in the Maradi subdivision in the Niger Territory, where there reigned a sultan, the administrator wanted a piece of land for an agricultural research station, and applied to the sultan, the only chief he knew. The sultan was a fine aristocratic figure, with curled locks, clad in a handsome embroidered robe and foaming turban, shod with boots of stamped leather, wearing his sword on his hip, and riding a stallion hung with leather and lengths of cotton cloth, followed by trumpet-blowers and a numerous retinue; he left his vaulted and terraced castle and led the Commandant to the outskirts of the town. A man was summoned to meet them there who was quite unknown to the administrator, a person without prestige or arms. He was the descendant of the original family, the earliest occupants of the soil. He was the master of the land, he alone had the power to lend a piece of it.*

In Hausa country, the canton chief is the *Serky*, the landlord. The Sultan of Maradi is called the *Serky n'Fulani*. Now the generic name of the village is *Gari*, but the village chief is not called *Serky n-Gari*, but *Mai-Gari*. A cameleer is the *Mai-rakumi*, a horseman is the *Maidoki*, that is, "the camel-man," "the horse-man." Thus it appears that the *Mai-Gari* is not the lord of the village, but the village-man, one with the village as the cameleer is one with his camel, and the horse-man one with his horse. I give the idea for what it is worth. I am trying to express the fact that among all the men of the village, the chief is the one who symbolizes the village itself. And I am trying to mark the difference in kind between the *Serky*, the seigneur, who may hold numerous villages, and the *Mai-Gari*, who is not a chief of an inferior grade, a bottom-of-the-ladder chief, but in fact the real chief of ancient rural Africa.

A passage from Ernest Renan's *Souvenirs d'Enfance et de Jeunesse*, throws light on the character of the true chief. Speaking of the old Breton chiefs, in connection with the "flax-bruiser's daughter," he writes that they were "keystones in the social structure of the people." The comparison holds good for negro Africa. If you succeed in building your administration round the chief, the whole population will be included. And if he goes with you, they will follow.

It does not matter if the chief is old, infirm or blind; the essential

* "The inalienability of land rights is so rooted in the mind of the African, that in his eyes even the conquest of a region cannot entail any rights whatsoever over the soil conquered." (Capt. N'Tchoréré, of the Colonial Infantry, "Le Problème des jeunes générations africaines" in the *Revue des Troupes coloniales*, Dec. 1938.)

thing is that he should be there.* If necessary he can take a young
and active man as his colleague. If he is illiterate and has some
difficulty in dealing with natives educated in our schools, let him be
given clerks and assistants. Only one thing counts, and it does not
depend on education, age or health: that is the sacred character of
his power. In the old Africa the community which the chief represents lives in him and there can be no life without a supernatural
element. Hence the force which binds the people to the chief;
hence the ritual which permeates social unity and solidarity, which
orders the form of greeting addressed by the people to the chief
and gives a religious sanction to the authority of the humblest
village chief, the chief of the cultivated and inhabited land.

What principles of action in colonial administration can be
drawn from these facts? We must proceed, so to speak, from the
"straw chief" to the chief of the land, who seems indeed to be the
product of the land itself, and it is almost always in the village that
he is to be found. Thus we are driven to make an important distinction between the village chief and the chief of a canton.

THE CHIEF OF A CANTON: A FEUDAL RULER WHO
DISCHARGES THE DUTIES OF AN OFFICIAL

As the village chief derives from a primitive feudal Africa based
on the holding of land, so the chief of a canton belongs to modern
Africa, and is part of the mechanism of colonial administration.

First, let us put a question of tactics. We often ask ourselves
whether the territorial Command should be concentrated in a
single station, or whether it should be deployed in a network of
small stations grouped about the principal one. Should there be a
cercle without subdivisions, or a *cercle* composed of subdivisions?
The solution of this problem varies according to the number and
importance of the canton chiefs.

Take as a starting point the following fact of experience: *The
presence of a European administrative organization beside a canton
chief tends to limit his independence while at the same time extend-*

---

* The best administrative instructions relating to chiefs and to territorial
administration are those issued by Gov. general J. van Vollenhoven (*Une
âme de Chef*, Plon, 1920) and Gov. general J. Brévié (*La Politique et
l'administration indigènes en A.O.F.*, 1931–5. Govt. Printer, Gorée). These
were followed, from 1940–1, by the Directives of Gov. general Felix Eboué.

ing his influence. The chief who lives in the neighbourhood of our offices adapts himself to their surveillance and profits from their activity. And if he becomes less free than other chiefs farther away, he nevertheless acquires pre-eminence over them. He can easily get in touch with the Commandant; he performs services for the colonials; he is introduced to the ways of the administration; he seems doubly chief because he is chief at headquarters.

In a district formed of a homogeneous country, of one race and religion, where the outstanding figure is a feudal grandee who has been appointed chief of a canton or several cantons, there is every advantage in establishing and concentrating the administration in the neighbourhood of the chief, and not constituting subdivisions. If, however, the chief's power seems troublesome or dangerous, the partition of the territory into different *cercles* or into subdivisions will certainly break it up. But it must be realized that then new chiefs will spring up round each subdivision headquarters, and that by lopping branches off the big tree one does not always clear a space for the people, but may only make room for feudal shoots to spring up.

In a district composed of different countries where a number of independent chiefs exist, it will be wise to create several subdivisions and put the headquarters of each in the canton that is most important from the economic point of view. If the differences between the countries are very marked, it may be better to establish a single district and a centralized command.

Is it expedient to lay down rules for all these possible circumstances? It could be argued that a multiplicity of small chiefs of different cantons calls for the same tactics of concentrated command as the existence of a single great chief. The only axiom that will guide us in every case is that the political value of a canton chief is tied up with the economic value of his chiefdom. We need not hesitate to move the headquarters of *cercles* or subdivisions according to the economic progress of the cantons. No native feudal tradition can stand against a railway station, a factory, a market.

If we consider the chiefs in relation to their functions and modes of appointment, we shall recognize other differences between the village chief and the chief of a canton, and shall grasp the fact that the canton chief has become an official.

The administration nominates all chiefs, whoever they may be and in all circumstances. The most frequent case is also the simplest; the Government has only to follow native custom, which varies from hereditary succession to election, according to the locality. Certain customs witness to a shrewd political spirit. Here is one that I never tire of quoting: In the Djerma country, the *Koye*, that is to say the chief, is chosen from the family of the ancestor who ruled the Djermas when they occupied the country many centuries ago. But he is chosen by a council, called the council of "Zendis," composed of the principal descendants of the original inhabitants. The Djermas are the invaders; the Zendis, the invaded. By calling the sons of the vanquished to choose from among the victors the chief over all, the unknown African sage who founded this custom invites us to follow it. Which is what we do. And the Djerma *Koye* of Dosso is at present one of the greatest chiefs of the Federation.

Greater care is needed where there is no hereditary dynasty or well-established rule to take into account. There are two cases to be considered: either the chief will be drawn from the country, or from outside. Except in very rare cases the village chief will never come from outside. If the family which provided the village head has died out, it is still from within the area that the branch must be chosen which will bear the new chief. And if the whole village is awakening to a new life, it will be possible to arrange for an election on a broad basis including not only notables and heads of families, but also the young people and women.

It is, however, in the exercise of his functions rather than by the method of his appointment that the chief of a canton differs from a village chief and acts as an agent of the Administration.

The primary function of a chief, whether he is chief of canton or village, is to be there, to be in residence. Nothing takes the place of the real presence. If the courtyard of a *cercle* Commandant is always paved with chiefs waiting for him to receive them, we can be sure that the administration is not good. The Commandant who keeps his chiefs at headquarters, far from their chiefdoms, injures their authority and his own. And indirectly he oppresses the villages. In fact, in order to put in an appearance at headquarters, the chiefs drain their territories, where they are represented by deputies who oppress the peasants. There is another method, which consists in requiring the canton chiefs to maintain representatives at headquarters. This procedure may be a bad one if these representatives are themselves a heavy charge, and if they encroach on the status of the chiefs.

In fact, we are confronted with opposing and mutually contradictory necessities: on the one hand we are well aware that it is essential to preserve the native character of the canton chief and to make use of the traditional feudal spirit which still survives in him; on the other hand the very fact of colonization forces us to shape him to our administrative outlook. Our major fault is lack of method in our dealings with him. We demand from him too many trivial tasks and we set too much store by the way in which he performs them. Instead of entrusting to him certain important tasks—a tax, a main road, a new crop—and judging his achievement on the spot in our tours, we make his authority a travesty by using him as an intermediary in small affairs—provisioning a camp, receiving a vaccinator, collecting witnesses for a petty court case, providing a supply of chickens. We think that because he is a native, we are carrying out a native policy with his assistance, while in fact by putting menial tasks on him we treat him as sub-European. And we tolerate a hypocritical manoeuvre: in theory, the canton chief executes administrative orders; in practice, he resorts to feudal methods to get them carried out. He turns the tax into feudal tribute, the labour service into a *corvée* and cultivation into requisitioning.

Should the traditional authority of the canton chief be restored? We have already shown that this is a negative programme. We could certainly reconstitute a décor of pomp and ceremony around them, but we should not be able to re-create the soul of their ancient authority. No, the tendency of the Administration is all towards making these feudalists into officials. But then we must face the thing. They should be specialized officials and exercise a distinctive function. We have already involved them in implicit officialdom; they receive rebates on the tax, which is not always without danger for the taxpayers; they are paid a salary and it is small enough; on the Ivory Coast there are 500 of them to share 1,500,000 francs, while the European administration of the *cercles* costs 7,430,000. They enjoy a status of a sort, in the sense that they do not come under the "Native Status Code,"* and that they can-

* Translator's note: This "Indigénat" is a disciplinary code, applied by administrative officials to all persons legally of native status, i.e. not French citizens, nor of any legally defined intermediate status.

not be arbitrarily deposed. They have a personal file in the records at the station and they are scrupulously given good and bad marks by their Commandants. They are decorated, they are welcomed at receptions on national holidays, they are invited to visit exhibitions; they are sent as delegates to Dakar and even to Paris; they are brought together on councils where they collaborate with Europeans. And they are rightly treated as important persons; but what is needed is not to re-establish them, but to establish them. Not to re-establish them in a social structure that is dying, but to establish them in a modern Africa that is being born. And it is there that we should make officials of them. This need not mean making them robots or abstractions. To make officials of them is first to define their official duties, and then to establish not only their administrative status but their social personality. We must reconsider with them—and for them, as for ourselves—the problem of the function of the chief.

The Village Chief: Let the Village Re-create Its Own Chief

For a long time to come, the territorial Administration will work through canton chiefs who, while no longer feudal, are not yet completely officials. But there is a basic Africa on which *cercles* and cantons will always rest: the Africa of the villages. It is in the village that the secret of African evolution is hidden. Do not let us be afraid to sweep Africa clean of its feudalists by officialising them, and to dig right down to the rock, to the foundations of ancient negro society. Here are rooted the local institutions which influence native policy and transform the conditions of territorial Administration. The councils of village notables have had a status in the administration for several years; they deliberate in each *cercle* on the plan of campaign for labour service and on the tax-rate. In the villages themselves these councils should not be the preserve of the notables, but should include all the heads of families. It is also necessary to revive and adapt to modern Africa a very old institution, the association of young people of the same age, which embodies the principles, the disciplines and the chartered liberties of a trade union. The councils and age associations will not take the place of the village chief, but they will help to bring him to life in a new form.

The feudal organization that we found in Africa is crumbling. And the village that supported it, and which we did not discover at first, is going to pieces. With our commercial economy, we have introduced an individualistic ferment which has now reached the village and is eating away the ancient community. The canton chief is losing his feudal character and the village chief his religious sanctions. But though it is conceivable that the canton chief may become an official, it is difficult to foresee what the village chief will become. It is not the case that there are great chiefs who could be chiefs of cantons, and small chiefs who could be village chiefs. There is one feudal Africa which may be compared to the feudal structure of French society at the close of the Middle Ages. Just as the French kings gathered into one unity the land of France, so in Africa the Colonial Government unites the country by eliminating the great territorial overlords and changing the feudatories into chiefs of cantons or officials. A colonial Africa is developing, over-lapping the rural Africa of the village chiefs, who themselves are also feudatories and whose importance—legal and social—is not to be measured by the size of their territories. The area which they rule is not large but it represents the land which was reclaimed from the bush by the first cultivators, whose lineage it perpetuates. The village chiefs have preserved the genius of the land and of labour. But to-day their position is shaken by new methods of labour and new forms of tenure. What new kind of man will arise as chief in this Africa? I do not think that he will be an official. He will emerge from the families who hold the land and from the world of labour. But in what form who can yet say?

A curious fact seems to me pregnant with meaning for the future. Good year or bad, there are 50,000 to 70,000 migrant groundnut labourers—*navetanes*—who go off from the Soudan to Senegal, and 100,000 cocoa *navetanes* who go from the Upper Volta to the Ivory Coast and the Gold Coast—a seasonal migration of agricultural labourers. These peasant labourers have chiefs, not the chiefs of their own original villages nor yet those of the villages in the south where they go to work. The village of their birth may be a thousand miles from the place where they work, and it will be a year before they are back there. The village where they work is foreign in race and customs. And yet the *navetanes* have their chief. The Administration had no hand in it, they found him them-selves. Men from the same Soudanese village or region have drawn from among themselves the chief of the work-team; he organizes their movements, buys the railway tickets or fixes the stages on the road, settles the team in at the place of work and oversees it. Thus rural labour, in this new form of seasonal migrants, can have new chiefs. And in the agrarian Africa of our time, there may be a work-chief distinct from the territorial chief. The capacity of Africa to produce new chiefs is not bound to the traditional form of the territorial administration.

What is certain is that the village will always have to have a chief. That is of moment not only to the colonial administration but to Africa itself. There will be a chief, that is to say there will be only one. In every country in the world, the ruler is a single individual. The old Africa, with its own forces of renewal, will perhaps construct a "municipium," a communal organization, but in it it will place the chief.

Do not let us be too closely mixed up in it. We can constitute the canton; we should leave the village to react and reconstitute itself. The *de facto* chief that the village gives birth to will be the legal chief in our eyes.

VII

The Right to Rule

Beginning with the Spanish jurists of the sixteenth century, European commentators on imperialism, if not the conquerors themselves, have been much concerned with the morality of their actions. In the background, the Judeo-Christian religious tradition and the Roman legal tradition were both important in making states wish to see their actions as moral and licit. Legality or claims to legality were also important, if a European state wished to have its overseas claims recognized and respected by other states. But the wish to appear moral was more than this. International law, after all, recognized the "right of conquest" as an adequate claim to sovereignty over territory. At bottom, states needed to assert their imperial rule as a matter of right simply because the men who ran them needed to feel that they were acting morally.

The arguments that recur in the moral justification of empire were few. Some simply said "might makes right," but this argument was seldom used in such a crass form. In the wake of Darwinian biology, it was easier to say that the struggle for survival was involved, where the victory of the "fittest" was part of Nature's law, if not of God's. From the beginning of European expansion, it had been convenient to justify empire as a way of spreading Christianity, and the nineteenth century shifted from Christianity to civilization. Finally, a moral duty to develop undeveloped or unused resources could be called upon.

The selections that follow are representative justifications for empire, each different from the others, and each seeing the problem in a different context of time and space. In addition, none of them is simply an argument for the morality of empire, so that each incorporates a variety of the themes in imperial thought of the nineteenth and twentieth centuries.

23. The Aborigines Committee and the Morality of Empire

The Select Committee on Aborigines was appointed through the influence of Thomas Fowell Buxton and the same group of humanitarians in the House of Commons who had obtained the act emancipating the slaves in 1833. The committee sat through three consecutive sessions before it presented its report in 1837.

Its terms of reference had to do mainly with the original inhabitants of the true colonies like Australia and Canada. The committee was appointed "to consider what measures ought to be adopted with regard to the native inhabitants of countries where British settlements are made, and to the neighbouring tribes, in order to secure to them the due observance of justice and the protection of their rights; to promote the spread of civilization among them, and to lead them to the peaceful and voluntary reception of the Christian religion." That in itself was a substantial program for empire, and the final result of the committee's work was predictable from the beginning. The report, moreover, is an interesting document summing up the conversionist position in Britain—especially the final paragraph.

The portion of the report quoted here is from Parliamentary Sessional Papers, 1837, vii (425), pp. 3–6 and 75–76.

THE SITUATION of Great Britain brings her beyond any other power into communication with the uncivilized nations of the earth. We are in contact with them in so many parts of the globe, that it has become of deep importance to ascertain the results of our relations with them, and to fix the rules of our conduct towards them. We are apt to class them under the sweeping term of savages, and perhaps, in so doing, to consider ourselves exempted from the obligations due to them as our fellow men. This assumption does not, however, it is obvious, alter our responsibility; and the question appears momentous, when we consider that the policy of Great Britain in this particular, as it has already affected the interests, and, we fear we may add, sacrificed the lives, of many thousands, may yet, in all probability, influence the character and the destiny of millions of the human race.

The extent of the question will be best comprehended by taking a survey of the globe, and by observing over how much of its surface an intercourse with Britain may become the greatest blessing, or the heaviest scourge. It will scarcely be denied in word, that, as an enlightened and Christian people, we are at least bound to do to the inhabitants of other lands, whether enlightened or not, as we should in similar circumstances desire to be done by; but, beyond the obligations of common honesty, we are bound by two considerations with regard to the uncivilized: first, that of the ability which we possess to confer upon them the most important benefits; and, secondly, that of their inability to resist any encroachments, however unjust, however mischievous, which we may be disposed to make. The disparity of the parties, the strength of the one, and the incapacity of the other, to enforce the observance of their rights, constitutes a new and irresistible appeal to our compassionate protection.

The duty of introducing into our relations with uncivilized nations the righteous and the profitable laws of justice is incontrovertible, and it has been repeatedly acknowledged in the abstract, but has, we fear, been rarely brought into practice; for, as a nation, we have not hesitated to invade many of the rights which they hold most dear.

Thus, while Acts of Parliament have laid down the general principles of equity, other and conflicting Acts have been framed, disposing of lands without any reference to the possessors and actual occupants, and without making any reserve of the proceeds of the property of the natives for their benefit.

Such omissions must surely be attributed to oversight; for it is not to be asserted that Great Britain has any disposition to sanction unfair dealing: nothing can be more plain, nothing can be more strong, than the language used by the Government of this country on the subject. We need only refer to the instructions of Charles II, addressed to the Council of Foreign Plantations in the year 1670.

"Forasmuch as most of our said Colonies do border upon the Indians, and peace is not to be expected without the due observance and preservation of justice to them, you are, in our name, to command all the governors, that they, at no time, give any just provocation to any of the said Indians that are at peace with us," &c.

Then, with respect to the Indians who desire to put themselves under our protection, that they "be received."

"And that the governors do by all ways seek firmly to oblige them.

"And that they do employ some persons to learn the languages of them.

"And that they do not only carefully protect and defend them from adversaries, but that they more especially take care that none of our own subjects, nor any of their servants, do any way harm them.

"And that if any shall dare to offer any violence to them in their persons, goods or possessions, the said governors do severely punish the said injuries, agreeably to justice and right.

"And you are to consider how the Indians and slaves may be best instructed and invited to the Christian religion, it being both for the honour of the Crown and of the Protestant religion itself, that all persons within any of our territories, though never so remote, should be taught the knowledge of God, and be acquainted with the mysteries of salvation."

Nor is modern authority wanting to the same effect: the Address of the House of Commons to the King, passed unanimously July 1834, states, "That His Majesty's faithful Commons in Parliament assembled, are deeply impressed with the duty of acting upon the principles of justice and humanity in the intercourse and relations of this country with the native inhabitants of its colonial settlements, of affording them protection in the enjoyment of their civil rights, and of imparting to them that degree of civilization, and that religion, with which Providence has blessed this nation, and humbly prays that His Majesty will take such measures, and give such directions to the governors and offices of His Majesty's colonies, settlements and plantations, as shall secure to the natives the due observance of justice and the protection of their rights, promote the spread of civilization amongst them, and lead them to the peaceful and voluntary reception of the Christian religion."

This Address, as the Chancellor of the Exchequer observed, so far from being the expression of any new principle, only embodies and recognizes principles on which the British Government has for a considerable time been disposed to act.

In furtherance of these views, your Committee was appointed to examine into the actual state of our relations with uncivilized nations; and it is from the evidence brought before this Committee during the last two Sessions, that we are enabled to compare our actions with our avowed principles, and to show what has been, and what will assuredly continue to be, unless strongly checked, the course of our conduct towards these defenceless people.

It is not too much to say, that the intercourse of Europeans in general, without any exception in favour of the subjects of Great Britain, has been, unless when attended by missionary exertions, a source of many calamities to uncivilized nations.

Too often, their territory has been usurped; their property seized; their numbers diminished; their character debased; the spread of civilization impeded. European vices and diseases have been introduced amongst them, and they have been familiarized with the use of our most potent instruments for the subtle or the violent destruction of human life, viz. brandy and gunpowder.

It will be only too easy to make out the proof of all these assertions, which may be established solely by the evidence above referred to. It will be easy also to show that the result to ourselves has been as contrary to our interest as to our duty; that our system has not only incurred a vast load of crime, but a vast expenditure of money and amount of loss.

On the other hand, we trust it will not be difficult to show by inference, and even to prove, by the results of some few experiments of an opposite course of conduct, that, setting aside all considerations of duty, a line of policy, more friendly and just towards the natives, would materially contribute to promote the civil and commercial interests of Great Britain.

It is difficult to form an estimate of the population of the less civilized nations, liable to be influenced for good or for evil, by contact and intercourse with the more civilized nations of the earth. It would appear that the barbarous regions likely to be more immediately affected by the policy of Great Britain, are the south and the west of Africa, Australia, the islands in the Pacific Ocean, a very extensive district of South America at the back of our Essequibo settlement, between the rivers Orinoco and Amazon, with the immense tract which constitutes the most northerly part of the American continent, and stretches from the Pacific to the Atlantic Oceans.

These are countries in which we have either planted colonies, or which we frequent for the purposes of traffic, and it is our business to inquire on what principles we have conducted our intercourse.

It might be presumed that the native inhabitants of any land have an incontrovertible right to their own soil: a plain and sacred right, however, which seems not to have been understood. Europeans have entered their borders uninvited, and, when there, have not only acted as if they were undoubted lords of the soil, but have punished the natives as aggressors if they have evinced a disposition to live in their own country.

"If they have been found upon their own property, they have been treated as thieves and robbers. They are driven back into the interior as if they were dogs or kangaroos."

From very large tracts we have, it appears, succeeded in eradicating them; and though from some parts their ejection has not been so apparently violent as from others, it has been equally complete, through our taking possession of their hunting-grounds, whereby we have despoiled them of the means of existence. . . .

"The main point which I would have in view," said a witness before your Committee, "would be trade, commerce, peace and civilization. The other alternative is extermination; for you can stop nowhere; you must go on; you may have a short respite when you have driven panic into the people, but you must come back to the same thing until you have shot the last man." From all the bulky evidence before us, we can come to no other conclusion; and considering the power, and the mighty resources of the British nation, we must believe that the choice rests with ourselves.

Great Britain has, in former times, countenanced evils of great magnitude,—slavery and the slave-trade; but for these she has made some atonement; for the latter, by abandoning the traffic; for the former, by the sacrifice of 20 millions of money. But for these offences there was this apology; they were evils of an ancient date, a kind of prescription might be pleaded for them, and great interests were entwined with them.

An evil remains very similar in character, and not altogether unfit to be compared with them in the amount of misery it produces. The oppression of the natives of barbarous countries is a practice which pleads no claim to indulgence; it is an evil of comparatively recent origin, imperceptible and unallowed in its growth; it never has had even the colour of sanction from the legislature of this country; no vested rights are associated with it, and we have not the poor excuse that it contributes to any interest of the state. On the contrary, in point of economy, of security, of commerce, of reputation, it is a short-sighted and disastrous policy.

As far as it has prevailed, it has been a burthen on the empire. It has thrown impediments in the way of successful colonization; it has engendered wars, in which great expenses were necessarily incurred, and no reputation could be won; and it has banished from our confines, or exterminated, the natives, who might have been profitable workmen, good customers, and good neighbours. These unhappy results have not flowed from any determination on the part of the government of this country to deal hardly with those who are in a less advanced state of society; but they seem to have arisen from ignorance, from the difficulty which distance interposes in checking the cupidity and punishing the crimes of that adventurous class of Europeans who lead the way in penetrating the territory of uncivilized man, and from the system of dealing with the rights of the natives. Many reasons unite for apprehending that the evils which we have described will increase if the duty of coming to a solemn determination as to the policy we shall adopt towards ruder nations be now neglected; the chief of these reasons is, the national necessity of finding some outlet for the superabundant population of Great Britain and Ireland. It is to be feared that, in the pursuit of this benevolent and laudable object, the rights of those who have not the means of advocating their interests or exciting sympathy for their sufferings, may be disregarded.

This, then, appears to be the moment for the nation to declare, that with all its desire to give encouragement to emigration, and to find a soil to which our surplus population may retreat, it will tolerate no scheme which implies violence or fraud in taking possession of such a territory; that it will no longer subject itself to the guilt of conniving at oppression, and that it will take upon itself the task of defending those who are too weak and too ignorant to defend themselves.

Your Committee have hitherto relied chiefly on arguments, showing that no national interest, even in its narrowest sense, is subserved by encroachments on the territory or disregard of the rights of the aboriginal inhabitants of barbarous countries; but they feel it their duty to add, that there is a class of motives of a higher order which conduce to the same conclusion.

The British empire has been signally blessed by Providence, and her eminence, her strength, her wealth, her prosperity, her intellectual, her moral and her religious advantages, are so many reasons for peculiar obedience to the laws of Him who guides the destinies of nations. These were given for some higher purpose than commercial prosperity and military renown. "It is not to be doubted that this country has been invested with wealth and power, with arts and knowledge, with the sway of distant lands, and the mastery of the restless waters, for some great and important purpose in the government of the world. Can we suppose otherwise than that it is our office to carry civilization and humanity, peace and good government, and, above all, the knowledge of the true God, to the uttermost ends of the earth?"* He who has made Great Britain what she is, will inquire at our hands how we have employed the influence He has lent to us in our dealings with the untutored and defenceless savage; whether it has been engaged in seizing their lands, warring upon their people, and transplanting unknown disease, and deeper degradation, through the remote regions of the earth; or whether we have, as far as we have been able, informed their ignorance, and invited and afforded them the opportunity of becoming partakers of that civilization, that innocent commerce, that knowledge and that faith with which it has pleased a gracious Providence to bless our own country.

24. Jules Harmand on the Morality of Empire and the Policy of Association

Jules Harmand (1845–1921) was the French imperial theorist who gave the name *association* to the new racist concept of imperial policy. His early career was spent as a naval doctor, which put him in touch with the biological aspects of pseudoscientific racism. His own field of imperial activity was East Asia, where he first made a reputation in the 1870's as a traveler and diplomatic agent in Siam, Cambodia, and Laos. In 1884, he acted as Commissaire-Général in Tonkin, and from 1894 to 1905 he was French Minister to Japan.

The selection below is a translation in full of Chapter VI, Section I, entitled "Native Policy," from his major work, *Domination et colonisation* (Paris, 1910), pp. 152–174. Reprinted by permission of Flammarion et cie. It is something more than a mere statement of the Associationist view of imperial morality; it also sums up the main tenets of that school.

* Rev. Mr. Whewell's Sermon before the Trinity Board.

It could therefore have been just as well placed in Part III of this book, to be read alongside Léopold de Saussure and Charles Temple, and it is equally pertinent as a companion piece to Lord Lugard's views on administrative policy in Part VI.

The sense of the title, and the interpretation Harmand used throughout his work, is the view that the colonies for European settlement must be sharply distinguished from true empire, where Europeans go only as rulers. His term for this latter kind of overseas territory is *domination*, which is translated here as "true empire" or "territorial empire."

1. Native Policy

THE PROBLEM to which all others are subordinate is that of setting up and maintaining a good native policy, and in a true empire the best policy will be that which makes best use of the conquered people, creating the least suffering on one hand, and giving them the greatest extent of well-being on the other. It will be that which succeeds in creating such a close relationship between the interests of the conqueror and those of the conquered that anything useful to the first will also be useful to the second, and *vice versa*.

Enough has been said of the "might" that makes "right" through conquest. But whatever explanations are given, or arguments made in its favor, the fact remains that, from a strictly moral point of view, these are mere side issues. It is certain that to deprive a people of its independence is in itself an evil deed, and to do so violently, most often with motives that are not beyond reproach, is immoral. It is a demonstration of that universal law of the struggle for survival in which we are all engaged, not only on account of our nature, which condemns us to win or die, but also on account of our civilization. It cannot permit such vast and fertile regions of the globe to be lost to us and to humanity by the incapacity of those who hold them and by the ill treatment given these lands so long as they are left to themselves.

The two ideas of true empire and of force, or at least of constraint, are correlative or complementary. According to the time, circumstance, and procedures, force can be more or less, strong or weak, open or hidden, but it can never disappear. On the day when constraint is no longer required, empire will no longer exist: only a single society will remain, a single political community. A new nationality will have been born, emerging from that of the conquerors. But that is too much to hope for, or even to conceive of, in the conditions which prevail where the enterprises considered in these reflections go forward. Political power, being exercised over races too different from that of the conquerors ever to join intimately with it, gives true empire an indelible characteristic of foreignness. The two elements present are irreducible, or, one may say, unassimilable.

The conqueror should have no illusions. Whatever his wisdom, experience, good conduct, or excellent government, he will never inspire those he claims to guide with the feelings of instinctive affection and easy solidarity that make a nation—not after having conquered them and forced them to submit. These feelings can occur only among men who differ but little in blood and historic culture, in customs and ideals.

Even after a lengthy occupation, after long periods of peace and security will have brought about the anticipated and desirable transformation and joined together the interests of the two communities insofar as it is possible, it would be folly for the conquerors to think that they might be loved, blinding themselves to the extent of believing that the dominated society will submit to their rule with pleasure and turn itself over to them with complete confidence.

No example can be mentioned, and one can rest assured that none will occur, of a conquest like these, over a people separated by oceans and continents, who consequently had no sort of community with their conquerors, but who nevertheless accepted them without a second thought. However weak or degraded or barbarous one may imagine the vanquished to be, however evil their natural rulers may be; or, on the contrary, however civilized in their fashion and intelligent; or however deprived one may imagine the people to be of any ethnic or patriotic sense, feudal or religious loyalty toward their princes, they will always consider the departure or disappearance of the alien power as a deliverance, and almost always and almost everywhere, they will even see the replacement of one foreign master by another as a kind of liberation.

This is a truth expressed recently by the *Times* in connection with the example of disturbances which India presents today as a demonstration and lesson of true empire after long experience, carried on under exceptionally favorable circumstances, when it wrote: "After all, it was by the sword that we conquered India, and it is by the sword that we hold it."

That is inexorable fate, which no policy can remove or any rhetoric hide. However high the conqueror's ambitions and aspirations, he must resign himself to it. It is the punishment for his violence, the bloodstain that nothing can remove from his hands.

But expansion by conquest, however necessary, seems especially unjust and disturbing to the conscience of democracies. Empire, hardly compatible with their egalitarian principles, is *ipso facto* autocratic in practice; it requires an absolute government. The conquerors, by the mere fact that they are foreign and conquerors, become an aristocracy, a privileged body with special powers, and their government in its very essence, and in order to carry out fruitfully the demands of the situation, can only be a patriarchal government, a government removed from the concept of equality and hence from political liberty; for this liberty is only a form and a manifestation of equality. They must be "good tyrants," intelligent, kind, enlightened, foresighted and charitable, comprehending and tolerant, but strong. Whatever else, they will always remain aristocrats and usurpers.

To place the republican emblem on government actions and public monuments may be allowable. But to transpose democratic institutions into such a setting is aberrant nonsense. The subject people are not and cannot become citizens in the democratic sense of the term.

France has tried to resolve the contradiction by assimilation, based on a previous faith in the equality of all men and their rapid perfectibility. Observation, experience, and science have convinced all those who are not content to pay for the inanity, sterility, and dangers of that chimera with mere words—and with the suffering it brings to those whom one would like to help.

The time has come to substitute other conceptions for these utopias, perhaps less generous but assuredly more useful and more fruitful, for they alone are in conformity with the nature of things.

The Right to True Empire Founded on Moral Superiority

It is necessary, then, to accept as a principle and point of departure the fact that there is a hierarchy of races and civilizations, and that we belong to the superior race and civilization, still recognizing that, while superiority confers rights, it imposes strict obligations in return. The basic legitimation of conquest over native peoples is the conviction of our superiority, not merely our mechanical, economic, and military superiority, but our moral superiority. Our dignity rests on that quality, and it underlies our right to direct the rest of humanity. Material power is nothing but a means to that end.

Peoples who lack this belief and this frankness about themselves should not try to conquer. The policy which suits them is that of Simeon Stylites. Whatever happens, they should stay at home. Otherwise, they will inevitably prepare the ruin of their empire and render it evil, because in such uncertain and irresolute hands it is never aboveboard or certain of consequence. Incapable of sustaining or prolonging empire, such people are shown in advance to be unworthy of the role they claim without right—a role that necessitates the uninterrupted use of force, if it is to be advantageous both to the mother country and to the natives, that requires discipline and the kind of justice that goes with command—with *imperium*.

Moral Responsibility

Former conquerors, even recent ones, sought conquest only for their own advantage. Modern nations, implanting their domination over distant lands at great risk and at great expense in men and money, no doubt pursue the same objective, but with an ideal that was missing among their predecessors, an ideal which was awakened in their conscience only a short time ago. It is well understood that they work for their own interests and expect to draw profit of various sorts from their sacrifice. But alongside these intentions something else has appeared; a new imperative inspires their conduct. They obey a new feeling almost unknown among their predecessors, and this is the sense of moral responsibility imposed by conquest.

Without doubt, they have their own ends in mind, but they think of these ends in a new light and try to gain them in new ways. They conceive that if a conquest is permitted by their superiority, if it is excused by its necessity, it remains nonetheless a very serious act, an abuse of power which may be absolved only by the well-being it procures for those who must suffer it. Remembering that in every case he can only take advantage of his possession through the agency of the native—which is the policy of exploitation—the foreign director also understands that the native's work becomes more and more productive to the extent that the native himself can be brought to understand things as they are, that his mind expands, that his faculties improve, and that he better understands how to control them—as he plans ahead, as he becomes willy-nilly an efficient collaborator in the benefits of empire, and as he is forced to comprehend and to judge its value. This is the policy of association or cooperation.

THE POLICY OF ASSOCIATION

While always having useful results, this policy only comes into its own and becomes the ideal choice when brought alive by moral inspiration and by the conviction that the conqueror, in undertaking the trusteeship of a people, also takes charge of their souls, their intellectual needs, their atavistic feelings, and, in promising to satisfy all these becomes their initiator, the *naleutes* of their minds.

The policy that might be called that of integral exploitation is slavery, and in its mitigated forms, agricultural or industrial serfdom, where the individual is tied to the farm or the factory without security for his personal property, an instrument of low productivity, whom the capitalist master considers only as a machine and as an individual separated from society. The policy of association, far from breaking the solidarity of native groups, seeks to consolidate them in order to serve its subjects as well as making them participate conscientiously in its work.

But if the writer of these lines may be permitted to lay further emphasis on this matter, when he put forward the idea that in order to be advantageous, while becoming moral, the relations of the conqueror and the conquered must be established as an association, he hardly doubted the future that awaited it, so much did it appear natural to him. Nevertheless, in becoming a generalized formula, it has had the fate of all such formulas. Badly understood, badly practiced, it could be interpreted by anyone in the sense that fitted his tendencies or his opinions, and often in a manner opposed to the observation and reflection that lay behind it. It has especially served as an improved argument for assimilation, seeking to endow that old passion with a new virginity.

APPLICATIONS

Association, understood as an economic principle and a moral guide, has, in fact, a quite general applicability. But as a political instrument, it only comes into full play when the conqueror finds himself in control of a homogeneous and coherent population, with its own quite advanced civilization, self-conscious of its personality and possessing a historical heritage. That is to say, it aims at precisely the circumstances in which empire meets the greatest obstacles and the most difficult opposition.

This policy, in my opinion, is especially concerned with the Annamese peoples, and we can even extend it to the Arabs with valuable results, for it resolves the great difficulty of our Mediterranean possession, at once a European colonization territory and a racial empire, by helping us to reconcile as much as possible the unfortunately opposed interests of our colonists and of our Arab and Berber subjects. It has a narrower and less ambitious application when its objects are the segmented and backward races, such as the greater part of the peoples and tribes of tropical Africa. Nevertheless, it always teaches tolerance and liberalism in autocracy. In particular, it prescribes a scrupulous respect for customs, manners, and religions. It everywhere substitutes mutual aid for exploitation pure and simple of natives' abilities, for the seizure of their goods and their private property. It encourages their intellectual development. Wishing to make their work more personal and more in their own interest, it tends to make them more productive. Seeking a meeting of minds and their union in a meeting of interests, it facilitates their submission.

But a realistic and wise policy of association reserves with an unshakable firmness all these rights that pertain to empire and takes account of all the exigencies of empire. It does not comprehend the preparation or realization of a never-to-be attained equality, but rather the establishment of a certain equivalence or compensation in reciprocal services. Rather than allowing a dissipation of empire, this policy seeks to reinforce the domination by making it less vexatious and more bearable.

The "Contract" of Association

Without falling into Rousseauan reveries, it is worth noting that association implies a contract, and this idea, though nothing more than an illustration, is more appropriately applied to the coexistence of two profoundly different societies thrown sharply and artificially into contact than it is to the single society formed by natural processes which Rousseau envisaged.

This is how the terms of this implicit agreement can be conceived. The European conqueror brings order, foresight, and security to a human society which, though ardently aspiring for these fundamental values without which no community can make progress, still lacks the aptitude to achieve them from within itself. It would vegetate day after day in universal fear, crushed under the weight of abuse and injustice. The European power transmits, along with public and private peace, the mechanical knowledge, the money, the science, and the hygiene which go to vivify the latent potential of its population, to multiply its numbers, and to transform its territory. With these mental and material instruments, which it lacked and now receives, it gains the idea and ambition for a better existence, and the means of achieving it.

We will obey you, say the subjects, if you begin by proving yourself worthy. We will obey you if you can succeed in convincing us of the superiority of that civilization of which you talk so much, and proving to us that, in imposing your rule, you are not following your own interest, as you constantly claim. We are willing to work for you, but with the prior condition that it is in our own interest, and because we cannot fail to recognize that under your management our work, having become more necessary, also becomes more fruitful and certain, and our property better protected. You are profoundly alien to our nature. Nevertheless, we will submit to your direction on condition that our entire way of life will not be overturned, that you will not attempt to impose ideas and institutions we cannot understand, or force us to consume products we do not want, that we have the least possible contact with you, and that most of us find out about your presence only through its results.

We will pay the taxes you require of us, but on condition that we are certain they benefit us and are spent among us, that they do not create an artificial inflation, that they be not spent on incomprehensible and useless luxuries which, insulting to our poverty, will also show you to be parasites and liars.

We will forget all that we suffered as soldiers opposing your conquest, and we will defend you and die fighting alongside your own men, here and even beyond our frontiers, if this service profits our own nation, preserves us from our neighbor, whom we fear, hate, and despise, and against whom we occasionally may have our revenge.

We will serve you faithfully, say the chiefs and the upper classes, if this service does not dishonor us, if, instead of covering us with disdain, ruining our fortunes and our pride, and making us your accomplices and traitors to our fellow countrymen, you will allow us to play a role, following the laws and organization of our country and preserving the social rank that we have acquired.

We will either help you or give you free rein, say the princes, if you will repay us for the loss of power with material advantages and illusions consoling to our vanity and if you persuade us that your protection, which we have not requested, offers the only chance for survival that remains to us. We will be resigned to your domination if it is strong and if it is demonstrably better for our country and our people than anything our weakness has hitherto allowed us to fear or hope for.

Such is the *schema* of the policy of association. It has the ambition of making empire better and more protective of mutual benefits, while at the same time making it more bearable by thus reducing to a minimum the ever-costly and sterile use of force.

It seeks to ameliorate the lot of the native in every way, but in every way that is profitable to him while leaving him to evolve in his own way, maintaining each individual in his own place, his own function, and his own role, touching only very lightly the habits and traditions of the subjects, using, rather, their own organization to attain its objectives. It is, then, a systematic repudiation of assimilation and tends to substitute an indirect rule for the necessarily rigid and oppressive direct administration, while conserving the institutions of the conquered people, though better watched over and better directed—and that with a respect for their own past.

It requires more delicate application, without doubt, than the brutal exploitation of administrative militarism. It calls for a perfect understanding of the natives and their psychology, a profound experience of their customs and ideas—experience and knowledge which can only be acquired through specialized preparation, by prolonged exposure to the setting, by permanence in office, all of these being conditions which can only be fulfilled by a particularized organization of the colonies. It can thus be seen that the concept of association brings us back in practice to that autonomy which was shown to be more urgent for France than for the other expanding states by deducing the necessities which condition general policy.

Order, the Basis of True Empire

If the moral foundation of colonial conquest is the faith of the conqueror in his own superiority, the experimental basis of association is the fact that the missing element in the most advanced and perfected native societies is the internal faculty for order and discipline. These peoples already have needs great enough and varied enough to appreciate and seek the benefits of security, but that security is only attainable under solid and well-organized governments, capable of assuring the regular dispensation of justice and the fair collection of taxes. Their chiefs are not lacking in either the idea or the intention of carrying out the public good; but it is not possible for them to wait long for results, and they also lack the reserves of capital and scientific knowledge to master an exuberant and capricious nature. Without even speaking of the external dangers which can paralyze them, they are obliged, if for no other reason by internal disorder, to live from day to day. Sometimes having theoretically excellent laws, perfectly translating and synthesizing their evolution, they lack the means to apply them, and this impotence contributes to their demoralization. Discouraged by a task beyond their strength, they end by looking only for personal advantage in their power, concentrating only on the perpetuation of the abuses from which they live, and finally by invading the whole system of government.

Under this regime, where violence and weakness, the arbitrary and the lax, are mixed, the people for their part work in a vacuum. Their activity, already contradicted and reduced, leaves almost nothing for the government, and the feeble revenues obtained are still more dispersed in collection. Not only is there no longer that concord between the interest of the administrators and those of the administered, without which good government is impossible; their interests are actually opposed. The impact of corruption becomes universal, and disorder is irremediable.

The Consequences of Order in True Empire

Only a foreign government, strong and well ordered, is in a position to draw this kind of population and country out of this vicious circle. By doing nothing more than penetrating the chaos with regularity, honesty, and the personal impartiality of its agents, it has an influence the results of which appear promptly and are shown to be extraordinary.

These populations seem to us to be sleeping, relaxed, resigned to a fate that is made bearable by the climate. They were, in fact, all of that, but more from circumstance and their belief in the sterility of effort than by nature. Hard-working nevertheless, but crushed under onerous taxes, never sure of keeping their earnings, both foresight and the desire for gain are asleep within them. When order and security are reborn, they will revive, so to speak, and show the qualities of energy and activity which have often confounded witnesses.

Foreign domination always produces this result, however little it is raised above the level of mere pillage and however long it remains; it can be encountered in the ancient world as it can in modern times. Only to take our own example, we have seen this happen in Cochin China, in spite of our general lack of experience in such enterprises, in spite of our ignorance of the setting, where we landed as though discoverers of the Americas, without the slightest idea of the customs and institutions of the natives, and in spite of special obstacles thrown in the way of our success by our prejudices, the defects of our central organization, and the upheaval in which we found this tiny country.

THE COCHIN CHINESE EXAMPLE

The Mekong delta, with fertility above average and ordinarily free of severe climatic problems (though, it is true, with insufficient population to exploit it properly), could furnish the court at Hué before our arrival no more than two million francs in direct taxes, paid in cereals and in zinc sapeks. After a few years, this same area and this same population provided the French administration with that amount tenfold in silver coin, even though peace was still troubled and before the land could be improved in ways rendered both costly and difficult by the nature of the country.

The natives, without our having yet undertaken to teach them protection against avoidable disease, began to multiply, to increase their paddies, and to acquire ideas about the value of time, money, and thrift.

Legislative Procedures

In order to obtain these happy results, the conqueror must first of all avoid introducing his own laws into the new possession. These laws were not created for it. Nor should he set his mind to constructing new laws. He must use only those which exist, recognizing that they alone are good for the community, because no law is good or bad in itself—or, rather, a law is good only to the extent that it is natural, which is to say resulting from the evolution of the nation, summing up its concepts and sentiments: it will then fit congruently and precisely the instinctive needs and ideals inherited from the ancestors.

The conqueror will no doubt fall short of his obligation and show himself unworthy if he does not seek to improve his legislation. Nevertheless, he must not ask for the improvements that are suggested by his own inventiveness, or by the artificial parallel of a foreign tradition, but rather those that follow from the observation and study of local laws and traditions and lead to their *restitutio ad integrum.* The wisest thing to do is to arrange them, codify them, and remove the irregularities introduced through the weakness and disorder of governments or the corruption of individuals—introduce a few slight, partial, and prudent improvements over time, as a consequence of changes produced by the progress of his own task and of the needs it calls forth. Even when held down to these modest proportions, it is still a very ambitious task. It is attractive and tempting, the most attractive and useful that may be suggested to a conqueror. But it also requires rare qualities of judgment, critical sense, erudition, and philosophical penetration of the native soul; for it is a matter of distinguishing that which constitutes the pure and solid core of the ethnic and political processes in these pupil societies, forged by history in the course of ages, and of eliminating that which is only the superficial rust and blemish.

From this point of view, no more appropriate political and social study can be indicated than that of the Chinese administrations of the Far East, or those impregnated by Chinese methods. In China, Annam, and Korea—and even in ancient Japan, though it passed through its own peculiar evolution thanks to its geographical position and to the remarkable character of its inhabitants—in these places one cannot fail to be struck by the contrast between the theoretical excellence of legal prescriptions and their degradation in practice, between the law and the fact, between the intentions of the laws and the innumerable abuses which have deformed them and in their turn taken on the force of law.

MATERIAL IMPROVEMENTS

But the legislative policy of imperial governments should be first of all economic and governed by its economic consequences. If preoccupation with these moral responsibilities, or the new consciousness of duty, just now called forth, remains our highest inspiration; if we now consider the intellectual progress of the natives and the enlargement of their interior life, carried out with whatever prudence is necessary, as our absolution for the initial crime of conquest; we must also consider that the surest means of reaching these ultimate results is the material improvement of the lot of the conquered. It is best to approach the problem from the material side, and the material results will show the best road to follow next. The policy of association has as its tool the "policy of enrichment" of the natives, and this implies their automatic enrichment, unleashed as it were by the administrative guarantee of our actions.

THE BUDGETARY CRITERION

The revenue of a possession is of the greatest importance for an imperial government. Government income is a translation of its efforts and the criterion of its success, provided of course that its receipts fall into place normally, without tactless annoyances or abusive taxation. The natural progress of this curve is upward, leaving aside accidental deviations caused by physical conditions against which man is still powerless, and it is the most certain indication not merely of the economic progress of the natives but also of their contentment and of their degree of acceptance of foreign domination. Even as budgetary increases demonstrate their well-being, population increase, extending cultivation, and the development of their industry and commerce, budgetary stability betrays their discontent, uneasiness, and the doubts that are found among their disturbed masses.

Can this policy make the individual native happier? That is quite another question, no doubt worthy of full examination but leading far afield. In any case, it must be admitted that the outcome would be doubtful. But man does not live by bread alone, and he only appears to fulfill his destiny by wearing himself out in the impossible task of crossing the abyss that lies between his desires and their realization—a canyon that only grows deeper as his attainments increase and his needs expand.

The policy of association—penetrating every act of the conqueror, making him seek his own advantage in that of the vanquished, raising his goals toward the progressive elevation of the conquered populations without denying their moral being or separating its discrete elements—also seems the most appropriate to combat the principled objections which democracies make against colonial expansion. It is, in fact, the policy best suited to conciliate the rights and interests of the most favored races with their most necessary tasks, and with the obligations which they have assumed in imposing the weight of their superiority on weaker peoples.

Dangers of the Policy of Association

Like every theoretically inspired political institution, where general ideas are translated into policies, the native policy of association carries with it dangers and disadvantages in application, for evil may follow from the best intentions.

The stumbling block of this formula, already shown by experience and especially with the French temperament, is to open the door to excessive liberalism and to favor certain tendencies to think of the native as a being like ourselves, on the same footing as ourselves, having the same rights in the association—tendencies so conducive to laziness, so convenient to the routine attitude of our administrators, and of all administrations.

If there exists a contract as the basis of the policy of association, a reciprocal agreement, it must be said that a contract never, in any kind of business, implies the equality of the participants. Its aim most often is to compensate for and to counterbalance the inequality of their means and to guarantee a just payment proportional to their different contributions.

The rights which the conqueror takes upon himself, as has been said and must be said again, rest upon his sense of his superiority, on the conviction that his domination is useful and good, and on his wish to prove the same. The first of his duties, in regard to his subjects (as to the state and to the nation), is to maintain his domination and make sure that it lasts: everything that has the consequence of consolidating and guaranteeing it is good; everything that may weaken or compromise it is bad. Such is the fundamental aphorism which must guide and set limits on every action of the ruler: it could well serve as a motto for his reflection.

In associating the native in our enterprise, one must guard against letting him step out of his place, specifically, for example, by not putting into his mind the germs of ambitions or unrealizable hopes by making promises to him that cannot be kept.

THE EXAMPLE OF BRITISH INDIA

We have no monopoly over colonial mistakes. Domination, in whatever circumstance, is always difficult, and as great an enterprise as the British domination over India is not exempt. English mistakes in India have been many and serious, and their critical examination to prevent their repetition among ourselves is no less profitable than the imitation of that which they have done better. Nothing, without doubt, has had more disastrous consequences than the promise, which they have inscribed and reiterated in solemn declarations, to consider the natives of India as equal in law to the conquerors and as qualified as themselves, on the same conditions as themselves, to the exercise of public office.

This imprudence, one must add, is not the act of the Indian government itself, a government too well informed and experienced to have done such a thing deliberately. It was imposed by England, where, according to the remark of Sir John Strachey, "one can always meet, as elsewhere, with people disposed to accept tranquilly the most singular political aberration, providing it substitutes sentiment for good sense and lowers national pride." This observation shows what snags autonomous governments can run into, and what precautions we must take to recognize the fact.

The first step along this unfortunate road goes back to 1834, when, by act of Parliament, the government declared "that no native of India, nor any natural British-born subject of His Majesty residing there, may be denied any post or employment of the East India Company for reason of his birth, descent, or color." That declaration, which is not far removed from the most celebrated political nonsense of the French Revolution, was renewed in 1850, in 1858, and yet again in 1877 in the name of Queen Victoria, at the very moment when the sovereign was proclaimed Empress of India with great pomp. It must nevertheless seem

certain to every European endowed with the most ordinary good
sense and having the slightest experience of India and the conditions under which a foreign government must function, that it
would be impossible in practice to keep such promises, which held
back no position, giving over not merely those of provincial chiefs,
governors, lieutenant-governors, chief secretaries, but even that of
governor-general or viceroy.

Whatever disdain one may have for the Hindu character, one
cannot doubt their subtle intelligence and ability to pass any examination at least as easily as the English, and one can easily imagine that they would not fail to interpret a commitment of this
kind in the broadest sense, and that one could hardly have put a
more ingenious and powerful weapon into their hands for use
against British domination. This was, in fact, the origin of the
movements that now disturb India; it is on this document, a ver-
itable revolutionary charter, that all eyes are fixed.

It sharpens the ambitions of every university graduate, as well as
the lying complaints against the "monopolies" or the abuses of the
masters of India. In keeping back the posts and functions of
command, the English are not guilty of any abuse; they have monop-
olized nothing; they have only acted in conformity with the necessary exercise of their role and with the protection of their
mission. They are caught between their word and the impossibility
of keeping it, so long as they wish not to betray the rights and obvious interests of their country. Governments of India have already
overstepped the reasonable limits of liberalism in making Englishmen submit to the judgments of Hindu magistrates and admitting
their native subjects to certain executive posts. The Hindu, de-
moralized by an assimilative education ill suited to his type of mind
and overexcited by the Japanese victories—which were not so
much victories against the Russians as against the whites, and
against their Anglo-Saxon allies themselves[1]—takes every concession as the sign of a new retreat by his masters and a new breach in
the edifice of the beneficent authority.

It is worth while pointing out this lesson, and we must heed it. It
should keep the policy of association, which circumstances have
made well known but ill understood, free of false interpretations,

1. Britain was allied to Japan at the time of the Russo-Japanese War,
though not an active participant.

toward which we are drawn all too much by our turn of mind and our old habits. At the moment when we find ourselves seized in the Far East with the same problems as the English, we should stop to think about it. Indo-China is of little moment compared with India, but the unity of the race that lives there makes its management more difficult, and we do not enjoy the same advantages in Europe as the English do. Let us make no such error! If we may come someday to such audacious reforms, may they not be imposed by imprudent and impolitic promises, and may we at least have the benefit and honor of our timely liberalism!

25. Lugard on the "Dual Mandate"

Lugard's *Dual Mandate in British Tropical Africa* was first published in 1922, when the unashamed imperialism represented by Harmand was no longer unquestioned. His concluding chapter, "The Value of British Rule in the Tropics to British Democracy and the Native Races," represents his defense of empire—the dual mandate being the contribution of empire to Britain and the "native races" alike. The arguments are far from new, but the tone and context of the discussion form a striking contrast to the evangelical morality of the Aborigines Committee. The chapter is quoted here in full, with the exception of some footnotes which have been deleted. Reprinted by permission of William Blackwood & Sons Ltd.

The Value of British Rule in the Tropics to British Democracy and the Native Races

THREE DECADES have passed since England assumed effective occupation and administration of those portions of the interior of tropical Africa for which she had accepted responsibility when the nations of Europe partitioned the continent between them. How has her task as trustee, on the one hand, for the advancement of the subject races, and on the other hand, for the development of its material resources for the benefit of mankind, been fulfilled? There is no one, I think, who has been privileged to bear a share in the task, with its immeasurable opportunities, who, looking back, would not echo Mr. Rhodes' dying words, "So much to do—so little done!"

In the foregoing chapters I have endeavoured to describe some

of the problems which confront the administrator, and with diffi-
dence to indicate the path by which, as it seems to me, the best
solution may in the course of time be found.

Viceroys and Governors of the older dependencies, of Colonies
and of Dominions, occupy posts of greater titular importance than
those who are entrusted with the charge of these tropical dependencies in Africa, but their own personal initiative is circumscribed
and controlled by Ministers, by effective assemblies and councils,
by a local press which reflects public opinion and criticism, and to a
greater or less extent by the Parliament and press of England. The
Governors in Africa are to-day gradually being brought under the
same guiding and controlling influences, but in the earlier begin-
nings of our rule these influences hardly existed. Neither the
Foreign Office nor the Colonial Office had any experience of Central African conditions and administration, when, at the close of
the nineteenth century, the summons for effective occupation
compelled this country to administer the hinterlands of the West
African colonies, and to assume control of vast areas on the Nile,
the Niger, the Zambesi, and the great lakes in the heart of Africa.

The self-governing Dominions grew by slow stages from small
municipalities to the status of United Nations. In India and the
Eastern colonies, territorial expansion was the slow increment of
many decades. But in Africa it was not a matter of *expansion* from
existing nuclei of administration, but of sudden creation and im-
provisation. Perhaps it was well that Great Britain, following the
tradition of the Empire, did not (as she might have been expected
to do) select from her most experienced servants, trained in the
school of Indian administration, those who should grapple with this
sudden emergency, but trusted to the men on the spot. The
pioneers of African administration came to their task with minds
unbiassed by traditions unsuited to the races and conditions of
Africa, and more ready to attempt to make bricks without straw.
The perspective of history will perhaps show more clearly the
magnitude of that task, and the opportunity it gave for initiative,
almost unprecedented in the annals of the Empire.

It was for these pioneers to cope with the internal slave-trade,
the very existence of which was hardly known in England, to
devise their own laws, to set up their courts of justice, to deal with
foreign aggression, to create an administration, and bring order out
of chaos. The funds at their disposal were wholly inadequate, the

staff poorly paid, painfully insufficient, and recruited somewhat at haphazard, whether for chartered companies or for Crown dependencies. The areas to be controlled were most of them many times the size of England, with populations numbered in millions, seething with internal strife, and wholly without roads or means of communication.

The nation is justified in demanding how, in such circumstances, the administrative officers and their colleagues in the judicial and educational departments on the one hand, and the engineers, the medical, agricultural, and forestry officers, and the rest of the technical staff on the other hand, have acquitted themselves in their respective responsibilities towards the native races, and the material progress of these countries.

We are all familiar with the creed of the "Little Englander." At each fresh access of responsibility and expansion of the Empire he has warned us that "the white man's burden" was already growing too heavy for this country to bear, that the British taxpayer was being called on to support the ambitions of chauvinists, and that the native races were misgoverned and robbed of their lands and their proper profits by the greed of exploiters.

Of late, since the war, it would almost seem as if an organised attempt was being made to promulgate these doctrines among the Labour Party, and to persuade them that the existence of the Empire is antagonistic alike to their own interests and to those of the subject races. That Party has not as yet had experience of overseas problems. Its "Research Department" for the investigation of these subjects appears to have fallen under the influence of those who hold these narrow views. They would persuade the British democracy that it is better to shirk Imperial responsibility, and relegate it to international committees; that material development benefits only the capitalist profiteer; and that British rule over subject races stands for spoliation and self-interest. Guided by these advisers—some of the more prominent of whom are apparently not of British race—the Labour Party has not hesitated to put forward its own thesis of Government of tropical dependencies under the Mandates. To these views I hope that I have already in some measure offered a reply, and I will endeavour briefly to summarise in these concluding pages.

"Nothing," says Sir C. Lucas, "should appeal so strongly as the Empire to democracy, for it is the greatest engine of democracy the world has ever known. . . . It has infected the whole world with liberty and democracy." There is no doubt that the control of the tropics, so far from being a charge on the British taxpayer, is to him a source of very great gain. I have in a previous chapter shown how the products of the tropics have raised the standard of comfort of the working man, added to the amenities of his life, and provided alike the raw materials on which the industry and wealth of the community depend, and the market for manufactures which ensure employment.

So keenly do other nations value the assured possession of these sources of supply and these markets, that they have been willing to expend enormous sums for their acquisition and development, and (unlike Great Britain) have built tariff walls around them to exclude other nations from participation. "Never in the world's history was there an Empire which in proportion to its size encroached so little upon the public time and the public cost."

The temporary subsidies which have been paid to some of these tropical possessions in their earlier years, as "grants-in-aid," have decreased yearly until the countries became self-supporting, since which time they have not cost the taxpayer a penny, and the temporary grants have been indirectly much more than repaid.

Prior to the war Nigeria was the latest addition to the Empire, and if against the original payment to the Chartered Company and all subsequent grants, be set the profit derived by the British Exchequer on the import of silver coin, and the contributions offered by Nigeria to the war, it will be found that the debit is on the other side, and the country, with all its potentialities and expanding markets, has cost the British taxpayer nothing. Its trade—already £42,000,000—the greater part of which is with the United Kingdom, is of the kind which is the most valuable possible to the workers of this country—raw materials and foodstuffs in exchange for textiles and hardware.

Democracy has learnt by the war how absolutely dependent it is on the supply of these vital necessities from overseas, and even for the material for munitions in time of war. We have realised that the import can only be maintained by command of the seas. Some of these tropical dependencies are essential as naval bases, as cable and wireless stations, and as aerodromes, for that command of sea and air and of world communications upon which these islands depend for their existence. Without them we could only survive on such terms as the powerful nations might choose to dictate.

Before the war the Little Englander was wont to argue that these world-wide outposts were a source of weakness, and in time of war their defence would be a burden which we could not sustain. But when Armageddon came, we required no additional garrisons to hold these vast territories in check; on the contrary, thousands of volunteers were ready to fight the Empire's battles. The West African colonies (relying, of course, on British supremacy at sea) were able, with the French, to capture the German Cameruns and Togoland, and to send thousands to fight or serve as transport units in German East Africa, and if need be in Palestine. These colonies asked for no financial assistance to help them through the crisis; indeed, they subscribed largely to the cost of the war and to war charities.

But let us return to the more normal conditions of peace and commerce. It is alleged that we could do an equally lucrative trade in the possessions of other Powers, instead of incurring the cost and responsibility of maintaining possessions of our own. But I have shown that foreign colonies are increasingly exclusive, and do not welcome British competition; that the cost of maintenance is borne by the revenues of the colonies themselves, and not by the British taxpayer; and, finally, it were easy to demonstrate that the largest proportion of their trade is done with the United Kingdom and not with foreign nations.

The fallacies put forward by these critics have long since been disproved, though the Labour Party may not be familiar with the statistics. It suffices here to point out that the trade of the single dependency of Nigeria for 1920 stood at over £42,200,000 in value, which, however, was probably abnormal and due to the "boom" of that year. Of this 96.74 per cent of the imports and 97.35 per cent of the exports were carried in British vessels—mainly, of course, to British ports.* For East Africa and Uganda the latest figures (1918-1919) show 84.3 per cent of imports and 91.1 per cent of exports from and to the Empire (United Kingdom 61 per cent and 53.5 per cent). How rapidly the trade of these

---

* Governor's address to Nigerian Council, December 1920. The destination is not stated, but in 1918 92.4 per cent of exports, and 87 per cent of imports, were to and from the Empire.—Cmd. 508/14 of 1919.

colonies is expanding may be judged from the fact that the trade of Nigeria in 1913 (pre-war) was under 13½ million.

As to the assertion that we do just as good trade with countries in tropical Africa which are not under the British flag, I find in the "Statistical Abstract for the British Empire" that the trade of the United Kingdom with all French possessions (including those in India and the Far East) was, in 1913, £6,730,244, while our trade with the single dependency of Nigeria for the same year stood at £8,278,813, in spite of the fact that in that year Germany had monopolised nearly half the Nigerian trade, which has since reverted to the United Kingdom.

The critics quote statistics showing the proportion that the trade of this or that tropical dependency bears to the whole volume of our foreign trade, as though any comparison could be instituted between our commerce with wealthy, populous, and highly industrialised countries like the United States, Germany, or France, and that of new and undeveloped markets in the tropics, whose present output or demands are no measure whatever of their future potentialities.

And though our markets are free to all the world, British merchants have no small advantage in the first-hand and early knowledge of the conditions and resources of each country, available in their own language. They can and do bring their influence to bear in order to secure as far as possible that the conditions of trade shall be made to suit their own convenience. The home market, provided it can hold its own as to quality, price, and rapidity of delivery, has the first opportunity of supply colonial demands.

These are indeed matters of such common knowledge that I refrain from dilating further upon them, and will content myself with referring to one or two other aspects which have perhaps received less recognition. The abounding progress of our tropical dependencies calls not only for millions of pounds worth of railway and other construction material, but for men to construct and to maintain the railways and other works. The expansion of administration equally demands officers for every branch—administrative, medical, educational, &c. The development of commerce requires local agents. The opening of mine-fields calls for expert workers.

In all these fields of activity openings are afforded for every class of the youth of England, whether from the universities, the technical schools, or the workshop. It is difficult to realise how severe would be the blow to the life of the nation if these thousands of avenues to independent initiative and individual enterprise and ambition were closed, as Germany has largely closed them to her people by her crime against the world.

I have already pointed out that this large field of opportunity and of responsibility must undoubtedly have contributed very greatly to the formation of the national character, which the late Lord Salisbury described in memorable words: "Our people, when they go into the possession of a new territory, carry with them such a power of initiative, such an extraordinary courage and resource in the solving of new problems and the facing of new difficulties, that if they are pitted against an equal number—I care not what race it is, or what the part of the world it is—and if you keep politics and negotiations off them, it will be our people that will be masters, it will be our commerce that will prevail, it will be our capital that will rule, though not a sword has been unsheathed, and though not a blow has been struck in their defence." He did but echo the words of Adam Smith, which I have quoted elsewhere, that the debt of the colonies to the motherland consists in the fact that "it bred and formed the men who were capable of achieving such great actions, and of laying the foundations of so great an Empire."

The British working man is told that the exploitation of Africa was undertaken by groups of financiers and capitalists, who desired to profiteer at the expense of the nation and of the native races alike. "Common greed," says the reviewer of the Labour Research Committee's report, summing up the gist of the argument, "came to be avowed openly as the most respectable of reasons for establishing colonies or protectorates anywhere and everywhere," in contrast with the nobler motives which prompted the bold adventurers of the spacious Elizabethan days.

I will not digress to discuss those motives here, or the navigation laws which treated the colonies merely as sources of profit, or the fortunes which Macaulay's "Nabobs" brought from India, or the quest for an "El Dorado." The partition of Africa was, as we all recognise, due primarily to the economic necessity of increasing the supplies of raw materials and food to meet the needs of the industrialised nations of Europe. It is a cheap form of rhetoric which stigmatises as "common greed" the honourable work by which men and nations earn their bread and improve their standard of life.

But while admitting this we must not lose sight of the fact that several of our West African colonies had been acquired solely as depots to assist in the suppression of the overseas slave-trade, others in support of missionary endeavours which were certainly not prompted by greed for profit. Others again, as I have shown, were necessary for the maintenance of our sea-power. In all these cases a higher civilisation was brought into contact with barbarism, with the inevitable result, as history teaches, that boundaries were enlarged in the effort to protect the weak from the tyranny of the strong, to extend the rule of justice and liberty, to protect traders, settlers, and missions, and to check anarchy and bloodshed on our frontiers, even though territorial expansion was not desired. Nor must we ignore the very real desire of the people of this country to assist in the suppression of slavery and barbarous practices. These are matters in which I am convinced that the British democracy has a deep interest, deeper perhaps than its political leaders credit it with. They cannot be disposed of with a sneer. But I return to the economic question, since this argument of "capitalist exploitation" appears to be a favourite one with which to capture the ear of Labour.

In the introductory chapter I cited statistics to show that, at the time of the first impulse of Imperial expansion in the reign of Queen Elizabeth, the small and chiefly agricultural population of these islands was able to supply its own essential needs in food and materials; that when the second impulse came 240 years later, after the Napoleonic wars, the population had quadrupled, while in the next seventy-five years of the nineteenth century, 1816–91 (when the partition of Africa began in earnest), it again nearly doubled itself. The congestion of the population, assisted by the discovery of the application of steam to industrial uses, led to the replacement of agriculture by manufacturing industry, with the consequent necessity for new markets for the product of the factory, and the importation of raw materials for industry, and of food to supplement the decreased home production, and feed the increased population. The same phenomenon was to be seen in Germany and elsewhere in Europe. I recapitulate these figures because their importance in this connection can hardly be over-estimated.

But mere increase in population alone, prodigious though it was, does not represent the full measure of the pressure on the Governments of the industrial nations of Europe. The standard of comfort, and what had come to be regarded as the absolute necessities of life by the mass of the population, had, during the nineteenth century, advanced in an even greater ratio. I cannot here attempt to depict the contrast. It is enough to recall the fact that 100 years ago a labourer's wage was 4s. to 6s. a week. He rarely tasted white bread, for the quartern loaf stood at 11d., and had been double that price a few years before. Still less could he afford to eat beef or mutton. Towards the close of the nineteenth century, tea, coffee, and cocoa, previously unknown luxuries, were his daily beverages and white bread his daily food. Sugar was cheap, and rice, sago, and other tropical products were in daily use. If my reader will turn to the pages of Miss Martineau's history, or to those of Carlyle, and contrast the condition of squalor and misery in which the bulk of the people of these islands lived in 1816 with the conditions prevailing in 1891, he will realise how insistent had become the demand alike for the food-supplies and for the raw materials which were the product of the tropics.

These products lay wasted and ungarnered in Africa because the natives did not know their use and value. Millions of tons of oil-nuts, for instance, grew wild without the labour of man, and lay rotting in the forests. Who can deny the right of the hungry people of Europe to utilise the wasted bounties of nature, or that the task of developing these resources was, as Mr. Chamberlain expressed it, a "trust for civilisation" and for the benefit of mankind? Europe benefited by the wonderful increase in the amenities of life for the mass of her people which followed the opening up of Africa at the end of the nineteenth century. Africa benefited by the influx of manufactured goods, and the substitution of law and order for the methods of barbarism.

Thus Europe was impelled to the development of Africa primarily by the necessities of her people, and not by the greed of the capitalist. Keen competition assured the maximum prices to the producer. It is only where monopolies are granted that it can be argued that profits are restricted to the few, and British policy has long been averse to monopolies in every form. The brains, the research, the capital, and the enterprise of the merchant, the miner, and the planter have discovered and utilised the surplus products of Africa. The profits have been divided among the shareholders

representing all classes of the people, and no small share of them
has gone to the native African merchant and the middleman as well
as to the producer. It is true to say that "a vast area of activity has
been opened up to the British workman, in which he shares with
the capitalist the profits of the development of tropical resources."

In accepting responsibility for the control of these new lands,
England obeyed the tradition of her race. British Africa was acquired not by groups of financiers, nor yet (as I have related in
chapter 1) by the efforts of her statesmen, but in spite of them. It
was the instinct of the British democracy which compelled us to
take our share. When Mr. Gladstone's Cabinet in 1893 had decided
to evacuate Uganda, he was told by his Scottish agent that if he did
so he would have to evacuate Downing Street too. Even were it
true—and I have shown that it is not—that we could do as lucrative a trade in the tropical possessions of other nations, there can be
no doubt that the verdict of the British people has been emphatic
that we will not ask the foreigner to open markets for our use, or
leave to him the responsibility and its reward. Nor will tariff walls,
like those of Jericho, fall flat at the sound of the trumpet of the
new Labour leaders.

"The general effects of European policy in Africa have been
almost wholly evil," says the Labour reporter, yet he admits that
"experience and temperament have made the rule of the British
over non-adult races an example of everything that is best in
modern imperialism." The verdict of another of the prophets of
Labour is to the same effect. The fundamental character of British
official policy in West Africa, he says, has primarily been influenced by a desire to promote the welfare and advancement of the
native races. England, he points out, led the way in the suppression
of the overseas slave-trade, paying enormous sums in compensation
to slave-owners in the West Indies, and at the Cape, and to Spain
and Portugal, and in patrolling the seas. She espoused the cause of
Congo reform, and of the indentured labour in Portuguese West
Africa. The extension of British control in the Gold Coast hinterland was (he adds) to secure protection of the natives, and in
Southern Nigeria to suppress war and human sacrifice.

The indictment against European misrule in Africa appears
therefore to lack consistency, and to be directed chiefly against
foreign Powers, though bitter charges, as we have seen, are made
against some of the Eastern British dependencies in Africa, which

have been fully discussed in these pages. In so far as they concern the territories of other Powers, this attitude of what Mr. Rhodes called "unctuous righteousness," which has the appearance of assuming that others are actuated by less generous motives than our own, is more likely to promote resentment than reform. That the aims of these critics are good will not be denied, but they write without actual experience, and they create prejudice where sympathy and appreciation would be more promising of results.

Let it be admitted at the outset that European brains, capital, and energy have not been, and never will be, expended in developing the resources of Africa from motives of pure philanthropy; that Europe is in Africa for the mutual benefit of her own industrial classes, and of the native races in their progress to a higher plane; that the benefit can be made reciprocal, and that it is the aim and desire of civilised administration to fulfil this dual mandate.

By railways and roads, by reclamation of swamps and irrigation of deserts, and by a system of fair trade and competition, we have added to the prosperity and wealth of these lands, and checked famine and disease. We have put an end to the awful misery of the slave-trade and inter-tribal war, to human sacrifice and the ordeals of the witch-doctor. Where these things survive they are severely suppressed. We are endeavouring to teach the native races to conduct their own affairs with justice and humanity, and to educate them alike in letters and in industry.

When I recall the state of Uganda at the time I made the treaty in 1890 which brought it under British control, or the state of Nigeria ten years later, and contrast them with the conditions of to-day, I feel that British effort—apart from benefits to British trade —has not been in vain. In Uganda a triangular civil war was raging —Protestants, Roman Catholics, and Moslems, representing the rival political factions of British, French, and Arabs, were murdering each other. Only a short time previously triumphant paganism had burnt Christians at the stake and revelled in holocausts of victims. To-day there is an ordered Government with its own native parliament. Liberty and justice have replaced chaos, bloodshed, and war. The wealth of the country steadily increases. The slave-raids and tyranny of the neighbouring kingdom of Unyoro have given place to similar progress and peace.

In Nigeria in 1902 slave-raiding armies of 10,000 or 15,000 men laid waste the country, and wiped out its population annually in the quest for slaves. Hundreds of square miles of rich well-watered land were depopulated. Barth bore witness to a similar condition of things fifty years ago. Men were impaled in the market-place of Kano. I have described its dungeon. Nowhere was there security for life and property. To-day the native Emirs vie with each other in the progress of their schools; the native courts administer justice, and themselves have liberated over 50,000 slaves. The Sultan of Sokoto and the other Emirs are keenly interested in such questions as afforestation, artesian well-boring, and vaccination. The native prisons have been pronounced by the medical authority to be a model for Government to imitate; the leper settlement in Bornu under purely native control is the most successful I know of.

I refer to these two countries because I happen to have personally witnessed their condition prior to the advent of British control, but similar results may be seen in every other British dependency in tropical Africa.

As Roman imperialism laid the foundations of modern civilisation, and led the wild barbarians of these islands along the path of progress, so in Africa to-day we are repaying the debt, and bringing to the dark places of the earth, the abode of barbarism and cruelty, the torch of culture and progress, while ministering to the material needs of our own civilisation. In this task the nations of Europe have pledged themselves to co-operation by a solemn covenant. Towards the common goal each will advance by the methods most consonant with its national genius. British methods have not perhaps in all cases produced ideal results, but I am profoundly convinced that there can be no question but that British rule has promoted the happiness and welfare of the primitive races. Let those who question it examine the results impartially. If there is unrest, and a desire for independence, as in India and Egypt, it is because we have taught the value of liberty and freedom, which for centuries these peoples had not known. Their very discontent is a measure of their progress.

We hold these countries because it is the genius of our race to colonise, to trade, and to govern. The task in which England is engaged in the tropics—alike in Africa and in the East—has become part of her tradition, and she has ever given of her best in the cause of liberty and civilisation. There will always be those who cry aloud that the task is being badly done, that it does not need doing, that we can get more profit by leaving others to do it, that it brings evil to subject races and breeds profiteers at home. These were not the principles which prompted our forefathers, and secured for us the place we hold in the world to-day in trust for those who shall come after us.

26. J. A. Hobson,
Trusteeship Under International Control

John Atkinson Hobson (1858–1940) has a place in the history of economic thought as well as in the history of imperialism, since some of his ideas foreshadowed aspects of the Keynesian economics that developed between the two World Wars. The work for which he is best known is nevertheless *Imperialism: A Study* (London, 1902), and that book is still attacked and defended as a crucial early work setting forth the hypothesis that the roots of European expansion in the imperial era lay in the European economy, and especially in its generation of funds available for investment overseas. The idea was taken up by Lenin during the First World War, and later became an article of faith in several shades of socialist doctrine.

But Hobson's *Imperialism* was a good deal more than an economic interpretation, and Hobson was an anti-imperialist only in the sense of opposing the way empires were run in his own time. In his chapter entitled "Imperialism and the Lower Races," he came to grips with the problem of immense cultural and technological differences between the more developed and less developed regions of the world. He concluded that simply refraining from the conquest of the non-Western world was not enough, and he ended with an appeal for a form of trusteeship—far different from the kinds of trusteeship practiced in his day, but trusteeship nevertheless.

Hobson therefore ended with a position that was not truly anti-imperialist but rather one advocating minimal empire, under international control. Even though it was written before the preceding selection from Lugard's *Dual Mandate*, it can be read in part as a critique of Lugard's position. The section quoted includes Parts I–IV and X of the chapter "Imperialism and the Lower Races," pp. 223–246 and p. 280 of the original, with some footnotes deleted.

Imperialism and the Lower Races

I

THE STATEMENT, often made, that the work of imperial expansion is virtually complete is not correct. It is true that most of the "backward" races have been placed in some sort of dependence upon one or other of the "civilized" Powers as colony, protectorate, hinterland, or sphere of influence. But this in most instances marks rather the beginning of a process of imperialization than a definite attainment of empire. The intensive growth of empire by which interference is increased and governmental control tightened over spheres of influence and protectorates is as important and as perilous an aspect of Imperialism as the extensive growth which takes shape in assertion of rule over new areas of territory and new populations.

The famous saying, attributed to Napoleon, that "great empires die of indigestion" serves to remind us of the importance of the imperialist processes which still remain after formal "expansion" has been completed. During the last twenty years of the last century Great Britain, Germany, France, and Russia had bitten off huge mouthfuls of Africa and Asia which are not yet chewed, digested, or assimilated. Moreover, great areas still remain whose independence, though threatened, is yet unimpaired.

Vast countries in Asia, such as Persia, Thibet, Siam, Afghanistan, are rapidly forging to the front of politics as likely subjects of armed controversy between European Powers with a view to subjugation; the Turkish dominions in Asia Minor, and perhaps in Europe, await a slow, precarious process of absorption; the paper partition of Central Africa teems with possibilities of conflict. The entrance of the United States into the imperial struggle throws virtually the whole of South America into the arena; for it is not reasonable to expect that European nations, with settlements and vast economic interests in the southern peninsula, will readily leave all this territory to the special protection or ultimate absorption of the United States, when the latter, abandoning her old consistent isolation, has plunged into the struggle for empire in the Pacific.

Beyond and above all this looms China. It is not easy to suppose that the lull and hesitancy of the Powers will last, or that the magnitude and manifest risks of disturbing this vast repository of incalculable forces will long deter adventurous groups of profit-seekers from driving their Governments along the slippery path of commercial treaties, leases, railway and mining concessions, which must entail a growing process of political interference.

It is not my purpose to examine here the entanglement of political and economic issues which each of these cases presents, but simply to illustrate the assertion that the policy of modern Imperialism is not ended but only just begun, and that it is concerned almost wholly with the rival claims of Empires to dominate "lower races" in tropical and sub-tropical countries, or in other countries occupied by manifestly unassimilable races.

In asking ourselves what are the sound principles of world policy and of national policy in this matter, we may at first ignore the important differences which should affect our conduct towards countries inhabited by what appear to be definitely low-typed unprogressive races, countries whose people manifest capacity of rapid progress from a present low condition, and countries like India and China, where an old civilization of a high type, widely differing from that of European nations, exists.

Before seeking for differences of policy which correspond to these conditions, let us try to find whether there are any general principles of guidance in dealing with countries occupied by "lower" or unprogressive peoples.

It is idle to consider as a general principle the attitude of mere *laissez faire*. It is not only impracticable in view of the actual forces which move politics, but it is ethically indefensible in the last resort.

To lay down as an absolute law that "the autonomy of every nation is inviolable" does not carry us very far. There can no more be absolute nationalism in the society of nations than absolute individualism in the single nation. Some measure of practical internationality, implying a "comity of nations," and some relations of "right" and "duty" between nations, are almost universally admitted. The rights of self-government, implied by the doctrine of autonomy, if binding in any sense legal or ethical on other nations, can only possess this character in virtue of some real international organization, however rudimentary.

It is difficult for the strongest advocate of national rights to assert that the people in actual occupation or political control over a given area of the earth are entitled to do what they will with "their own," entirely disregarding the direct and indirect consequences of their actions upon the rest of the world.

It is not necessary to take extreme cases of a national policy which directly affects the welfare of a neighbouring State, as where a people on the upper reaches of a river like the Nile or the Niger might so damage or direct the flow as to cause plague or famine to the lower lands belonging to another nation. Few, if any, would question some right of interference from without in such a case. Or take another case which falls outside the range of directly other-regarding actions. Suppose a famine or flood or other catastrophe deprives a population of the means of living on their land, while unutilized land lies in plenty beyond their borders in another country; are the rulers of the latter entitled to refuse an entrance or a necessary settlement? As in the case of individuals, so of nations, it will be generally allowed that necessity knows no laws, which, rightly interpreted, means that the right of self-preservation transcends all other rights as the prime condition of their emergence and exercise.

This carries us on an inclined plane of logic to the real issue as ably presented by Mr. Kidd, Professor Giddings, and the "Fabian" Imperialists. It is an expansion of this plea of material necessity that constitutes the first claim to a control of the tropics by "civilized" nations. The European races have grown up with a standard of material civilization based largely upon the consumption and use of foods, raw materials of manufacture, and other goods which are natural products of tropical countries. The industries and the trade which furnish these commodities are of vital importance to the maintenance and progress of Western civilization. The large part played in our import trade by such typically tropical products as sugar, tea, coffee, indiarubber, rice, tobacco, indicates the dependence of such countries as Great Britain upon the tropics. Partly from sheer growth of population in temperate zones, partly from the rising standard of material life, this dependence of the temperate on the tropical countries must grow. In order to satisfy these growing needs larger and larger tracts of tropical country must be cultivated, the cultivation must be better and more regular, and peaceful and effective trade relations with these countries must be maintained. Now the ease with which human life can be maintained in the tropics breeds indolence and torpor of character. The inhabitants of these countries are not "progressive people"; they neither develop the arts of industry at any satisfactory pace, nor do they evolve new wants or desires, the satisfaction of which might force them to labour. We cannot therefore rely upon the ordinary economic motives and methods of free exchange to supply the growing demand for tropical goods. The resources of the tropics will not be developed voluntarily by the natives themselves.

"If we look to the native social systems of the tropical East, the primitive savagery of Central Africa, to the West Indian Islands in the past in process of being assisted into the position of modern States by Great Britain, or the black republic of Hayti in the present, or to modern Liberia in the future, the lesson seems everywhere the same; it is that there will be no development of the resources of the tropics under native government."*

We cannot, it is held, leave these lands barren; it is our duty to see that they are developed for the good of the world. White men cannot "colonize" these lands and, thus settling, develop the natural resources by the labour of their own hands; they can only organize and superintend the labour of the natives. By doing this they can educate the natives in the arts of industry and stimulate in them a desire for material and moral progress, implanting new "wants" which form in every society the roots of civilization.

It is quite evident that there is much force in this presentation of the case, not only on material but on moral grounds; nor can it be brushed aside because it is liable to certain obvious and gross abuses. It implies, however, two kinds of interference which require justification. To step in and utilize natural resources which are left undeveloped is one thing, to compel the inhabitants to develop them is another. The former is easily justified, involving the application on a wider scale of a principle whose equity, as well as expediency, is recognized and enforced in most civilized nations. The other interference whereby men who prefer to live on a low standard of life with little labour shall be forced to harder or more continuous labour, is far more difficult of justification.

I have set the economic compulsion in the foreground, because in point of history it is the *causa causans* of the Imperialism that accompanies or follows.

In considering the ethics and politics of this interference, we must not be bluffed or blinded by critics who fasten on the palpable dishonesty of many practices of the gospel of "the dignity of labour" and "the mission of civilization." The real issue is whether, and under what circumstances, it is justifiable for Western nations to use compulsory government for the control and education in the arts of industrial and political civilization of the inhabitants of tropical countries and other so-called lower races. Because Rhode-

* Kidd, *The Control of the Tropics*, p. 53 (Macmillan & Co.).

sian mine-owners or Cuban sugar-growers stimulate the British or American Government to Imperialism by parading motives and results which do not really concern them, it does not follow that these motives under proper guidance are unsound, or that the results are undesirable.

There is nothing unworthy, quite the contrary, in the notion that nations which, through a more stimulative environment, have advanced further in certain arts of industry, politics, or morals, should communicate these to nations which from their circumstances were more backward, so as to aid them in developing alike the material resources of their land and the human resources of their people. Nor is it clear that in this work some "inducement, stimulus, or pressure" (to quote a well-known phrase) or in a single word, "compulsion," is wholly illegitimate. Force is itself no remedy, coercion is not education, but it may be a prior condition to the operation of educative forces. Those, at any rate, who assign any place to force in the education or the political government of individuals in a nation can hardly deny that the same instrument may find a place in the civilization of backward by progressive nations.

Assuming that the arts of "progress," or some of them, are communicable, a fact which is hardly disputable, there can be no inherent natural right in a people to refuse that measure of compulsory education which shall raise it from childhood to manhood in the order of nationalities. The analogy furnished by the education of a child is prima facie a sound one, and is not invalidated by the dangerous abuses to which it is exposed in practice.

The real issue is one of safeguards, of motives, and of methods. What are the conditions under which a nation may help to develop the resources of another, and even apply some element of compulsion in doing so? The question, abstract as it may sound, is quite the most important of all practical questions for this generation. For that such development will take place, and such compulsion, legitimate or illegitimate, be exercised, more and more throughout this new century in many quarters of this globe, is beyond the shadow of a doubt. It is the great practical business of the country to explore and develop, by every method which science can devise, the hidden natural and human resources of the globe.

That the white Western nations will abandon a quest on which they have already gone so far is a view which does not deserve consideration. That this process of development may be so conducted as to yield a gain to world-civilization, instead of some terrible *débâcle* in which revolted slave races may trample down their parasitic and degenerate white masters, should be the supreme aim of far-sighted scientific statecraft.

II

To those who utter the single cry of warning, "*laissez faire*, hands off, let these people develop their resources themselves with such assistance as they ask or hire, undisturbed by the importunate and arrogant control of foreign nations," it is a sufficient answer to point out the impossibility of maintaining such an attitude.

If organized Governments of civilized Powers refused the task, they would let loose a horde of private adventurers, slavers, piratical traders, treasure hunters, concession mongers, who, animated by mere greed of gold or power, would set about the work of exploitation under no public control and with no regard to the future; playing havoc with the political, economic, and moral institutions of the peoples, instilling civilized vices and civilized diseases, importing spirits and firearms as the trade of readiest acceptance, fostering internecine strife for their own political and industrial purposes, and even setting up private despotisms sustained by organized armed forces. It is unnecessary to revert to the buccaneering times of the sixteenth century, when a "new world" was thrown open to the plunder of the old, and private gentlemen of Spain or England competed with their Governments in the most gigantic business of spoliation that history records. The story of Samoa, of Hawaii, and a score of South Sea Islands in quite recent years, proves that, at a time when every sea is a highway, it is impossible for the most remote land to escape the intrusion of "civilized" nations, represented by precisely their most reckless and debased specimens, who gravitate thither in order to reap the rapid fruits of licence. The contact with white races cannot be avoided, and it is more perilous and more injurious in proportion as it lacks governmental sanction and control. The most gigantic modern experiment in private adventure slowly yielded its full tale of horrors in the Congo Free State, while the handing over of large regions in Africa to the virtually unchecked government of Chartered Companies has exposed everywhere the dangers of a contact based on private commercialism.

To abandon the backward races to these perils of private exploitation, it is argued forcibly, is a barbarous dereliction of a public duty on behalf of humanity and the civilization of the world. Not merely does it leave the tropics to be the helpless prey of the offscourings of civilized nations; it opens grave dangers in the future, from the political or military ambitions of native or imported rulers, who, playing upon the religious fanaticism or the combative instincts of great hordes of semi-savages, may impose upon them so effective a military discipline as to give terrible significance to some black or yellow "peril." Complete isolation is no longer possible even for the remotest island; absolute self-sufficiency is no more possible for a nation than for an individual: in each case society has the right and the need to safeguard its interests against an injurious assertion of individuality.

Again, though there is some force in the contention that the backward natives could and would protect themselves against the encroachments of private adventurers, if they had the assurance that the latter could not call upon their Government for assistance or for vengeance, history does not lead us to believe that these powers of self-protection however adequate against forcible invasions, would suffice to meet the more insidious wiles by which traders, prospectors, and political adventurers insinuate their poisons into primitive societies like that of Samoa or Ashanti.

So far, we have established two tentative principles. First, that all interference on the part of civilized white nations with "lower races" is not prima facie illegitimate. Second, that such interference cannot safely be left to private enterprise of individual whites. If these principles be admitted, it follows that civilized Governments *may* undertake the political and economic control of lower races—in a word, that the characteristic form of modern Imperialism is not under all conditions illegitimate.

What, then, are the conditions which render it legitimate? They may be provisionally stated thus: Such interference with the government of a lower race must be directed primarily to secure the safety and progress of the civilization of the world, and not the special interest of the interfering nation. Such interference must be attended by an improvement and elevation of the character of the people who are brought under this control. Lastly, the determination of the two preceding conditions must not be left to the arbitrary will or judgment of the interfering nation, but must proceed from some organized representation of civilized humanity.

The first condition is deduced directly from the principle of social utility expanded to its widest range, so as to be synonymous with "the good of humanity." Regarding the conduct of one nation towards another we can find no other standard. Whatever uncertainty or other imperfection appertains to such a standard, regarded as a rule for international policy, any narrower standard is, of necessity, more uncertain and more imperfect. No purely legal contentions touching the misapplication of the term "right" to international relations, in the absence of any form of "sanction," affects our issue. Unless we are prepared to re-affirm in the case of nations, as the all-sufficient guide of conduct, that doctrine of "enlightened selfishness" which has been almost universally abandoned in the case of individuals, and to insist that the unchecked self-assertion of each nation, following the line of its own private present interest, is the best guarantee of the general progress of humanity, we must set up, as a supreme standard of moral appeal, some conception of the welfare of humanity regarded as an organic unity. It is, however, needless to insist upon the analogy between the relation of an individual to the other individuals of his society, and that of one society towards another in the commonwealth of nations. For, though cynical statesmen of the modern Machiavelli school may assert the visible interest of their country as the supreme guide of conduct, they do not seriously suggest that the good of humanity is thus attained, but only that this wider end has no meaning or appeal for them. In the light of this attitude all discussion of general principles "justifying" conduct is out of place, for "just" and "justice" are ruled out *ab initio*. The standard here proposed would not, however, in point of fact, be formally rejected by any school of political thinkers who were invited to find a general law for the treatment of lower races. No one would assert in so many words that we had a right to sacrifice the good of any other nation, or of the world at large, to our own private national gain.

In England, certainly, Lord Rosebery's declaration that the British Empire is "the greatest secular agency for good known to the world" would everywhere be adopted as the fundamental justification of empire.

Lord Salisbury expressly endorsed the principle, asserting that "the course of events, which I should prefer to call the acts of Providence, have called this country to exercise an influence over the character and progress of the world such as has never been exercised in any Empire before"; while the Archbishop of Canterbury propounded a doctrine of "imperial Christianity" based upon the same assumptions. It may, then, fairly be understood that every act of "Imperialism" consisting of forcible interference with another people can only be justified by showing that it contributes to "the civilization of the world."

Equally, it is admitted that some special advantage must be conferred upon the people who are the subject of this interference. On highest ground of theory, the repression, even the extinction, of some unprogressive or retrogressive nation, yielding place to another more socially efficient and more capable of utilizing for the general good the natural resources of the land, might seem permissible, if we accepted unimpaired and unimproved the biological struggle for existence as the sole or chief instrument of progress. But, if we admit that in the highest walks of human progress the constant tendency is to substitute more and more the struggle with natural and moral environment for the internecine struggle of living individuals and species, and that the efficient conduct of this struggle requires the suspension of the lower struggle and a growing solidarity of sentiment and sympathy throughout entire humanity, we shall perceive two important truths. First, "expansion," in order to absorb for the more "progressive" races an ever larger portion of the globe, is not the "necessity" it once appeared, because progress will take place more and more upon the qualitative plane, with more intensive cultivation alike of natural resources and of human life. The supposed natural necessity for crowding out the lower races is based on a narrow, low, and purely quantitative analysis of human progress.

Secondly, in the progress of humanity, the services of nationality, as a means of education and of self-development, will be recognized as of such supreme importance that nothing short of direct physical necessity in self-defence can justify the extinction of a nation. In a word, it will be recognized that "le grand crime internationael est de détruire une nationalité."* But even those

* M. Brunetière, quoted *Edinburgh Review*, April, 1900.

who would not go so far in their valuation of the factor of nationality will agree that it is a sound practical test of conduct to insist
that interference with the freedom of another nation shall justify
itself by showing some separate advantage conferred upon the
nation thus placed in an inferior position: partly, because it seems
obvious that the gain to the general cause of civilization will chiefly
be contained in or compassed by an improvement in the character
or condition of the nation which is the subject of interference;
partly, because the maxim which recognizes the individual person
as an end, and requires State government to justify itself by showing that the coercion it exercises does in reality enlarge the liberty
of those whom it restrains, is applicable also to the larger society of
nations. Without unduly pressing the analogy of individual and
nation as organisms, it may safely be asserted that imperial interference with a "lower race" must justify itself by showing that it is
acting for the real good of the subject race. Mr. Chamberlain is no
sentimentalist, and his declaration may rank as a *locus classicus*
upon this matter. "Our rule over the territories [native] can only
be justified if we can show that it adds to the happiness and prosperity of the people."

The moral defence of Imperialism is generally based upon the
assertion that in point of fact these two conditions are fulfilled, viz.
that the political and economic control forcibly assumed by
"higher" over "lower races" does promote at once the civilization
of the world and the special good of the subject races. The real
answer, upon which British Imperialists rely in defending expansion, is to point to actual services rendered to India, Egypt, Uganda,
etc., and to aver that other dependencies where British government is less successful would have fared worse if left either to
themselves or to another European Power.

Before considering the practical validity of this position, and the
special facts that determine and qualify the work of "civilizing"
other races, it is right to point out the fundamental flaw in this
theory of "Imperialism," viz. the non-fulfilment of the third condition laid down above. Can we safely trust to the honour, the public
spirit, and the insight of any of the competing imperial races the
subordination of its private interests and ends to the wider interests
of humanity or the particular good of each subject race brought
within its sway?

No one, as we point out, contends that so perfect a natural

harmony exists that every nation, consciously following its own chief interest, is "led" as "by an invisible hand" to a course of conduct which necessarily subserves the common interest, and in particular the interest of the subject race. What security, then, can possibly exist for the practices of a sound Imperialism fulfilling the conditions laid down? Does any one contend that the special self-interest of the expanding and annexing nation is not a chief, or indeed the chief conscious determinant in each step of practical Imperialism? Prima facie it would seem reasonable to suppose that many cases would occur in which the special temporary interests of the expanding nation would collide with those of the world-civilization, and that the former would be preferred. It is surely unreasonable to take as proof of the fulfilment of the conditions of sane Imperialism the untested and unverified *ipse dixit* of an interested party.

III

While it is generally agreed that the progress of world-civilization is the only valid moral ground for political interference with "lower races," and that the only valid evidence of such progress is found in the political, industrial, and moral education of the race that is subjected to this interference, the true conditions for the exercise of such a "trust" are entirely lacking.

The actual situation is, indeed, replete with absurdity. Each imperialist nation claims to determine for itself what are the lower races it will take under its separate protection, or agrees with two or three neighbours to partition some huge African tract into separate spheres of influence; the kind of civilization that is imposed is never based on any sober endeavour to understand the active or latent progressive forces of the subject race, and to develop and direct them, but is imported from Europe in the shape of set arts of industry, definite political institutions, fixed religious dogmas, which are engrafted on alien institutions. In political government progress is everywhere avowedly sacrificed to order, and both alike are subservient to the quick development of certain profitable trading industries, or to the mere lust of territorial aggrandisement. The recurrent quarrels of the armed white nations, each insisting on his claim to take up the white man's burden in some fresh quarter of the globe; the trading companies seeking to oust each other from a new market, the very missionaries competing by sects and nationalities for "mission fields," and using political intrigue and armed force to back their special claims, present a curious commentary upon the "trust for civilization" theory.

It is quite evident that this self-assertive sway lacks the first essentials of a trust, viz. security that the "trustee" represents fairly all the interested parties, and is responsible to some judicial body for the faithful fulfilment of the terms of the trust. Otherwise what safeguard exists against the abuse of the powers of the trustee? The notorious fact that half the friction between European nations arises from conflicting claims to undertake the office of "trustee for civilization" over lower races and their possessions augurs ill alike for the sincerity of the profession and the moral capacity to fulfill it. It is surely no mark of cynicism to question closely this extreme anxiety to bear one another's burdens among the nations.

This claim to justify aggression, annexation, and forcible government by talk of duty, trust, or mission can only be made good by proving that the claimant is accredited by a body genuinely representative of civilization, to which it acknowledges a real responsibility, and that it is in fact capable of executing such a trust.

In a word, until some genuine international council exists, which shall accredit a civilized nation with the duty of educating a lower race, the claim of a "trust" is nothing else than an impudent act of self-assertion. One may well be sceptical about the early feasibility of any such representative council; but until it exists it would be far more honest for "expanding" nations to avow commercial necessity or political ambition as the real determinant of their protection of lower races than to feign a "trust" which has no reality. Even were international relations more advanced, and the movement begun at the Hague Conference solidified in a permanent authoritative body, representative of all the Powers, to which might be referred not only the quarrels between nations, but the entire partition of this "civilizing" work, the issue would still remain precarious. There would still be grave danger lest the "Powers," arrogating to themselves an exclusive possession of "civilization," might condemn to unwholesome and unjust subjection some people causing temporary trouble to the world by slow growth, turbulence or obnoxious institutions, for which liberty might be the most essential condition of progress. Apart from such genuine misapprehensions, there would exist the peril of the establishment of a self-chosen oligarchy among the nations which, under the cloak of the civilizing process, might learn to live parasitically upon the lower races, imposing upon them "for their own good" all the harder or more servile work of industry, and arrogating to themselves the honours and emoluments of government and supervision.

Clear analysis of present tendencies points indeed to some such collusion of the dominant nations as the largest and gravest peril of the early future. The series of treaties and conventions between the chief European Powers, beginning with the Berlin African Conference of 1885, which fixed a standard for the "amicable division" of West African territory, and the similar treaty in 1890, fixing boundaries for English, German and Italian encroachments in East Africa, doubtless mark a genuine advance in the relations of the European Powers, but the objects and methods they embody throw a strange light upon the trust theory. If to the care of Africa we add that of China, where the European Powers took common action in "the interest of civilization," the future becomes still more menacing. While the protection of Europeans was the object in the foreground, and imposed a brief genuine community of policy upon the diverse nations, no sooner was the immediate object won than the deeper and divergent motives of the nations became manifest. The entire history of European relations with China in modern times is little else than one long cynical commentary upon the theory that we are engaged in the civilization of the Far East. Piratical expeditions to force trade upon a nation whose one principle of foreign policy was to keep clear of foreigners, culminating in a war to compel the reception of Indian opium; abuse of the generous hospitality given for centuries to peaceful missionaries by wanton insults offered to the religious and political institutions of the country, the forcible exaction of commercial and political "concessions" as punishment for spasmodic acts of reprisal, the cold-blooded barter of murdered missionaries for the opening of new treaty ports, territory at Kiao Chow, or a new reach of the Yang-Tse for British trading vessels; the mixture of menace, cajolery, and bribery by which England, Russia, Germany, France, and Japan laboured to gain some special and separate railway or mining concessions, upon terms excluding or damaging the interest of the others; the definite assumption by Christian bishops and missionaries of political authority, and the arrogant and extensive use of the so-called right of "extra-territoriality," whereby they claim, not only for themselves but for their alleged converts and protégés, immunity from the laws of the land—all these things sufficiently expose the hollowness in actual history of the claims that considerations of a trust for civilization animate and regulate the foreign policy of Christendom, or of its component nations. What actually confronts us everywhere in modern history is selfish, materialistic, short-sighted, national competition, varied by occasional collusion. When any common international policy is adopted for dealing with lower races it has partaken of the nature, not of a moral trust, but of a business "deal."

It seems quite likely that this policy of "deals" may become as frequent and as systematic in the world of politics as in the world of commerce, and that treaties and alliances have regard to the political government and industrial exploitation of countries occupied by lower races may constitute a rude sort of effective internationalism in the early future.

Now, such political arrangements fall short in two important respects of that genuine trust for civilization which alone could give moral validity to a "civilized" control of lower peoples. In the first place, its assignment of a sphere of interest or a protectorate to England, to Germany, or Russia, is chiefly determined by some particular separate interest of that country by reason of contiguity or other private convenience, and not by any impartial consideration of its special competence for the work of civilization. If, for example, European Powers were really animated by the desire to extend Western civilization to China for her own good and that of the world, they might more favourably essay this task by promoting the influence of Japan than by inserting their own alien occidentalism. But no one proposes to delegate to Japan this "trust"; every nation thinks of its own present commercial interests and political prestige.

Secondly, the civilization of the lower races, even according to accepted Western lights, is nowhere adopted as the real aim of government. Even where good political order is established and maintained, as in Egypt or India, its primary avowed end and its universally accepted standard of success are the immediate economic benefits attributed thereto. The political government of the country is primarily directed everywhere to the rapid, secure, effective development of the national resources, and their profitable expolitation by native labour under white management. It is maintained and believed that this course is beneficial to the natives, as well as to the commerce of the controlling power and of the world at large. That Indians or Egyptians are better off to-day than they were before our autocratic sway, not merely in economic resources but in substantial justice, may be quite true; it may even be accredited to us that many of our governors and officials have displayed some disinterested concern for the immediate well-being of the races committed (by ourselves) to our trust. But it can nowhere be sincerely contended that either we or any other Christian nation are governing these lower races upon the same enlightened principles which we profess and sometimes practise in governing ourselves. I allude here not to methods of government, but to ends. In the more enlightened European States and their genuine colonies, though present economic considerations bulk largely enough, they do not absorb the present and the future of public policy; provision is made for some play of non-economic forces, for the genuine culture of human life and character, for progress alike in individual growth and in the social growth which comes by free processes of self-government. These are regarded as essential conditions of the healthy growth of a nation. They are not less essential in the case of lower nations, and their exercise demands more thought and more experiment. The chief indictment of Imperialism in relation to the lower races consists in this, that it does not even pretend to apply to them the principles of education and of progress it applies at home.

IV

If we or any other nation really undertook the care and education of a "lower race" as a trust, how should we set about the execution of the trust? By studying the religions, political and other social institutions and habits of the people, and by endeavouring to penetrate into their present mind and capacities of adaptation, by learning their language and their history, we should seek to place them in the natural history of man; by similar close attention to the country in which they live, and not to its agricultural and mining resources alone, we should get a real grip upon their environment. Then, carefully approaching them so as to gain what confidence we could for friendly motives, and openly discouraging any premature private attempts of exploiting companies to work mines, or secure concessions, or otherwise to impair our disinterested conduct, we should endeavour to assume the position of advisers. Even if it were necessary to enforce some degree of authority, we should keep such force in the background as a last resort, and make it our first aim to understand and to promote the healthy free operations of all internal forces for progress which we might discover.

Natural growth in self-government and industry along tropical lines would be the end to which the enlightened policy of civilized assistance would address itself.

Now, what are the facts? Nowhere has any serious organized attempt been made, even by Great Britain, by far the largest of the trustees, to bring this scientific disinterested spirit of inquiry to bear upon the races whose destiny she dominates. The publications of the Aborigines Protection Society, and the report of the Native Races Committee, dealing with South Africa, indicate the vast range of unexplored knowledge, and the feeble fumblings which have hitherto taken the place of ordered investigations. It is natural that this should be so. White pioneers in these countries are seldom qualified to do the work required; the bias of the trader, the soldier, or the professional traveller, is fatal to sober, disinterested study of human life, while the missionary, who has contributed more than the rest, has seldom been endowed with a requisite amount of the scientific spirit or the scientific training.

Even the knowledge which we do possess is seldom utilized for light and leading in our actual government of native races. There have indeed been signs of an awakening intelligence in certain spots of our Empire; administrators like Sir George Grey, Lord Ripon, and Sir Marshall Clarke brought sympathy and knowledge to the establishment of careful experiments in self-government. The forms of protectorate exercised over Basutoland and Khama's Country in South Africa, the restoration of the province of Mysore to native government, and the more careful abstention from interference with the internal policy of feudatory States in India, were favourable signs of a more enlightened policy.

In particular, the trend of liberal sentiment regarding government of lower races was undergoing a marked change. The notion that there exists one sound, just, rational system of government,

suitable for all sorts and conditions of men, embodied in the elec-
tive representative institutions of Great Britain, and that our duty
was to impose this system as soon as possible, and with the least
possible modifications, upon lower races, without any regard to
their past history and their present capabilities and sentiments, was
tending to disappear in this country, though the new headstrong
Imperialism of America was still exposed to the taunt that "Americans think the United States has a mission to carry 'canned' civilization to the heathen." The recognition that there may be many
paths to civilization, that strong racial and environmental differences preclude a hasty grafting of alien institutions, regardless of
continuity and selection of existing agencies and forms—these genuinely scientific and humane considerations are beginning to take
shape in a demand that native races within our Empire shall have
larger liberty of self-development assured to them, and that the
imperial Government shall confine its interference to protection
against enemies from without, and preservation of the elements of
good order within.

The true "imperial" policy is best illustrated in the case of
Basutoland, which was rescued in 1884 from the aggressive designs
of Cape Colony, stimulated by industrial exploiters.

Here British imperial government was exercised by a Commissioner, with several British magistrates to deal with grave offences
against order, and a small body of native police under British
officers. For the rest, the old political and economic institutions are
preserved—government by chiefs, under a paramount chief, subject to the informal control or influence of public opinion in a
national assembly; ordinary administration, chiefly consisting in
allotment of land, and ordinary jurisdiction are left to the chiefs.

"As far back as 1855 Moshesh forbade the 'smelling-out' of
witches, and now the British authorities have suppressed the more
noxious or offensive kinds of ceremonies practised by the Kaffirs.
Otherwise, they interfere as little as possible with native ways,
trusting to time, peace, and the missionaries to secure the gradual
civilization of the people." "No Europeans are allowed to hold
land, and a licence is needed even for the keeping of a store.
Neither are any mines worked. European prospectors are not permitted to come in and search for minerals, for the policy of the
authorities has been to keep the country for the natives, and nothing alarms the chiefs so much as the occasional appearance of these

speculative gentry, who, if admitted, would soon dispossess them."*

These sentences serve to point the path by which most of our Imperialism has diverged from the ideal of a "trust for civilization."

The widest and ultimately the most important of the struggles in South Africa is that between the policy of Basutoland and that of Johannesburg and Rhodesia; for there, if anywhere, we lay our finger on the difference between a "sane" Imperialism, devoted to the protection, education, and self-development of a "lower race," and an "insane" Imperialism, which hands over these races to the economic exploitation of white colonists who will use them as "live tools" and their lands as repositories of mining or other profitable treasure. . . .

X

In setting forth the theory which sought to justify Imperialism as the exercise of forcible control over lower races, by regarding this control as a trust for the civilization of the world, we pointed out three conditions essential to the validity of such a trust: first, the control must be directed to the general good, and not to the special good of the "imperialist" nation; secondly, it must confer some net advantage to the nation so controlled; lastly, there must exist some organization representative of international interests, which shall sanction the undertaking of a trust by the nation exercising such control.

* Mr. Bryce, *Impressions of South Africa*, p. 422.

Index

DOCUMENTARY HISTORY OF WESTERN CIVILIZATION
Edited by Eugene C. Black and Leonard W. Levy

ANCIENT AND MEDIEVAL HISTORY OF THE WEST

Morton Smith: ANCIENT GREECE *

A. H. M. Jones: A HISTORY OF ROME THROUGH THE FIFTH CENTURY
Vol. I: The Republic
Vol. II: The Empire

Deno Geanakoplos: BYZANTINE EMPIRE *

Marshall W. Baldwin: CHRISTIANITY THROUGH THE THIRTEENTH CENTURY

Bernard Lewis: ISLAM TO 1453 *

David Herlihy: HISTORY OF FEUDALISM

William M. Bowsky: RISE OF COMMERCE AND TOWNS *

David Herlihy: MEDIEVAL CULTURE AND SOCIETY

EARLY MODERN HISTORY

Hanna H. Gray: CULTURAL HISTORY OF THE RENAISSANCE *

Florence Edler de Roover: MONEY, BANKING,
AND COMMERCE, THIRTEENTH THROUGH SIXTEENTH CENTURIES *

V. J. Parry: THE OTTOMAN EMPIRE *

Ralph E. Giesey: EVOLUTION OF THE DYNASTIC STATE *

J. H. Parry: THE EUROPEAN RECONNAISSANCE: Selected Documents

Hans J. Hillerbrand: THE PROTESTANT REFORMATION

John C. Olin: THE CATHOLIC COUNTER REFORMATION *

Orest Ranum: THE CENTURY OF LOUIS XIV *

Thomas Hegarty: RUSSIAN HISTORY THROUGH PETER THE GREAT *

Marie Boas Hall: NATURE AND NATURE'S LAWS

Barry E. Supple: HISTORY OF MERCANTILISM *

Geoffrey Symcox: IMPERIALISM, WAR, AND DIPLOMACY, 1550-1763 *

Herbert H. Rowen: THE LOW COUNTRIES *

C. A. Macartney: THE HABSBURG AND HOHENZOLLERN DYNASTIES
IN THE SEVENTEENTH AND EIGHTEENTH CENTURIES

Lester G. Crocker: THE AGE OF ENLIGHTENMENT

Robert and Elborg Forster: EUROPEAN SOCIETY IN THE EIGHTEENTH CENTURY

* In preparation